# THE FATE OF AMERICA

**Also by Michael Gellert**
*Modern Mysticism: Jung, Zen and the Still Good Hand of God*

# THE FATE OF AMERICA

## An Inquiry into National Character

*Michael Gellert*

BRASSEY'S, INC.
WASHINGTON, D.C.

**Library of Congress Cataloging-in-Publication Data**

Gellert, Michael
    The fate of America: an inquiry into national character/Michael Gellert.—lst ed.
      p. cm.
    Includes bibliographical references (p.) and index.
    ISBN 1-57488-356-9 (acid-free paper)
      1. National characteristics, American. 2. United States—Civilization. 3.
    Heroes—Mythology—United States. 4. Idealism—Social aspects—United
        States. 5. Comparative civilization. I. Title.

    E169.1 .G4514 2001
    973—dc21                                            2001025545

ISBN 1-57488-356-9 (alk. paper)

Printed in the United States of America on acid-free paper that meets the American National Standards Institute Z39-48 Standard.

Brassey's, Inc.
22841 Quicksilver Drive
Dulles, Virginia 20166

First Edition

10 9 8 7 6 5 4 3 2 1

*In memory of Kōun Yamada, who taught me,
among other things, that the patient cultivation of character
is both the fruit and the critical ingredient of a spiritual life.*

*. . . I flatter myself that a Superintending Providence is ordering everything for the best and that, in due time, all will end well.*

—George Washington

*In order to arrive at that which thou knowest not*
*Thou must go by a way that thou knowest not.*
*In order to arrive at that which thou possessest not*
*Thou must go by a way that thou possessest not.*
*In order to arrive at that which thou art not*
*Thou must go through that which thou art not.*

—St. John of the Cross

# ★ Contents ★

# Part III: The Underside of Innocence

## Part IV: The Fate of America

# ★ Introduction ★

*Character is fate.*

—Heraclitus

Of all the books that cannot be written, the historian Jacques Barzun has said, those about nations and national character are the most impossible. If this is true, then the topic of this book is perhaps *the* most impossible, for it is about America and the American national character.

The difficulty of this subject begins with the issue of national character itself, an issue upon which nobody can agree. That every nation or ethnic group has a distinct temperament, with unique qualities, talents, and predispositions, is a fact that has by and large been accepted. But aside from this fact, what do we know about the nature of national character? Is it genetic, or is it acquired? Is it a fixed thing, or does it change over time? Does it exist in the psyche, or is it a purely social phenomenon? What is it rooted in—climate, geography, historical events? These are only questions of definition. Questions of how to evaluate national character are even more vexing. How does one measure the mettle of a nation's character? Does one use moral backbone as the yardstick, as David Hume suggested in the eighteenth century? Or does one use the quality of genius possessed by a people, as Voltaire suggested? Or, finally, as Hegel would contend, does one look above all to the spirit of the people, to their collective consciousness and emotional, intellectual, and aesthetic sensibilities? As one can see, the notion of national character is one of the vaguest and most mysterious in the history of ideas.

The fact then that this book is about *America's* national character immensely magnifies the complexity of its inquiry. As the Swiss psychologist Carl Jung wrote, America, in spite of the European's impression of it as childlike, impetuous, and naive, has probably the most complicated psychology of all nations. As a pluralistic society composed of so many ethnic groups, America is a world within itself. Furthermore, its history, though short by comparison with most nations, has had a number of distinct phases with marked shifts from one another. And the factors shaping this history have been complicated, including the Puritan origins of the nation, the political philosophy of the Founding Fathers, the institution of slavery, and the transformative events of the Civil War, the New Deal, the civil rights movement, the Vietnam War, and America's emergence as the leading nation and stalwart defender of democracy in the world. There is, ostensibly, no such thing as "the" American experience, but only *many* American experiences. American identity is so heterogeneous, in flux, and perplexing that it may altogether defy characterization.

Nevertheless, the difficult problems facing the nation as it begins the twenty-first century necessitate an examination of its complex character precisely because the latter has a great deal to do with them. Indeed, these problems are largely self-imposed. Despite the recent increase in prosperity, America is plagued by crime, drug abuse, racial tensions, poverty, the erosion of vital institutions such as the family and education, a diminished sense of vision and direction, and the deterioration of community life if not the quality of life in general. Incidents such as the 1992 Los Angeles riots, the Oklahoma City bombing in 1995, and the Columbine High School shootings in 1999 reveal the explosive potential of discontent in the nation. Thus, this book is not only a study of national character, but an attempt to understand how national character relates to the nation's problems; it is an attempt to confront these problems by going to one of their root causes.

The book's central thesis is that America suffers from a crisis in heroism, in what it means to be heroic. The American "heroic ideal"—the nation's aspiration toward greatness and its sense of purpose—no longer holds up the way it did in former times, and consequently there is confusion in the values, morals, and norms of society. The nation's heroic ideal is too simplistic and "young" for modern times. Furthermore, the basic national character out of which this heroic ideal emerged is also gripped by the spirit or principle of youth. This principle is appropriate for a young country, but it can thwart maturation by persisting in its hold long after this has become historically and psychologically inappropriate. America has thus become fixed in a protracted youth that affects every aspect of its experience. The book explores this problem in its diverse effects and aspects. It elucidates the dangers it poses to the nation—in particular, to its democracy—and addresses what the nation must focus on in its public discourse and the education of its citizens. Vital to the book's inquiry is a question central to all great civilizations: what constitutes, in Plato's words, the "good life"? Though not a Platonist, Jefferson also held this concern dear to his heart. He knew that an enlightened citizenry, refined in its culture and character, was an essential requirement for democracy.

Part I, "America's Heroic Ideal," discusses the origins and development of American heroism and how it is informed by the spirit of youth. From the Founding Fathers to the cowboy and to modern heroes of all kinds, one sees not an evolution but a devolution in heroic values and consciousness. Accordingly, American society and culture are pervaded by a simplistic, young, and anachronistic heroic ideal, and the understanding of what greatness consists of is at odds with the complexities and demands of contemporary life.

With an overview of America's heroic ideal thus established, Parts II and III then engage in an extensive probe into the numerous and complex ways this heroic ideal has gone awry. These parts describe two large categories of the ways America is addicted to the spirit of youth. In specific, Part II, "The High Life," concerns the addiction to height. The image of height is used here as a metaphor for humanity's aspiration to reach beyond itself. Whether we speak of attaining great heights of achievement or status, or of the inflation of the economy that leads to periodic depressions, or of getting high with drugs, we employ this ancient metaphor. The problem of going too high or beyond what is humanly adaptive, that is, of becoming inflated, is the theme of such ancient stories as the Tower of Babel and the myth of Icarus. Thus, the addiction to height is by no means a recent development in history. Numerous empires, Rome being perhaps the most illustrious example and the Soviet Union the most recent, collapsed from some form of addiction to height, some form of living beyond their means. Whether occurring in the material or moral dimension, this addiction has ungrounding and insidious effects. Part II examines America's distinct forms of addiction to height.

Part III, "The Underside of Innocence," explores the second category of America's addiction to youth. This is the addiction to innocence, to what

Bertrand Russell called naive realism, the belief that things are the way they appear. Innocence reflects the original condition of all human beings, the condition of childhood, and it can operate on a collective level as naturally as on an individual level. In a state of innocence, one's actions appear righteous or sacrosanct because they are stamped with the imprimatur of childhood's purity. But unbridled innocence can have a very dark side, for it limits one to a simplistic, one-dimensional view of the world and permits one to engage in immoral acts but with a sense of entitlement and justification. Among the various forms of innocence that Part III examines are certain basic assumptions of America's founding vision and the modern cults of novelty, freedom, and happiness derived from them. The underpinnings of innocence in slavery, segregation, and current race relations are discussed, too.

Part IV, "The Fate of America," consists of the concluding chapter, "America in the Third Millennium." The evidence of heroic failure that has been documented in the book up to this point naturally has profound implications for the future of the nation, and the discussion now turns to the likelihood that America is at a historic crossroads. This section addresses the notion that the true meaning of democracy and the American vision must be realized in the personal sphere of each individual's spiritual and ethical experience. A nation can only be as spiritually evolved, ethical, and free as its individual citizens. The nation's problems cannot be solved solely by public policies or government programs administered from the top-down, no matter how innovative or effective they might be. Real social change must come from people, forged through public discourse and studied at all levels of education. It must involve not a faceless crowd, but persons. As Gandhi said, "We must be the change we wish to see in the world." An inner-based, spiritual rebirth is the challenge, above all others, that America faces.

But the book does not only conclude on a spiritual note. Its very approach from the outset treats both the American character and its problems as expressions of the human spirit. It seeks to understand the inner forces at work in America's national character—indeed, the spirit of youth is just one of them—and it tries to show how these forces manifest in the life of the nation, for better or worse. Only by seeing our problems in the larger context of our spiritual condition can we begin to deal with them in a more comprehensive and authentic way. Albert Einstein once said that the world that we have made as a result of the level of thinking we have attained thus far creates problems that cannot be solved at the same level at which they were created. The problems can only be solved when understood from the vantage point of the next higher level. The underlying premise of this book is that the solutions to America's problems must come from a level of thinking that addresses the human spirit and its special needs. This has nothing to do with spiritual or religious belief systems per se. It is a spiritual *way* of thinking that is needed rather than a particular school of religious thought or practice.

America's fate in the century and millennium ahead will depend upon its ability to shift to this level of thinking in some form or another. As the historian Arnold Toynbee and others have made clear, civilizations and nation-states that fail to meet the creative and spiritual challenges that new eras bring sooner or later fall by history's wayside. Toynbee alone has charted the course of some thirty-four civilizations and many nation-states since the beginning of recorded history. Half of these civilizations no longer exist, and among the other half, only a few can claim uninterrupted continuity since ancient times. Nation-states are even more transient. One wonders, how will America respond to the challenges of fate that now knock on its door?

Of course, to respond successfully to these challenges, it is not enough for us to merely study our national character and the forces affecting us. We need to enter into an active dialogue with these forces so we can truly grasp their inner workings, which are essentially our own inner workings. A purely intellectual approach might cast light upon our problems, but would not enable us to embrace them. We not only need to question and examine, but to grope and wrestle. Only in this way can our presently unconscious relationship to these forces become conscious and undergo change. Indeed, only such an approach can provide the understanding and involvement needed to help us meet the challenges of our problems and the future.

Los Angeles, 2001

★

# Part I

## America's Heroic Ideal

*The fact is that this is what society is and always has been: a symbolic action system, a structure of statuses and roles, customs and rules for behavior, designed to serve as a vehicle for earthly heroism. Each script is somewhat unique, each culture has a different hero system. . . . It doesn't matter whether the cultural hero-system is frankly magical, religious, and primitive or secular, scientific, and civilized. It is still a mythical hero-system in which people serve in order to earn a feeling of primary value, of cosmic specialness, of ultimate usefulness to creation, of unshakable meaning. . . . In this sense everything that man does is religious and heroic, and yet in danger of being fictitious and fallible.*

—Ernest Becker

*[The hero has to] awaken the sleeping images of the future which can and must come forth from the night, in order to give the world a new and better face.*

—Ernst Barlach

# ★ Prelude: The Aspiration Toward Greatness ★

In American history there have been three developments which more than any others demanded that Americans critically reflect upon the course they were on. They were the American Revolution, the Civil War, and the New Deal. All were precipitated by crises that could have been met by responses leading to failure just as easily as to success. All were radical responses, but the changes they brought had an interesting blend of liberalism and conservatism, of reform and restraint. And lastly, all were brought on by factors beginning long before a crisis developed. This last fact is not very consoling with regard to the Civil War and the New Deal, developments that occurred once the nation was born. As Senator Daniel Moynihan said, "The test of a democracy is to act *before* a crisis occurs." If this is so, then American democracy has once again failed this test, for it has failed to act in advance of the crisis that is now threatening it. This crisis is in one sense the most dangerous the nation has ever had, for its effects are so subtle and insidious that they are not recognized for what they are. Even considering that the crisis is already present and steadily growing, there is little motivation for any reflection of the kind that made the Revolution, the Civil War, and the New Deal viable options.

The current crisis has to do with the American understanding of the meaning of heroism, with what it means to be heroic. It has to do with what Jung called the American "Heroic Ideal." As a European experiencing America from an outsider's perspective, Jung assessed the nation's basic psychological orientation in these terms:

> America has a principle or idea or attitude, but it is surely not money. Often, when I was searching through the conscious and the unconscious mind of my American patients and pupils, I found something which I can only describe as a sort of Heroic Ideal. Your most idealistic effort is concerned with bringing out the best in every man, and when you find a good man you naturally support him and push him on, until at last he is liable to collapse from sheer exertion, success, and triumph. It is done in every family, where ambitious mothers egg their boys on with the idea that they must be heroes of some sort, or you find it in the factory, where the whole system anxiously tries to get the best man into the best place. Or again in the schools where every child is trained to be brave, courageous, efficient, and a "good sport," a hero in short. There is no record which people will not kill themselves to break, even if it is the most appalling nonsense. The moving pictures abound with

heroes of every description. American applause holds the world record. The "great" and "famous" man gets mobbed by enthusiastic crowds, whatever he may be "great" in; even Valentino got his full share. In Germany you are great if your titles are two yards long, in England if you are a gentleman as well, in France if you coincide with the prestige of the country. In small countries there is, as a rule, no greatness when you are alive, because things need to be small, therefore it is usually posthumous. America is perhaps the only country where "greatness" is unrestricted, because it expresses the most fundamental hopes, desires, ambitions, and convictions of the nation.

Jung wrote these words in 1930. They are as true today as then.

It is important here to appreciate that the American aspiration to be heroic or great is an ideal not limited to specific persons and deeds. It *precedes* the persons and deeds as the motivating factor that inspires them. It is the hunger in the American heart that gives heroic persons and deeds their value in the first place. The heroic mindset exists well before heroic status is fixed upon any image. This mindset is part of the American national character, and distinctly sets it apart from the character of other nations or civilizations. By contrast, other civilizations built up their cultures upon other ideals. These may not be the only factors influencing these civilizations, but they are identifying trademarks in a general sense. For example, ancient Israel had predominantly a religious ideal, ancient China had a philosophical ideal, and modern France very much has aesthetic and intellectual ideals.

There can be no doubt that America's position in the world is attributable in no small measure to its heroic ideal. America's attainment of greatness thus far has been made possible not only because the nation has been blessed by abundant resources, or a diverse population eager to "make good" in the New World, or historic opportunities to assume center stage in the global theater. America's greatness is also a direct expression of its heroic ideal, of the drive for greatness inculcated into Americans from an early age. The greatness Americans have achieved in commerce, technology and science, military power, international affairs, space exploration, entertainment, and sports is surely also a result of the fact that Americans simply strive to be great and to apply their talents to this purpose. But the heroic ideal is not merely a drive to assert one's stature in the world, to be in a dominant or superior position in relation to others or even in a position of comfort within oneself. It is not merely a reflection of the psychologist Alfred Adler's famous dictum, "To be a man means to suffer from an inferiority feeling which constantly drives him to overcome it." The impetus to be heroic is rooted in mysterious yearnings that originate deep within the soul.

In mythology and folklore, the quest or journey of the hero is a universal motif for the adventure of youth, and is a symbol of youth's transformation into maturity and mastery. The hero's slaying of the dragon, for example, is such a symbol. It is an allegorical tale of the test of character and of the victorious movement from what one is to what one can become. Ultimately, the hero conquers himself and grows into himself by reaching his full stride. This redeems him and gives his life value. Indeed, it is the desire for value or meaning that secretly underlies the hunger for greatness and that gives the hero his passion and willingness to risk death. This pushes him on as an inner urge: he *must* fight the dragon.

Thus, inasmuch as it is about finding one's purpose in life, the hero's tale is also an allegory of fate. By "fate," I do not here mean "fatalism" or "destiny." I am not referring to the Calvinist, Muslim, or Hindu notion that the course of one's life is divinely preordained or karmically predetermined. I am referring rather to the notion of fate as a calling to bring something forth into the world. It is a spiritual and creative imperative. Its possibilities may be God-given, but the successful pursuit and mastery of it are another matter. One's "fate" in this sense is not prefigured as a *fait accompli*, but is a challenge which one must rise to and meet. Because it is ultimately a challenge to find one's purpose, it is not so much about what one does, but about who one wishes to be.

For this reason, the particular heroes of a nation tell us about "who" that nation wishes to be. They tell us about that nation's sense of its fate, and about its maturity and mastery of that fate. For example, Gandhi attained heroic stature in India riding the winds of change (namely, the nation's desire for independence and social reform), but his unique heroism, with its emphasis on nonviolence and religious principles, was steeped in the civility and wisdom of the nation's 3,000-year-old tradition, Hinduism. What made Gandhi a great hero *by India's standards* was that he spearheaded a modern cause while being true to the nation's level of maturity and its spiritual calling or fate. It is the universal appeal of these same high standards that has also made Gandhi a hero and standard-bearer for social protesters of his kind elsewhere in the world, most notably, Martin Luther King.

It is precisely in connection to its understanding of its fate and "who" it wishes to be that America today is in a state of crisis. One could say that the nation is suffering from a kind of heroic-identity crisis: the ideal of what is heroic, of what constitutes "greatness," is no longer clear. What was once heroic is no longer applicable in modern times. The heroes, conquests, and enemies of former times have become anachronisms. The North American continent no longer offers boundless opportunity for exploration. Even space travel has become routine and tends to be looked upon as if it were business-as-usual. The debacle in Vietnam was America's first major experience of heroic failure on the international scene, followed by others. The Persian Gulf War, hailed by George Bush as the end of the "Vietnam syndrome," held the public's attention only for its short duration and did not leave a deep impression; whatever military and political merits it may have had, it could not satisfy the nation's unsettled and disillusioned heroic imagination. Certainly, it did not assure the reelection of Bush the way the victory of World War II made Eisenhower a shoo-in in 1952 and again in 1956.

More significantly, as political pundits often point out, with the Soviet Union and the global threat of communism now gone, America's role in the world has also entered a stage of uncertainty and redefinition. Power blocs are shifting and, with terrorism increasing, ethnic wars promoting genocide, and "rogue" states threatening regional destabilization (not to mention nuclear and biochemical war), priorities are not the same. In the economic sphere as well, the old paradigm is changing. Competition from Asian and Third World markets and recurring periods of recession and depression have sent Americans a strong message that greatness in the material world will require ever-greater or better means of production, management, and commercial mastery. Although America has clearly demonstrated in the 1990s that it can meet this challenge, the new paradigm of globalization and interdependence has compelled the nation to redefine its image as an economic giant that can rule as it wishes.

On the domestic front too, America is in a state of transition. Here one finds an explicit sense of disenchantment. Since Watergate, public officials and leaders have become subject to scrutiny in unprecedented ways, and naturally, it does not take much to discover that they have feet of clay. One investigation after another leads to the discrediting or resignation of congressmen, senators, and presidential aides. Presidents themselves are increasingly being exposed as liars. Cynicism has become the order of the day, and greatness, however it may be defined, appears unattainable. The kind of greatness that is propagated in the media is even more unattainable because it is so much larger than life, promoting what the actor and director

Sean Penn called "un-heartfelt lies." Or, if this greatness is not too fantastic and removed from the everyday world, it is simply not desirable: the media are full of pseudoheroes, self-destructive heroes, and criminal antiheroes. Most network television is banal and, aside from a few good films a year, the best Hollywood can offer is a deafening parade of violence, sex, and empty hero worship.

The fall of America's heroic ideal pervades every aspect of society. Drug abuse, crime, racial hatred and division, the rootlessness and cultural vacuity of the nation's youth, the proliferation of cults, gangs, and militia groups, the decline of the American family as a two-parent, tight-knit unit, and the general, mindless pursuit of ambition for its own sake are all signs of heroic failure. The fact that authors such as William Bennett and Ben Wattenberg have issued best-selling books on values, virtue, and normal, commonsense morality indicates the dearth of these things, and that Americans are hungry for them. A most revealing illustration of heroic failure comes from a 1996 survey of 3300 high-achieving high school students. Three out of every four of them admitted to having cheated in school. Sixty-six percent admitted to copying homework, 39 percent to cheating on tests, and 16 percent to plagiarizing. Forty-one percent acknowledged that they cheated to get higher grades; 66 percent said cheating was simply not a "big deal." Of 6 percent caught in the act, only 5 percent of those were punished, and mildly, with a failing grade only for the test or paper on which they cheated. The survey also asked the students to identify the greatest crisis facing the nation and their own generation. Curiously, their top concern was the decline of social values and morals.

The main argument of this book is that America's most pressing crisis and challenge to survive as a society and civilization is to transform its failing heroic ideal. The notion of greatness and the ways to attain greatness have become, on both the collective and individual levels, obfuscated. The culture is arrested in a static heroic ideal that is without relevance and effectiveness in our rapidly changing, complex "Information Age." This old ideal fixates on the most simplistic elements from former periods of American history. Although America's original heroic ideal as expounded by the nation's founders had a powerful redeeming and guiding vision, the nation is at a loss as to what this means in a twenty-first century context. Though schools may teach the history of the founders, the question of what constitutes greatness for the individual and society—or in Platonic terms, what defines the good life—is not addressed and studied as a necessity of life.

Our inquiry will largely involve an examination of the complex nature of America's heroic ideal—its history, its current condition and the ways it is expressed, the evidence and causes of its failure in modern times, and what its regeneration would demand. In this context, regeneration is not just an attempt to correct failure and survive, but is itself part of the drama of the heroic, as is failure itself ("there's no success like failure," Bob Dylan sings). This is the wonderful thing about the hero in all of the hero myths and legends of the world: failure and regeneration, death and rebirth, are natural parts of his adventure. Death here does not mean physical death, but inner death, spiritual or psychological death. It is this that makes a deep and genuine transformation possible. The hero is not unlike the phoenix who must crash and burn before he rises. In the tale of the hero, it is always a false or immature inner condition or attitude that needs to be killed in order for the hero to be reborn *as a hero*. Ultimately, it can be to their benefit that Americans love the drama of the heroic.

However, to be able to more fully appreciate America's heroic ideal and the crisis connected to it, it is first necessary to explore the American national character.

# Chapter 1

## Two Souls Within the Human Breast

*The same political parties which now agitate the United States, have existed through all time. . . . And in fact, the terms of whig and tory belong to natural as well as to civil history. They denote the temper and constitution of mind of different individuals.*

—Thomas Jefferson

### The Spirits of Youth and Authority

The American national character is one of the most polarized in the world. This condition ultimately stems from the polarization of two principles of human nature, principles that have been present and active since the dawn of man. These principles may be thought of as spirits, by which I do not mean something supernatural. On the contrary, my use here of the term "spirits" refers to natural forces of evolution that drive human beings in specific ways and with specific intents—indeed, *as if* they were supernatural spirits with a mind and will of their own. Mostly, however, they may be thought of as spirits because they imbue humans with a particular spirit, that is, a particular mood, attitude, and outlook. The two principles or spirits most active in the American national character, and consequently in the unfolding of American history, are the spirits of youth and authority. They are, as Goethe's Faust would say, two souls that dwell within the human breast. They are two distinct, powerful, instinctual forces or tendencies that constitute the human condition. Together these spirits make a dynamic whole, for they are in fact complementary opposites that balance and complete each other. But when polarized and split apart from each other, they can have detrimental effects.

Let us take a look at what these spirits are and how they operate. The spirits of youth and authority are brought into play as a dialectical process that is universal. All people and peoples experience this process as phases of development. The spirit of youth usually propels the early, burgeoning, and most dynamic phase of development. It is concerned with newness, growth, and ambition. It seeks to attain mastery and a sense of achievement, and thus is preoccupied with industry and action, with "doing." It sings the praise of progress and prizes new discoveries and inventions not only for their concrete benefits but for their own sake, simply because they open new possibilities.

A person or nation under the influence of this spirit is in a state of evolution and is future-oriented. As with the person, so with the nation: its identity is in flux and it is in quest of its role in the world. Its pursuits in this regard can be highly idealistic and yet opportunistic. Jung found that the spirit of youth is portrayed in mythology as a child god or hero, or as a *puer aeternus*—that is, an adolescent or young adult who is eternally young ("*puer aeternus*" is Latin for "eternal youth"). Jung called this spirit the child archetype. Certainly, it has a childlike energy, innocence, and optimism. A nation that captures this spirit, or as the case may be, is captured by it, is usually in its childhood or adolescence. As a young nation, America is clearly animated by the spirit of youth. Among European nations, Germany too is driven by this spirit. Of course, neither nation is exclusively youth-oriented and without the spirit of authority.

In contrast to the spirit of youth, the spirit of authority usually rules the later, more mature, settled phase of development. It is concerned with tradition, culture, and order. The continuity of social order is highly valued by this spirit precisely because it has taken so long for such order to evolve out of the chaos of youth. The element of change is thus not as attractive to this spirit as it is to the more adventurous, free spirit of youth that has its future wide open before it. Conservation—the principle supposedly behind conservatism—carries more weight than experimentation. Containment is more important than expansion; cultivation more important than distant goals; "being" more important than "doing."

With order and tradition comes a natural appreciation for law, ethics, and religion. A person or nation that lives in the spirit of authority has very probably survived the tests of time, formed a solid sense of identity, and acquired a measure of experience, knowledge, and culture; herein lies the authority. Something of enduring value has been authored or created. One may think of India and Great Britain as nations that project this spirit. They have age on their side. Based on its image in mythology, Jung called this spirit the archetype of the wise old man or woman. (The Latin term for such a figure is "*senex,*" which is also the root of such words as senior, senator, senescence, and senile.) The image of the wise old man or woman is closely allied to that of God, the supreme authority and author of creation.

Speaking of them also as archetypes of the collective unconscious, the psychologist James Hillman revealed that the spirits of youth and authority are related to each other in a bipolar yet interdependent way. The order of their relationship is thus only circumstantially sequential or developmental, that is, arranged so that one spirit comes before or gives rise to the other. Theirs is as much a spiritual or psychological dialectic as a historical one. The spirits of youth and authority are two halves of a single whole. They are defined by contrast to each other, just as young and old are meaningful categories only relative to each other. Furthermore, we are speaking here of spirits—spiritual or psychological states—and not physical, temporal conditions. To be young at heart means that regardless of your age you have the spirit of youth. Thus, "youth" and "young" are not exactly the same thing. This is true for authority and old age as well.

What this means is that in the same way youth gives rise to authority— an obvious fact given our commonsense experience—authority can give rise to youth. If we think of authority as the father principle and youth as the son principle, it becomes apparent how authority gives rise to youth, or the old to the new. For example, Christianity maintains that the Father God of the Old Testament gave birth to the Son God of the New Testament, and it was only upon completion of his life mission that the Son returned to the Father, to the original source and ultimate author. It was also no accident that the Son did away with the heavy emphasis placed upon the practice of the Mosaic Law: the Law belonged to the old order. The son principle or spirit of youth often comes as a reformer or revolutionary. Fifteen hundred years later, after centuries of rebel and reform movements against Catholic orthodoxy, it would triumph again in the form of Martin Luther. His decree was against a Church that had acquired a monopolized role as the chief authority in the Western Christian world.

In the same way that the spirit of youth moves toward the spirit of authority for guidance and completion, the spirit of authority moves toward the spirit of youth for rejuvenation and rebirth. Youth without authority stays forever young and becomes stagnant; authority without youth dries up and dies. This interplay of spirits makes it possible for a nation like China, whose character has been predominantly defined by the spirit of authority for at least the last three thousand years, to again and again reinvent itself. So strong is its youthful capacity for regeneration that it almost wiped out its entire tradition of authority with two single strokes: the Communist ascendancy to power in 1949 and the Cultural Revolution in 1966. A nation's ability to access the spirit that is *not* the one most intrinsic to its character is what may enable it to survive in the long run. It is the opposite spirit that complements the nation's temperament and orientation with a fresh viewpoint. Toynbee's challenge-and-response premise is that for a nation to survive a critical and overwhelming challenge—and history sooner or later serves every great nation with at least one—it must respond creatively and nonhabitually. In Toynbee's view, the human spirit is on the whole more important in this matter than particular strategies, be they military, economic, or other.

## One Plus One Equals Three

The movement between the spirits of youth and authority is cyclic and not strictly linear or unidirectional. As the German philosopher Hegel postulated, this is what constitutes a dialectic: the thesis generates its opposite, the antithesis, optimally leading to a reconciliation of opposites, the synthesis. Taking it a step further, the process then repeats, hopefully at a more evolved level. The process is not only cyclic—going back and forth—but spiraling, moving somewhere.

The moment of synthesis is very important because it is out of the synthesis that something new emerges. History demonstrates that a synthesis of youth and authority is almost always a critical ingredient in the birth of great visions, movements, and epochs. For example, the theologian Arthur Webster suggests that the idea of Jesus Christ as the Redeemer and Son of God became conceivable during the Greco-Roman period as a result of the fusion of ideas from two great traditions: the Greek, Platonic idea of the *metaxy* was fused with the Jewish idea of the Messiah. The *metaxy* was believed to be a "middle region" between the human and the divine, a crossover dimension or meeting place somewhere *in-between* that which is mortal and that which is beyond mortality. This idea, integrated into the notion of the human Messiah that the Jews expected, made possible the conceptual appreciation of Jesus Christ, a redeeming figure who was not merely human, nor exclusively divine, but in-between the two.

This synthesis, incidentally, did not occur as the result of a direct influence of Greece upon Israel, even though Plato predated Jesus by about 350 years and Jesus lived in a Hellenic milieu (as his Greek title of "Christ" or *christos* implies). As the philosopher and historian Eric Voegelin explains, the discovery of the "In-Between reality" occurred independently in Israel. In the Bible, the process of this discovery began with the unique personal encounter of the Prophets with God, and finally culminated in the event of Jesus Christ and its insight that man is the active partner of God. The Jewish version of this insight was developed in the rabbinic tradition of the Talmud, which profiles the human-divine partnership in its own distinct ways. In any case, the dynamic idea of the *metaxy* or in-between reality was an impetus of youth that, when applied to the authoritative or established ideas of Jewish messianism, gave birth to Christianity. In this instance, the movement between the spirits of youth and authority was not exactly dialectical in the Hegelian sense because it was not between a thesis and its antithesis, but between one thesis and another; yet the result was still a synergistic synthesis.

A similar kind of phenomenon occurred some 1700 years earlier, when the patriarch Abraham emerged from Babylonia and migrated to Canaan, an event that marked the beginning of the Hebrew people and eventually gave rise to the Mosaic religion. Here the synthesis was the result of a direct influence of one culture upon another. Modern historical scholarship shows that Abraham probably brought with him a host of ideas from Babylonia—most notably, ideas about creation and primordial history, the idea of a personal god, and ethics and morals. The Mosaic Law in particular has striking similarities in content, terminology, and even arrangement to the prior-established law code of the Babylonian King Hammurabi, who lived around the time of Abraham. Thus, when Abraham incorporated these older elements of the Babylonian order into his experience of Yahweh—an experience that was radical in its exclusive monotheism and fierce devotion—the Hebrew religion was born. And then, much later, when this new synthesis would become the old established order, the introduction of the above-mentioned Platonic idea would give birth to the new Christian religion, which would in turn again become the old established order against which Martin Luther would rebel. In this way, on this large canvas, we may see history as a cyclic but evolving movement between authority and youth, thesis and antithesis (or other thesis). It is the synthesis between these two that catapults this movement to a new level or in a new direction.

And yet, nothing new is ultimately created. This is the paradox. The very idea of newness or novelty, of history as something moving somewhere new, is itself a kind of fantasy of the spirit of youth. By contrast, the spirit of authority sees history as changelessness in change, as eternity in time. From its viewpoint, human nature is like a well that doesn't change. Water may be drawn from it—always a different serving, and this is what gives us our sense of history, of storytelling—but the well itself doesn't change. As David Hume wrote, "It is universally acknowledged that there is a great uniformity among the actions of men, in all nations and ages, and that human nature remains still the same, in its principles and operations. The same motives always produce the same actions; the same events follow from the same causes. Ambition, avarice, self-love, vanity, friendship, generosity, public spirit—these passions, mixed in various degrees and distributed through society, have been, from the beginning of the world, and still are, the source of all the actions and enterprises which have ever been observed among mankind."

Of course, from a historical perspective, the synthesis of the spirits of youth and authority is a distinct event of monumental significance, an event that signals a newfound sense of wholeness or completeness. On a national level this often occurs as an experience of national purpose, but a purpose grounded in both spirits. The birth of America was such an experience. (This shall become clear in following chapters as we discuss how the contributions of the Founding Fathers consisted of a unique synthesis of youth and authority.) When the spirits of youth and authority meet in an integrated way, a new, third factor is created. It is not quite youth, not quite authority, but something of the two and yet different. In Christianity, the synthesis of youth and authority is represented by the Holy Spirit, a free, agile spirit with divine authority. In Jungian or mythological terms, the image that symbolizes this synthesis is a child or childlike being with a wise old soul. Examples include the Etruscan god Tages, a boy with gray hair; Islam's Khidr, a handsome youth with a white beard; and Taoism's Lao-tzu, whose name means "old master-child." An American version of this image is the child George Washington, who cut down his father's cherry tree but whose integrity would not permit him to lie about it. The symbolic significance of this tree belonging to his father should not escape us.

Of course, historical high points during which the two spirits are united in an experience of strong national purpose do not last indefinitely. Given human nature—indeed, all of nature—it is difficult to sustain any particular state or equilibrium indefinitely. Things change. That one spirit will be set more in motion than another and come to predominate is a natural by-product of the course of events. The synthesis of spirits is like the full moon, which is but a brief interlude in the cycle of the moon's waxing and waning.

Indeed, it is curious that the Latin root of the words "authority" and "author" is *augere,* which means to increase or to wax. The inevitable tendency after any synthesis is for the newly created, third factor to increase its mass until it develops inertia and becomes the established authority which youth must come to revivify.

## America's Alternating Current

Not only is synthesis brief, but it is rare. Synthesis only occurs if there is a union of spirits. The mood of a nation can change back and forth from one spirit to another indefinitely without going through the full moon of a synthesis. Or, both spirits can also coexist simultaneously without there being a synthesis, though this is less frequent. In the American experience, the first scenario has been the most common.

When any one pole of a pair of opposites becomes too extreme, it flips into the opposite pole. This phenomenon was first observed in the West by Heraclitus (he called it "enantiodromia") and in the East by all its major religions. American history has tended to follow this pattern with many different themes. The psychologist Erik Erikson highlights the following as important pairs of opposites that characterize American identity: open roads of immigration and jealous islands of tradition; outgoing internationalism and defiant isolationism; boisterous competition and self-effacing cooperation; migratory and sedentary; individualistic and standardized; freethinking and pious; cynical and responsible; and mobocratic and aristocratic. The historian Michael Kammen adds these: hedonistic and puritanical; idealistic and pragmatic; conflict-prone and consensus-minded; rebellious and disciplined; innovative and reactionary; and plebeian and patrician. (The latter pair is similar to mobocratic and aristocratic.) However, all these polarities are obviously, upon closer examination, variations of the larger, spiritual polarity that is their common source: the spirit of youth and the spirit of authority. Historically, the characteristics that fall under the wing of the spirit of youth dominate the American scene more or less all at the same time, as is the case with the characteristics that fall under the wing of the spirit of authority. Now one spirit is predominant, then another. When one becomes extreme or exhausted, it flips into its opposite.

The movement between the spirits of youth and authority can be seen in any lengthy span of time to follow distinct and measurable cycles. The historian Arthur Schlesinger, Jr. charted the course of a set of opposites in American politics that also essentially expresses the spiritual polarity of youth and authority. The opposites he identified are public action and private interest. The former consists of the liberal inclination toward the collective good and social progress, while the latter consists of the conservative inclination toward the good of the individual and laissez-faire. The cause of public action is the impetus behind the Democratic Party, and the protection of private interest, the impetus behind the Republican Party. Their ruling periods by and large reflect the cycles of the nation. A cycle lasts one human generation—approximately 30 years in this century and 24 in former centuries—with half the cycle represented by one party and half by the other. The pattern of one party leap-frogging over the back of another every 12 years was also prevalent when the Federalist and Democratic-Republican Parties dominated the scene; it was a pattern first observed by John Adams.

The alternations between public action and private interest have allowed for there to be periods of dramatic, innovative change followed by periods in which the change is digested by limiting it and letting it settle. The latter periods thus focus on individual self-fulfillment. Schlesinger remarks that periods such as the "Roaring Twenties" and the "Me-Decade" (the 1980s) always coincide with periods of private interest. Schlesinger's accounting for the cycles in this century are earmarked, for the periods of public purpose, by Theodore Roosevelt in 1901, Franklin Roosevelt in 1933, and John Kennedy in 1961, and for the periods of conservative restoration, by the 1920s, the 1950s, and the 1980s. Prior to this century, the periods of public interest were as follows: the creation of an efficient Constitution, 1776–1788; a reaction against the newly formed government, 1788–1800; a period of sweeping change, 1800–1812; a period of Jeffersonian retreat after the War of 1812; the democratizing age of Jackson, 1829–1841; increasing domination of the national government by slaveholders, 1841–1861; abolition of slavery, 1861–1869; and conservative rule, 1869–1901.

It should be noted, as Schlesinger indicates, that the party in power doesn't always reflect the mood or cycle of the nation: twists of fate such as the Vietnam War and Watergate can topple a party's presidential candidate even if that party speaks more directly to the cycle that the nation is in. Nixon benefited from Johnson's failure in Vietnam and was elected during the liberal phase of a cycle. And then Carter took advantage of Nixon's fall from grace with Watergate and was elected at the beginning of a conservative period. But the rhythm of the nation seemed to remain intact. The cycles of American history, like the spirits of youth and authority they are grounded in, operate with a momentum of their own. It was no accident,

Schlesinger argues, that Nixon implemented rather liberal domestic policies (the Environmental Protection Act, the Occupational Safety and Health Act, the Comprehensive Employment and Training Act, and the Family Assistance Program). Nor was it an accident that Carter was the most conservative Democratic president in the twentieth century (rejecting the affirmative role of government, advocating deregulation, increasing interest rates, and bringing the discussion of religion into public affairs).

A more recent example of how presidential politics are affected by the mood or cycle of the nation was the 2000 election. This took place during a period of public action that, historically speaking, should have overwhelmingly favored the incumbent vice president. However, three factors in tandem contributed, above all others, to the extremely close race between Al Gore and George W. Bush. Firstly, Gore ran against the backdrop of "Clinton fatigue," that is, a general disillusionment with Clinton's moral failures; many voters, though pleased with Clinton's economic performance, had a strong wish for leadership that would be a complete departure from the previous administration. Secondly, Bush's campaign of "compassionate conservatism" advocated public action policies—reform of Medicare, education, and health care—that competed with Gore's policies; this then made Bush an attractive alternative candidate at the time. And thirdly, Ralph Nader, a Green Party candidate whose appeal was largely based on his public action proposals, drew a significant number of votes that would otherwise have gone to Gore; this diminished the latter's edge over Bush. Inasmuch as partisanship influenced the legal proceedings that then concluded the presidential race, a fourth factor playing upon the polarity of youth and authority was involved. Certainly with regard to the final U.S. Supreme Court ruling in favor of Bush's appeal to stop the Florida recount, all of the five judges who formed the majority opinion were Republicans appointed by Presidents Nixon, Reagan, or Bush. As Justice John Paul Stevens noted in his dissenting opinion regarding that decision, the nation's confidence in the judge as an impartial arbiter was the real loser in this contest. All these factors conspired to make the 2000 election one of the most controversial ever.

## America's Bias

A less pleasant but vital facet of the spirit of youth is its barbaric and primitive core. If we think of the spirits of youth and authority as a single continuum, the higher end would consist of the most evolved degree of authority, namely, sainthood. Of course, few among us have attained this state, but all of us have experienced, in varying degrees and certainly in childhood, the lower end of the continuum. This is the most basic level of youth, the instinctual, primitive foundation of human nature. It is our animal side, or at least the part of us that is not far removed from the animal side. Jung too defined the child archetype as the instinctual, preconscious, childhood aspect of the collective psyche. By this he meant that there is a layer in the psyche—everybody's psyche—that corresponds to the state that humanity was in during its childhood phase. Although we have evolved as a species beyond this state, it always exists within us at an elemental level, and could break out or show itself under certain conditions. Children naturally live in this state as part of their development. The individual in his or her development naturally progresses through the different levels of consciousness through which humanity as a whole has evolved. Ontogenetic development recapitulates phylogenetic development.

Our primal youth or childhood probably began around four and a half million years ago when our ancestor the ape began to evolve into the human. It is believed that around that time the primate made the transition from being four-legged to two-legged—the human qualifier that anthropologists routinely assign to *Homo sapiens* and his immediate predecessors, such as *Homo erectus*. It is safe to say that the human species is not far removed from its childhood condition: the first civilizations emerged with the beginning of the Bronze Age around 4500 B.C., which, as one can see, is relatively recent in the schema of human evolution. Prior to this, humanity lived for eons in a Stone Age whose primitivity one can only imagine. This extensive period was our childhood.

The fact that this period still thrives within us at some level of the psyche gives cause for consideration. Our civilized selves are but a thin veneer upon this much older layer that is our childhood. With all its jungle or cave-dwelling instincts and its sexual and other appetites, it is the "Africa within" that awed Joseph Conrad in *Heart of Darkness*. It is the "id" Freud was so soberly cautious about when he said its repression and sublimation were not only a consequence of civilization but its prerequisite. Civilized man had to struggle to rise out of his original, primitive condition. To hold down his fundamental, bestial nature and to prevent himself from slipping back into it he had to create strong cultural and psychological barriers—prohibitive taboos, moral codes, and laws. Thus, it was the latent and later-emerging spirit of authority that served as the civilizing function for the primordial spirit of youth. It operated as a sort of guiding, teleological principle, just as innate as the spirit of youth even if not as immediately apparent in the course of human evolution. Indeed, where else could the impulse to civilize have come from but human nature if this impulse itself is so contrary to human nature? Our animal nature would not be able to tolerate the restraints of civilization were there not an equally strong drive toward civilization. The evolutionary drive to rise above instincts is also, as Jung and the paleontologist Pierre Teilhard de Chardin observed, a kind of instinct or urge. This paradox qualifies the two spirits to be among the great opposites that riddle the human condition.

The civilizing function that the spirit of authority serves for the spirit of youth has had a most interesting twist in the American psyche. Listen to how the historian Daniel Boorstin describes the early American experience:

> When the intellectually and spiritually mature man of Europe first settled in America, he was forced to relive the childhood of the race, to confront once again the primitive and intractable wilderness of his cave-dwelling ancestors. In America he became an anachronism. This quaint juxtaposition of culture and barbarism— the Bible in the wilderness—which characterized the earliest settlement of the continent, has left a heritage of conflict and paradox for our own time.

The "intellectually and spiritually mature man of Europe" who first settled in America clearly embodied the spirit of authority; his was the language of civilization, order, and tradition. However, confronted with the fierce wilderness of the American continent, "he was forced to relive the childhood of the race"; that is to say, the spirit of youth was naturally evoked. Although this may be viewed as a regression, it was also, of course, an adaptation. Only the spirit of youth could meet the spirit of the land with equanimity. The raw energies of this spirit were needed to transform the land and build the new nation. But the consequence of this for the American character has been, as Boorstin indicates, a disposition toward barbarism juxtaposed by a heritage of culture and spirituality—in other words, a schism between the spirits.

The American temperament established its footing predominantly in the spirit of youth in three ways. Firstly, in the manner described above, the spirit of youth was constellated in response to the natural environment. Secondly, the spirit of youth was constellated by the American Revolution and the distinct course this revolution took. As England more and more cast itself into the role of the tyrannical authority, the colonies acquired a thirst for independence. But the painful confrontation with British authority gave rise to a suspicion of authority in general—so much so that the new republic was designed to inhibit authority. The cultural anthropologist Geoffrey Gorer explains the history of this attitude:

> In the course of a protracted and often desperate war the allegiance to England was thrown off by the greater number of the colonists, including the most influential. This throwing off of the English allegiance was the rejection of the only embodied authority which was generally recognized; it was not, in those years, the replacement of one authority by another. The birth of the American republic was signalized by the rejection of authority as such: authority was coercive, arbitrary, despotic, morally wrong.
>
> For eleven years the thirteen independent colonies pursued often mutually contradictory policies, linked only in a powerless voluntary confederation; but the almost complete bankruptcy to which this near anarchy brought the Confederation showed that it was impossible for them to survive without some sort of central authority; and in 1787 a Constitutional Convention was held to devise a federal government which would have the minimum of authority necessary for the independent survival of the United States. The remarkable document which was the outcome of these deliberations—the American Constitution—is especially noteworthy for the ingenuity with which authority is jealously circumscribed; the system of checks and balances and the principle of divided powers were intended to erect insuperable legal barriers to the excessive authority of one person or group.

Said otherwise, the suspicion of authority that characterized the American Revolution has been permanently institutionalized in the body politic through the nation's Constitution and system of government. Much of the ferocity unleashed in the ongoing political debate on what should be the degree of government intervention in the public's life stems from this youthful attitude. Curiously, today it is conservatives who most exhibit this attitude, whereas in the early days of the republic it tended to be the liberals, as observable in the case of Jefferson and other members of the Democratic-Republican or Anti-Federalist Party. Part of the reason for this is that today we know that "big government" is more costly, and conservatives simply prefer fiscal conservatism. But another part is surely that the suspicion of authority is so ingrained in the American character that it can take hold of just about any political persuasion. Indeed, as Gorer illustrates, it is not only a strong factor in politics, but in nearly every sphere of American life. In business and industry, in the role of parenting, and even in the mass media's caricatures of family relations, the original experience of revolt against authority translates into an ambivalent or uneasy relationship with the exercise of power and control. In short, the American wishes to maintain a youthful distance and freedom from the constraints of authority.

The third way the American temperament is rooted in the spirit of youth is with regard to the novel form of the American enterprise. The creation of a democratic political and economic system in the liberal spirit of the Enlightenment was a new experiment in history. The Enlightenment was itself an expression of the revisionary spirit of youth, advocating humanitarian political goals, social progress, and a reliance on reason and experience rather than dogma and tradition. The American republic was founded on this cornerstone of liberalism, particularly on the ideas of Smith, Locke, Rousseau, Montesquieu, and Hume. If the Puritans were more an embodiment of the spirit of authority with their reliance on religious tradition, then the Founding Fathers anchored America in the free-thinking, intellectual tradition of the Enlightenment. Regardless of how conservative the nation has periodically been in the course of its mood swings between the spirits of youth and authority, in the long run it has been this youthful spirit of Enlightenment liberalism that has defined the direction of the nation.

## The Fallout from Falling Out of Balance

The American experience is marked by periodic, extreme dissociations between the spirits of youth and authority. During such episodes, the spirits lose their complementarity and become sheer opposites. This can have two effects. The first is that each spirit paradoxically becomes its opposite in a negative way—a phenomenon initially observed by Hillman—and the second is that they explosively repel each other. These effects can occur on the national scene simultaneously. Let's examine the first effect.

When the spirits of youth and authority become split apart from each other, they lose the benefit of being balanced and rounded out by each other. They become one-sided, each a mere half that is missing its other half. Without the balance, the process of movement-limitation-movement that makes constructive change possible goes awry. Human development depends on the rhythm of this process. Without it, history stands still and, together with the human condition, may soon even begin to regress.

The spirit of youth without authority loses its sense of weight and limitation. Because it aspires to achieve everything, it risks spreading itself too thin. It is forever young, meaning that it is forever changing and in a state of permanent potential. Change that never finally arrives anywhere becomes itself a constant and thus, paradoxically, changeless. In this way it becomes identical to authority, but in a negative way. The plot-and-climax dynamic of the human drama breaks down. Plot without climax becomes anticlimactic, as beginning without end becomes an end in itself. Youth becomes the sole authority. What you finally end up with is a tyranny of youth.

A nation that is tyrannically gripped by the spirit of youth will worship it and be addicted to it in a broad variety of forms. It will not be able to satisfy its appetites, live within its means, or set limits upon itself, either material or moral. It will always look to the future to solve its ever-increasing problems, not realizing that there is a law of diminishing returns in both the material and moral spheres. Its leadership and populace fail to recognize that after a certain point, irreversible entropy will set in and there will be no return, no possibility for rebirth. In the end it becomes food for the god whom it so relentlessly served. Rome, the Napoleonic Empire, and Nazi Germany are history's best examples of this. As adventurous, sporting, militant powers, they were driven by the spirit of youth. Unlimited, this evoked the dark side of the spirit of authority: all three powers strove for imperial dominion over the earth and were among the worst tyrannies in history, with Germany in particular embracing evil in heretofore unimaginable ways. With all of them we see how the spirit of youth and the spirit of authority became negatively identical.

One of the more insidious and dangerous consequences of being possessed by the spirit of youth is that a nation loses its sense of the historical, a problem America very much has. A nation becomes so oriented toward the here-and-now and a timeless future that it loses touch with the past and its lessons. Santayana's maxim has sadly become a cliché, but it needs to be said: those who don't learn from history are bound to repeat it.

Regarding the very lesson of learning from history to avoid past mistakes, Americans may wish to remember what happened to Rome when it lost its sense of the historical. A gradual process of social disintegration occurring over a few centuries should have warned the Romans of collapse. Rome had become the greatest power on earth, politically unifying the Hellenic world in a way which even the Greeks could not do. Yet it became too big for its britches and fell victim to carelessness. Its middle classes became displaced by its system of slavery, and work had come to be regarded as something disdainful. Loose sexual norms and general moral decay undermined the family as an institution and transmitter of values from one generation to the next. The corrupt and unjust system of taxation that held the Empire together eventually corroded it, as the conquered nations of the Empire began to rebel. Rome's warring nature set it up as a target for barbarian invaders, and sacking Rome became a regular occurrence. Clearly, Rome was in decline. However, the denial of this and the widespread belief in its own immortality were so strong that, as Toynbee points out, its final collapse in the fifth century caught everybody by surprise—not only its citizens, but its subjects in the far reaches of the Empire. Perhaps the most astounding features of the spirit of youth are its blind faith and naiveté.

If the spirit of youth without authority loses its sense of weight and limitation, then the spirit of authority without youth is *all* weight and limitation. And thus, it too in the final analysis falls lame. The answers to all questions great and small are known à priori, and things are set according to a fixed order of rules, or at least a firm preconception of the way they should be and how they should be done. There is no room for further authoring, as decisions are made according to a closed system, be it a philosophy, theology, moral code, or political agenda. There is no perceived need for the spirit of youth, which like children "should be seen and not heard." Rebirth is unnecessary. The correctness upon which the spirit of authority rests its mantle is eternally valid and never needs to adapt to the changing winds of time. If the spirit of youth without authority is forever changing, then the spirit of authority without youth is never changing.

Clearly, the spirit of authority without youth loses its inner authority, its wisdom. This wisdom, being the knowledge and love of truth, comprises both wisdom from within and the living wisdom of the ages; these are, in fact, one and the same. But for wisdom to be ageless, it must remain open to change. As Jung said, referring to Heraclitus' law of everlasting change, "it seems that all the true things must change and that only that which changes remains true." Without this flexibility and connection to ageless wisdom, the spirit of authority becomes merely the voice of external authority and conventional wisdom. Its strength lies only in its institutional arm, and it merely preserves the status quo, regardless of whether this is merited or not. Conformity replaces originality as dogma replaces insight. A defensive posture is taken against anything new or unknown.

If this spirit becomes fanatical or despotic, it then reaches its darkest nadir in the form of authoritarianism. Authoritarianism is the spirit of authority rigidified, depotentiated, and afraid of its own lack of authenticity— hence its need for absolute power and control. Its conservatism is extreme not because it desires to preserve tradition—which, most would agree, is a good thing—but because it wishes to impose its values and beliefs upon others at all costs and against their will. "It's for your own good," is the arrogant assumption of such authority. This is the perverse side of Father Knows Best. In its grandiosity, the authority in power believes that it alone is qualified to have all power of authority. Inevitably, the polarized spirit of authority is prone toward hysteria and paranoia. Its campaigns of repression, to no surprise, wear the banner of serving and protecting truth. One need only recall that the Holy Inquisition was, as its official title conveys, proclaimed in the name of God, or that Senator McCarthy conducted his investigations in defense of freedom and the American way of life. It is not only the spirit of youth that becomes blind when it is one-sided.

When the spirit of authority relies purely on might, on the power principle, it regresses to a form of authority that is barbaric. It is more in alignment with the laws of the primal horde and the jungle than those of civilization. The monarchies and dynasties that prevailed through most of recorded history were at least based on an orderly method—usually, the inherited, divine right of kings—and future rulers had to be reared from birth in the ways of nobility and skillful leadership. Though history has shown how tyrannical absolute monarchs could be, modern totalitarianism has hardly been an improvement, almost altogether lacking in the cultivation of wise leadership. The most charismatic and cunning too often win, as Hitler and Stalin amply demonstrated. The regimes of such dictators naturally descend to the most barbarous levels.

In another vein, the primitive emerges when authoritarian movements, both secular and religious, are seized by the numinous power of their beliefs. In deriving their authority from a strict, fundamentalist interpretation of doctrine, they employ ideas in a way similar to how chiefs and shamans in primitive tribes use the "power-word," the magic formula. Their authority is less irrational than suprarational, and there is no argument against it. "It is so because it is written," or because "God said so." St. Anselm's golden rule, *fides quaerens intellectum,* or faith seeking understanding, degenerates into faith without understanding—that is, once again, blind faith.

In regressing to the barbaric and the primitive, the spirit of authority becomes archaic, both in the sense of being antiquated and of belonging to an earlier period or mode of thinking. What is earlier here is the spirit of youth in its primal stage. In becoming arrested in archaic modes, the spirit of authority becomes identical with the spirit of youth, but in a negative way.

In the final analysis, the identification of each spirit with its opposite in a negative way creates a situation in which youth predominates in its darker aspects. The pole that is primal in nature or evolution reigns, but in a tyrannical way. The tyranny that youth becomes is a tyranny of youth, and the tyranny that authority becomes is an archaic authority that consists of the barbaric and primitive features of youth. Either way, immaturity prevails. When youth and authority become dissociated, in the long run, youth wins and both lose, along with the society in which the dissociation occurs.

## A Big Bang

The second possible effect of a dissociation between the spirits of youth and authority is intense conflict. In the above condition where one spirit becomes negatively identical to the other, there is little or no tension between the opposites; in this scenario, there is too much. Whereas the former can be likened to a violin whose strings are too loose, here the strings of the violin are too taut. In the first case there can be no sound at all, and in the second case, only screeching noise. For there to be the harmony of music, there must be a certain degree of tension, but not too much. The situation of too much tension or conflict between the spirits of youth and authority also finds an analogy in physics as an irresistible force meeting an immovable object, or matter encountering antimatter: the result is explosive, cataclysmic violence.

The Civil War was an episode of such violence. Combining hand-to-hand combat with the indiscriminate killing of industrialized war, it was one of the first instances of modern warfare. Deadly artillery rounds and rifled muskets rendered Napoleonic tactics obsolete. Entire regiments were butchered. In a nation whose population was 30 million, over 600,000 were killed and over 400,000 wounded, to date America's deadliest conflict. In Europe, writers like Dostoevsky commented on the irony of a civil war in the so-called United States of America. The fierce patriotism each side felt was not only toward separate views on slavery and the politics of expansion, and to different visions of the future of America, but to the different spirits influencing those views and visions. The Union had assumed the firm, ethical stance of authority while the Confederacy incarnated the rebellious spirit of youth. (Actually, Lincoln's considerations at the outset of the war were determined pragmatically rather than ethically, his priority being the preservation of the Union. Prior to the Emancipation Proclamation, he declared: "If I could save the Union without freeing any slave, I would do it; and if I could save it by freeing all the slaves I would do it; and if I could save it by freeing some and leaving others alone, I would also do that.")

Nevertheless, there can be no doubt that in the end the North carried the ethical conscience and weight of authority, with the South taking an attitude toward the North similar to the one the colonies had taken toward England a hundred years earlier: the South saw the North, if not as a tyrannical oppressor from whom it must break free, then as a tyrannical economic competitor whose demand to contain or eliminate slavery would firmly establish the North's dominance over the South. This demand also threatened the South's fundamental way of life. Whereas in the American Revolution the colonies were united as a single force of youth against British authority, here this duality was replicated within the nation. Virtue, of course, is determined here by moral imperatives and not by the spirits per se: in the American Revolution, the rebels were the righteous, while in the Civil War, the authority was the righteous. For a nation whose predominant orientation was toward the spirit of youth, the victory of authority in the Civil War signaled a very important fact, namely, that the spirit of authority was strong enough in the backbone of the nation to assert itself against the spirit of youth, and win.

However, this limitation upon youth and its demands for freedom—including the freedom to practice slavery—saved the nation not only because it won but because, indeed, it had virtue on its side. As the scientist Garrett Hardin said, *freedom is the recognition of necessity.* That freedom itself must by necessity be limited, is also a principle of freedom. The Founding Fathers understood this when they acknowledged that democratic government cannot embrace all points of view, especially those intolerant to democracy itself. Without the same understanding, Lincoln would not have been able to insist that the principles of freedom and equality are nonnegotiable, that they do not depend on the people's choice or their vote but are the precondition of their having the right to choose and vote in the first place. This principled way of thinking gave Lincoln the authority to limit the South's excesses and abuse of freedom. This is what kept the Union together.

The tendency toward friction and explosiveness between the spirits of youth and authority did not of course end once and for all with the Civil War. These spirits reverberate throughout American history and culture like echoes. They are always the same voices but in different contexts. The situations and the opposing parties change but the nature of the polarity remains the same. Groups and sections of society that perpetually antagonize each other usually face off according to youth-authority distinctions. The more intense the spiritual schism, the more intense the alienation, hostility, and violence between camps that fall on opposing sides of the youth-authority dialectic. In ways more subtle and diverse, America today is still a battlefield. The State of the Union very much depends on the state of the union of the spirits of youth and authority.

## The American Heroic Ideal, Yesterday and Today

The spirit of youth, as Jung pointed out, is traditionally depicted in the form of a young god or hero. Ancient and medieval cultures produced a rich variety of such figures. Those that are divine include Iacchus, Tammuz, Adonis, Attis, Dionysus and Bacchus, Hermes and Mercury, Athena and Minerva, Persephone, Artemis and Diana, Odin and Wotan, Baldur, Krishna, and again, Jesus Christ. Among the heroes (some of them historical), one can count Gilgamesh, Samson, King David, Hercules, Alexander the Great, Arjuna, Siegfried, St. George the Dragonslayer, and the Arthurian Knights of the Round Table. The spirit of youth is a force that seeks its own self-expression.

In America, the spirit of youth has also naturally expressed itself through a youthful heroic ideal. However, what makes America truly remarkable is that its original heroic ideal, as embodied in the Founding Fathers, represented a unique synthesis of the spirits of youth and authority. Though it was predominantly youthful, as the heroic aspiration toward greatness always is, it was tempered by a sensible understanding of what the ancients considered greatness and the *limits* to greatness. Ambition was coupled with intellectual and moral reflection and an earthy, commonsense wisdom, and there was a genuine sense of purpose and direction that aimed to serve the common good and not just the individual. Indeed, the Founding Fathers highly valued what the Romans meant by common sense, or *sensus communis*—namely, not only that which makes good sense, but an intellectual and moral sensibility and a sense of what is good for the community or humanity.

Today we find America in different circumstances. With the spirits of youth and authority almost entirely split apart from each other, America's definition of greatness is caught in a heroic ideal that is one-sided in its youthfulness. This brings out the negative aspects of both spirits. On the one hand, there is an ambitious optimism and innocence that permeate society. With little or no critical reflection and few authoritative reference points from which to ask the right questions—the ancient or ageless questions—America is unable to grasp what is happening to it. As it has become fixed in a condition of perennial youth, the unrestricted greatness of which Jung spoke in 1930 has today become a great restriction. There are no limits on anything, there is at best only a vague sense of purpose and direction, and a void of common sense pervades public policy and affairs. On the other hand, a dissociated spirit of authority always comes back to haunt society with efforts to compensate the latter's missing heroism, but these efforts also tend to be immature and are, moreover, senile and sterile. They are rigid, ossified forms of authority, often relying on black-and-white thinking and measures to get a hold on a culture that is experienced as running amok.

In the remaining chapters of Part I, we will examine America's original heroic ideal and its devolution into the heroic ideal prevalent today.

# Chapter 2

## The Revolutionary

*Tis not in mortals to command success,*
*But we'll do more, Sempronius, we'll deserve it.*

—Cato, in Joseph
Addison's *Cato*

*I think of a hero as someone who understands the degree of*
*responsibility that comes with his freedom. . . .*

—Bob Dylan

### A Distant Galaxy

It is not only because of chronology that the revolutionary patriot is the prototype of the American heroic ideal. It is true that the patriots, in bravely revolting against British tyranny and leading the colonies to nationhood, earned the right to become America's first heroes. And there was a long trail of them, beginning as early as with Nathaniel Bacon, who led an uprising against the Governor of the Virginia Colony in 1676. His rebellion was of historic significance not only because it was the most serious challenge to royal authority prior to the Revolution, but also because it was the first instance in which blacks and whites fought together side by side.

Naturally, the patriots who were more pivotal to the Revolution itself are the ones that are thought of as America's original heroes. They include such figures as Samuel Adams and his cohorts at the Boston Tea Party, the English immigrant Thomas Paine whose pamphlet *Common Sense* helped ignite the fire of revolution in the hearts of many colonists, and Paul Revere who alerted the minutemen that the British were coming. If not them, then the many who followed in their footsteps were heroes in the traditional sense of their era: As military history shows, many heroes never survived the wars that made them heroes. Theirs were acts of self-sacrifice, often lacking glory and done with no guarantee of helping anyone. The soldiers of the American Revolution were for the large part such unsung heroes.

Of course, the revolutionary patriots who most influenced the American heroic ideal were the Founding Fathers. They were the heroes of the heroes, revered even in their day as a breed apart from ordinary men. As the historian Herman Hover writes, "One of the mysteries of colonial America is why, with a population less than half that of modern Los Angeles, it provided a galaxy of distinguished leaders—including Benjamin Franklin, George Washington, John Adams, Thomas Jefferson, Alexander Hamilton, James Madison, George Mason, and John Marshall—that we cannot begin to duplicate today." The Founding Fathers are special heroes because of the great qualities of character that they embodied, and it is above all for this reason that they are the prototype of the American heroic ideal. They are admired not only for their deeds but because they were great men.

A great man or woman and a hero are not always the same, and indeed, today they are rarely the same. A hero today is glorified either for accomplishing a certain feat, noble or not, or for imitating the heroic by exuding a certain radiance that raises him or her out of the sphere of the commonplace. The latter qualification is what, for example, elevates celebrities to the status of idols. The German sociologist Max Weber first used the term "charisma" to designate this radiance, and defined it as "a certain quality of an individual personality by virtue of which he is set apart from ordinary men and treated as endowed with supernatural, superhuman, or at least specifically exceptional powers or qualities." From charismatic personality to genuine hero, however, is a long leap, and the latter does not necessarily presuppose the former. For instance, Jefferson, with his soft voice, was a notoriously uncharismatic public figure, which may have had something to do with why he became the literary intellectual and philosopher of the American Revolution.

The mystery Hover alludes to becomes a little more fathomable when we consider the spiritual constitution of the Founding Fathers. Regardless of whatever religious and ideological differences they may have personally had, on the whole their behavior and their efforts to solve their problems demonstrated a remarkably high degree of integrity. It can be argued that no American hero since them, except for Abraham Lincoln, held that degree of integrity. At the minimum, integrity here needs to be understood the way it was by the classical philosophers whom the Founding Fathers so emulated: that is, as a moral obligation and a standard of how to live in the world, a standard of the good life. Integrity in this sense implies the practice of virtue and of bringing harmony to human nature. But the Founding Fathers also understood integrity in its more modern sense, as an expression of psychological and ethical wholeness. The literary critic Robert Grudin insists that this sense of integrity depends upon three things: an inner, psychological harmony or wholeness; a conformity of personal expression with psychological reality—of act with desire, of word with thought, of face with mind, of outer self with inner self; and lastly, continuity of all this over time. Certainly these qualities were exhibited in varying degrees by the Founding Fathers, but in the perception of many Americans today, are sorely lacking in our contemporary leaders.

The psychologist John Beebe points out that most heroic integrity violates psychological and ethical wholeness because it takes a limited part, party, theme, or issue and makes it all-important, as in the case, for example, of nationalism. Genuine integrity is broader than that kind of integrity. The heroism of the Founding Fathers aspired toward genuine integrity insofar as it strove to rise above partial perspectives and gave form to universal principles that spoke to all human beings. It is true that they failed to include all Americans in their democratic enterprise; they were, like the nation they represented, divided on the issue of slavery, and they considered women second-class citizens. But the documents and institutions they passed down to history were inseminated with the seeds of inclusivity. Once they uttered the word "equality," their heroism was bound to serve a larger cause and move beyond the restricted way this word was originally used. And Jefferson, who made equality the cornerstone of the Declaration of Independence, knew emancipation would have to occur. Himself a conflicted slaveowner, he knew that one day the moral incompatibility between slavery and the principles of the American Revolution would come to a head, and he feared, bloodily. In the Virginia Assembly, the federal Congress, and his published *Notes on the State of Virginia,* he expressed his views in favor of the abolition of the slave trade and emancipation. Given the strong public resistance he was met with, he eventually took the position that the problem would have to be passed along to the next generation of American statesmen, which needless to say is what happened. The integrity was there, but unfortunately, not the possibility for its integration into society, at least not yet. It can be argued that even the integrity was not yet fully developed or mature. To many, the fact that Jefferson never freed his own slaves suggests this.

In spite of such human flaws, the Founding Fathers still stand out among history's great leaders and innovators. There are two tracks by which we may come to understand the unique synthesis of youth and authority that distinguished them. The first is their character, and the second, their vision. The latter consists of the heroic mission or fate they envisioned for America, and, combining an emphasis on moral enlightenment or authority with a variety of youthful features, it will be discussed in later chapters. These tracks naturally intersect, and the question of which comes first is, to a degree, a chicken-egg question. Is character the deciding factor of fate, as Heraclitus believed, or do the possibilities and challenges of fate—the forces of history—shape the development of character? Both seem to be true, but I am inclined to believe that at least in the case of the Founding Fathers, the element of character was primary. They were, with all their shortcomings, men of character. Their character, no doubt a cultured product of their times but also something that had a quality of divine grace or blessedness about it, shaped their vision. This vision was not quite there to begin with. It emerged as the reality of the United States of America became a distinct possibility. George Washington recognized how important the issue of character was to the formation of the United States: "We now have a National character to establish," he wrote when the Revolution was coming to its conclusion, "and it is of the utmost importance to stamp favorable impressions upon it." And he knew, like Jefferson and other Founding Fathers who were more populist in inclination, that these impressions must come from the people and not solely from the leaders of the Revolution; the "We" he referred to is the same We as in "We the People." And yet, he knew that he and his fellow founders, as the chosen representatives and leaders of the people, were most responsible for setting the precedents of which impressions would be stamped on the national character.

## The Recognition of Necessity

One obvious way the Founding Fathers stamped their character on the nation was with their belief in freedom with restraint. Freedom is an aspect of youth, and restraint an aspect of authority. A word about each is in order.

What the Founding Fathers meant by freedom is often misunderstood. There is a general confusion between liberty and democracy. As the historian Richard Hofstadter points out in his classic study, *The American Political Tradition*, the Founding Fathers subcribed to a political theory that in a crucial sense directly opposes mainstream American democratic faith. The Founding Fathers, though revolutionaries, were not freedom fighters, or at least fighters for freedom at large. In fact, the liberty they were most concerned with, the right to ownership and protection of property, was in their view threatened by democracy. They did not, for example, believe in the right of the masses to have free access to the nation's unappropriated wealth, or of the squatter to occupy unused land. Though "all men are created equal," they also possess different natural faculties and abilities to acquire wealth, and the Founding Fathers believed that the liberty to exercise these differences also required protection. Majority rule, the basic premise of democracy, would surely bring arbitrary redistribution of property, destroying the very essence of liberty.

The liberties the Founding Fathers wished to obtain are best described in terms of their negative gains. Hofstadter writes: "They wanted freedom from fiscal uncertainty and irregularities in the currency, from trade wars among the states, from economic discrimination by more powerful foreign governments, from attacks on the creditor class or on property, from popular insurrection. They aimed to create a government that would act as an honest broker among a variety of propertied interests, giving them all protection from their common enemies and preventing any one of them from becoming too powerful." Freedom was thus very narrowly conceived. The Constitution did not require that it be extended to those classes in America that most needed it, namely, slaves and indentured servants. Nor did it, in its original form, insist on civil liberties. It was the opponents of the Constitution, Hofstadter notes, who were most vocal about the need for such essential liberties as freedom of religion, freedom of speech and press, jury trial, due process, and protection from unreasonable searches and seizures. These had to be added into the first ten amendments because the Constitutional Convention failed to include them in the original document. In other words, freedom to the Founding Fathers was not the idealistic, all-embracing idea that one might expect would have burst forth from a youthful, revolutionary movement. As with the integrity of their position on slavery, the Founding Fathers' conception of freedom needed to ripen and mature. All things that are born are born young, and a democracy is no exception. The new republic of the Founding Fathers would look forward not only to the promising prospects of youth, but to youth's many hurdles and growing pains.

The Founding Fathers' sense of restraint perhaps came easier than their efforts to define freedom. It was rooted in their sober understanding of the human condition. Adams, for example, wrote the following to the more idealistic Jefferson in an attempt to caution him, as Jefferson was generally opposed to restraining man within any institutional or social design: "Power always thinks it has a great soul, and vast views, beyond the comprehension of the weak; and that it is doing God's service, when it is violating all His laws. Our passions, ambition, avarice, love, resentment, etc., possess so much metaphysical subtlety, and so much overpowering eloquence, that they insinuate themselves into the understanding and the conscience, and convert both to their party." How similar are Adams' words to those of the Puritan John Cotton a century earlier: "Let all the world give mortall man no greater power than they are content they shall use, for use it they will." As noted in the last chapter, this healthy suspicion of the human tendency to abuse power is what lies behind the careful devices of the Constitution. The Constitution, the journalist Horace White observed, "is based upon the philosophy of Hobbes and the religion of Calvin. It assumes that the natural state of mankind is a state of war, and that the carnal mind is at enmity with God." In other words, the Constitution is an instrument of authority designed to curtail not only the excesses of authority itself, but the darker impulses of youth, including primal youth.

The Founding Fathers recognized that for democracy to be a viable alternative to authoritarianism on the one hand and anarchy on the other, it needed to have a built-in authority that established restraints and balances. Carefully blending freedom and restraint together into a cohesive and practicable system of government was a work of true genius and a monumental historical achievement. The separation of church and state, the division of government into executive, judicial, and legislative branches, and the protection of states' rights against federal intrusion, all aimed to create a democracy with sound, well-defined limits and safeguards. James Madison is generally acknowledged as the chief mastermind behind the Constitution. He understood his task in no uncertain terms: "In framing a government which is to be administered by men over men, the great difficulty lies in this: you must first enable the government to control the governed; and in the next place oblige it to control itself."

The division of the legislature into a Senate and a House of Representatives was also intended to oblige the government to control or check itself.

Thomas Paine, believing that democracy did not need to be so regulated, denounced this division as a deception and called for single-chamber representation of the people. Adams, however, felt that Paine's plan was "so democratical, without any restraint or even an attempt at any equilibrium or counter-poise, that it must produce confusion and every evil work." Adams believed that popular assemblies needed to be checked because they were "productive of hasty results and absurd judgements." Needless to say, Adams' position won. In the end, the popular assembly was divided into two houses coexisting with a strong executive armed with veto power. The whole system was then counterweighted yet again by an independent judiciary. All this would not only maintain order against popular uprisings and against majority rule by a single faction, but would offset the inevitable tendency of the rich and the poor to plunder each other. The principle of democratic government with effective checks and balances can be traced back to sources as ancient as Aristotle and Polybius. However, the recognition of necessity that makes it possible to value this principle could not have been simply gleaned from history books. The Founding Fathers evidently "worked" with this virtue in their souls.

## The Cultivation of Character

The Founding Fathers stamped their character on the nation in ways other than their contributions to constitutional government and policymaking. Their example in matters of social and political conduct—particularly Washington in setting the style, limits, and modest tone of the presidency as compared to that of the monarchies of his day—has been duly noted by historians. Jefferson's impact on American education and his emphasis on open, public discourse to keep the spirit of democracy fresh and alive cannot be overstated. Like Jefferson, Benjamin Franklin was a Renaissance man—a statesman, scientist, inventor, publisher, printer, and the first Postmaster General. A well-rounded character was considered among the virtues of a number of the Founding Fathers. But it was with their virtues in general that the Founding Fathers made their deepest if not most visible impression on the American heroic ideal. This had less to do with legendary tales like the young Washington confessing to cutting down his father's cherry tree than with the fact that they were serious students of history, the classics, philosophy, and ethics.

The appreciation the Founding Fathers had for the virtues and vocation of the Greeks and Romans—a vocation that aspired to find truth and create a moral society—was fed by the ambience of the Enlightenment. Montesquieu, who stands out as one of the stronger influences on the Founding Fathers, deplored the loss of this vocation in European civilization. Washington was not impervious to such influences. Though he was chosen to be the first president because of his heroic stature and his qualities of honor, modesty, and calmness, and not because of his intellectual stature, he was, like the second and third presidents who were intellectuals, an acknowledged lover of things Roman. Of course, we are here speaking of Roman civilization at its height, and not during its decadent phases when it was in decline. Being well-acquainted with this civilization, the Founding Fathers knew too well what transpired when it lost its virtue. The famous quip Franklin made to Eliza Powel during the Constitutional Convention in response to what the Americans had created—"a republic, if you can keep it"—was referring largely to this. The Romans had built a great republic that lasted a few centuries, but they could not sustain it. The Founding Fathers hoped to do better.

Thus, they knew that they should learn from the Roman example and, with respect to ethics and virtues, not only avoid reinventing the wheel, but improve upon the vehicle if possible. Washington was compared even in his own day to Cincinnatus, the Roman statesman and general who after serving selflessly relinquished power to return to his fields. Washington was a great admirer of the first-century Roman philosopher and playwright Seneca, whose ideas of virtue were made available in a seventeenth-century translation of his essays, *Seneca's Morals.* He was also greatly taken by Joseph Addison's 1713 drama *Cato* about the Roman statesman and philosopher of the same name, and quoted from it throughout his lifetime. It is a story about the failure to live virtuously, or rather, about living by a code of virtues that is incomplete and even inhumane in its practical applications.

Jefferson, who with Adams was particularly passionate among the Founding Fathers in the study and advocacy of the means to lead a moral, principled life, made no pretensions about what he thought about both the greatness and limitations of Greek and Roman ethics. Speaking of Pythagoras, Socrates, Epicurus, Cicero, Epictetus, Seneca, and Antoninus, Jefferson bluntly expressed his view in two points:

> 1. Their precepts related chiefly to ourselves, and the government of those passions which, unrestrained, would disturb our tranquillity of mind. In this branch of philosophy they were really great.

2. In developing our duties to others, they were short and defective. They embraced, indeed, the circles of kindred and friends, and inculcated patriotism, or the love of our country in the aggregate, as a primary obligation; towards our neighbors and countrymen they taught justice, but scarcely viewed them as within the circle of benevolence. Still less have they inculcated peace, charity, and love to our fellow-men, or embraced with benevolence the whole family of mankind.

Jefferson went on to compile his secularized, demystified version of the gospel of Jesus, emphasizing the latter's moral teachings. These he felt were "more pure and perfect than those of the most correct of the philosophers." It was on its humanitarian grounds and not its theological grounds that Jefferson accepted Christianity. When he called himself a Christian—"a *real* Christian"—he meant that he was an adherent of the morality of Jesus. Sympathizing with this approach, Adams accentuated the value of this morality on a national level: "One great advantage of the Christian religion is, that it brings the great principle of the law of nature and nations,—Love your neighbor as yourself, and do to others as you would that others should do to you,—to the knowledge, belief, and veneration of the whole people." Intrinsic to this view is the understanding that nations, and not just individuals, flourish or fall on the character of their morality. It was not per se a Christian nation that the Founding Fathers advocated, but a moral nation.

If one had to sum up the Founding Fathers' ideal of what constituted heroism, it was simply the cultivation of character or virtue in a practical way. "Practical" here means the art of living, and not just *making* a living. It is not true what Max Weber said about Benjamin Franklin's "art of virtue." All of Franklin's moral attitudes, Weber wrote in *The Protestant Ethic and the Spirit of Capitalism*, "are coloured with utilitarianism. Honesty is useful, because it assures credit; so are punctuality, industry, frugality, and that is the reason they are virtues. . . . According to Franklin, those virtues, like all others, are only in so far virtues as they are actually useful to the individual. . . . Man is dominated by the making of money, by acquisition as the ultimate purpose of his life." (A somewhat similar opinion was expressed by D.H. Lawrence in his study of American literature.) It is true that Franklin extolled such virtues as industry and frugality as prerequisites for acquiring one's material comfort and fortune. But to claim that the aim of these virtues was solely material gain is to put the cart before the horse and overlook what Franklin believed was the implicit purpose that connected money-making with social skills and scientific and creative invention. Wealth was valued, but chiefly as one of the necessary preconditions for moral and intellectual development, that is, for the cultivation of character. As the historian Christopher Lasch writes, "Self-improvement is not the same thing as self-advancement, in Franklin's eyes; indeed, ambition, in the eighteenth century, was a Hamiltonian much more than a Franklinian or Jeffersonian virtue."

The Franklinian and Jeffersonian hero's handbook or vade mecum was a guide to moral health. It included such virtues as self-discipline, common sense and the cultivation of reason (the latter being the Enlightenment's equivalent to the alchemist's gold), evenness of temper, knowledge and usefulness, moderation, sincerity, justness, living within one's means, devotion to community, cheerfulness, and wisdom. There was nothing mysterious or esoteric about this code of living. For example, the Virginia Declaration of Rights, authored by George Mason, boldly states that "no free government, or the blessings of liberty, can be preserved by any people but by firm adherence to justice, moderation, temperance, frugality, and virtue, and by frequent recurrence to fundamental principles." And the Declaration of Independence itself concludes with a profound commitment of purpose on the parts of the Founding Fathers: "And for the support of this Declaration, with a firm reliance on the protection of divine Providence, we mutually pledge to each other our Lives, our Fortunes and our sacred Honor." How many people are there in America today who feel strongly enough about something altruistic to dedicate themselves to it with this kind of selflessness?

It needs to be stressed that the heroic ideal of the Founding Fathers was not to be confused with hero worship or the idealization of particular heroes, not even the Founding Fathers themselves. For the greater part they were not men who were deluded about their own limitations, and moreover, they knew that every individual must cultivate virtue and integrity as an expression of his or her own humanity. With his philosophy of tolerance, Jefferson would never have imposed upon others an expectation to conform to his own personal program of self-improvement. Even the cultivation of virtue and integrity needs to be a democratic process. Rather than imitate heroes, people should strive to become themselves, or rather, the best of themselves. *This* was the heroic ideal of the Founding Fathers.

# Chapter 3

## The Frontiersman

*The history of any public character involves not only the facts about him but what the public has taken to be the facts.*

—J. Frank Dobie

### The Backwoods Boasters

Mr. Speaker.

Who—Who—Whoop—Bow—Wow—Wow—Yough. I say, Mr. Speaker; I've had a speech in soak this six months, and it has swelled me like a drowned horse; if I don't deliver it I shall burst and smash the windows. The gentleman from Massachussetts talks of summing up the merits of the question, but I'll sum up my own. In one word I'm a screamer, and have got the roughest racking horse, the prettiest sister, the surest rifle and the ugliest dog in the district. I'm a leetle the savagest crittur you ever *did see*. My father can whip any man in Kentucky, and I can lick my father. I can out-speak any man on this floor, and give him two hours start. I can run faster, dive deeper, stay longer under, and come out drier, than any *chap* this side the big *Swamp*. I can outlook a panther and out-stare a flash of lightning, tote a steamboat on my back and play at rough and tumble with a lion, and an occasional kick from a *zebra*. To sum up all in one word *I'm a horse*. Goliah was a pretty hard colt but I could choke him. I can take the rag off—frighten the old folks—astonish the natives—and beat the Dutch all to smash—

make nothing of sleeping under a blanket of snow—and don't mind being frozen more than a rotten apple.

Congress allows *lemonade* to the members and has it charged under the head of stationary—I move also that *whiskey* be allowed under the item of *fuel*. For *bitters* I can suck away at a noggin of aquafortis, sweetened with brimstone, stirred with a lightning rod, and skimmed with a hurricane. I've soaked my head and shoulders in Salt River, so much that I'm always corned. I can walk like an ox, run like a fox, swim like an eel, yell like an Indian, fight like a devil, spout like an earthquake, make love like a mad bull, and swallow a nigger whole without choking if you butter his head and pin his ears back.

That was reportedly the beginning of a speech by Davy Crockett to the U.S. Congress, of which he became a three-term elected member. Needless to say, it is colorful, brash, and, at least in its use of language, racist. The frontiersman was a notorious braggart, admired as much for this, strangely enough, as for the incredible feats he bragged about. He was an earthy, rough-and-tumble, populist hero. The greatness and wildness of the American continent became his own. In becoming larger than life and consciously creating his image as such, he became the blueprint of many American heroes. Andrew Jackson ("Old Hickory") was a frontiersman; Abraham Lincoln, with his many "true grit" qualities, was the son of a frontiersman; all the cowboys—Kit Carson, Wild Bill Hickok, Buffalo Bill, and Wyatt Earp, to mention just a few—were frontiersmen; and Theodore Roosevelt, with his love of nature, hunting, ranching, and adventure, was perhaps one of the last frontiersmen. Though their kind has passed into history with the conquest of the frontier, the heroic ideal that they represented lives on through the characteristics Americans still look for and emulate in their heroes.

The American folklorist B.A. Botkin has accurately described how the "backwoods boasters" have influenced the American heroic ideal: "A composite picture of the American hero would show him to be a plain, tough, practical fellow, equally good at a bargain or a fight, a star-performer on the job and a hell-raiser off it, and something of a salesman and a showman, with a flair for prodigious stories, jokes, and stunts and a general capacity for putting himself over." We see these characteristics in so many American hero figures, ranging from film stars like John Wayne and Clark Gable to entrepreneurs like Henry Ford and Ross Perot to politicians like Lyndon Johnson and Ronald Reagan (the latter often pictured on horseback and in cowboy gear on his western ranch). The frontiersman captured par excellence the extroverted temperament of the American, and introduced the inclination toward things fantastic that would henceforth color the American's aspiration toward greatness.

The frontiersman was basically a pioneer, and his heroism reflected the pioneer spirit. His fierce courage and independence, his "diamond-in-the-rough" chivalry, and his skill with a rifle all became the stuff of legends, but were in fact rooted in the harsh realities of life on the American frontier. Not only was America's environment still untamed, but most of it had not yet even been claimed and charted, and so it was with good reason that the frontiersman became a hero. Jefferson himself held the frontiersman in high regard. Of Daniel Boone, he said, "We have recently seen a single person go and decide on a settlement in Kentucky. Though perpetually harassed by Indians, that settlement in the course of ten years has acquired 30,000 inhabitants." Jefferson estimated that if other men were brave enough to follow Boone's example, the entire continent would be America's within two generations.

Jefferson's enthusiasm for Boone is not surprising in light of the meaning he assigned Boone's trailblazing. The frontier, particularly the Western frontier with its seemingly endless possibilities, was to Jefferson an inoculum against the national aging process, at least for the remainder of the nineteenth century. It was, in the words of the historian Joseph Ellis, "America's fountain of youth." Expansion for Jefferson, as his Louisiana Purchase demonstrated, was a practical or political matter of enlarging America and insuring its future vitality. But it was not only this. The development of the continent also expressed his spiritual belief that the highest form of human endeavor is activity—not the activity of urban life, which he felt was antithetical to an agrarian way of living in harmony with nature, but activity which brings to fruition man's innate capacities. Jefferson's idea of progress was not industrial progress, but, in the vein of the Enlightenment, progress of the human condition. This would surely occur through the advancement of knowledge, especially knowledge of nature and science. Nature was man's proper place. His proper destiny or purpose thus consisted of activity that was grounded in nature and natural things. "Natural things" included life, liberty, and happiness.

For Jefferson, happiness did not mean what it means today. It did not imply happiness in the individualistic sense of personal well-being, or the hedonism of modern pleasure-seeking. It meant rather "the happiness of the species" or "the happiness of mankind" through material prosperity and resilient survival. The abundant land and resources afforded by the American continent were the great discovery of the day, for they would make such happiness possible on a large scale. Given the predatory nature and other limitations of societies in Europe, this pursuit could never occur there. The means to happiness in America would be through development of its seemingly boundless abundance. "The assignment which man found in America," Boorstin writes, "was less the attainment of any specific destination, than simple and effective activity. . . . The Jeffersonian philosophy was an incentive toward populating a continent and building a society." Daniel Boone, in Jefferson's eyes, was a pioneer of this assignment and incentive; his kind was the leading edge in the pursuit of happiness.

We see here even more clearly the unique synthesis of youth and authority in the character of the Founding Fathers. This synthesis was evident in their philosophy of living as much as their philosophy of government. The Jeffersonian and Franklinian virtues can be assessed as a relationship between the spirits of youth and authority. Although Weber's contention that Franklin's art of virtue was purely for utilitarian purposes is not true, it is true that its utilitarian aspect was a key requirement for the development of the nation. The success of the American venture would depend upon that ever-so-strong virtue of youth: "simple and effective activity"; "building a society"; "the pursuit of happiness." These are all one and the same. Virtues of youth are concerned with doing; they tend to be economic virtues, such as industriousness, inventiveness, and so forth. Virtues of authority are concerned mostly with being, that is, the state of one's being; they enhance the quality of life, for example, generosity, compassion, and wisdom. Jefferson and Franklin knew that with the virtues of youth as the primary guidelines of American ambition, Americans would need to have the balancing virtues of authority, and that is why, in addition to their intrinsic value, they placed such emphasis on them. Again, they did not want America to repeat the fate of Rome.

Boone, one of the first frontiersmen, was unfortunately also one of the last that Jefferson would feel had captured this balance of virtues. With the frontiersmen who came after Boone—namely, the Davy Crockett-type that paved the way for the election of Andrew Jackson—the heroic ideal of the Founding Fathers would begin to dramatically change. The historian Richard Slotkin astutely described the manifest forms of this transformation:

> The land speculators and ambitious cotton planters and artisan-entrepreneurs who rose to meet the opportunity of the frontier windfall (and a generally expanding commerical economy) did not accept the limitations implied in Jeffersonian ideology. They did not deal deferentially with the established leaders of society, nor adapt manners and morals to the requirements of high culture.

Their urge to exploit resources of land and of labor was limited only by self-interest, calculated (by and large) for the short term. They were willing to proceed with the dispossession of the Indians without waiting for the operations of an enlightened Indian policy to justify and ameliorate the process. They were willing to risk the outbreak of class and interest-group conflict in their drive for financial success. Andrew Jackson was, for Jefferson, the type of this rising class, and he regarded Jackson as a sinister figure: a border warrior without Boone's philosophic restraint, who had scrapped his way from low estate to membership in the slaveholding class, but who remained a frontier brawler, duelist, speculator, and demagogue.

Simply stated, the new breed of frontiersmen did not fulfill Jefferson's ideal of an enlightened citizenry in whom the economic virtues and moral virtues were balanced.

## The Quintessential American Hero

With the emergence of the cowboy in the second half of the nineteenth century, the American heroic ideal further transformed. The youth-authority synthesis of the Founding Fathers during this period deteriorated and became polarized in a number of social contexts, the most significant of which was the Civil War. The Civil War soldier, like the revolutionary patriot, also became a hero figure, but in the final analysis he did not add anything to the character of the American heroic ideal that wasn't already there. In spite of the noble causes for which they may be fighting, soldiers at war are so universal or homogenous in character that the impressions they leave on the heroic ideals of their nations are more similar than distinct from each other. Their courageous deeds are usually in service to well-defined national interests, and thus, war heroes are venerated in much the same way in every nation. The cowboy, on the other hand, is an American original. An embodiment of pure youth, he eventually became, with the advent of radio, movies, and television, the unbridled hero of millions of American youngsters. But it is not fair to say that he spoke only their language. He appealed to American audiences at large because he spoke the language of the American spirit of youth.

The cowboy was the quintessential free spirit. He stereotypically roamed where he wanted, worked when he wanted, and lived an adventurous if hard life. In retrospect, by modern standards, the cowboy life appears somewhat antiquated and dull, which is one reason the Western genre hardly appears today in film or television. Intergalactic space has become the new frontier, and Captain Picard and his like the new cowboys. Nevertheless, their prototype *is* the cowboy.

As the American heroic ideal shifted from a synthesis of youth and authority to a one-sidedness of youth, the element of fantasy—one of youth's favorite forms of creative expression—also increased, reconfiguring the cowboy into an altogether new breed of American hero. By this I do not mean that the cowboy was believed to perform extraordinary or impossible feats, although he was saddled with his fair share of these, no pun intended. The truly fantastic was left for America's fairytale heroes, its mythical giants and strong men, like Paul Bunyan and, more recently, Superman and Batman. The cowboy dwelled in the borderland between imagination and history. The way fantasy entered into the picture with him was with what the American psyche did with him: it transformed him from a roughneck into a smooth-mannered fellow of high character. What started off as a love of bravado in the tall tales of Davy Crockett became the spellbound veneration of a kind of demigod whose stature was measured by his brawniness, instinctual intelligence, and calm, cool, collected demeanor.

This romanticizing of the cowboy predates the heroes that were fabricated by Hollywood. The legend-making began well before Gene Autry, Hopalong Cassidy, Matt Dillon, Maverick, the Lone Ranger, and Roy Rogers. Walter Noble Burns wrote this about an episode he experienced with Billy the Kid:

> A little while before we made a dash for our lives, the Kid rolled a cigarette. I watched him. It seemed just then as if he had about a minute and a half to live. But when he poured the tabacco from his pouch into the cigarette paper he did not spill a flake. His hand was as steady as steel. A blazing chunk of roof fell on the table beside him, barely missing his head. "Much obliged," he said; and he bent over and lighted his cigarette from the flame. Then he looked at me and grinned as if he thought that was a good joke. He didn't roll that cigarette because he was nervous but because he wanted a good smoke. You could tell by the way he inhaled the smoke and let it roll out of his mouth that he was getting real pleasure out of it. If you had seen Billy the Kid roll that cigarette and smoke it, senōr, you would have known at once that he was a brave man.

Billy the Kid was just the first of a string of killers that was on the wrong side of the law, and glorified for it. Jesse James, Sam Bass, and Butch Cassidy and the Sundance Kid were some other notorious outlaws who were beloved. They tend to fall, at least in the American imagination, into the second category of a hero typology developed by B.A. Botkin, whose general description of the American hero was cited above. In all, Botkin saw three specific types of American heroes: the poor boy who makes good, the good boy gone wrong, and the kind that is too good or too bad to be true. In some measure, the good boy gone wrong is the good boy gone primitive. The primal youth that emerged when the frontiersman confronted the primitive, intractable wilderness of the American continent is most vividly expressed in the wild tales of the outlaws. They became what they beheld. Also, their outlaw status is an expression of the outsider archetype or motif, itself perennially older than their particular stories and experiences, as the biblical story of Cain illustrates. Indeed, the frontiersmen *were* outsiders in a vast, hostile environment, and the glorification of the outlaw is a twisted sort of celebration of their "go-it-alone," "against-all-odds" stand against nature and the established social order. This is what has made the outlaw a favored figure in the country western, folk, and rock ballads of Johnny Cash, Bob Dylan, the Eagles, and others. Although this heroism of the rugged individualist is clearly a development of the frontier, one can argue that its seeds were planted as early as with the colonial experience of revolt against British authority, if not earlier. After all, from the British standpoint, the Founding Fathers were outlaws.

Of course, the Founding Fathers were hardly deviants or derelicts, even in light of the recent, revisionary trend of scholarship that has portrayed them as self-serving aristocrats or at least as human beings with flaws like everyone else. If the cowboy is an American original, then the outlaw is unmistakably an American frontier original. He dramatically reflects the emerging schism in the American heroic ideal. The frontier outlaw prefigures the American gangster; viewed together, the two show that from Botkin's good boy who has gone wrong to the boy who is too bad to be true is not such a far leap.

Certainly, the American fascination with villains strikes Europeans most curiously. Europeans of course also have novels, movies, and television shows about criminals, but the awe and glamor accorded them in America are largely absent in Europe, and they are far less idealized. Films like "Bonnie and Clyde," "The Godfather," "Silence of the Lambs," and even "Pulp Fiction" which reveals the banality of criminal types, may be appreciated in Europe, but everybody there knows that such films are distinctly American products. "The Americans," Oscar Wilde said, "are certainly great hero worshippers, and always take their heroes from the criminal classes." This is slightly overstated but expresses the basic European sentiment.

The kind of hero that is too bad to be true trumpets humanity's dark side, its propensity toward evil or—in the words of Horace White—toward being in a natural state of war against itself and of enmity with God. Jung called this side of human nature the shadow. All people and peoples have it, and no nation has the privilege of being exempt from it. Nor is the *fascination* with evil unique to the American people. The problem of evil has in one way or another gripped the minds of people in every civilization— much as it should have, for it is a profound and serious problem. But the confluence of the heroic ideal with the dark or evil side of human nature seems to be an altogether different matter. The release of this dark side in the form of an idealized image in American culture became that much more possible with the decline of the authority principle that began, in at least one of its strains, with the emergence of the frontiersman. It is important to recognize that it is not just some ethereal image or ideal that has been re-leased in this trend. The heroic ideal conveys a culture's sense of what is right and wrong, what is acceptable and not. The rise of the criminal hero-image coincides with the rise of crime in America. The much-debated argu-ment of whether the media inspires crime or merely reflects it is predicated on a chicken-egg assumption. The rise of crime in society and the criminal-ization of the heroic ideal go together as figure and ground. One could not exist without the other.

## The Mysterious Indianization of the American People

No discussion of the American frontiersman could be complete without consideration of the Native American or Indian. Recent times have wit-nessed a reinstatement of the Indian as a human being with cultural in-tegrity, value, and pride. Films like "Dances with Wolves" portray him as a heroic figure in his own right. But there is something of a sleight of hand going on here in that this fad appears to transfer the heroic ideal of the fron-tiersman, when he was at his best, onto the Indian when in fact the transfer-ence was the other way around. A close look at Indian cultures and their in-fluence on the white man's frontier culture reveals that the frontiersman, particularly the cowboy, subconsciously absorbed the virtues and style of the Indian heroic ideal and made them his own. Jung was the first to ob-serve this influence, describing it as the "mysterious Indianization of the American people." The author Robert Pirsig also studied this phenomenon and came to the same conclusion. Both agreed that the legendary virtues of the Indian—his self-composure, extraordinary concentration, tenacity of purpose, and unflinching endurance of the greatest hardships—were sub-liminally infused into the American character. As far as history is con-cerned, this would not have been an unusual occurrence. Whenever one culture meets and dwells with another on the same soil, there is a merging of collective psyches. Or, if not this, the natural forces or "spirit" of the land that influenced the first culture now exert a similar influence on the second culture. "The foreign land," Jung wrote, "assimilates its conqueror." The communications theorist Marshall McLuhan expressed the same idea with his quip, "To the spoils belongs the victor."

It is no accident that an Indian head was for many years an emblem on American coins; that many places in the United States are named after In-dian tribes and leaders; that a number of American automobiles have also been named after Indian chiefs and tribes, not to mention totem animals (for example, Pontiac, Cherokee, Thunderbird); and that American sports, in their character and rigors, are closer to Indian games than European sports. The American incorporated the Indian temperament into his heroic ideal, and molded himself after it. With his cool silence, modest manner, and dangerous potential for violence, the cowboy, Pirsig writes, "is a rendi-tion of the cultural style of an American Indian." In their cowboy roles, John Wayne, Gary Cooper, Robert Redford, and Clint Eastwood mimicked this style, and insofar as Americans watched them with a rapt attention that bordered on religious awe, they partook in a spiritual bonding with the In-dian, albeit unconsciously.

This cultural style has now become so typically American that Ameri-cans are the last to recognize its Indian origins. In other matters of tem-perament as well, the American is as close to the Indian as to the Euro-pean, falling halfway between the two. "If you take a list of all the things European observers have stated to be the characteristics of white Ameri-cans," Pirsig argues, "you'll find that there is a correlation with the charac-teristics white American observers have customarily assigned to the Indi-ans. And if, furthermore, you take another list of all the characteristics that Americans use to describe Europeans you'll get a pretty good correlation with Indian opinions of white Americans." Europeans tend to think of Americans as untidy, too direct and plain-spoken, bad-mannered and inso-lent, childlike and naive, and violent and unable to control their impulses. During World War II Europeans noted that American troops drank too much and made trouble, but under fire were highly reliable. These are all features that Americans have also attributed to the Indian. Americans on the other hand often complain that Europeans are snobby, indirect, and "phony," qual-ities that the Indian feels belong to the "fork-tongued" white American.

The heroic ideal of the Indian has impressed itself upon the American in spiritual ways too. Jung points out that American college fraternity initiations, with their emphasis on trial by ordeal, parallel the initiation rites of Indian tribes. One may add the hazing rituals in the military that are so excessive that they have recently been the subject of media attention. Similarly, the American penchant for secret societies such as the Ku Klux Klan, the Masons, and the Knights of Columbus, many replete with initiation rites, finds its source as well in native mystery religions. And the shaman or medicine man as a conjurer of spirits has been transposed into American religion in the form of Christian evangelists, charismatics, and more recently, New Age "healers" who directly base their practices on Native American spirituality. The magical power of the word that propels these forms of religion is a cornerstone of Indian belief systems. Both the spoken and written word are accepted today in America with oracle-like authority, in secular and religious matters alike. As Jung writes, "There is no country on earth where the 'power-word,' the magic formula, the slogan or advertisement is more effective than in America." Contemporary American politics have become defined by this power-word, it now being called the "sound bite."

Last but not least, the Indian heroic ideal may have had a subtle role in the genesis of American democracy. Although the Founding Fathers borrowed much in their political thinking from other sources, the Indian's fundamental beliefs in freedom and social equality probably had some influence on even these other sources. Pirsig makes an interesting connection when he argues that Rousseau did not base his idea of social equality on the history of Europe, Asia, or Africa: "He got it from the impact of the New World upon Europe and from contemplation of one particular kind of individual who lived in the New World, the person he called the 'Noble Savage.' " The Indians lived in a social structure that was relatively free of the kind of hierarchical order that rendered one class of individuals socially inferior to another. Theirs was a more or less egalitarian society ("more or less" because, as the anthropologist George Murdock illustrated, no society is completely egalitarian and without hierarchy; and the Indians certainly had tribal chiefs and medicine men and women who held distinctive positions). The Indians did not need to formally institute equality and liberty; these were *always* self-evident truths because Native American societies were modeled upon an imitation of nature rather than a subjugation of it. To the Enlightenment thinker, the Noble Savage represented the "natural man" to whom natural rights were a given condition.

The Indians may have had influences on American democracy other than this philosophical connection. The relationship between the colonists and various Indian tribes was often extensive, and a number of early settlers had the opportunity to closely observe everyday life in Native American culture. It has been speculated that the Indians provided a role model for certain democratic practices of the colonists. For example, the word "caucus," some suggest, comes not from the supposed medieval Greek *kaukos* ("drinking cup"), but from the Algonquian *cau-cau-asu*, which means "meeting of the tribal elders." Certainly, the latter more accurately denotes what a caucus is.

Having said all this about the Indian, it is easier to conjecture from where the stereotype of the Indian as an amoral, bloodthirsty savage came. To be sure, this stereotype did have *some* foundation in fact, as revealed by the experience of Jesuits and others in Canada who had the misfortune of falling into the hands of the Iroquois. The film "Black Robe," based on documented accounts, shows how brutal and sadistic the warriors of this nation could be. But this by far was not the European settler's typical experience of the Indian. Something else motivated the need to make the Indian a *persona non grata* and worse, a nonperson altogether. If it is true that the Native American was the source of the frontiersman's heroic ideal, then the most expeditious way for the latter to make this ideal appear legitimately and solely his own was to denigrate all that was Native American. The Indian *had* to become an object of contempt—a scalper, an "Indian giver," a heathen. General Custer and the cruel campaign to make the Indian altogether invisible by relegating him to reservations were merely the next logical step. No one likes to be reminded that the best part of himself is not his own.

# Chapter 4

## Contemporary Heroic Idealism

*Turning and turning in the widening gyre*
*The falcon cannot hear the falconer;*
*Things fall apart; the centre cannot hold;*
*Mere anarchy is loosed upon the world.*

—W.B. Yeats

### The Continuing Saga of the Cowboy

The historical thread of the American heroic ideal, having unfolded from the revolutionary patriot of the eighteenth century into the frontiersman of the nineteenth century, branched out into numerous, diverse forms in the twentieth century. Although this was a natural, inevitable development accomodating the expressive needs of a modern, pluralistic society, it involved a fraying of the thread, a fragmentation or splintering that has left the nation without any real sense of what is and is not indeed heroic. This fraying can be seen on two levels. The first is the concrete level of hero-images—who or what constitutes a hero—and the second is a more subtle level in which the ideal is manifested in the culture through myriad forms, namely, the values, lifestyles, and trends of the society.

Hero-images are easy to identify. They are abundant, although in fact their blueprints number substantially fewer. Most hero-images in popular culture are derived from the frontiersman—the cowboy to be specific—or are some combination of the frontiersman with the hero-image of the day. But the hybrid is only a contemporary variation of the blueprint, and has added little to it that is new. For example, General Patton, with his pearl-handled pistol and brash manners and outspokenness, nicely recast the frontiersman-cowboy in the guise of a modern soldier. His heroic ethos played an important role in the Nixon administration. Nixon's favorite film was "Patton." He reportedly saw it many times, drawing upon it for inspiration and using it as a sort of divining rod in his decision to invade Cambodia and increase the bombing of Vietnam. "We will not be humiliated," Nixon said; America will not be a "pitiful, helpless giant." And Kissinger's diplomacy, too, was imbued with the ethos of the cowboy. Asked in an interview how he explained his "incredible movie-star status," he said: "Americans like the cowboy who leads the wagon train by riding ahead alone on his horse, the cowboy who rides all alone into the town. . . . and does everything by himself."

The Vietnam War was the result of a number of complex factors, but certainly the style it was conducted in is reminiscent of a kind of John Wayne, cowboy machismo. As the psychologist Thayer Greene reflects, "There is something still young, almost adolescent, in such nostalgic and heroic flexings of our national and military muscle." The indestructibility and invincibility of the cowboy are indeed not unlike that of the adolescent. In spite of the lessons America may have learned from the Vietnam War, it still draws upon this sense of heroic identity both in its global actions and its cultural expressions. The invasion of Grenada and the Persian Gulf War exuded a good deal of such machismo, even though the latter with its forged web of international alliances had less of a Lone Ranger quality than former American interventions abroad. Culturally, for every movie like "Apocalypse Now" or "Platoon" that cast a critical eye upon this heroic ideal, there has been a series of "Rambos." No doubt, this is the way a culture shifts its ideal—gradually and peripatetically, by going back and forth between old and new perspectives until a new ideal emerges.

Bill Clinton's first act as president seemed like a distinct step toward exorcising the ghost of the cowboy from the military. Though his attempt to legalize the status of gays in the military was short-lived and dismissed as a foolhardy blow to his young presidency, it legitimized the issue as worthy of presidential attention and sounded a note that would forever change the military. After this and such scandals as Tailhook, women's rights and integration into the military also became a prominent focus, as did the propriety of sexual behavior on the part of men toward women in the armed services. The traditional model of the American soldier as ruthlessly tough, tight-lipped, competitive, and a sexual conqueror was beginning to make way for a new model. The military itself was becoming more civilized or genteel.

# A Simple Problem

But in truth, the American psyche can no more exorcize from its character the basic orientation of its heroic ideal than modern man can root out from his brain the instincts of aggression and hoarding that he inherited from his hunting and gathering days. Heroic ideals serve history the way instincts serve evolution, and you can't fool Father Time any easier than you can fool Mother Nature.

Essentially, the historical thread of America's heroic ideal has consisted of the interplay between complexity and simplicity, between a more highly differentiated mindset and a simple one. The Founding Fathers' heroic ideal, from its understanding of political and personal character to its vision for the nation, was complex and simple at the same time. It was calibrated to the problems and evils of human nature, encouraging their acknowledgment while advocating institutional safeguards against them. Freedom and the workings of democracy were conceived not as an open book to be determined as the tide of events might dictate—*que sera sera*—but as a well-structured set of guidelines. This heroic ideal reflected a struggle with the details of human existence, a struggle that was as naturally riddled with paradox and contradiction as the details themselves. And yet, the same heroic ideal nurtured an optimistic and simple faith that the human condition is not immutable and can be improved or advanced. It boldly professed universal truths and aspired toward things to which all people could relate. This counterpoise between complexity and simplicity gave this heroic ideal its sophistication, depth, and accessibility.

The movement toward less differentiated forms of heroic idealism that came after the Founding Fathers was a gravitation toward one-dimensional thought and often no thought at all. Davy Crockett and John Wayne were colorful but they were hardly textured. Simplicity in America's choice of heroes eventually became the order of the day. In an essay entitled "I'm Just That Simple," Jeff Greenfield writes:

> American popular culture is dense with unassuming, homespun heroes and heroines: from James Fenimore Cooper's Deerslayer to Mark Twain's Tom and Huck, to Will Rogers and Ma and Pa Kettle and the Clampetts of Beverly Hills, to Forrest Gump, who took the myth one step further by demonstrating that a double-digit IQ could lead to immense worldly success if accompanied by a good heart and simple decency. It is the essence of Capra's best-loved heroes. Jefferson Smith must contend with the schemes of Senator Paine, his onetime hero who plays a scene decked out in white tie and tails. In *Meet John Doe*, Gary Cooper battles the fascistic

schemes of the super-rich Edward Arnold, who is seen in an elegant dining room complete with tuxedo and cigar. In *Mr. Deeds Goes to Town,* Cooper must defend himself against a courtroom full of slickly dressed, high-priced, big-city lawyers. In *It's a Wonderful Life,* Jimmy Stewart's George Bailey learns that without his good heart and small-town values, the whole town of Bedford Falls would have fallen to the corrupt greed of Mr. Potter.

Simplicity, when the situation calls for it, is a virtue, but when it becomes mere escapism from the complex demands of life, it quickly degenerates into simple-mindedness. In today's world, the truths of John Doe, Mr. Deeds, and George Bailey appear not only simple but simplistic, and yet American culture keeps churning out such heroes in one form or another. In the movies they are usually angelically good, but just as often they can be diabolically sinister. The media has the liberty to play to the extremes of the human imagination, as Arnold Schwarzenegger and others like him have amply demonstrated. With living heroes, the opposites are there too; they are just more muted, banal, and mixed with each other. One would expect this mix since in the real world nobody is one-sidedly good or sinister, though even with living American heroes, this mix still occurs in a simplistic way. The only thing surprising about Oliver North's 1994 bid for a seat in the Senate was that nobody found it surprising. North had a simplified view of right and wrong—simplified to suit his needs or wishes—and hopelessly confused them when the situation became complicated in its opportunities and ethical considerations. Either he could not understand how his actions in the Iran-contra affair might have had detrimental, harrowing effects, or he could not understand why others might have found them detrimental and harrowing. Or, he simply didn't care. In this regard, he was similar to Nixon during Watergate. Both suffered from the same kind of heroic confusion and failure. But there are other kinds, too.

## The Heroism of Sports

Simple heroism finds its most popular form in the zeal Americans have for sports and sports heroes. What can be more pleasing than a Michael Jordan leading his team to six titles, or a Jimmy Connors making the U.S. Open Semifinals at the age of 39? The level of refinement or primitivity of the sport has nothing to do with the idealization of the hero. Tiger Woods is held in a qualitatively similar regard as Sugar Ray Leonard. Both are quite simply the best, not only at their respective sports but also, their fans like to believe, at being humans. But nowadays, athletes also mirror the nation's heroic crisis. They too have problems with drugs, gambling, sexual miscon-duct, and violence, except theirs end up in the news. Indeed, it seems as if the predisposition toward these problems is now even greater among ath-letes than the rest of the population. Young athletes are quickly pushed into the spotlight, and are ill-prepared to deal with the attention and pressures of stardom. These are probably amplified by the fact that an increasing number of athletes today come from economically deprived backgrounds that do not promote the kind of skills needed to cope with such success, with getting too much too fast. The number of athletes getting into trouble with the law is thus greater than ever before. In the 1999–2000 NFL season, to use a glaring example, two dozen football players were arrested and charged with crimes ranging from theft to murder. However, the trend of sports-related crime has sadly extended beyond the professional arena and transcends parame-ters of socioeconomic class. Also in 2000, a Massachusetts father, Michael Costin, was killed by another father in a confrontation over their sons' hockey game. As the priest officiating the funeral said, "Sports can build up or take away." But is it sports that take away in such instances, or a tragic misunderstanding of the heroic ideal that motivates the sports?

The decline of heroism is a problem that has assaulted sports in every quarter. Because the question of what it means to be a hero can no longer be clearly and simply answered, the professional athlete's playing field is no longer an adequate stage for the exercise of heroism. The mixture of money and sports has become such a focus that the acquisition of money has be-come a sport in its own right, for both athletes and team owners. The for-mer accuse the latter of being greedy and then, defining their own value strictly in monetary terms, fall prey to the same false heroism. When the NBA in 1998 cancelled the first two weeks of the season's games because of stalled negotiations on players' salaries, one Celtic player complained that the ceiling imposed at that time would not allow him to continue as a player. Whether he felt this way for moral reasons or because his salary was simply not enough to support his lifestyle, or both, was unclear. Needless to say, he was earning a multimillion-dollar annual salary; his contract re-portedly earned him more than the owners had paid for the team.

In other ways too, sportsmanship has made way for gamesmanship or game-playing and false heroics. One might expect this more perhaps from gladiatorial sports like wrestling and boxing, where there is a fine line between the cultivation of the sport and the cultivation of brute power. Mike Tyson biting off a piece of Evander Holyfield's ear could only happen in such a primitive, contact sport; in the days of the Roman Colosseum, from which modern boxing is derived, such an act would not even have

been noticed. The surprised reaction of Americans to this incident is an indication of the degree to which they believe that something primitive can
be made civilized simply by imposing high standards of sportsmanship on
it. Boxing, as Howard Cosell pointed out, will always be a blood sport.

More telling illustrations of the decline of sportsmanship come from
baseball, a sport that once set a standard for sportsmanship based on its intricate, stylized maneuvers, slow, rhapsodic rhythm, and team spirit. (Indeed, ballplayers became living icons whose very images made baseball
cards collector's items.) To cite but two examples: Before the 1996 playoffs,
the world of baseball went into another of its heroic crises (and in its history
there have been more than a few). This time the problem involved the possibility of a strike by the umpires over a matter other than money, the usual
source of grievance. A star player for the Baltimore Orioles had spit in the
face of an umpire and, according to the umpires' union, was given only a
slap on the wrist as punishment. Then in 2000 a brawl broke out between
practically the entire Dodgers team and fans of an opposing team. The
penalties the Dodgers received for this outburst were among the harshest in
baseball history. Such episodes show what American heroism has come to:
ballplayers who were once the role models for millions of youngsters now
behave in ways that make America's favorite pastime a spectacle of the
lowest kind. The joyously simple has become the simply grotesque.

Of course, this deterioration of the heroic, as this last episode illustrates,
has occurred not just on the part of the athletes. It has occurred in the entire
culture of spectator sports, and is equally observable in the behavior of the
fans and what is seen as acceptable behavior on the part of the fans. One incident that took place during the actual 1996 playoffs themselves speaks directly to this. A youngster in the first row of the bleachers interfered with
an outfielder's catch, dramatically affecting the outcome of a game. The
team that lost that game because of this interference was, coincidentally, the
Baltimore Orioles. However, of significance here is the fact that the youngster was rewarded with attention and gifts, indeed, as if he were a hero. Of
course, he was just being a youngster, and even the outfielder had a sports-
manlike attitude toward the incident. But in another time, this misdeed
would not have been perceived in such a positive light.

Throughout much of competitive sport, the meaning of competition has
decidedly shifted in focus. Competition was once innately understood as
the challenge to attain one's highest performance level and, if possible, surpass one's former achievement. One was in competition with oneself, to
break one's own record; the other team or challenger was to all intents and
purposes seen as the external goad that spurred on this competition with

oneself. The game or the contest, of course, provided the structure for this competition and naturally made it exciting and entertaining. But it was in the athlete's reaching his pinnacle that fans took delight more than anything. Today, it is mostly the external competition and the game of one-upmanship that excites fans. The meaning of the heroic as a challenge to oneself has become obscured. This is particularly evident in team sports. As the former basketball player Bill Bradley observed, "Something seems wrong somehow these days. Instead of regarding your opponent as an honorable adversary, athletes seem to enjoy degrading each other. In pro basketball these days, trash talk profanes the game. . . . Football players rarely offer a hand to help an opponent to his feet." When heroic confusion looms large, the degradation of sport is inevitable.

## The Divided Hero

The twentieth century's devolution into the heroics of the simple has left a vacuum in the heroics of the complex. Yet because complexity is as essential to the orientation of the American heroic ideal as simplicity and cannot just be exorcized, this vacuum is not mere emptiness. It is a pregnant emptiness that acts upon the collective psyche from the inside in subtle, gnawing ways. There is, as the British psychologist Andrew Samuels observed, a hunger for complexity in America. But this hunger is neither conscious nor being consciously satisfied. The results are an unconscious dynamic of complexity and an unconscious way of gratifying the yearning for the complex.

One sees this most conspicuously in the phenomenon of the divided hero. An ancient theme, the hero who is torn within himself has become something of an expectation in American culture, an ideal that evokes a certain aura of mystery and fascination. The divided hero of ancient times was a figure tormented by profound doubts or crises that arose from the human condition. His dilemma had a moral and often tragic, Shakespearean quality. His conflict spoke to all people because it struck at universal, core issues in human experience, such as, in the instances of Job and Oedipus, finding the right attitude and response to evil.

The American hero who most suffered the burden of dividedness was Abraham Lincoln. The nation's pain became his own as he conducted a war while openly agonizing about its morality and impact. He even called for national days of repentence which, as the historian Garry Wills points out, was extraordinary in view of the fact that so doing risked demoralizing his side and undermining its will to press on for victory. Yet Lincoln had the gift to inspire while demanding a fierce moral scrutiny that was not without its ambivalence. Although he went to war against the South, he always understood the reasoning if not the righteousness of its position, and he compassionately sought to alleviate tensions and lessen differences between the two sides immediately following the war. He held opposites together as have few leaders in world history. As the psychologist Edward Edinger commented, this capacity of Lincoln's made possible one of the outstanding differences between America and ancient Israel: both nations were founded on spiritual visions, but Lincoln was able to hold his nation together whereas Israel splintered in two. In spite of the toll of anguish that the nation's dividedness exacted upon him, Lincoln was not a man divided against himself.

By contrast, an increasing number of America's modern leaders are not just divided heroes but self-divided heroes. Kennedy's alleged associations with the Mafia have posthumously cast a pall on his Camelot image and call for a new kind of leadership. There was first the speculation that his father employed connections with the crime world to influence labor votes and ensure the 1960 election; then the involvement of Mafia figures in the Bay of Pigs fiasco raised questions about Kennedy's integrity and judgment, as did never actualized CIA plots to deploy Mafia hit men to assassinate Fidel Castro. The procession of presidents after Kennedy included, in the words of the journalist Lance Morrow, "men of rather peculiar and divided psyche. Lyndon Johnson, Richard Nixon and Jimmy Carter [and we may now add George Bush and Bill Clinton] were personalities utterly different from one another, but they all shared, to some degree, an odd, self-thwarting trait. Each became his own worst enemy." Of course, once again, the hero and the heroic ideal of the culture go together as figure and ground. Kennedy's connection with the criminal underworld is no more surprising than America's tolerance of this underworld to begin with. Johnson's political suicide, spurred by his Vietnam policies, paralleled the nation's swing from an arrogant belief in its invincibility to a deflating admission of its all-too-human fallibility. What can one say about Nixon's undoing in Watergate when the heroic ideal of the culture itself instills the value of winning at any cost? It is suggestive that America's involvement in Vietnam, an experience that divided the nation against itself unlike anything since the Civil War, was perfectly timed with the presidencies of these latter three self-divided figures.

Self-dividedness, then, is one of the ways complexity resurfaces in the American culture in subtle, and not so subtle, gnawing ways. Whatever personal factors may shape his individual psychology, the hero who is "his own worst enemy" can, logically speaking, only thrive in a culture that at some conscious or unconscious level tolerates this sort of complicated, self-defeating heroism. Leaders not only lead their societies but are their products. A society divided against itself or against the basic orientation of its own character would be expected to create self-divided leaders or heroes. Not surprisingly, the society doesn't see its self-dividedness any more clearly than its leaders see theirs. If America's experience is any example, it seems that when an innately complex culture becomes too simplistic—that is, too innocent—in its understanding of itself or the world, it naturally generates complicated, tormented heroes as a form of compensation. They live out the culture's simplicity and innocence in a thwarted and byzantine way. As with any compensation, this provides a vent for the problem, a cue that signals its existence, and an attempt to balance it.

Other heroic types tend to convey their culture's psychological condition in a more direct way. When a demagogue, for example, captures and gives voice to the imagination of his people, he directly reflects and appeals to their condition. Hitler embodied and spoke to the desperation of a dying Weimar Germany in a straightforward manner, in spite of the fact that this manner was laden with his histrionic and paranoid pathology. There was nothing divided about Hitler's self-presentation. Indeed, he was, right from the beginning with *Mein Kampf*, remarkably candid and single-minded in the pursuit of his dark ambitions. And it appears that the millions who followed him were just as undivided, as illustrated in the controversial book by Daniel Jonah Goldhagen, *Hitler's Willing Executioners*. The German people's naiveté and pseudo-innocence corresponded directly with Hitler's own inasmuch as they blindly believed in his promises of salvation for Germany.

But a self-divided hero is a trickier phenomenon. Even his people often don't believe him and are divided against him. Americans did not understand and always remained fascinated by the question of what made "Tricky Dick" Nixon tick. This is the nature of the dynamic of self-dividedness: it operates ubiquitously, affecting the leader, the people, and the relationship between them. Kennedy, Johnson, Nixon, Carter, Bush, and Clinton were all heroic reflections of the self-divided society that gave rise to them; but as the heroes, they carried society's self-dividedness and were scapegoated for it. All were in some sense at odds with their constituents, ranging from Kennedy who was hated by some as deeply as he was loved by others (indeed, he won the presidency by a very narrow margin of votes), to Clinton, who in spite of never earning the public's trust and affection, managed to achieve high performance ratings throughout much of his presidency. It is curious that the last president most Americans would agree was a great leader—that is, in the top tier of American presidents—was Truman. The second half of the twentieth century had every bit the same need for great leadership as the first, which produced not only Truman but the two Roosevelts and Wilson. With the rise of the self-divided hero and the consequent focus on human foibles and frailties, the presidency itself has become an institution hampered by vulnerability and divided between its priorities of governing and defending itself.

The self-divided hero, given all of this, is an indirect way for the culture to confront its innate complexity. It is most often not a legitimate way because it does not involve critical self-examination; everything that has gone awry is blamed on the hero. The culture's dissociated complexity is seen in its hero. "Bill Clinton cannot give us a straight answer," people complained well before the Lewinsky affair. "He lies through his teeth." But as one political commentator observed, it should not have been surprising that he lied. If the electorate to whom he lied is seen as his boss, Clinton just did what many Americans would do to keep their jobs if they got into trouble. Why should Americans expect their presidents to be so different from themselves, with moral standards that are head and shoulders above what they demand from themselves? The Founding Fathers stand out luminously with their high moral standards, but theirs were standards—certainly if Benjamin Franklin would have had his way—for everyone, and not just for those belonging to an elevated world that was head and shoulders above the general population. It was recognized that these standards needed to be cultivated by the people too. Today, similarly high standards reflecting an equally high heroic ideal continue to be expected, but mostly from leaders as opposed to the citizenry itself, and mostly in a simple-minded way: it is assumed that these standards should be there automatically, without the complex and arduous process of self-examination required to make them a living social reality. So the heroic ideal of America is still, at heart, much the same as it was 200 years ago, except the people are dissociated from it in these ways. There is a direct thread between the moral standards of the Founding Fathers and what is expected in America today, but this thread is increasingly frayed.

## The Divided Society

A divided heroic ideal presupposes a divided society, and then reinforces it. The dividedness of American society is not a recent phenomenon. America has been a society with diverse polarities since its beginnings. It is the current extremity of this phenomenon that once again gives life in America an embattled quality much as it had during the Civil War era. This quality appears to exist in the psyches of all Americans, even the privileged. Robin Winks, a Yale University historian, wrote the following in 1989: "Recently I asked 15 bright undergraduates to write short autobiographies, and 10, without comparing notes, chose the divided life as their theme." By "divided life," Winks meant a dual, secretive existence, such as the life a spy lives. Certainly, supersleuths such as James Bond and the Mission Impossible team became the mysterious heroes of the Cold War, not only in America, but in Britain and elsewhere. In the post-Cold War period, however, their relevance and appeal greatly diminished. The real-world analogue to this was what happened in the CIA after the collapse of the Soviet Union. There was, as observed *Washington Post* journalist David Ignatius, a paralyzing loss of morale and purpose, with accompanying organizational disarray and downsizing. This heroic disillusionment and confusion paralleled American society at large. The experience of diminishment that Russia underwent after the demise of the Soviet Union had its counterpart in the United States, quite contrary to the elation one might expect from the victor of an epic struggle like the Cold War. Heroism that derives its sense of identity from fighting an enemy always requires an adversary and is at a loss without one.

This kind of heroism naturally goes together with divided heroism. In a society that nurtures the ideal of the divided hero, one would expect to find schisms manifesting throughout the entire society. One way to be one's own worst enemy is to consistently make enemies with others or to create situations where feelings of enmity become the ruling principle. The 1990s were defined by this dynamic. The Rodney King trial that led to the Los Angeles riots is typically thought of in terms of racial dividedness. The pent-up resentment it released resurfaced in the O.J. Simpson trial. His case was virtually built and won on the same experience of black resentment at white injustice. When the not-guilty verdict in this case was announced, the roles had clearly been reversed: whites now screamed at the injustice they felt was delivered by a mostly black jury. Tit for tat seemed to continue throughout the decade. Not long after this, black churches were burned down in a number of Southern states.

All these episodes, however, reflect the crisis in American heroism as much as the crisis in race relations. The two are intimately connected. Justice goes hand-in-hand with the heroic. When one is obscured, so is the other. The use of an enemy to define the American heroic ideal inevitably has repercussions in race relations. The polarization between black and white in America is also a polarization between "us" and "them." When taken to an extreme, this in turn becomes a polarization between hero and villain; each race sees the other as the villain. Of course, under such conditions there can be no justice for all. Only when this split is somehow healed can justice be truly served.

For the sake of argument, I wish to put aside here the racial dimension of the Simpson trial, but certainly not because it is unimportant. On the contrary: racism and race relations are central among America's problems, but they are complex and will be explored later. Here I want to focus on the heroic dimension of the Simpson case. It graphically illustrates the workings of a divided heroic ideal and society.

The relentless splitting between hero and villain that characterized this case made it impossible for society to arrive at any cohesive understanding of what it was about. To begin with, Simpson himself fit the image of a divided hero. His behaviors, ranging from spouse abuse to the suicide letter and the Bronco chase, were the signs of a man divided against himself or at least acting against his own best interests. He gripped society's imagination on a number of levels. He had been a great sports hero, and now he was in trouble. He had the shimmer of a fallen hero, a tragic figure—always a compelling image. However, as the psychologist Gilda Frantz and others have noted, the deepest source of society's fascination with Simpson was the mystery of evil: horrendous crimes always ignite the public's interest because they offer a peek into the darkest, hiddenmost corners of human nature.

Simpson's lawyers, as well as the prosecuting attorneys, played out the divided hero syndrome in numerous ways, as if the whole legal process had become contaminated with it. Indeed, the process was probably more contaminated with this dynamic than was, allegedly, the evidence tainted. The argument that there had been police impropriety was dependent on finding a villain other than Simpson, somebody who, either through incompetence or malicious intent, compromised the collection of evidence. And no doubt, the defense team's revelations about Mark Fuhrman—a self-divided figure in his own right—were shady enough to add the specter of malice to the impression of incompetence already given by the Los Angeles Police Department. The members of the "dream team" were so invested in divisive heroics that they even turned against each other, with members publicly vilifying each other. The search for a villain other than Simpson seemed to throw the prosecuting team off balance, and succeeded in diverting its attention away from proving Simpson's guilt. The prosecution, as Vincent Bugliosi argued in *Outrage*, was insufficiently directed toward illuminating the facts—and just the facts—of Simpson's behaviors in connection with the crime. These never came to light, at least in the criminal trial.

Instead, what the public saw and viscerally understood were the strong passions that are usually stirred up when the mindset becomes "us vs. them."

If Simpson was the figure who most benefited from this mindset, probably the figure who most suffered was Christopher Darden. A black prosecutor who was identified, at least by many blacks, as serving a white cause, Darden had the difficult task of navigating a course between the "us" and "them" sides of the case. He had to fight for what he believed in while being perceived as a traitor or villain by his own people. Subsequently called "the Darden factor," this aspect of the Simpson case has implications for other black professionals fulfilling a role that may appear contrary to popular black sentiments. In any event, Darden was the polar opposite and complement of Simpson. Whites called Simpson a white black man; blacks called Darden a black white man. Both were divided heroes in a divided society governed by a divided heroic ideal.

## The Diffusion of the Heroic Ideal

Earlier I stated that the historical thread of the heroic ideal has frayed on two levels: the concrete level of hero-images and the more subtle level of cultural values, lifestyles, and trends. Turning more explicitly to this second level, we can see that fraying also occurs in the diffusion of the ideal. To a large extent, the diffusion of a heroic ideal into the culture is natural; one would expect the values, lifestyles, and trends of a culture to be permeated by its heroic ideal. But when the thread or continuity of that ideal has been frayed, the diffusion is so acute—diverse, sublimated, and masked—that unless one knows what one is looking for, the ideal becomes imperceptible. It is as if it has acquired a gaseous state, becoming not only invisible but so pervasive that you don't even know it's there. Of course, it *is* there, and just as formidably. Again, it is part of the national character and cannot be exorcised. It does not disappear simply because it no longer expresses its voice in a solid and authentic manner. Rather, it transmutes or, at worst, transmogrifies into unrecognizable forms.

In Parts II and III, I'd like to explore the heroic ideal's diffusion in the culture, focusing on two forms in particular. They are the addiction to height (as in the "height of greatness"), and the addiction to innocence. I speak of addiction here in a psychological and spiritual sense, and not as a physiological craving. Addiction is essentially an expression of heroic failure, a surrender of freedom, creativity, and self-determination. Addiction means to give assent or say "yes" to something in an automatic, unreflective way that then becomes a matter of habit (*ad* in Latin means "to," and diction or *dicere* means "say"). The many addictions to which Americans say "yes"—and indeed, most of them are not physiological—are almost all variations of the greater addictions to height and innocence. These are, ultimately, addictions to the spirit of youth, since the aspiration toward height and the state of innocence are primary features of this spirit. When a culture becomes addicted to height and innocence and becomes their servomechanism, it no longer has the spirit of youth. The spirit of youth has it.

In other words, what I am advocating here is that America's heroic crisis is a spiritual problem. Youthfulness is a blessing, but when a nation loses its inner compass—the principles of authority that balance and guide it—and it gets stuck in its youthful ways, even its heroic gifts and talents cannot help it. In fact, its heroic virtues turn into vices precisely because they are imbalanced and without purpose. The aspiration toward height or greatness becomes an addiction, a compulsive drive that has no real sense of purpose about what that greatness is for. Likewise, the state of innocence, which speaks to a certain openness and purity of heart, becomes a blind naiveté and habitual simplemindedness that beg for and inevitably lead to corruption. Let us try to understand how these crucial features of the American heroic ideal operate. As we shall see, they influence practically every facet of American culture.

★

# Part II

## The High Life

*I am willing to allow your Phylosophers your opinion of the universal Gravitation of Matter, if you will allow mine that there is in some souls a principle of absolute Levity that buoys them irresistably into the Clouds . . . an uncontroulable Tendency to ascend.*

—John Adams

*On with the dance! Let joy be unconfined; No sleep till morn, when youth and pleasure meet to chase the glowing hours with flying feet.*

—Lord Byron

*All we know about the world, about the mind, the body, about anything whatsoever,* including the spirit *and the nature of the divine, comes through images and is organized by fantasies into one pattern or another. . . . We are always in one or another root-metaphor, archetypal fantasy, mythic perspective.*

—James Hillman

# ★ Prelude: The Metaphor of Height ★

America's aspiration toward greatness is expressed through the metaphor of height. This metaphor, of course, is not unique to America. Since time immemorial, height has represented that which is beyond man, or perhaps just within his reach but barely. Essentially, the metaphor of height is an image of the psyche, both in the sense of being a product of the psyche and a self-portrait of it. The psyche, soul, or spirit has height, metaphorically speaking. When Marc Chagall paints a canvas of people flying in the sky, or when we have dreams of flying, a statement is being made about the height of the psyche.

In the history of religion and mythology, the metaphor of height was usually experienced in connection to the heavens. To catch even a glimpse of something heavenly confirmed to man his God-given ability to transcend himself, to surpass, even if momentarily, his natural limitations. Every religious tradition is thus rich with images of height. Their meanings vary, but generally, they speak to the realm of things godly or godlike. Height is where the divine resides, whether it is Yahweh on Mt. Sinai or the Greek gods on Mt. Olympus. A wide range of religious experiences, particularly the visionary kind that pertain to man's burning questions about immortality or the afterlife, are also for this reason often couched in images of height.

Because the metaphor of height symbolizes godly or godlike things, it lends itself to all of man's drives and desires to make his mark, to leave behind something immortal. The human aspiration toward greatness is above all a flirtation with immortality, an attempt to stay young forever. The spirit of youth moves in man in no small measure through his desire for immortality and his aspiration toward greatness. Indeed, this spirit is a part of man that never ages; perhaps it is itself the fountain of eternal youth. From it springs those drives and desires that make man feel youthful, alive, immortal, and godlike. And all of them, when experienced in fullness, are described in terms of the metaphor of height: the height of power, the height of achievement, the height of creativity, the height of knowledge, the height of culture and civilization, the height of aesthetics, the height of passion, the height of pleasure, the height of sensuality. Height is the imagination's way of referring to immortality, greatness, and immortal greatness.

It should thus come as no surprise that the central symbol and heroic emblem of America is the eagle. The eagle is a symbolic image as ancient as civilization itself. The Sumerians, Egyptians, Hittites, Israelites, Greeks, Romans, early Christians, Byzantine Christians, Copts, Gnostics, Vikings, Teutons, and American Indians all chose the eagle to represent some high ideal or noble idea in their culture. Naturally, what was a high ideal or a noble idea in one culture wasn't always seen that way by other cultures or by the hand that writes history. The Roman, Napoleonic, and Nazi eagles had ominous connotations, signifying absolute power and imperialism. One might say that the eagle in these instances was admired for its keen predatory skills and its dominion over other creatures. The eagle that symbolizes Saddam Hussein's regime falls into this category as well.

Although America is not without its history of foreign interventionism, its eagle is more widely associated with freedom and democracy than power. The eagle here depicts the freedom to soar to great heights and to glide through the skies uninhibited, abilities at which it is among the greatest of flying creatures. The principle of freedom makes possible the attainment of greatness as it is understood by Americans: the high civilization that the Founding Fathers envisioned for America could only be the creative product of a nation with democratic ideals. Height in the American imagination is the height of achievement made possible by the freedom to pursue one's ambitions. Michael Kammen urges us to "notice the repetitive use of the word 'rise' in books and essays about American history and culture: *The Rise of American Civilization* by Charles and Mary Beard (1927); *The Rise of the Common Man* by Carl R. Fish (1927); *The Rise of the City, 1878–1898* by Arthur M. Schlesinger (1933); and James Truslow Adams's essay for the *New York Times* (1939), titled '1789–1939: A Nation Rises.' " All this rising motion is the movement of the American eagle in flight.

As the psychologist Jacques Lacan once said, we don't form the images from our imagination; they form us. Certainly this is true not only in the case of the image of the eagle, but also with other images of height that shape the American experience. These images illustrate how the American experience has been driven by the aspiration to constantly attain new and greater heights. The modern city with its skyscrapers is largely an American innovation. In America, a city's beauty and glamour are measured by its skyline. Cities vie to have the tallest building or structure, celebrating whenever a record is broken. There is considerable public excitement whenever a new height might be attained. One major news source rushed to judgment when it erroneously announced in 1996 that Las Vegas had completed its construction of the largest free-standing tower in the world, the Stratosphere. Toronto's CN (Canadian National) Tower is some 300 feet taller than the Stratosphere.

This particular form of the aspiration toward height can be explained in different ways. No doubt, logistics dictated that an island like Manhattan— the pioneer and champion of skyscraper cities—had limited space for urban development, and that upward growth was imperative. But from a psychological viewpoint, Erik Erikson's studies of children playing with toys suggest that boys build cities with tall structures to express their need to prove themselves strong and aggressive and to achieve "high standing"; girls by contrast construct house interiors to represent the anticipated task of taking care of a home and rearing children. Erikson hypothesized that the spatial tendencies governing these constructions closely parallel the morphology of the sex organs, that is, that the "genital modes" of the phallus and the womb respectively influence the play style of boys and girls.

From here it is only a short leap to suggest that the masculine genital mode, enacted on a larger, social scale, is similarly at work in the design of real cities. But this view is too narrow and reductive, which is at least in part why it has become clichéd. It fails to recognize that it is the experience of ecstasy, transcendence, and primal creativity that makes the phallic so numinous and charged in the first place. To say that tall, erect structures symbolize the penis only begs the question of what the penis symbolizes. In the end, we are led back to our starting point, that the aspiration toward height is an imitation of and reach for the gods. Los Angeles and Phoenix, though not particularly known for their tall buildings, exhibit the same aspiration as other American cities simply by being named after creatures of height.

The city is only one place where the American heroic ideal is played out through the metaphor of height. Beginning with Wilbur and Orville Wright, America has always been a world leader in aviation. The Wright brothers succeeded in doing what Icarus could not. Their natural extension was Charles Lindbergh. Could anyone doubt that when he flew nonstop across the Atlantic he would become a national hero? The Spirit of St. Louis (the name of his plane) *is* the spirit of youth, the spirit of height, freedom, and achievement. It is the eagle in the form of technology.

America's dominance in the skies was ushered in by the two world wars. This in turn dovetailed into the space program. The book and film *The Right Stuff* nicely portrayed the development of America's new industry of height. Project Mercury was appropriately named after the Roman god Mercury, whose winged sandals and helmet offered grace and swiftness in flight. As the messenger of the gods, he was known to fly "as fleet as thought." Project Mercury with its seven astronauts was designed if not destined to receive a hero's welcome from the American public. President Kennedy promoted it as the "most hazardous and dangerous and greatest adventure on which man has ever embarked." It was as if this adventure were tailor-made for America, a nation whose very conception and vision were based on a belief in its special relationship with the heavens.

Knowing full well that the success of the space program depended on its ability to connect to the American heroic ideal, NASA carefully orchestrated its public relations. The astronauts were hailed as the new frontiersmen exploring the new and final frontier. The pinnacle of the program's success was of course reached with the Apollo XI mission to the moon. America had attained a new height, not only on its own behalf but humanity's: as Neil Armstrong said, "That's one small step for man, one giant leap for mankind." (He had allegedly meant to say, "That's one small step for a man, one giant leap for mankind," which makes more sense.)

On the other hand and on a more pragmatic note, success in space was very much linked to winning the Cold War. The Russians may have launched the space race with Sputnik, but the Americans were determined to win it precisely because this race symbolized the effort to win the Cold War. This was true from the beginning right through to the close of the Reagan era. In the end, the Soviets balked at the prospect of having to economically and militarily compete with a costly, ultrahigh technology initiative like Star Wars. After the collapse of the "evil empire," to use Reagan's Cold War terminology, the Americans and Russians could comfortably collaborate with each other in space. The war was over.

Amelia Earhart and John Glenn are not the only kind of hero to have scaled the heights. Nor for that matter are Batman and Luke Skywalker. Whether factual or fictional, these heroes express the aspiration toward height in its most concrete, visible form. But forms that work directly upon the imagination are, as one might expect, more compelling. Again, height is but a metaphor for greatness, for the extraordinary, for that which is inspired and in turn inspires. Probably no American hero in recent times has radiated this quality more than Kennedy. With his call for a new generation of leadership and his vision to set America on a new course—not to mention his commitment to send a man to the moon by the end of the 1960s—he was himself a Mercury-like messenger who illustriously embodied the metaphor of height. In the words of *The Washington Post's* Ben Bradlee, he "lit the skies of this land bright with hope and promise as no other political man has done in this century."

When Kennedy was killed, millions of Americans felt that the light of that hope and promise had been killed with him. Certainly, some of the heaviness and despondency that settled upon the nation following his death lasted through the 1960s and well into the 1970s. Dallas, the assassinations of Martin Luther King and Robert Kennedy, the riots that raged across the nation, the war in Vietnam, and finally, Watergate, together constituted one of the lowest periods of morale in American history. It was largely in response to the decline of heroism during these years that the counterculture staged its movement with its alternative lifestyles and means of "getting high." But this period itself was merely one section of a larger chapter of American history, earmarking a theme that had been building for some time and which, with the birth of this new century, is still unfolding. The theme is not just about a low point in American heroic idealism resulting from the fraying of the latter's historical thread. It is about the crisis American society is undergoing—or should be undergoing—regarding the very meaning of the heroic. The current chapter of America's history might suitably be entitled, "What defines a hero at the dawn of the twenty-first century?" Unfortunately, as we shall see, much of the answer lies in the ways the heroic ideal has been diffused into the culture through the metaphor of height.

# Chapter 5

## The Commercialism of America's Heroic Ideal

*Civilization and profits go hand in hand.*

—Calvin Coolidge

*There used to be a time when the idea of heroes was impor-
tant. People grew up sharing those myths and legends and
ideals. Now they grow up sharing McDonald's and
Disneyland.*

—Bob Dylan

### The Cult of Prosperity

America is the most prosperous nation in the history of the world. The fact
that it owes its prosperity at least in some measure to its heroic ideal is a
source of both celebration and consternation.

The American aspiration toward high achievement in the form of material acquisition is rooted in a combination of things. Firstly, it is rooted in
human nature. People desire the comfort and pleasure of good things. In
this there is nothing new. Secondly, it is rooted in the demand that the continent imposed upon the American to sustain himself by the ascendance of
his skills and savvy. This demand was met by the uninhibited conquest of
the land and the fervent transformation of its resources into material goods
and infrastructure.

The people who undertook the task of building a continental nation
were ideally suited to it, and were *themselves* a great factor contributing
to American prosperity. For the most part, they were not adventurers but

immigrants escaping persecution, famine, poverty, and wars in their home countries. Their refugee mentality predisposed them and their descendants, the subsequent generations of Americans, to a fear of falling back into conditions of want. The drive to be prosperous was inculcated into the American psyche.

Another crucial factor responsible for American prosperity is the famous Protestant ethic. The Puritans established the colonies according to the Reformation view that man gains his salvation not only through grace but good deeds and hard work. The worldly things the latter brings are not sinful but are to be enjoyed as God's blessings. This view, as Max Weber showed, helped fuel American capitalism.

And then there is the nature of capitalism itself. Free enterprise has characterized the practice of modern democracy, and as a general rule, the health of one can be measured by the health of the other. This seems to be true even with the more socialist democracies. Democracy sets the people's ambitions free, allowing them to pursue the highest material goals they can fix their eyes upon. As Alexis de Tocqueville noted over 150 years ago, "In democracies nothing is greater or more brilliant than commerce; it attracts the attention of the public and fills the imagination of the multitude; all energetic passions are directed towards it."

But this, Tocqueville observed, spawns particular problems. In the old aristocratic societies of Europe, the value of an individual was not determined solely by wealth. Dignity and distinction were more often a function of rank and privilege, acquired by way of inheritance. Of course, wealth usually came with this, but it was one among a number of factors that defined an individual's merit. "When, on the contrary," Tocqueville wrote, "the distinctions of ranks are obliterated and privileges are destroyed, when hereditary property is subdivided and education and freedom are widely diffused, the desire of acquiring the comforts of the world haunts the imagination of the poor, and the dread of losing them that of the rich. . . . The love of well-being has now become the predominant taste of the nation; the great current of human passions runs in that channel and sweeps everything along in its course." In other words, in a democracy, money and goods tend to become the primary criteria of personal value because, for the large part, there are no other criteria.

This creates what historian Murray Levin described as a new pseudoaristocracy, a bourgeois class that is characterized by consumerism. The high achievement people strive for is not measured in terms of character or culture, but wealth. And they are not as much inspired as driven in an anxious, addicted way. The anxiety and drivenness are intrinsic to democracy; they are effects of democracy's Catch-22. Tocqueville writes:

> The same equality that allows every citizen to conceive these lofty hopes renders all the citizens less able to realize them. . . . They have swept away the privileges of some of their fellow creatures which stood in their way, but they have opened the door to universal competition; the barrier has changed its shape rather than its position. When men are nearly alike and all follow the same track, it is very difficult for any one individual to walk quickly and cleave a way through the dense throng that surrounds and presses on him. This constant strife between the inclination springing from the equality of condition and the means it supplies to satisfy them harasses and wearies the mind. . . . When inequality of conditions is the common law of society, the most marked inequalities do not strike the eye; when everything is nearly on the same level, the slightest are marked enough to hurt it. Hence the desire of equality always becomes more insatiable in proportion as equality is more complete.
>
> Among democratic nations, men easily attain a certain equality of condition, but they can never attain as much as they desire. It perpetually retires from before them, yet without hiding itself from their sight, and in retiring draws them on. At every moment they think they are about to grasp it; it escapes at every moment from their hold. They are near enough to see its charms, but too far off to enjoy them; and before they have fully tasted its delights, they die. . . .
>
> In democratic times enjoyments are more intense than in the ages of aristocracy, and the number of those who partake in them is vastly larger: but, on the other hand, it must be admitted that man's hopes and desires are oftener blasted, the soul is more stricken and perturbed, and trouble is felt more keenly.

Tocqueville here was discussing democracy in general, but as implied by the title of his book, *Democracy in America,* he was referring specifically to America as the first example of a modern democracy. America's clear detachment from an older, aristocratic order with established rules of merit, plus the seemingly infinite possibilities provided by the new continent, added to his impression of Americans as a people who can become lost at sea in their freedom and prosperity. "In America," he said, " I saw the freest and most enlightened men placed in the happiest circumstances that the world affords; it seemed to me as if a cloud habitually hung upon their

brow, and I thought them serious and almost sad, even in their pleasures."
Tocqueville's observations are as germane today as when he made them,
for the uprooting freedom and hungry prosperity-seeking that were first
spawned by democracy continue to be endemic to it.

A final factor contributing to American prosperity, and the only one capable of offsetting the above problems, is the American heroic ideal. Only a
strong heroic ideal that emphasizes character development, ethical living,
and reflective, critical thinking can curb the negative effects of consumerism.
But the problem here is that the same heroic ideal that can ameliorate the ills
and anxieties of consumerism is infected with them. At the core of the American heroic ideal is the very principle that makes consumerism the all-
consuming force it has become. William H. Kennedy explains:

> We are surrounded by voices, papers, causes, proposals, all urging
> us toward a better life. There is cancer cure, for example, and all the
> other causes concerned with physical health and with stamping out
> disease. There are politicians and investigative groups from all lev-
> els of government urging us to fight graft, crime, communism,
> profiteering, exploitation, poverty, monopolies, usually, of course,
> in the other fellow. The commercial interests of our consumer soci-
> ety implore us to fight bad breath with Listerine, body odors with
> Right Guard, dental decay with UltraBrite, old age with Geritol,
> boredom with travel and every kind of entertainment; we're even
> invited to get away from just ordinary everyday life via Pan Am's
> escape plan in 747s through the stratosphere. All sorts of religious,
> philosophical, mystical, and just plain superstitious groups and in-
> dividuals and corporate interests urge us to learn to touch, feel, do
> exercises, seek, find, create, wake up, tap latent powers, and even
> to turn away from the whole damn catastrophe via drugs and so
> on. And there are always with us the traditional and perennial ex-
> hortations to help other people, to love one another, to have faith,
> and so on. . . .
>
> In respect to the United States of America, it seems to me
> that . . . most of the movements that come up, are movements
> based on hope, the hope of defeating something like old age or
> poverty or the hope of building something for the future. But, in
> any case, the element of the hope for a better world characterizes, I
> think, the vast majority of all these vocal pleas and exhortations by
> which we're surrounded.

Defeating old age and poverty and building for the future are typical
pursuits of the spirit of youth. A heroic ideal that focuses on these at the ex-

pense of character development, ethical living, and reflective, critical thinking runs the risk of creating a society that in appearance may be democratic
but in fact suffers from the tyranny of mass-mindedness, the essential feature of the consumer mentality. The funny thing about all those vocal pleas
and exhortations is how they beckon us to become individuals, but in such
a conforming way that we all become exactly the same individual. The
height of achievement, when marketed as a consumer commodity, is nothing more than the height of mediocrity.

One cannot argue that the American heroic ideal was, with the rise of
consumerism, suddenly vanquished by it or somehow enlisted to join its
cause. It didn't happen like that. The American heroic ideal always was
centrally occupied with the attainment of prosperity, and as this increasingly turned into the unbridled materialism of the frontier and modern periods, the heroic ideal quietly followed suit. But the seeds of this tendency
always were there, from the beginning. They were germinated not only by
human nature, by the abundant riches promised by the continental task, by
the temperament of the nation's immigrants, by the Protestant ethic, and by
capitalism and democracy. They were germinated by the Founding Fathers
themselves, who used material interests—the ownership of property and
wealth—as the bottom line in their design of how the American republic
would work. While it is true that their heroic ideal placed a strong emphasis on character development, ethical living, and critical, reflective thinking,
these strains were always more implicit than explicit, more assumed than
touted, and more evident in their private reflections and writings than in
the official, public documents and institutions they created.

Furthermore, they had no idea, at least in the beginning, how things
would unfold. Boorstin writes that, as regards Jefferson, his was "a philosophy and a mode of thought suited not for eternity but for man's potentiali-
ties at a particular stage in history and at a particular place on earth. The
Jeffersonian philosophy was an incentive toward populating a continent
and building a society; but it must have been hard even for the Jeffersonian
not to surmise that once that work was achieved, much of the vitality of his
philosophy might be lost." The American heroic ideal from its earliest
stages saw the American as a doer, a man of action. His can-do approach
would transform the wilderness into an empire of well-being and define the
height of American achievement in terms of material prosperity. Boorstin
adds that "by refusing to declare the *duties* of man, by refusing to face the
large question of social purpose, [Jefferson] had presupposed the whole
end to be prosperity and the perpetuation of the species." In other words,

the American project was conceived, although with a distinct vision, without clearly expressed objectives that would concretize that vision in the practical, social sphere. The duties or responsibilities that would on the citizen's part help bring the vision about were not addressed. Whatever concreteness there was was too concrete: it went literally into the material world, into the pursuit of happiness through prosperity. Jefferson himself would later become known for his penchant for improving the human condition through scientific and agricultural innovations, technological inventions, and labor-saving devices.

It is of course unfair to blame the Founding Fathers because their heroic ideal was not sufficiently exposed or far-reaching in its objectives. Probably they assumed that they could leave it to future generations of Americans to articulate and revitalize the American heroic mission as the course of progress demanded. But there can be no doubt that by the end of their lives at least a few of them suspected that something was amiss and that the course of progress was one-sidedly materialistic. Within a generation of the nation's founding, Jefferson was lamenting that "money, not morality, is the principle of commercial nations." Evidently, in his prime he had not foreseen how the keen relationship between democracy and commerce would evolve, and that it would take time for this to become apparent. After all, Tocqueville's seminal work only appeared, in its entirety, fourteen years after Jefferson's death.

## The Fantasy of Unlimited Possibilities

The accomplishment of the continental task and the rise of prosperity have placed America into a peculiar and troubling predicament. As Boorstin indicated, a philosophy or heroic ideal predicated on these goals may lose its vitality once they have been reached. It is curious that as America reached one of its peaks of prosperity—at least with regards to the white middle and upper middle classes—in the late 1950s, the current wave of heroic problems plaguing the nation was unleashed: crime, the breakdown of the family, urban and environmental decay, and the loss of national purpose or vision. The counterculture movement of the 1960s came as an immediate reaction to the emptiness and numbness that young people sensed at the culmination of America's long march up the yellow brick road. The heroic ideal did not equip American society with any objectives of what to do with the greatness it finally achieved, that is, how to apply it toward creating the truly great civilization envisioned by the Founding Fathers. A Greek or Roman might have asked, what is all this prosperity for, after all?

Unless it evolves, the heroic ideal will stay fixed upon its original goal, the attainment of prosperity, a goal that, as Tocqueville explained, can never be fully satisfied or satisfying and has a miragelike quality. The result will be a never-ending cycle of prosperity-seeking: more, more, and more. The bumper sticker says it all: "The one who accumulates the most toys wins." However, this belief in the unlimited possibilities of prosperity is so ingrained in the American psyche that its adaptibility to new priorities is questionable. It is connected with notions of fated success and being specially privileged or blessed. The psychologist Fritz Redl thus writes of this belief as a "destiny complex."

> In the United States, the dream of "unlimited possibilities" has been preached to our young presumably from the day on which the first immigrants landed on these shores. Life is what you make of it; the sky is the limit. If you do not reach it, you have no one to blame but yourself. No doubt, this philosophy has always proved a special stimulant to most, a nightmare to some; and it must have sounded like a bad joke to the disinherited at any historical time.

The sense of entitlement to unlimited possibilities in prosperity—and I emphasize that it is the entitlement to unlimited possibilities and not to prosperity itself—is a social problem of the greatest magnitude. A nation that defines the good life and the good society in terms of a perpetual acquisition of material wealth is bound to hit a ceiling of diminishing returns in the quality of life—the quality of satisfaction and meaningfulness—if not the quantity of goods. Something must be wrong when the level of prosperity well exceeds the sum total requirements for well-being of all the individuals in that nation, and still the nation as a whole is hungrily seeking prosperity. Certainly, one can argue that this has a great deal to do with the *distribution* of prosperity: when 10 percent of American households own two-thirds of the nation's total assets, there is bound to be a high level of dissatisfaction. But nations have always had noble or upper classes that owned the large majority of wealth, and they were not, as Tocqueville indicated, afflicted with the kind of discontent that pervades American society. Besides, there is still, in comparison to other nations and periods of history, a high level of prosperity distributed throughout the American population. The remaining one-third of the wealth owned by 90 percent of American households has created a large middle class. Discontent in this group owes its existence not so much to factors of distribution as to the drivenness of endlessly pursuing greater and greater wealth.

Societies built upon the principle of individual, material gain at the expense of what is good for all their members have, as Noam Chomsky pointed out, inevitably declined and perished. "Good" here is not only what is democratically good or economically fair for all members of society, but what is heroically good. A society cannot thrive on a heroism of material acquisition alone. And moreover, it cannot thrive on a heroism of unlimited possibilities. This was clearly understood by the ancient Chinese, who notably gave birth to a civilization that is both the oldest in the world and, notwithstanding its numerous dynasties and regimes, still extant. A modern commentary on the Confucian *I Ching* or *Book of Changes* states: "Unlimited possibilities are not suited to man; if they existed, his life would dissolve in the boundless. To become strong, a man's life needs the limitations ordained by duty and voluntarily accepted. The individual attains significance as a free spirit only by surrounding himself with these limitations and by determining for himself what his duty is." Again we find that special attention is given to the precise determination of social duties, which as mentioned, has not been well-delineated in America.

All this weighs heavily on the current state of affairs and priorities in America, amounting to nothing less than an indictment of the nation's addiction to height. The compulsive, habitual drive toward unlimited prosperity has no end. This is also, by default, an addiction to youth, a way of becoming arrested in it by forever seeking, forever growing, forever staying young. When the youthful pursuit of prosperity has no end or purpose other than itself, and leads to no transformation in the quality of civilization, it eventually becomes static. This is why, in addition to Tocqueville's observations, a society that is bent on unlimited prosperity invariably becomes restless. The laws that govern human life are the same on the collective level as on the individual level. There are many folk tales and stories from around the world that tell of the downfall of the hero who has become too hungry and restless in his pursuit of wealth. Eventually he becomes blinded in his insatiability and loses the fortune he has amassed if not also himself. It is not just simple avarice that is at work here, but a profound unconsciousness of what he is really looking for. If the hero is lucky he wakes up before it is too late and at least saves himself, a wiser if less wealthy man. The film "Bright Leaf" with Gary Cooper was just such a story. "Citizen Kane" and the true-life story of Howard Hughes were more tragic.

## The Culture and Economics of Excess

Society's inability to satisfy the fantasy of unlimited possibilities has rendered the American Dream inadequate. The disillusionment caused by this has been compensated in the form of what has become a culture of excess: if the Dream with the house and the white picket fence is not enough, go for more. Instead of a qualitative change, Americans persist in a quantitative approach that turns prosperity into a kind of mirage in which one can never finally arrive at one's destination. *Prosperity and money itself lose their significance in direct proportion to the degree that the fantasy of unlimited possibilities is believed to be real and takes on a life of its own.*

In some instances, the fantasy may even become a "real," profit-oriented business in its own right. Perhaps the most stunning illustration of this is the international arms trade during the Cold War. Needless to say, America was (and continues to be) the world's leading arms supplier. From the American geopolitical point of view, there was a need to check Soviet expansionism and back U.S. allies and proxies with military support. However, from an *economic* point of view, *all* the nations producing and selling armaments believed that doing so would grow their economies (and in particular, their military industrial complexes) without inflation. Thus, this business had dramatic effects upon not only the client nations, whose proxy wars would not have been so easy to wage had they not been so abundantly armed, but the sellers as well. The historian John Ralston Saul writes:

> The end of colonialism meant the rise of new states. New states meant new armies in need of new weaponry. These young governments were eager to buy but short of cash. That turned out to be a simple technical problem. The same Western governments which sold them the weapons would finance their expenditures through aid programs or general bank loans or specific armament-financing agreements, all facilitated by subsidized low pricing.
>
> In other words the sellers were not actually financing their own military needs through foreign sales, because they were also financing the buyers. According to their rational accounting system, a fighter sold abroad more or less paid for a fighter in the home air force. In reality the seller government was paying for both. The whole process was and is little more than an inflationary chain in which money, in the form of debt, must be printed to finance the production of nonproductive goods to be stored at home or in other countries.

Much of this particular fantasy of unlimited possibilities ended with the fall of the Soviet Union, and of course, it can be argued that this fantasy with its high costs was consciously sustained as a necessary evil—a necessary price to pay—in order to keep the Western alliance of nations in a superior military position. In other words, the Cold War had to be won no matter what inflationary methods needed to be employed. Nevertheless, the "whole process" about which Saul writes was, with all the taxes, inflation, and debt it incurred, part and parcel of the culture of excess that characterized this period of American history perhaps more than any other. Americans accepted it as a natural way of life that the military portion of the federal budget ranged from 58.7 percent in 1955 to 43.9 percent in 1970. Then in the 1980s, few anticipated that Reagan's expansive build-up of the military (combined with tax cuts), though boosting the economy at the time, would help create a huge deficit in the federal budget. There was little recollection or awareness of the fact that exorbitant military spending has throughout history always been disastrous for economies.

Thus, the tendency toward excess and the denial it fosters cannot be attributed only to the government, as if the latter operates in a vacuum. The fantasy of unlimited possibilities perpetuates the business cycle of expansion beyond reasonable limits in the private sector as well as the public sector, resulting in inflation. This then is followed by the necessary contraction that adjusts the economy back to proper levels. This is experienced as a recession or depression. The ongoing alternation between inflation and depression has been a general phenomenon that began in America as early as with the crisis and Flour Riot of 1837, when the price of flour more than doubled and huge numbers were unemployed (as many as one-third of the labor force, or 50,000, in New York City alone). With massive wage cuts and strikes, the depression of 1857 was also devastating. By the end of the nineteenth century, frontier expansion finally came to a close and the fantasy of unlimited possibilities was now turned to the industrial development of the nation. Industrial barons such as Eastman, Carnegie, and Rockefeller were products of this change, along with their *Social Register*, exclusive clubs, and extravagant, high society balls. The Gilded Age, however, gave rise not only to the popular belief that America's streets were paved with gold, but to the recklessness responsible for the Panic of 1873, the Panic of 1893, and the ensuing depressions of 1907, 1919, and 1929.

Shortly after the First World War came the Roaring Twenties, another economic and social boom period. During this period such monuments of height as the Chrysler Building and Empire State Building were erected (they were completed, respectively, in 1930 and 1931). Living "high on the hog"—gambling, drinking at speak-easies, a soaring stock market—was the cultural style of the Roaring Twenties. But in truth, the prosperity was concentrated at the top: only the upper 10 percent of the population enjoyed any significant increase in real income. Forty-two percent of American families earned less than $1,000 a year; the average per capita income in 1929 was $705, which in 1999 terms equaled $6,680. The fateful end of this era of top-heavy prosperity came with the crash of the stock market and the Great Depression.

Roosevelt's answer to the Depression, the New Deal, only reduced unemployment from 13 million to 9 million. It was the industrial production demands of the Second World War that put the nation back to work. With the end of the war and the disintegration of the British Empire, America clearly emerged as the leading nation in the world. The period that followed was characterized by rapid economic expansion, growth of prosperity, and the baby boom.

But the inflationary chain of which Saul spoke also grew, and because it is linked to other chains in the machinery of the economy, it is possible to pass the buck from one area to the other. Inflation of prices, higher interest rates, and rising unemployment are all interrelated, and thus, excessiveness in any one of these will significantly affect the others. A huge multiple-chain reaction involving all of these occurred during the Vietnam War, a venture that was financed through the issue of new government debt as opposed to raising taxes. This act of borrowing caused interest rates to rise. At the same time, the demand for war materiel as well as the normal consumer demand for automobiles, houses, and so forth led to high inflation—from 4 percent in 1971 (when Nixon imposed price controls) to 12 percent in 1974. (If taxes had been raised instead, consumers would have cut back their demand for consumer goods, and there would have been less inflation.) All this was further compounded when Nixon took the U.S. dollar off the gold standard and confidence fell in its value against other world currencies. The quadrupling of oil prices by the oil-producing nations was at least in part a direct result of the diminished value of the dollar. Unemployment rose as well as prices and interest rates, and the stock market fell. Usually inflation and recession alternate in an oscillating cycle, but this unusual convergence was given the term "stagflation" by economists.

The inflation of the Vietnam War period was finally brought down in 1974 by the U.S. Federal Reserve's increase of short-term interest rates to a then unprecedented 12 percent. This brought about the worst economic downturn since the 1930s. Nevertheless, inflation continued, prompting the Federal Reserve during the early Reagan years to again increase interest rates to over 20 percent. This in turn produced very high unemployment, again showing how the problem of excess can be spread from one area to the other. The inflated condition of the economy had become so widely accepted as the norm that it became bankable. The demand for money in order to buy assets (real estate, companies, etc.) was so strong that people were willing to pay the exorbitantly high interest rates, reflecting an expectation that inflation would continue into the future. This is another instance of how the fantasy of unlimited possibilities became a business motivated by its own belief in inflationary-driven profits. But in the end, as with the arms trade, it was not all that profitable. Two results were the recession of 1981–82 and the savings and loan scandal in the late 1980s, the latter of which was a terrible catastrophe for those who were its victims.

The irony of inflation—worldwide and not just in America—is that although the profits reaped by continual expansion have increased the standards of living for many, most people need to earn more and work harder than ever to maintain these standards. Although there are a number of reasons why both parents in the average household now work outside the home, keeping up with these standards is certainly one of the predominant. And the nation has gone into great debt to keep up with these high standards. In 1997, it had $370 billion of credit card debt. The average household owed $6,000. In fact, every sector of the economy was in the red. The federal debt for the same year was $5.4 trillion. American corporate debt had broken the $2 trillion mark five years earlier. On this alone, 32 percent of corporate cash flow was absorbed by interest payments. This spending-and-debting borrows from the future. The issues of Social Security payments and rising health care costs are even greater concerns for the future. Although these do not borrow from the future, they put an excessive strain on the nation's ability to pay for them.

In spite of these figures, the late 1990s was an unprecedented period of peacetime economic expansion and prosperity. With the stock market boom and sustained low inflation, the entire model or theory of the economy was presumed to have changed, leading to what has been called the "new economy." The former model, in which the economy's stability depended on keeping demand and supply roughly balanced, has made way, ostensibly, for a model in which gauging either spending (demand) or productive capacity (supply) has become more and more difficult. New factors obfuscate the nature of productivity growth or its permanence. These include the computer and communications technologies (advances may occur in irregular spasms); the decline of unemployment without inflationary wage increases; globalization (which heightens America's exposure to foreign economic changes); and the "wealth effect" from the stock market (which emboldens people to save less and borrow and spend more). The long-range effects of these factors remain to be seen. Certainly, as noted by economist John Kenneth Galbraith, there has never been a period of growth in which the expansion did not eventually end. The 1990s may not have exhibited inflation as we know it, but there was a kind of inflation in the financial markets which led to what Federal Reserve Chairman Alan Greenspan called "irrational exuberance."

The fantasy of unlimited possibilities is a fantasy of youth, a hormonal but untested conviction—typically observable with adolescents—that the sky is the limit and that one is forever young and can afford to pay for today with tomorrow. As one airline advertisement put it, "Fly now, pay later"—a promotion of height in more ways than one. On a national level, the fantasy of unlimited possibilities had a certain plausibility and dynamism while America was in the throes of its continental task. In the words of Governor Mario Cuomo, "We built an America of great expectations. America was always the future." But today, one wonders if this ceaseless orientation toward the future is not becoming old and tired, and indeed, even aging the nation before its time. Americans spend tremendous energy worrying about their future well-being. The foremost concern on people's minds is whether they will continue to be able to earn a good living and whether their children will have the same opportunities they had. America and the world it is increasingly interdependent with are changing, and it is becoming apparent that what once were unlimited possibilities are now limited by nature itself. Saul writes:

> The gross world product has increased twenty-one times since 1900, the use of fossil fuels nearly thirtyfold, industrial production fifty times. The resulting goods were consumed by both a dramatic rise in general standards of living and a population explosion—from 1.6 billion to 5 billion in eighty years. That most of the production came from the West further exaggerated the effects of this growth. We sold our products to the whole world in return for their cheap natural resources. These combined circumstances created a run of exceptional profits. And so in the subsequent era—our own—devoid as it is of linear memory, the business community began to treat fast growth and massive profits as basic characteristics of successful business. . . .
>
> The developing world's population continues to grow in a way which impoverishes rather than enriches them. The population level of the West has paused at saturation level. Our production needs can't help but pause as well. This is only a catastrophe if capitalism is treated as a machine which must produce constant and

giant profits. Were we to return to more standard expectations, we would find it easier to accept modest returns.

Jung said it more bluntly: "What America needs in the face of the tremendous urge towards uniformity, desire of things, the desire for complications in life, for being like one's neighbours, for making records, et cetera, is one great healthy ability to say 'no.' "

## A Healthy Ability to Say "No": A Gift of Depression

President Kennedy's proclamation that "Prosperity is the only real way to balance the budget," may reflect standard economic thinking, but at the same time, the facts show that decades of increasing national prosperity have done little to balance the budget. The only real way to balance the budget is to balance priorities, expenditures, and appetites, that is, to "just say no." But even when America says "no," it is often in a way that is characterized by excess. With the seductive assumption that more is better, "no" somehow gets transformed into "yes."

A good example of this was the staggering sums spent on investigating potential wrongdoing in high places of government. The appointment of independent counsels to examine possible misdeeds in the executive branch began with Watergate and was later continued under the aegis of the Ethics in Government Act of 1978. Although the chief purpose of the latter was to check corruption and illegal activities, it also aimed to curtail excess, yet was itself so expensive that it defeated this aim. The government's own General Accounting Office reported that by 1996, investigations conducted by approximately two dozen independent counsels had cost taxpayers $132 million. The most highly publicized cases included Leon Jaworski investigating Watergate, Lawrence Walsh investigating Iran-contra, and Kenneth Starr investigating Whitewater (by the time Robert Ray concluded the latter investigation in 2000, it had cost $52 million). However, many of the other, less publicized cases were far from monumental in significance, but the amount of time and money spent on them was extravagant. For instance, the investigation of whether Agriculture Secretary Mike Espy received gifts worth around $10,000 in exchange for corporate favors took two and a half years and cost over $6.6 million. To find out how much Housing Secretary Henry Cisneros spent on his mistress—$200,000 was the amount eventually disclosed—the investigation took three years and cost $6 million. It took three years and $2.8 million before investigators cleared Bush administration officials of improperly searching Bill Clinton's passport file. The chief independent counsel in that case himself admitted that the independent counsel law covered too many people in the executive branch. Others claimed that Justice Department prosecutors could have completed such investigations far more quickly and cost-effectively. Evidently, to buy public confidence in their officials, Americans were willing to be penny-wise and pound-foolish. Naturally, Congress would not extend the Ethics in Government Act when it expired in 1999, at least not in its existing form.

The problem of excess is an addiction to height regardless of the form in which it manifests. The above are just a few of the many readily available examples in which America cannot say "no" to its own inflated mindset. Indulgence and waste are taken for granted as part of the American way of life even with the most ordinary functions of daily existence. It has been estimated that Americans waste approximately one-quarter of their food, throwing out even one-day-old bread; 5 percent of what they waste could feed 4 million people. American grandiosity has even crept into death: Americans spend on an average $6,000 for a funeral that should cost $2,000. Unfortunately, the grander the mindset, the greater is the unconsciousness or lack, of awareness of it. This naturally has detrimental global effects. Comprising 5 percent of the world's population, America consumes 25 percent of the earth's natural resources and produces 50 percent of the gases that are responsible for the greenhouse effect. At the 1992 United Nations Earth Summit Conference, America took a leading role in voicing the need for the nations of the world to control this effect, itself promising to cut greenhouse gases back to 1990 levels by 2000. At the time of the 1997 Conference, 10 percent more carbon was being emitted by American smokestacks and tailpipes than in 1990. Of course, Third World nations attending the Conference were hesitant to listen to America's urgent recommendations on this matter when it had been so negligent in implementing them itself.

It is curious that the words "inflation" and "depression" mean the same thing in economics as in psychology. In an inflated condition, the economy or psyche is swelled with a false confidence in its value. It is too heady or lofty for its own good, like Icarus soaring into the sun with his wings of wax or the builders of the Tower of Babel. A person in this condition is described as being full of himself or on an "ego trip." Everybody except him can see his inflation. In matters of economy it is the same: containing excess and the fantasy of unlimited possibilities that underlies it is not likely to occur during a period of expansion because the economy is flush and everybody is flying high. Economic and psychological inflation go hand-in-hand.

The discipline to say "no" and redefine parameters is more likely to emerge in response to a state of depression, as was obviously the case with the New Deal. The New Deal did not change the system of unlimited prosperity-seeking, inequality, and waste that brought the Depression on, but it did alleviate the immediate crisis and institute enduring reforms. It is doubtful whether these reforms would have been introduced at that time were it not for the Depression and its massive despair. Economic and psychological depression here went hand-in-hand as a compensation to inflation. As Jung pointed out, the word "depression" literally means "being forced downwards."

The suffering inflicted by depression compels self-examination like nothing else. In numerous myths and stories of the hero's journey, depression is analogous to psychological death and always precedes rebirth. Cecil B. DeMille, for example, understood this well when in his epic, "The Ten Commandments," he portrayed a demoralized and sun-scorched Moses wandering in the desert after his banishment from Egypt. Egypt was not only the House of Bondage but a house of inflation, and Moses' depression was an inevitable consequence of and reaction to it; after all, prior to his odyssey Moses had been a prince of Egypt.

Another illustration of the process of depression is the story of Jonah. His inflated refusal to go to Nineveh as God commanded resulted in his being swallowed by a whale. In the depths of the ocean, or in the "belly of hell" as the Bible describes it, he was forced to reevaluate his ways and come to terms with his religious calling and heroic mission. Depression is thus an attempt on the part of the psyche—regardless of whether it is the individual or collective psyche—to correct an imbalance, deviation, or faulty attitude. Its purpose is to return the psyche to its original course or set it on a new course to advance its development.

The episodes and varieties of inflation that America experiences are perversions of its aspiration toward height or greatness. They are compensated by periodic depressions that are economic *and* psychological: everybody feels deflated when they occur. In effect, they aim to pull the national psyche down into its depths. Only here can the nation reconnect to its heroic mission and ask, what indeed is all this prosperity for? People naturally view these periods of depression as a problem, and certainly, they impose grave hardships upon many. But, from a psychological and spiritual viewpoint, the real problem is that the low-spiritedness of depression has not been sunk into *enough*. These depressions can have spiritual value, but that value often remains buried. The nation is usually too quick to get out of its suffering to appreciate the latter's redeeming aspects.

# Chapter 6

## Heroic Mania

*The pilot-hero was made unique by a whole mythology of speed as an experience, of space devoured, of intoxicating motion; the* jet-man, *on the other hand, is defined by a coenaesthesis of motionlessness ('at 2,000 km per hour, in level flight, no impression of speed at all'), as if the extravagance of his vocation precisely consisted in over taking motion, in going faster than speed. . . .*

*No wonder if, carried to such a pitch, the myth of the aviator loses all humanism. The hero of classical speed could remain a 'gentleman,' inasmuch as motion was for him an occasional exploit, for which courage alone was required. . . .*

*The* jet-man, *on the other hand, no longer seems to know either adventure or destiny, but only a condition.*

—Roland Barthes

*Hunger pays a heavy price to the falling gods of speed and steel.*

—Bob Dylan

## The Cult of Motion and Speed

Americans live at breakneck speeds, quickly coursing through not only their collective suffering but even their common, daily activities. The urgency with which the nation pursues prosperity and then seeks to escape from the resulting problems extends to many areas of life. Like the fantasy of unlimited possibilities, this urgency takes on a life of its own, namely, as a cult of motion and speed. Extraordinary motion and speed express the aspiration toward height or greatness inasmuch as they are godlike abilities and attempts to surpass human limitation.

Americans have a love-hate relationship with the cult of motion and speed. They complain about the fast-paced, manic quality of modern life—rush hour and road rage on the freeways, the pressure to meet daily obligations, the feeling that there is never enough time. All the statistics on longevity and mortality indicate that stress-related disease, as it is now fashionably called, is a function of lifestyle. Of course, life itself is a cause of stress and mortality, and has always been, but there is little doubt that the recent increase in stress-related disease (ulcers, chronic backaches and headaches, heart disease, alcoholism, etc.) goes hand-in-hand with the increased tempo of modern life.

Yet Americans not only tolerate life in the fast track but glamorize it. Whether it is fast cars or fast food, motion and speed are good. They not only save time and promote productivity that leads to prosperity, but are signs of vitality and youth. America prides itself on being a nation "on the move." And of course, one of the nation's greatest prides, New York City, is a shrine of motion and speed. The love-hate relationship New Yorkers commonly feel toward their home reflects their ambivalence toward this cult. The city that never sleeps, it is the ultimate urban adrenaline-booster. Police, ambulance, and fire-truck sirens signal its intensity at all hours. The famous "New York minute" is the shortest in the world: drivers honk their horns in fury at the slightest delay. New Yorkers are commonly in a rush, and are highly ambitious, creative, and extravagant. The extremes of the Big Apple make it a microcosm of America, a rat race as well as a cornucopia of human achievement. It is a city of both high culture and empty pretense; America's best and worst, class and crass, exist side by side. "If I can make it there," Frank Sinatra sings, "I can make it anywhere."

But the pressures of living in New York are fundamentally no different than those of living anywhere else in the nation; they are only more intensely concentrated. The cult of motion and speed does not diversify the quality of life in America but homogenizes it. It spreads uniformity quickly and with a technological absolutism, as a drumbeat to which everybody and everything in the culture conform. As McLuhan observed decades ago, electric technology transforms the world into a global village by speeding up the exchange of information and all other activities that connect people.

Everything occurs simultaneously in the global village. The death of Princess Diana was known in America at the same instant as in England, and in fact, even sooner, because people were sleeping when it was announced in England. Electronic media and technology have turned the world into a single network. With the Internet, cyberspace, e-mail, and the emergence of a highly interdependent, global economy, this is even more true today than when McLuhan first made his observations.

In spite of its global scope, the cult of motion and speed has become a much more potent force in America than elsewhere. Perhaps Japan is the exception that is at least as hurried as America, but even there, the cult of motion and speed is moderated by strong ties between people and between present and past. The built-in traditions of Japanese culture—the arts, religion, and the intact, multigenerational structure of the family—serve as mechanisms to soothe the frenzy and duress of modern life. The cult of motion and speed in America is, as everywhere in the world, the child borne by the marriage of the cults of technology and prosperity: the capacity to make a fast buck is technologically amplified on a massive, collective level. But in America, unlike most other nations, this child has been raised in a house that doesn't have traditional roots and whose windows are open to the winds of change (read democracy) that blow through it in a most unsettling way. Tocqueville writes:

Among aristocratic nations, as families remain for centuries in the same condition, often on the same spot, all generations become, as it were, contemporaneous. A man almost always knows his forefathers and respects them; he thinks he already sees his remote descendants and he loves them. He willingly imposes duties on himself towards the former and the latter, and he will frequently sacrifice his personal gratifications to those who went before and to those who will come after him. Aristocratic institutions, moreover, have the effect of closely binding every man to several of his fellow citizens. As the classes of an aristocratic people are strongly marked and permanent, each of them is regarded by its own members as a sort of lesser country, more tangible and more cherished than the country at large. As in aristocratic communities all the citizens occupy fixed positions, one above another, the result is that each of them always sees a man above himself whose patronage is necessary to him, and below himself another man whose co-operation he may claim. Men living in aristocratic ages are therefore almost always closely attached to something placed out of their own sphere, and they are often disposed to forget themselves.

Among democratic nations, however, new families constantly crop up while others crumble, and those that remain change their condition with every new circumstance. The track of generations is lost, and concern for humanity is often confined to those in close proximity to oneself. Class distinctions dissolve and the aristocratic sense of order and belonging is shattered. "Thus," Tocqueville concludes, "not only does democracy make everyman forget his ancestors, but it hides his descendants and separates his contemporaries from him; it throws him back forever upon himself alone and threatens in the end to confine him entirely within the solitude of his own heart." In effect, there occurs a fragmentation or atomization of society: the glue that binds society together is weakened and the individual is made to feel small and insignificant. He becomes isolated.

Furthermore, the capitalist ethos fostered by democracy and technological modernity is prone to creating a purely survivalist world akin to the grim state of nature depicted by Thomas Hobbes: the individual is reduced to living according to the basic drives of fear and personal gratification. There is little sense of social responsibility and actions have few moral consequences. Each person lives in his or her own separate reality. The hero-systems of civilization—community, family, religion, education—lose their compelling force and what remains is the pseudoheroism of climbing up the socioeconomic ladder. The German sociologist Ferdinand Toennies coined the term *Gesellschaft* for this kind of society. It is impersonal, dispersed, competitive, and highly institutionalized. By contrast, *Gemeinschaft* represents the togetherness or communal kinship of the localized, rooted society that prevailed before the rise of democracy and industry.

Add to America's rootless condition and hunger for wealth the cult of motion and speed, and you have a portrait of the dissociated, restless society that Hobbes and Toennies feared would become the hallmark of modern times. Once again, Tocqueville had his finger right on America's pulse:

> In the United States a man builds a house in which to spend his old age, and he sells it before the roof is on; he plants a garden and lets it just as the trees are coming into bearing; he brings a field into tillage and leaves other men to gather the crops; he embraces a profession and gives it up; he settles in a place, which he soon afterwards leaves to carry his changeable longings elsewhere. If his private affairs leave him any leisure, he instantly plunges into the vortex of politics; and if at the end of a year of unremitting labor he finds he has a few days' vacation, his eager curiosity whirls him over the vast extent of the United States, and he will travel fifteen hundred miles in a few days to shake off his happiness. Death at

length overtakes him, but it is before he is weary of his bootless chase of that complete felicity which forever escapes him.

The transience of American society is well-illustrated by the answers to a questionnaire the medical doctor and researcher Dean Ornish administered to a group of people in Iowa in the mid–1990s. Four questions were asked:

1. Do you live in the same neighborhood you were born in?
2. Do you attend the same church or synagogue you did ten years ago, with the same congregants?
3. Do you work at the same job you did ten years ago, with the same coworkers?
4. Do you live near the members of your extended family and see them regularly?

Ninety percent of the people quizzed said "no" to all questions, whereas, Ornish argued, 40 years earlier 90 percent would have said "yes." He compared this lifestyle to other nations, particularly those of the Third World, and connected it to the high rate of heart disease in America. Speaking in the language of poetry, one could see how the heart would suffer from loneliness and other emotional wounds that result from the loosening and breaking of family and social ties. Ornish's work of course speaks to the psychosomatic component of heart disease.

The cult of motion and speed accelerates not only the pace of the world but of being human, that is, it impacts upon age-old rhythms conditioned by evolution. Surely life in the fast lane, with all its pressures and uncertainties, must affect the equilibrium of the psyche and of the human organism in general. Is it any wonder that anxiety has become one of the leading mental health problems in America? Some 19 million adults and 13 million children—one in seven Americans—are affected by anxiety disorders each year, and according to a study by the World Health Organization, the chances of developing such a disorder have doubled since 1960. It is in view of this that psychologists and social thinkers have called the modern period the Age of Anxiety. Not only are there the stressors of daily life, but there is no longer a "container" to hold the existential angst that Kierkegaard so brilliantly illuminated as the perennial essence of the human condition. In its race towards the future, the cult of motion and speed has made traditional religion seem anachronistic and irrelevant.

Children are susceptible to the pace and pressures of modern life in distinct ways. In this Information Age they are exposed to much more than ever before and grow up much faster—in all regards except the development of character, which requires *knowledge* as opposed to information and which is one of the few real indicators of maturity. Children almost seem to absorb the effects of the cult of motion and speed by osmosis, and then to somaticize them. Attention-deficit/hyperactivity disorder has increased in recent decades, at least in frequency of diagnosis if not actual occurrence. However, it has been estimated that the drug Ritalin, used to counter the hyperactivity, is prescribed to children in the United States 50 to 60 percent more than is medically necessary. The psychologist Ann Walker believes that some of these unnecessarily medicated children are in fact not hyperactive due to any biochemical imbalances, but because modern-day parents are so busy and rushed that they do not have adequate time to attend to their children's needs. The children then react with rushed agitation of their own in the form of hyperactivity.

The course of human relationships also speeds up, attaining a pace and an emotional quality that is something other than what is "normally" human. At the speed of modernity, depth is sacrificed and we are perpetually in a state of what Alvin Toffler called future shock, of being pounced upon by new changes before we have had a chance to digest the old ones. People get divorced as suddenly as they get married, Las Vegas style. A stand-up comic tells the following joke:

> A young man goes into the bank and has to wait in line to see the teller. As he is waiting, he notices that the teller is attractive and he starts to fantasize about her. In his mind he sees himself approaching her window and asking her for a date. He sees their first date. He then sees himself courting her and falling in love. He sees their first kiss, their first embrace, their wedding, their honeymoon, their first year together. Then he sees that one day she cheats on him, and he catches her with her lover. He sees himself divorcing her. Now his turn in line comes, he approaches the teller, and he shouts at her: "We're through! It's finished between us! I'm glad I never asked you out!"

The blurring of fantasy and reality makes this joke funny, but its humor also lies in the rote way relationships quickly degenerate in modern times. They are over before they even begin. The young man's fantasy mirrors a cultural pattern. The rapid tempo and superficiality of relationships in contemporary America can be observed in most American movies and television programs. Art here imitates life, and these movies and programs reveal a total absence of depth in human relatedness. It is no wonder that "intimacy" and "commitment" have become the main buzzwords of pop psychology.

## The Dangers of Motion and Speed

The very prospect of democracy is threatened by the cult of motion and speed. A fragmented, Hobbesian world can easily lead to fascism and fanaticism of all kinds, because when people feel small and insignificant, they long to become part of something that will restore their sense of purpose. Fascist movements such as Nazism and fanatical strains such as American militia groups appeal to people's desire for dignity and their wish to be part of something greater than themselves, however defined or ill-defined. These movements almost always develop when a formerly well-ordered world has become meaningless and chaotic; the historical need for a response is authentic, but the form of the response is twisted. These movements are, at least in part, the twisted effects of the cult of motion and speed, themselves manifesting in a primitive, Hobbesian way.

The American political landscape is today defined by the cult of motion and speed. It follows its dictates without reflection or judgment. The political atmosphere and mindset regularly change almost overnight. Everybody can recall how the 1994 Contract with America and Republican congressional victory seemed to set the stage for a new era. Two years later, Gingrich was all but washed up and Clinton was easily reelected. Ideological convictions are transient in an age of itinerant motion and speed. The flexibility to change like a chameleon can spell the difference between failure and success for a modern politician. Here is how *Time* described one of the key differences between Clinton and Dole in the 1996 presidential campaign:

> Clinton, a restless man defined by his energy and appetites, concludes that the only constant about life today is its unremitting motion. For his generation even the revolutions came from within and aren't over yet—civil rights, sexual freedom and now the one under way, driven by silicon and imagination. And so the beautiful thing about Clinton and the horrible thing about him too is that he moves with these changes almost daily, modulating his positions to fit the changing moods. If Dole, in his style and syntax, often seems strangely off-key, Clinton is a tuning fork, banging himself again and again against the edge of the table to see if he can get even closer to perfect pitch.

Their particular qualities have helped and hurt them along the way. But if Clinton ends Dole's political life next week, the President's victory will reflect how well he managed to turn his own inconstancy into a virtue and how Dole has converted his steadfastness into a liability.

The media, particularly television, have had a great deal to do with the rapid shape-shifting character of contemporary politics. "Just as nature abhors a vacuum," William Safire has said, "the media abhors no change. No change is no news." The media thus requires a steady diet of change. As McLuhan pointed out, a culture's way of perceiving things is affected not so much by the content of its media but by their sensory dynamics ("the medium is the message"). A culture predominantly under the influence of the spoken or printed word will experience the world with a different sensibility and momentum than a culture that has been thoroughly modernized. In the case of television, the sensory dynamic is one of rapidly moving images. A TV culture perceives the world through TV, that is, as a rapid succession of moving images. In this way TV shapes the events of the world, or at least determines which are real and which not. "Real" here is what moves rapidly enough to hold our attention on TV. But this is very fleeting: an image on the screen five minutes ago is now only a vague memory trace. Life assumes the quality of a passing parade of images that have little enduring substance. Everything is in constant motion.

Movement in television, however, is not only visual but dramatic. Good TV news has to be dramatically moving either in the sense that it emotionally moves us or that its story line moves with intensity. Political scandals make good television, as do wars, disasters, and terrorism. But as soon as a terrorist event becomes too drawn out and loses its action-packed quality, it ceases to be newsworthy. When Peruvian terrorists besieged the Japanese ambassador's residence in Lima in 1996 and held a number of hostages for 126 days, coverage of the event disappeared from television for extended periods every time there was a lull in negotiations. Most of the wars being waged at any given moment around the globe hardly get any coverage because their status changes too slowly and with insufficient action to warrant the assignment of a camera team. By the same token, policy issues, conferences, and events that require complex verbal explanations and updates do not make good television news. They do not fit into easily discernible categories of black vs. white, Left vs. Right, good vs. bad. The finer details that constitute most of the real happenings of the world are too slow-going and thus anathema to TV's visual and dramatic inclinations.

Like politics, the economic arena is frenetically driven by the cult of motion and speed—perhaps even more so because of the profit motive. The profit motive gives rise to the cult of motion and speed and then becomes regulated and challenged by it. As brought to the public's attention by consumer advocates in the 1960s, the automobile industry depends on a timely turn-around of cars and parts to assure profits. The "built-in obsolescence" of cars is designed so that they will last only a finite lifespan before the consumer is forced once again to purchase a new car. The Volkswagen beetle—the "people's car"—made its claim to fame as an easily affordable car with a bankable long life. This was clearly not an invention of Detroit's. Americans feel they need to have a new car every four to seven years whether they actually need one or not. This compulsion is not restricted to cars. The consumer economy thrives on products that sell at a premium, wear out quickly, and are thrown away, offering with each new generation some marginal improvement in usefulness.

The challenge of speed hurls industry into a hazardous race to break its own records of productivity and profit-making. John Ralston Saul tells of a typical example with the Boeing Company, whose quality construction of airplanes had by 1988 created not only $30 billion in revenue but such demand that there was a list of back orders for 1,000 planes:

> To meet this demand it went on a massive hiring binge, to the extent that some forty percent of the workers soon had less than two years' experience. There was enormous pressure on everyone to keep the assembly line going and going fast. The result was an abrupt drop in quality. Crossed wires on warning systems. Crossed wires on fire extinguisher systems. Thirty cases of backward plumbing. Engine-casing temperature sensors installed in reverse order. A disintegrating wing flap on a plane's first day of service. Metal fatigue disintegration of a 737 in flight. Disintegration of part of a 747 in flight. The U.S. aviation agency began reviewing Boeing's assembly procedures.

Such situations combine the cult of motion and speed with the cult of prosperity and the fantasy of unlimited possibilities. Managers lose their common sense and capacity for restraint as they are swallowed by these impersonal forces. Even the Federal Aviation Administration can't resist thinking in impersonal terms that in the end support the aviation industry's methods: in 1997 it reportedly estimated the monetary value of an individual life to be $2.7 million. Decisions to compel the industry to meet the rising costs of safety are considered with this sum in mind.

From all that has been said, it is evident that motion and speed are ways of getting high. A high speed not only invigorates us but intoxicates us. It triggers an ecstatic feeling of transcendence or immortality, momentary as this may be. Racing sports of all kinds owe their popularity to the fact that they give us not only a physical rush but a spiritual one. And certainly, a strange love of danger and sense of invincibility go with the godlike power of motion and speed. Think of those youthful men on motorcycles whizzing by everyone on the highway, stretching their limits while flirting with death. There's no time to think. Indeed, in their state of motion and speed, there's no time at all. The word "highway" accurately describes the road of inflation they are on.

Of all the forms of addiction to height, motion and speed are among the most narcotic. I use the word "narcotic" here in its Greek sense as *narkoun*, which means to benumb. The Indo-European root of this word is supposedly *nerk*, which means to twist, entwine, snare. Combining these meanings, we may say that narcosis is a state of numbness in which one is twisted, entwined, or snared. As the documentary filmmaker Godfrey Reggio illustrated, narcosis is probably the most prominent effect of the cult of motion and speed. His film "Koyaanisqatsi" takes its title from the Hopi word for a frenetic way of life. The film—a series of visual images of modern life in America—leaves the viewer numb. Apparently this was Reggio's intention.

The numbness induced by intense motion and speed is a response to overstimulation. When we are overwhelmed, we become desensitized in order to adapt. The hyperkinesis of modern American life numbs or desensitizes the psyche through sensory and gratification overload. More specifically, because the stimulation is gratifying but delivered in rapid bursts, like a machine gun going off, the cult of motion and speed produces a desensitization to *quick* gratification. But as can be observed, this is actually a maladaptation. People seek to gratify their senses and appetites, but no sooner are these satisfied than they are seeking the next quick fix—a job promotion, a new car, a better house, a more exciting vacation, a different lover. America has become an Epicurean culture in the most twisted, entwined, and snared sense of the meaning. But even Epicurus advocated moderation in the pursuit of pleasure.

Related to this is the expectation of immediacy: "I want it now, today." Particularly troubling is a tendency to find immediate, short-term solutions to problems without taking the time to understand the big picture. This problem of shortsightedness pervades every field of endeavor in America, from economics to education and from the environment to health care. Take for example the issue of nuclear waste and garbage disposal. The risk of nuclear dumps and regular landfills leaking toxins into the environment is a mounting concern as the production of waste steadily increases. We are here not even speaking about the disposal of refuse that for decades has been poisoning America's rivers and lakes. Yet the response has been, with nuclear waste, to package and hide it better, and with industrial waste, to chemically treat it and *then* dump it. On one occasion in 1987, America even tried to ship its garbage abroad on a barge, as if somebody else would want it.

The greatest scheme of all, however, was the government's plan to turn Yucca Mountain in Nevada into a nuclear waste repository by 2010. Nuclear waste accumulates in the United States at a rate of six tons per day. The government wanted to transport 70,000 tons of the nation's nuclear waste to Yucca Mountain. The total radioactivity of this waste is equivalent to one million atomic bombs of the type that destroyed Hiroshima. It would take 10,000 years for this material to cease to be harmful to human life—longer than the period of recorded human history. The flushed waste of Yucca Mountain, critics feared, would have been washed down to Los Angeles, and a transportation accident could have had a catastrophic effect on the surrounding region. Also feared was the risk of damage to the repository from an earthquake. The project was finally vetoed by Clinton only a few months before the end of his second term, but it is by no means certain that future presidents won't attempt to reinstate plans to proceed with this or similar projects. After all, the problem of nuclear waste itself cannot be vetoed away, and something must be done with this waste.

Experts tell us that the solutions to such problems require a fundamental overhaul of America's methods of energy production, consumption, and waste disposal. Looking at alternate sources of energy, such as the sun and wind, and recycling on a much larger scale than currently practiced, have been long recommended. But such changes demand not only an investment of money but of other kinds of human energy, particularly, time and critical thinking. American taxpayers do not react well to demands for their money, let alone time and thought. In the end, it will take a major environmental and health crisis to prompt the American public and its elected officials to take action. By then, of course, the status of these problems will be far worse. Saying "no" and delaying gratification are never pleasurable, but insisting upon the short-term gain because it is immediate is usually more costly in the long run. As the saying goes, the longest distance between two points is a shortcut.

If narcosis is the most prominent effect of the cult of motion and speed, the loss of historical memory is the most subtle. It too is a form of numbness, but to the sense of historical time. When everything is constantly in motion and speeded up, time flies, and when time flies, there is no sense of history. Events leave no tracks on the ground, just a dim sense of something having whizzed by overhead. The pace of time itself seems to have accelerated, and history has become like a wheel in spinning motion, moving so fast that it appears not to be moving at all, that is, it seems static. Americans do not experience themselves in the continuum of history. This is an estranged condition of which they remain unaware. Thus could Henry Ford so assuredly claim that "History is bunk."

In ahistorical time, the events of 50 years ago—for example, World War II and the Holocaust—seem like they belong to another epoch. They become a collection of vague and abstract facts, things that reportedly happened to other people far removed from oneself. This unconscious attitude can be dangerous for a nation. "For history," Arthur Schlesinger, Jr. writes, "is to the nation rather as memory is to the individual. As an individual deprived of memory becomes disoriented and lost, not knowing where he has been or where he is going, so a nation denied a conception of its past will be disabled in dealing with its present and its future."

America's loss of vision is undoubtedly the most important symptom of this ahistorical perception of time. This loss is the result of forgetfulness: the spiritual vision posited for America by the Puritans and the Founding Fathers has all but slipped from the nation's mind. Although the practical duties or responsibilities connected with this vision were always vague, the vision itself was not. A nation whose memory is impaired will not be able to draw upon such assets; it will be dissociated from them much like a man who has lost his memory is dissociated from the wisdom and learning of his past experience. Thus does Studs Terkel speak of America as suffering from a kind of national Alzheimer's disease, a collective amnesia in which the nation has forgotten its past and consequently lives in a directionless future.

In such a state of forgetfulness, a nation is bound to relive its past, to repeat history in order to learn its lessons. Is not, for example, the racial divisiveness that afflicts America today a replay of the fundamental issue that sundered the nation during the Civil War? The failure to implement the principles of equality extolled in the Declaration of Independence certainly has less intense or severe consequences today than 150 years ago, but for many it is still just as harsh in its implications. "Whenever we give up, leave behind, and forget too much," Jung writes, "there is always the danger that the things we have neglected will return with added force." The shock of white Americans at images of Los Angeles burning in 1992 or from the verdict of the Simpson trial was essentially a reaction to a forgotten piece of history returning with added force.

In the final analysis, Americans may wish to critically reflect upon and evaluate their glorification of motion and speed. Motion and speed are not compulsory prerequisites for the good life or for a high civilization, as the ancients demonstrated. They do not have any intrinsic moral value nor do they enhance the development of character. Though they aspire to great heights, what is heroic about them is their simulation of godlikeness rather than the creation of something that helps humans become more human. In a perpetual state of motion and speed, people are reduced to Hobbesian beings rushing about in their isolated, self-centered worlds. They become like rats in a rat race or dogs in a dog-eat-dog world.

Americans have a choice as to how they can live. But making good choices requires consciousness and the will to exercise restraint. People can decide to use speed with discretion, going fast when it is definitely advantageous and slowing down when it is not. They can proceed slowly in order to see if they are doing the right thing in the right way. And if not, they can make changes. It is the blind pursuit of motion and speed for their own sake that has turned these into a cult that can undermine democracy and singlehandedly prevent the spiritual prospects of the American vision from ever becoming real.

# Chapter 7

## The Imitation of Heroism

*But what are the celebrities? The celebrities are the Names that need no further identification.*

—C. Wright Mills

### The Cult of Celebrity

By now it should be evident that I am using the word "cult" inclusively to describe a number of different phenomena in American culture. The words "cult," "culture," and "cultivate" are all derived from the Latin *colere*, which means "wheel" and "to till," as in tilling soil. The development of culture was initially connected with the rise of agricultural technology that permitted the shift from hunting and gathering societies to more stable, sedentary ones. Taking some liberty with the image, we could say that a cult is a wheel within the wheel of the larger culture, moving according to its own dynamics and exhibiting its own subculture of beliefs and values. These are cultivated in a glorified way because they convey deeply felt, spiritual convictions and because an identity has to be forged apart from the larger culture. Thus, it is not uncommon that the wheel within the wheel rolls off on its own and asserts itself with an authority akin to that of the larger culture. For example, Protestantism was originally considered a heretical cult, but with time it became in many countries the dominant cultural force. With a similar history the Puritans established themselves as the founders of New England.

But this is only one of the ways "cult" may be understood. Another way is in its more secular and insidious sense. A cult here is not defined by clear organizational or social structures, but is diffuse. It moves as part and parcel of the larger culture without being recognized. When it overtakes or overwhelms the larger culture, questions of its legitimacy become a real concern, but to whom? Nobody in the culture recognizes the cult for what it is, as it has become all-pervasive. As a Zen parable says, the fish is the last to know that it is in water. Except for those discussed in the next chapter, the cults I examine in this book are of this kind.

Like the cults of prosperity and motion and speed, the cult of celebrity is diffused throughout American culture. The objects of its glorification are not heroic ideals like wealth or godlike abilities, but people. All the same, celebrity is a cult of height because it is connected firstly with achievement and secondly with status. "Status," if we go to the Latin roots once again, means "to stand," and to stand tall is an attainment of height. Keeping up with the Joneses is about keeping *up*. The most valued thing in America after prosperity is status. The ultimate version of the good life is to be rich and famous. Fame or celebrity is status publically celebrated.

The problem with this celebration as it is now carried on in America is that it has become divorced from any real sense of what genuine achievement or status means. Celebrity is idolized and cultivated for its own sake. Being famous is itself the great thing, not what one is famous for. Elizabeth Taylor, for example, draws huge attention simply by virtue of being beautiful, glamorous, and Elizabeth Taylor. Her endorsement of perfume products and causes such as AIDS research gives them status in spite of the facts that she has not appeared in any memorable roles in the last thirty years and most people can offhand recall, at most, only two or three of her films.

Some historians have noted that in former times, the only people whose fame was guaranteed irrespective of what they did to earn it were monarchs. It is no coincidence that Hollywood stars are treated as American royalty, and are likened to the British monarchy as the latter functions today, namely, in a purely celebratory capacity. "They don't do much," it has been said about both, "but what they do they do well." Both act their parts gloriously, and it often seems to be the same role: royalty itself. What makes tabloids so fascinating to the public is not that movie stars are great people who are revealed to have ordinary problems like the rest of us. Everyone knows that great people suffer great burdens and it is the salt-of-the-earth way in which they suffer them that makes them great. Rather, tabloids are fascinating because they portray celebrities as kings and queens who have fallen from grace. The scandals, rumors, and intrigues the tabloids invent to busy the public mind are no different than the kind circulated by courtesans in the courts of monarchs whose power was absolute because they were believed to be divine or divinely appointed.

The fact that the adulation formerly reserved for monarchs is now showered upon celebrities illustrates that such adulation serves a very deep human need independent of its justification. We are creatures who need to have heroes who represent and incarnate godhood. These are different than the heroes who throughout history were esteemed for their great deeds; even they bowed in honor of their monarchs. Though we worshiped historical heroes in no small measure because we longed to be like them, they were closer and more accessible to us. They were natural heroes. Given the right circumstances, we *could* have been just like them, or so we hoped. But everyone knew that the absolute monarchs, those beyond great deeds and any obligation to honor and serve others, could never be even remotely approximated. The dividing line was clearly not crossable; the worship was of a wholly other and higher being.

In America, democracy has eliminated this category of a wholly other and higher being. Furthermore, the once-accessible heroic ideal originally imprinted upon the nation's character by its founders has degenerated and been forgotten. A nation once blessed with an abundance of heroes to admire now finds itself with so few. The media has in turn rushed in to fill the void with a plethora of celebrity figures. For the most part, they are not of the ilk of accessible, natural heroes but of absolute monarchs, demigods who are surreal both in the sense of being above reality and in the absurd images they present. Madonna and Michael Jackson are demigods. Sylvester Stallone and Arnold Schwarzenegger, cowboys in the guise of gladiator-soldiers, are demigods. Having lost sight of the genuinely and naturally heroic, the culture leaps immediately to the absolute monarch in its type of heroism if not its exact form. This voices the more basic and ancient need for a hero who represents and incarnates godhood. This explains the obsessive public interest in the personal aspects of famous people's lives, and why the cult of celebrity is primarily a cult of personality. When there is little that is genuinely heroic, the personality becomes the main focus and gets raised to the level of godhood. The media are only partly to blame for this; they are merely feeding a widespread, consuming hunger.

With this cultural milieu, the paparazzi phenomenon is inevitable. Celebrity-hounding photographers are only the leading edge of a culture that supports them and is inundated by the cult of celebrity. In this sense, we are all paparazzi. The mass consumption of celebrity rewards the hunt for trivia most generously, as illustrated by the going rates for paparazzi photographs. A photograph of Madonna can easily bring $20,000. The first photo of Brooke Shields with André Agassi brought $100,000; the one of John Kennedy, Jr. arguing in Central Park with his then-fiancée earned its photographer $100,000 by one account and $250,000 by another. The first photo of Michael Jackson with his wife and newborn baby generated $2 million. A good photograph of Princess Diana with Dodi Fayed was reportedly worth $5 million, instigating a chase for money that in turn may have fueled the chase that some believe killed her.

Everything to do with celebrity acquires an aura of being special, often without regard for actual merit. O.J. Simpson's autograph after his civil trial was estimated to be worth $60. His ex-girlfriend Paula Barbieri received $3 million for her memoirs. On the other hand, where merit exists in at least some measure there is a great need to highlight it by making it official. The industries that promote and depend upon celebrity regularly host a variety of self-congratulatory events for this reason. Included are the Academy Awards, the Golden Globe Awards, the New York Film Critics' Circle Awards, the Screen Actors Guild Awards, the Tony Awards, the Emmy Awards, the Grammy Awards, the American Music Awards, and the People's Choice Awards. Americans love awards, for they not only bring status and celebrity but are the apotheosis of celebration itself. The American enthusiasm for lists is similarly motivated. (The words "apotheosis" and "enthusiasm," both derived from the Greek root *theos* or "god," are quite appropriate here: the first of course means to deify or raise to the status of a god, and the second means, in its original use, "to be possessed by a god.") *Fortune Magazine*'s list of the 500 largest U.S. industrial corporations, *Forbes'* list of the 400 richest people in the U.S., *Time*'s list of the 25 most influential people each year, lists of the best-dressed people, and numerous other lists show who's who in America. Celebrated figures are neatly placed in orbit around a shining sun of greatness, or what the public is led to believe is greatness.

If the cult of celebrity is sustained by make-believe, its effects are very real. Advertising thrives on celebrity, juxtaposing celebrity images and products that often have nothing to do with one another. Nothing promotes an automobile, for example, better than the face or voice of a celebrity. This waving of the king's or queen's endorsement wand inspires public confidence in and desire for the product. Celebrity masquerades as authority. And of course, with all the different ways it appeals to us, it also informs aesthetics. Fashion in clothes, cosmetics, and hair styles is defined by celebrities the same way it was once defined by monarchs, except now it is made public by the media and is accessible to a much larger, consumer class. *InStyle Magazine* described how undergarments can go in and out of style depending on their celebrity status: "Clark Gable unbuttoned his shirt to reveal a bare chest in *It*

*Happened One Night* (1934)—and sales of undershirts plummeted. Seventeen years later, in 1951, a mumbling Method actor and brooding bad boy named Marlon Brando brought them back when he appeared onscreen—in nothing more than a scowl, tight jeans and a grimy tee—as the brutish, smoldering, sexy Stanley Kowalski in *A Streetcar Named Desire*."

But celebrity impacts more than just advertising and fashion. In a culture that is becoming increasingly devoid of genuine heroes, celebrities are confused in the public imagination with the heroes they portray onscreen. Can anyone doubt that Charlton Heston's public announcements on behalf of the National Rifle Association radiate a certain romantic intensity and authority derived from his image as Moses and Ben Hur? Celebrities may even be expected to live up to their heroic images offscreen and help people as heroes do. James Doohan, the actor who played Scotty the engineer on the original "Star Trek" series, offers a poignant example. He tells of a despondent fan who wrote him a letter threatening suicide. Doohan called and urged her to come to a Star Trek convention at which he was to appear. She did. Sensing her precarious condition and dependence upon him—or rather, one might conjecture, upon Scotty—he then urged her to come to the next convention, too. She did. After this he did not hear from her for a number of years. Finally, one day, he received a letter from her thanking him: she had gotten her life in order, gone back to school, and become an engineer.

As the line between fantasy and reality dissolves, the world quite literally becomes a stage on which everyone is an actor playing an actor's part. Celebrity determines what is socially relevant and style and image replace substance. The criterion for excellence becomes the ability to excel at celebrity and the charisma that pumps it up. Kennedy understood this well, turning his natural charm into an asset and becoming the first politician-celebrity of the television age. Perhaps only George Washington enjoyed as much celebrity status while in office. But Washington's celebrity came from his reputation as a great general and his legacy as the military leader of the American Revolution. Kennedy's celebrity was largely mystique. He was as handsome as any movie star, he moved in celebrity circles, and he had a stylish wife who became a celebrity in her own right. Together they became a royal couple whose magical reign in the White House became appropriately known as "Camelot"—an analogy Mrs. Kennedy first made herself.

McLuhan explained why those who listened to the Kennedy-Nixon debates on radio thought Nixon won, while those who watched them on TV thought Kennedy won. On television, Kennedy presented an image closer to a TV hero, something akin to the shy young sheriff, whereas Nixon, with his dark, staring eyes and clever circumlocution, resembled the railway lawyer who brokers a deal that is not in the interests of small town folks. On radio, however, Nixon sounded sharper and intellectually superior. Radio can be a powerful medium for charisma as well, as Hitler demonstrated. Franklin Roosevelt with his fireside chats used radio very effectively. But as TV became the medium of choice for political events such as debates and campaigns, he who won on TV, won.

Nixon learned this lesson well from his 1960 experience. He softened his image and played the celebrity card in 1963 with a piano performance on "The Tonight Show." Then again in 1968, while campaigning for the presidency, he appeared on Rowan and Martin's "Laugh-In" for a quick spoof. Nixon saying "Sock it to me!" was undoubtedly aimed at broadcasting a Nixon into the living room who had a sense of humor and to whom it would be easier to relate. It would not be long before a B-grade movie actor would become a highly popular, two-term president known for his smooth delivery as "the Great Communicator" and for a "teflon-coating" that could repel scandals that would debilitate most other presidents. To some extent Reagan squeaked through the Iran-contra affair untarnished because of his popularity with the public and the press, evidence that in the politics of celebrity, image can shape reality.

Other presidents knew how to use their public image to their advantage and contributed in their own ways to the convergence of politics and celebrity. Not only did Franklin Roosevelt masterfully use the media, but Theodore Roosevelt, too. The latter's exploits, varying from being the first sitting president to venture abroad (to Panama) to the creation of the "Teddy Bear" when he refused while hunting to kill an adolescent cub, helped establish the presidency as a pulpit not only for policy but pageantry. But Reagan marked a solidifying point in the merging of politics and celebrity. Politics took on a role heretofore reserved for performance artists, namely, to make people feel good. It is true that Kennedy also had this effect, but Reagan, it seems, deliberately cultivated it. He knew how to apply his craft to one of the salient problems of his day, the nation's low morale. Making people feel optimistic in such situations can prove to be a real asset, but if too predominant a leadership tool or style, it makes politics conform to theater and entertainment more than it already does. Neal Gabler explains:

> Reagan's revelation was that politics didn't have to be about governance. It could be about raising spirits. . . . Indeed, this might

even be called the other Reagan Revolution: He turned politics into a placebo by regarding Americans not as a constituency to be served but as an audience to be uplifted. . . . Less obviously, the Reagan Revolution, in the process of making performance skills a prerequisite for office, also managed to displace the tedious details of policy with grand masterplots that resembled the plots of old movies and were intended to provide the same catharsis. For Reagan himself, the big plots were the citizen politician taking an ax to big government and the United States facing down the Evil Empire of the Soviet Union. But it wasn't so much the specifics of these plots that mattered as it was their message, which was that in politics, as in the movies, heroes are leaders who make things happen.

The cult of celebrity is another that poses a danger to democracy. It creates an environment in which politicians have to become celebrities, and celebrities are confused with heroes. Heroic idealism is concretized in and as the personality, and the charisma of the celluloid hero becomes a substitute for genuine authority. Social issues become important only when they attain celebrity status, often not even registering on the social barometer until they are endorsed by celebrities. One sees more and more celebrities testifying before Congressional committees that the problem in vogue today is "real," as if political leaders need the supposed expertise of celebrities to enlighten them. Serious public discourse is thwarted when celebrities become more popular and significant in influencing society's direction than those who hold public office. That our political leaders fail to recognize this and succumb themselves to the celebrity craze is remarkable and troubling. Few celebrities have the wit or wisdom to restrain this use of their influence (as when Brad Pitt, responding to a question about the political implications of one of his films, said "What do I know? I'm an actor.").

As the events of celebrity—the movies and TV programs with their make-believe content, the talk shows and gossipy news items, the awards and lists—increasingly become the source of the nation's mythology, history and its very real imperatives are obscured in a haze. From this too the nation falls into the collective amnesia discussed earlier. And it falls into spiritual impoverishment. Though only one contributing factor in this, celebrity breeds narcissistic values and not spiritual and moral ones. Or it mixes them up, as observable in New Age cults that center around celebrity-style gurus and healers or in Christian "televangelism" of the kind filled with self-loathing—self-loathing that is really a mask for self-preoccupation. But this brings us to an altogether different problem of height.

# Chapter 8

## Heroic Tunnel Vision

*Religious slavery, slavery to God and slavery to the church,
that is to a servile idea of God and a servile idea of the
church, has been a most burdensome form of slavery for
man and one of the sources of human slavery. It has been
slavery to the object, to the common, to externality and to
alienation. It is for this reason that the mystics have taught
that man should cut himself off even from God. This is the
path man has to tread.*

—Nikolai Berdyaev

### The Cults of Fundamentalism

Spirituality and religion remain the superlative expressions of the aspiration toward height because they not only represent but channel the effort of the human spirit to connect to that which is above and beyond itself. The American variation of this effort is a textured phenomenon, including in its historical and social fabric the Puritans, the Quakers, the Virginia Deists or Jeffersonians, the Transcendentalists, a variety of fire-and-brimstone types that checkered the frontier, the Mormons and other such sects, the mainstream denominations of Protestantism, and the diverse groupings of people whose beliefs fall under the rubric of modern secular humanism. Humanism is a loose creed whose lineage can be traced to the Renaissance and Enlightenment and whose language is clearly non-Christian and non-theistic. American art, literature, philosophy, psychology, and education all profess humanism's rational faith that man is capable of self-fulfillment and ethical conduct without recourse to supernatural forces. The human potential movement of the 1970s was a natural spinoff of this. From that movement it was not a far reach to the New Age movement: the latter infuses human potential with a new set of spiritual beliefs and practices. Instead of Christianity it offers a syncretism of ideas from so many sources that it is difficult to identify a distinct thread that unites them. As one can see, the pluralism of American spirituality and religion goes hand-in-hand with the pluralism of democracy and the society at large.

As with any aspiration toward height, the religious aspiration can become unbalanced and extreme. It can become ungrounded in the everyday world, or, in striving to integrate its values into the everyday world, do so in an unbalanced and extreme way. The forms this most commonly takes are fundamentalism and fanaticism. Tocqueville surmised that the American has a predisposition towards these as a compensatory reaction to his largely one-sided pursuit of materialism. These forms of spirituality are of interest not only for their own sake, but because they reveal, in boldface, certain features that are shared in common with American spirituality on the whole. As is often the case, the exception or the extreme proves the rule. If we conceive of American spirituality as a single continuum, its extremes accentuate characteristics that are present in milder form throughout the continuum, that is, in mainstream religion as well. After all, the extremes of a continuum are not something other than the continuum, but merely its ends.

Fundamentalism is basically the distillation of the broad range of considerations that constitute a religious or spiritual tradition down to a select, crucial few. This favoring or exaltation of select views occurs at the expense of all the others, so that what is sacrificed is an overall, balanced understanding of what that tradition has to say. Whereas most traditions have had to at least intermittently embrace an inclusiveness of views in order to survive, fundamentalist thinking is exclusionary and often intolerant of views that are different from its own. Too often, the thing that makes religious or spiritual matters a volatile topic at a dinner party is that fundamental truths are discussed in a fundamentalist way, and people cannot tell the difference. This is not limited, incidentally, to particular belief systems. Atheists can be just as fundamentalist as devout believers.

Among devout believers in America today, Christian evangelicals and followers of the New Age movement are two fundamentalist strains that stand out. Their numbers are in the millions, especially when one considers that the basic beliefs of evangelicals are the same that undergird what has come to be known as the New Christian Right. The temperament and beliefs of each strain are of course different from the other, as evangelism is a fundamentalism of Christianity and the New Age movement is, paradoxical as this may sound, a fundamentalism of freethinking. It is a spinoff of humanism. Christian fundamentalism is a fundamentalism of the spirit of authority while the New Age movement is a fundamentalism of the spirit of youth. And naturally, Christian fundamentalism has been around longer than the New Age movement. But this is where the differences end. In their underlying nature, beneath the appearance of things, they are more the same than different. This is because they are two ends or extremes of a single continuum, the continuum of American spirituality. It is not the shared continuum that makes them the same, for there are religious groups situated more toward the center of the continuum—that is, more in the mainstream of American spirituality—that are very different from each other, for example, Jews and Catholics. It is in their extremes that they are the same, for again, as Heraclitus observed, any extreme sooner or later flips into its opposite. It is as if the continuum were a piece of rope laid out in a circle with the opposite ends touching each other: they meet at a common point.

The common point at which the Christian evangelical and New Age movements meet is their distorted aspiration toward height. All religious belief systems express the aspiration toward height in some form or another. The human spirit naturally strives upward to connect with its kindred spirit, the divine, regardless of how the latter may be conceived. But the history of religion shows that religious experience as it has occurred through the ages is always grounded in and speaks to the hard truths and hardships of everyday life. The writings of saints, sages, mystics, and theologians in every tradition tell us that genuine religious experience does not seek to escape the world but to grasp it in its fullness. It does not diminish common sense and critical, inner reflection but deepens them. It does not displace or avoid the moral problems of human existence but embraces them. Christian evangelism and the New Age movement, on the other hand, are closed systems. They are closed in by virtue of their own fundamentalist beliefs and they are closed off from the kind of religious experience that has flourished throughout history. This, however, is of no consequence to evangelicals and New Age followers. They think only in a forward-looking way, evangelicals in terms of the Second Coming of Christ and New Age followers simply in terms of the dawn of a new age. Neither look back. Religious understanding is derived from what is believed to be coming or what is believed to be new. This is bound to be superficial. As

Jung said, "Any renewal not deeply rooted in the best spiritual tradition is ephemeral." It does not occur to either group that history might have something valuable to say about their orientation.

Fundamentalist Christians seem to be unaware that Christians in the first century A.D. had to redefine the purpose of the Christian religion in terms other than the Second Coming of Christ. Jesus himself in the Gospels gave the impression that his return was historically imminent, that it would take place within the lifetime of his immediate followers. When this did not happen, early Christians began the long process of reframing the meaning of the Second Coming in more cosmic terms, a process that is still going on today in various theological circles. Contrary to dealing a deathblow to Christianity, the need to reinterpret Scripture in a less literal and more open way deepened it and insured its survival. Fundamentalists in all periods of history, however, have fallen prey to the notion that it is only by holding on to the strictest possible interpretation of Scripture that they could endure the turbulent times in which they were living. The first century of Christianity was extremely turbulent, but it was the flexibility of the early Christians that enabled them to adapt and survive.

Similarly, followers of the New Age seem to be unaware that their movement has historical precedents that may prove valuable to know about. In fact, their movement offers little that is new. There have been other "new age" movements—in some instances with teachings and practices that very much resemble theirs—occurring often at the turn of a century or whenever the world has seemed threatened with annihilation, for example, during the Black Plague. Today's New Age movement seems to be a repetition of history. This is not to say that there *isn't* a new age or eon of consciousness dawning. Thinkers ranging from Marx and Nietzsche to Spengler and Jung have expressed the view that Western civilization is in decline and in transition toward a new civilization, and certainly, the current new age movement advocates itself as a harbinger of this change. But as Toynbee illustrated, it is upon the most creative achievements of the old civilization that the emerging new civilization builds its foundation. The teachings and practices of the New Age movement are so doctrinaire and facile that they can hardly claim to represent the highest achievements of Western civilization. It does not take a great historian like Toynbee to surmise that this movement would be washed away with the rest of the flotsam and jetsam of Western civilization should this epochal change in fact occur.

Christian evangelism and the New Age movement distort the aspiration toward height in identical ways. To begin with, both are encumbered by a rigid, dogmatic way of thinking. In the case of the former, this is rooted in a basic fear of life, of the fact that life is much harder when it is acknowledged to be a mysterious force that cannot be boxed into simple categories of right and wrong, good and bad, black and white. (The mutual tendency of both evangelism and television to approach life in these terms is what makes them such good bedfellows.) Acknowledging this mystery—itself a requirement of faith, it would seem—places an unwelcome burden upon man: *he too,* along with God, must be active in deciding what is right and wrong and good and bad. This burden is too much for fundamentalists, and they wish to put it exclusively upon God's shoulders. It was early in the Hebrew Bible that the patriarch Abraham demonstrated that man has the freedom and even the responsibility to participate with God in determining moral correctness. Bent on destroying Sodom and Gomorrah without regard for the righteous who lived there, God was convinced by Abraham to spare the cities if even ten righteous people could be found in them. "Shall not the Judge of all the earth do right?," Abraham pleaded. In confronting and influencing God in this way, Abraham established that man is in partnership with him. What Gandhi said is true even for God: "The insistence on truth teaches one to appreciate the beauty of compromise."

The shunning of this freedom and responsibility gives God all power and makes man powerless. It casts Christian fundamentalism into a rigid mold and pushes it into a preoccupation with sin. The psychologist Erich Fromm explains:

> When man has thus projected his own most valuable powers onto God, what of his relationship to his own powers? They have become separated from him and in this process he has become *alienated* from himself. Everything he has is now God's and nothing is left in him. *His only access to himself is through God.* In worshipping God he tries to get in touch with that part of himself which he has lost through projection. After having given God all he has, he begs God to return to him some of what originally was his own. But having lost his own he is completely at God's mercy. He necessarily feels like a "sinner" since he has deprived himself of everything that is good, and it is only through God's mercy or grace that he can regain that which alone can make him human. And in order to persuade God to give him some of his love, he must prove to him how utterly deprived he is of love; in order to persuade God to guide him by his superior wisdom he must prove to him how deprived he is of wisdom when he is left to himself. . . .
>
> Thus the attempt to obtain forgiveness results in the activation of the very attitude from which his sin stems. He is caught in a

painful dilemma. The more he praises God, the emptier he becomes. The emptier he becomes, the more sinful he feels. The more sinful he feels the more he praises his God—and the less able is he to regain himself.

In other words, the doctrine of original sin, developed to explain the element of evil in human nature, here becomes a self-fulfilling prophecy in the fate of man not because it is a universal principle but because it is the primary principle. Instead of being one element in human nature, sin becomes more or less the sole element. It is no wonder that Jim Bakker and Jimmy Swaggart, after having built their careers on denouncing sin—mostly in others—fell victim to it in the most flagrant and yet banal ways. Theirs was more than simply a case of "pride goeth before a fall." To constantly harp on evil in a manner that avoids the real reason for one's fascination with it—namely, one's personal identification with it, as Fromm indicates—is like going into a lion's cage pretending to be invisible. It is as if this evokes the "evil eye" even more. People like this are bound to end up playing poker with the devil, and of course, they are bound to lose. Or worse, they end up becoming instruments of the devil, as in the case of fanatics who believe they are doing God's work when they bomb abortion clinics and murder innocent people. The combination of self-righteousness and a displaced obsession with evil or sin can be deadly. But such violence can be justified in the closed system of beliefs to which extremists adhere. The violence implied in the Day of Judgment is transformed into a militant attitude about all moral issues. The salvation of the world hinges upon the moral superiority of God's followers—or as it were, soldiers—and upon their ability to spread his word in the world, tolerantly or not, peacefully or not. Not surprisingly, this mindset gave rise to the Crusades, the Inquisition, and the multitude of other holy wars and witch hunts that have pockmarked history.

Christian fundamentalists are not wrong in their appraisal of the darkness and severity of the problem of evil. However, where they themselves depart from the fundaments of the Judeo-Christian traditions is in their personal identification with evil, as if it were some kind of ungodly intrusion into the human condition that they must take upon themselves to personally exorcise. Fundamentalists tend to treat evil like a fire that can and must be stamped out. But if the Bible is to be believed, even God has a cruel, capricious side and an ambiguous relationship with evil. In the Book of Job, for example, we see a God who is susceptible to the persuasive influences of the "Adversary"—the devil—in ways not unlike man. This suggests that the problem of evil is even greater and more complex and mysterious than fundamentalists imagine. It seems as if the challenge is to learn, as did Job, to stand the fire and, indeed, stand against it, but not get consumed in a personal identification with it. After all, if God has a dark side, why should we be without one?

If Christian fundamentalism is preoccupied with sin in a slavish way, the New Age movement gives it absolutely no attention at all. The result for both is ultimately the same: a gross misunderstanding of the problem of evil. While Christian fundamentalism is high and mighty in its condemnation of evil, the New Age movement is so above this problem that the movement becomes ungrounded in the real world. This is what gives it its light and flaky quality. Human beings cast no shadow, and life has no darkness. Or rather, suffering and darkness are seen not as being inherent to life—for example, as Judaism, Christianity, and Buddhism teach—but as an acquired problem that the individual could and should, again, eliminate. The New Age movement professes that if you're suffering or you're ill, it's probably because you've done something wrong or are not doing something right in some formula of right living. That is also why you're not rich or successful, and if you just do things a certain, mechanical way, everything will turn out alright. (As the philosopher Stephan Hoeller points out, the New Age movement in this regard shares the Calvinist ethic that by doing good works one will be blessed by God and become prosperous.) Popular teachings such as Deepak Chopra's "Seven Spiritual Laws of Success" and James Redfield's "Ten Insights"—most of which are refashioned truths from the world's great religious traditions or just good old-fashioned common sense—are neatly packaged to guarantee quick gratification. And they are marketed to compete in a spiritual supermarket that services the cults of prosperity and motion and speed: self-improvement is a $2.5 billion-per-year industry. The large number of self-help books with a psychological bent line the shelves of bookstores and employ the same method of teaching an inner road map to solve all problems. One self-help book editor at a publishing house admits that "all of our books follow a formula, a basic dogma of 'Change the way you think and you will change the way you feel.' " The New Age and self-help movements recruit psychology and then transform it into "how-to" techniques or a simplified, pulp psychology for mass consumption.

In the real world of course everything does not always turn out alright and not all problems can be solved. Changing the way you think does not in most cases make your illness go away and never makes your loved ones who have died come back. In an authentic inner life where contemplation has to embrace the real details of existence, there is little if any quick gratification. Mystics through the ages have always been people who have struggled and suffered *more*, not less. They experienced the problems of suffering, evil, and death intensely and didn't pretend that there were simple solutions to them. Rather, they aimed to help us live with these problems in a more fully conscious and responsible way, so that we could discover our divine nature not *in spite of* these problems, but *in full view* of them. Theirs were not easy teachings, and that is why there have been so few genuine mystics in history. The New Age movement by contrast preaches that life should be ideal. This is a euphoric, airy notion that comes not only from an inflation in the heavenly heights where it is imagined there is no conflict, but from what shall be discussed in Part III as the addiction to innocence and the cult of happiness.

## The Trappings of Fundamentalism

It was stated above that Christian evangelism is a fundamentalism of the spirit of authority and the New Age movement a fundamentalism of the spirit of youth. It should now be more evident why this is so. Not only do the historical traditions they are derived from correspond, respectively, to these spirits, but so do their styles. Their extremism makes these styles particularly distinct. Evangelicals are not only authoritarian but speak as if they have been vested with the authority of God the Father. The New Christian Right also feels it has this special authority to influence decisions and policies that affect the nation. The New Age movement has a different style, but not entirely. Though it is not authoritarian, its ideas and practices have a certain rigidity that is probably there to compensate for their fragility, much the way young children buttress their fragility with rigid proclamations and behaviors. As colorful and creative as these ideas and practices are, they are fixed in magical thinking and an unabashed belief in all possibilities. The New Age movement has the exuberance of a divine child at play in the fields of the Lord. The developmental psychologist Jean Piaget would see New Age thinking as typical of adolescent psychology: "Adolescent egocentricity is manifested by belief in the omnipotence of reflection, as though the world should submit itself to idealistic schemes rather than to systems of reality. It is the metaphysical age *par excellence*."

The New Christian Right has greater social significance. With its authoritarian tendencies it runs against the spirit of democracy, while the

Chapter 8 Heroic Tunnel Vision ★ 115

New Age movement simply remains disconnected and irrelevant in matters of social concern. The political agenda of the Christian Right is to infuse American government, policymaking, and public life with Christian values. As Jefferson and Adams pointed out, a nation whose life is informed by Christianity might not be a bad thing if the emphasis were on the moral principles of Christianity and the core teachings of Jesus. George Bernard Shaw expressed the same sympathies when asked what he thought of Christianity. "[It] might be a good thing if anyone ever tried it," he said. Truly, after two thousand years, Christianity has yet to be authentically practiced on a wide social scale.

And yet, in its aim to see Christianity practiced on a wide social scale, the agenda of the Christian Right is calibrated by an orientation that is much like that of Christianity, indeed, two thousand years ago: the Christian Right seems preoccupied with establishing or asserting its authority in the world. Its expression of its authority, which it sees as rooted in divine authority, has the same messianic and missionary character that Christianity displayed in its early days and throughout much of its history. Although the the followers of the Christian Right claim to draw their moral authority from a personal relationship with God, their desire to act as an external authority for others suggests that their own sense of authority is not as grounded in an inner, spiritual experience as they would like to think. A genuine religious experience, one would imagine, promotes tolerance rather than the lack of it. But the Christian Right often expresses itself in a tone that leaves one with the impression that it is less interested in a Christian democracy than a Christian theocracy. It demonstrates little or no recognition of the fact that the United States was explicitly established without a state religion in order to assure religious freedom for all its citizens, Christian and non-Christian alike. It behaves as if one of the basic tenets of the American creed, namely, the separation of church and state, was a matter of choice and merely a formality. In its approach to the issues of school prayer, school subsidies, the official display of religious symbols, and abortion, it rides roughshod over this tenet and is not democratic but autocratic. In the words of the former Republican Senator Alphonse D'Amato, the problem with ultraconservatives like Pat Buchanan and Pat Robertson is that "they believe that their values are the *only* acceptable set of values [and] should be imposed by the government." John Adams, too, was very wary of evangelical Christianity for this reason.

Of course, one could argue that fundamental Christian values were always part of the historical situation in America—that in the past abortion was illegal, prayers were routinely said in school, Christmas was celebrated distinctly as Christ's birth and not merely festively as part of "the holidays," and that all this went on without the nation falling under authoritative control by churches. In fact, as shall be discussed shortly, the emergence of a strong Christian Right occurred to a large extent as a reaction to secularism. In particular, it rose in defense of an attack by the secular left on traditional Christian beliefs and practices such as those just described. This attack used the courts rather than the legislature—a more democratic means—to attain its goal of removing religion from public life. And, as the chess player knows, the best defense is a good offense or an even more vociferous attack, which explains the aggressiveness of people like Pat Buchanan. Regardless of whether or not they actually believe they can succeed, they wish to return the nation to its earlier historical situation.

The struggle to infuse religion into state affairs has been an ongoing theme in American history. Even the Masons, a quasi-religious, secret society, have tried their hand at politics, giving rise in the first half of the nineteenth century to an anti-Mason movement that was as paranoid as the Masons were aggressive. The impulse to insert or reinsert religion into state affairs over the centuries is not easy to shake. As history's first attempt at democracy in the modern era, America was the first to make the separation of church and state one of its cornerstones. Continuing the old order that united church and state might have been easier than what the Founding Fathers envisioned. History's difficulty in taking its next step toward their ideal of an individually based moral order manifests as a tendency toward historical regression or fixation: namely, the desire among many for a collective state religion or political order that is a mouthpiece for their religion.

This desire is not the only way that Christian fundamentalism is contrary to the spirit with which the American enterprise was founded. Fundamentalism typically wishes to take a shortcut to arrive at truth. It demands truth in simple, concise, and incontrovertible terms. The one thing fundamentalism cannot tolerate is doubt. It resists an intellectual approach to truth-seeking that entertains doubt and that insists on exploring the full range of possibilities. It fails to recognize, however, that faith—the intuitive leap toward Something mysterious and beyond rational proof—implies doubt. Without doubt, faith loses its character and becomes a mere profession of dogmatic beliefs. The theologian Paul Tillich understood faith and existential doubt as two poles of the same reality, the state of "ultimate concern." St. Paul's definition of faith as "the substance of things hoped for, the evidence of things not seen," renders the bond between man and God very tenuous indeed. And Eric Voegelin minced no words when he said "Uncertainty is the very essence of Christianity."

True faith is not only intimately related to doubt but is deepened by intimately relating *to it*. Thus did the great intellectual traditions within Judaism and Christianity, such as rabbinism and the scholasticism of St. Augustine and the Jesuits, seek to reconcile the faith of the heart with a questioning mind. Again, one is reminded of St. Anselm's golden rule, *fides quaerens intellectum,* or faith seeking understanding. St. Thomas Aquinas even thought that an inquiring mind was the only safe guarantee of love and union with the divine; only it could guard against an unbalanced emphasis on love and an unwise faith. To him, there was no such thing as a sanctity that was not intelligent.

Americans who think that the only place such intellectual traditions existed was Europe need to look more closely into their own history. As Jacob Heilbrunn writes, "The reason Puritans occupy such a forbidding image in American memory is precisely because they constituted a religious class of intellectuals who emphasized learning. The Puritans established Harvard University, where young Americans could read Aristotle and Homer in the original Greek. The Puritans frowned on the ecstatic forms of religion, and emphasized sobriety and scholarship." While it is true that the Puritans were a fundamentalist sect in their own right and were to a large extent the forebears of fundamentalism in modern America, their Calvinist piety—deeply religious, morbidly self-examining, and substantiated by personal effort—gave them a dimensional complexity that one is hard-pressed to find in modern American fundamentalism.

The fundamentalism of the New Age movement is pseudointellectual, or at best, simply nonintellectual. But Christian fundamentalism is overtly anti-intellectual. In campaigning against the spirit of scholastic understanding, it opposes the kind of intellectually sound and free society that the founders—both the Puritans and the Founding Fathers—wished America to be. The Scopes "monkey" trial in 1925 epitomized the Christian fundamentalist stand. Brought to trial on charges of teaching the theory of evolution in Tennessee, John Thomas Scopes stood against the biblical literalism that pervaded the South. The popular politician William Jennings Bryan, famous for his fundamentalist views, denounced the theory of evolution and attacked Scopes' defenders as a "little irresponsible oligarchy of self-styled 'intellectuals.' " Earlier he traveled around the nation giving lectures at colleges with the message, "No teacher should be allowed on the faculty of any American university unless he is a Christian."

The particular issue behind this trial by no means belongs to another era. Not until 2001 did the Kansas State Board of Education finally approve the teaching of evolution, and other school boards in the South have been resistant as well. The larger issue is also extant: a significant minority of Americans feel that a literal interpretation of the Bible should provide the basis for determining school curricula as well as the agenda of the nation. And their numbers are growing. In 1962, 45 percent of Americans were mainstream Protestants and 29 percent were evangelical Protestants. By 1992, the number of mainstream Protestants had declined to 24 percent, while evangelicals had risen to 33 percent. The trend in government is similar. A survey of Republican congressmen revealed that in the early 1960s, 72 percent were mainstream Protestants and 13 percent were evangelicals. By 1992 the mainstream Protestants had declined to 39 percent while the evangelicals comprised 27 percent. Although the actual beliefs of members of the Christian Right vary with regard to public policy, one can assume that these beliefs tend to conform to fundamentalist guidelines. Evangelical congressmen do not necessarily reject evolution, but their views on most other issues involving religion and public policy—abortion, school prayer, etc.—seem inclined toward merging the two.

In his speech at the 1992 Republican Convention, Pat Buchanan boldly asserted that "There is a religious war going on in this country. It is a cultural war." He of course failed to acknowledge his role in helping to inflame that war, but his observation was accurate. At first glance, this war appears to be between the values of fundamentalism and those of mainstream thinking. It is easy to see mainstream America's resistance to fundamentalists as an aversion to returning to the Dark Ages and to predemocratic times. This conflict further illustrates the phenomenon of the divided hero and society. It is a conflict of Americans against Americans, of different visions of what America should be. A closer look, however, reveals that the clash of values between the two groups is really a wider conflict, and only by appreciating this can we understand the significance of fundamentalism and why it is on the rise.

In addition to the psychological mechanisms that create a fundamentalist outlook and that were described above, one must consider the social factors contibuting to fundamentalism's appeal. There is an objective reason why people want to adopt a religious style that organizes life in simple, concise, and incontrovertible terms. Life today has become so complex and unstable that people are grabbing onto anything that promises meaning and order. In fact, the trend towards fundamentalism is very much a reaction to the breakdown of authority in the culture, that is, of genuine authority or wisdom that defines what a principled life and society are. Fundamentalism is a compensation for the failure of mainstream society to connect to fundamental truths. It offers an alternative to the lifestyle now prevailing in America. Fundamentalist cults are a revolt against the effects of the other cults that shape American culture; they are attempts to respond to the moral decline and Godlessness that have resulted from the cults of materialism and prosperity, technology and progress, motion and speed, and celebrity. Comprising the cults of modernity, the latter have subtly taken on a religious character of their own, as all cults do. In listening to the grievances of fundamentalists, what one basically hears is outrage against the pseudoreligions of modernity and secularism.

And indeed, these grievances are legitimate. The need for a response is authentic, but, as noted earlier in regard to fascist movements and fanatical elements such as militia groups, the form of this response is not. It simply will not work. While the cults of modernity drive civilization forward in a frenzied, out-of-control manner, fundamentalism is a flight into the past and into archaic, simplistic modes of understanding. Fundamentalism is not only a reaction, but reactionary. It reacts to the current challenge of history with the fixed response of another era instead of seeking a fresh response that might once again, like Christianity in the first century and later on as well, adapt faith to changing times. Its lack of real authority has pushed it into an authoritarian stance. Needless to say, its efforts to impose its will on the majority culture in an almost papal fashion have no impact upon the effects of modernity. Fundamentalists are as much under their sway as the majority culture they so self-righteously want to rehabilitate. In the final analysis, beneath the trappings of fundamentalism lie the more pernicious trappings to which fundamentalism is a reaction.

## Religious Mediocrity

As mentioned, the cults of fundamentalism are of interest not only for their own sake, but because they share common features with American spirituality as a whole. Again, the ends of the spiritual continuum are not something other than the continuum; they are merely its extremes. In a milder, less sharply defined form, mainstream American spirituality has the same tendency toward formulaic thinking as the cults of fundamentalism. There may be less rigidity and evangelical zeal, but the desire to neatly explain the mystery of the divine still prevails. Americans are not comfortable with doubt, and the ontological insecurity of the human condition is quickly covered over not only by the cults of modernity and fundamentalism, but by mainstream Judaism and Christianity as well. American Judaism—particularly Reform and Reconstructive Judaism—is so couched in a historical explanation of religious experience that it often appears that history altogether replaces God as the focus of the religious imagination. It is curious that many of the teachers and practitioners of Eastern religions in the United States are Jews; the sense of the transcendent that they are not able to find in their own tradition they seek elsewhere. Such disillusionment was certainly less pronounced in European Judaism, whose spiritual flowers included Hasidism, the Kabbalah, and the more religious components of the *Haskalah* or Jewish Enlightenment.

Mainstream Protestantism, the religion of the majority of Americans, has also been relegated to a comfort zone of predictability and formality. As Tocqueville observed, it is confined to being a Sunday affair during which the American "meets with sublime and affecting descriptions of the greatness and goodness of the Creator, of the infinite magnificence of the handiwork of God, and of the lofty destinies of man, his duties, and his immortal privileges. Thus it is that the American at times steals an hour from himself, and, laying aside for a while the petty passions which agitate his life, and the ephemeral interests which engross it, he strays at once into an ideal world, where all is great, eternal, and pure." Spirituality and religion remain idealized, and the great, eternal, and pure are rarely integrated into everyday life.

The notion of evil that is so distorted by the fundamentalists has in mainstream Protestantism become parochial, a shell of an idea that no longer resonates with what goes on in the real world. (Indeed, fundamentalism's preoccupation with evil seems to compensate for this.) There is a casual, haphazard approach to evil, so that the fact of its existence can easily be called upon when suitable and disregarded when not. America quickly condemned the force of evil at work in the Cold War because its self-interest was directly threatened, but barely fifty years after the Holocaust, it demonstrated unduly prolonged hesitation before committing its troops to Bosnia-Herzogovina. This hedging in the face of the magnitude of evil there added tens of thousands to the death toll. And on the streets of America's inner cities, the existence of evil is treated as if it were equally negligible, as is the fact that the entire nation is responsible for this situation, not just a single racial group. As long as religious idealism and the problem of evil remain purely a matter for the pulpit, religion in America will continue to be insulated. It is the hero's calling to do battle with evil, and it is a religious attitude that helps the hero rise to this calling. The generally disengaged state of religion in America goes hand-in-hand with the decline of the heroic ideal. It is a condition of religious mediocrity. If religious fanaticism is a sort of soul-on-fire phenomenon, then religious medi-ocrity, its opposite, bespeaks a soul whose spiritual spark has burned out. It has lost both its spiritual passion and moral authority.

It may be argued that these are not singularly American problems, that the deteriorated condition of religion in America reflects the trends of de-mythologization and secularization occurring worldwide. Certainly, there is truth to this. Is the state of Christianity really any different in America than in Europe, for example? It is our entire civilization that is going through an upheaval and not just a single nation. But it is also true that America, in its unrootedness and addiction to height, seizes upon the worst elements in Christianity and freethinking. It is a lamentable fact that in what is supposedly the freest nation in the history of the world, a religious or spiritual understanding of life and the freedoms this can bring have not been genuinely advanced in any real sense. On the contrary, thus far, free-dom has seemed to work in the opposite direction.

# Chapter 9

## The Escape from Heroism

*It is well to repeat constantly that man is a being who is full of contradictions and that he is in a state of conflict with himself. Man seeks freedom. There is within him an immense drive towards freedom, and yet not only does he easily fall into slavery, but he loves slavery. Man is a king and a slave.*

—Nikolai Berdyaev

### Getting High: The Cult of Passion

It is no accident that one of psychology's great innovators, Abraham Maslow, was an American. His contribution, though drawing much on European psychology and even Eastern civilization, is distinctly American in character, or let us say, what he discovered would have been more apparent to an American eye than to that of any other nationality. His central concept, the "peak experience," denotes the quintessential experience of height. That he developed it in the 1960s is also no accident. America was then undergoing an explosion in height: the space program, the reach for power in Vietnam and elsewhere, and a counterculture that so emphasized the experience of getting high on drugs. The peak experience represents the summit of human perception, rising above the ordinary to a state of mind that is rich, intense, seemingly full in its scope of awareness, exhilarating, and even ecstatic. In more traditional language, one might have described the peak experience as a state of grace. It is usually brief, a passing glimpse of the hidden wonders of the world or of Being, as the existentialist Maslow would say. Nevertheless, if one has had a peak experience—and many people have in some form or another—it is unforgettable.

What makes a peak experience so exhilarating and high is the fact that it releases or liberates one from the usual shackles of perception. It allows one to forget oneself and experience unification—momentary as this may be—with some object beyond the ego or known self. This "object" may be a loved one, or some activity, or an ideal that may be found within oneself but is still beyond the ordinary range of the ego's perception, such as God. "Man's basic drive," the psychologist David Cole Gordon writes, "is for unification, to be one in mind and body, to be one with the world, to be one with others and to resolve the subject-object bifurcation that divides him from others since his birth. This drive for unification is also the mainspring of man's behavior, which is characterized by his search for happiness and ultimate reality. Much of his activity is unconscious in that man is not aware of the real object of his quest, except insofar as he feels incomplete, alienated, restless and unhappy." Many things we desire, we desire because they give us this sense of release and unification. This is what makes them fulfilling. Eating a good meal, playing tennis or golf or poker or chess, watching a basketball game, consummating a business deal, listening to a Beethoven sonata or going to a rock concert, painting a picture or going to the museum, and, as one might expect, having sex, are all experiences that to varying degrees provide release and unification. They are all things that connect us to the world, to life, and to ourselves.

It is, however, the rarer experiences of total or near-total release and unification that tend to be peak experiences. They not only connect us to the world or life or ourselves, but to something beyond, often a sense of immortality or superhuman ability, if not God himself. Such experiences have a distinctly religious or spiritual character even though they may not occur in a religious setting or have any overt connection to religion as commonly conceived. Mountain climbing and sky diving, for example, are often spoken of by their practitioners in glowing, numinous terms because they provide this kind of peak experience. The rarer or higher the experience, the more it is valued, and as is often the case with human nature, the higher one goes, the higher one wants to go. The aspiration toward height, when unlimited, is the aspiration toward ever rarer or higher peak experiences. Thus must mountain climbers always conquer higher, more dangerous peaks in order to get a charge, as flyboys must always go higher and faster in their planes. One regularly reads of these types in the newspapers when they have surpassed their limits and fallen or crashed. Nation-states are the same, as discussed earlier with regard to Rome, the Napoleonic Empire, and Nazi Germany.

Involvement in religion, speaking here in the more formal sense, is also definitely a pursuit of peak experience, as are the cults of modernity. They uplift us, make us feel heroic, and, supposedly, provide a sense of release from the ordinary through a unification with immortality. But the cults of modernity exemplify what Gordon called an unconscious pursuit of peak experience: people do not know that this is what they are actually seeking. To know this might alter the pursuit. People might ask, does this pursuit really provide a peak experience or the kind of peak experience they were really hoping for? In other words, because their desire would no longer be blind, they might exercise greater discretion in their choices. When one understands the motivating factor *behind* one's desires and behaviors, a different light is cast upon the objects of desire *in front of* oneself. Consciousness or awareness, the goal of all psychological introspection, changes the picture dramatically. One can more clearly see where one is coming from and where one is going.

Unfortunately, modern American society is in blind pursuit of peak experiences without even knowing it. It does not realize that its cults of height are, firstly, cults, and secondly, cults of *height*. It knows neither what motivates it nor what it is really after. The ability of a society to distinguish such things about itself marks the difference between an enlightened society and one that lives in the darkness or primitivity of its own impulses. Greece and Rome at their height (no pun intended) were enlightened societies. They had a clear sense of their purpose or direction. As Toynbee observed, without this, societies disintegrate or merge into the sea of history sooner rather than later. A strong, conscious grasp of why a people are here and where they are going and can enable them to adapt to history's challenges indefinitely. The Chinese and the Jews, both ancient peoples, are living examples of this.

Probably the most glaring demonstration of the blind pursuit of peak experiences is the cult of passion. Our passions, as Shakespeare and others have shown, can be our greatest and most humanizing assets, or they can be our greatest sources of distraction and downfall. Because of the former quality, the Romantics glorified passion, and because of the latter, the Buddhists teach detachment from passion. But whether seen as a source of strength or weakness, our passions let us know that we are alive. The symptom people who are clinically depressed most complain of is their loss of passion. However, depression is itself a kind of passion, a dark passion. Because it is dark does not mean it is not a passion. As Aristotle said, pain is a passion of the soul. Indeed, the Greek root of the word "passion" is *pathos,* or suffering. Christ's suffering was just such a passion of the soul, a passion of suffering. To be fully human, one needs to be able to endure this kind of passion, to carry it consciously and heroically without trying to escape it, just as to enjoy the more delightful passions one needs to not be swept away by them. This is central to the ancient thinking on passion. The Latin root of "passion" is *passus* or *pati,* which means to endure. Buddhist teaching in this regard is similar to that of the Christian mystics: the best way to endure suffering or passion is to experience it but in a detached, disinterested manner. "Disinterested" is not the same here as "uninterested," but rather means free from self and self-interest. The Christian mystic Meister Eckhart, for example, taught that no one can be truly interested in or passionate about anything until he or she is disinterested.

Our passions are closely bound up with our instincts; we know them through our physiological nervous system. We *feel* our passions not only emotionally but bodily. America's cult of passion is an addiction to intense feelings, or as the case may be, to a narcotic numbing of intense feelings when the latter cause suffering. The act of extinguishing passion when it is dark is still a salute to the cult of passion because the individual is still gripped by passion in an uncontrollable way, which is why he or she feels driven to extinguish it; one is still as much in service to it as if he gave in to it. As we know, most efforts to numb suffering do not make it go away. The passion just comes out in another form, such as the behavioral addictions that comprise America's cult of passion and that are so commonly rampant today. The cures to the problem of suffering become the new problem.

Whether in search of a peak experience or an escape from suffering, America's cult of passion manifests in the variety of behavioral addictions that plague the nation. These are the most concrete forms of the addiction to height. Not unlike the cults of fundamentalism, they too are at least in part a reaction to the loss of order and meaning spawned by the cults of modernity. As McLuhan said, " 'Numbed to death by booze and tranquilizers' is an average strategy for 'keeping in touch' with a runaway world." But alcohol and drugs are only one "strategy." All the behavioral addictions serve the same function, and they are even more numerous and prevalent than in McLuhan's day. Gambling, sex addiction, food addiction, shopping addiction, addictive relationships, workaholism, exercise addiction, are now all recognizable features of the American cultural landscape. New addictions continue to form: computer addicts are offered help from Interneters Anonymous, the Center for On-Line Addiction, and the F12

Online Anonymous Twelve Step Program—services that, ironically, are provided online. All behavioral addictions are ways in which Americans seek to get high or keep *up* with a runaway world. Keeping up with the world is usually translated as "coping," and includes seeking relief from suffering regardless of how ill-founded or self-destructive the means.

The American appetite for peak experiences surpasses that of any other nation. As President Clinton acknowledged during his visit to Mexico in 1997, America has 5 percent of the world's population but consumes 50 percent of the world's drugs. His statement was meant to curtail the expectations of those who believed that high-level talks with the Mexican authorities on the international drug trade could alone solve America's problem of drug abuse. The crux of the problem is drug demand, not supply, for wherever there is strong demand, there will be a supply, even if it has to be manufactured synthetically and domestically. A national survey in 1997 by the Department of Health and Human Services revealed that 76 percent of high school students admitted to keeping, using, or selling drugs on school grounds, and 46 percent of middle school students reported drug availability at their schools. Another government survey found that drug use among 12- to 17-year-olds had risen 78 percent from 1992 to 1995. Of course, substance abuse among adolescents as a group exceeds the rest of the nation because of the particular nature of the adolescent appetite. But statistics on the rest of the nation show that it, too, has a strong adolescent appetite. America has over 20 million alcoholics and 10 million drug addicts; cirrhosis of the liver is the eighth leading cause of death in the nation, and motor vehicle accidents often involving intoxication is a top killer.

Gambling can be just as addictive as chemical substances but is condoned by society because it is a perceived as less destructive. But the fact that one is permitted and the other not only goes to show how little society understands the common nature of both. The excitement of gambling creates physiological reactions in the body similar to certain narcotics. People get high gambling. The sense of release and unification it provides has long been known. Dostoevsky, himself a compulsive gambler, made a good study of this in his novel *The Gambler*. After alcohol and drugs, nothing distracts one from one's problems and the humdrum of life like the thrill of taking a chance. America's gambling fever, *Newsweek* writes, "is part of the weekly, even daily routine of tens of millions of Americans." "We are becoming a nation of compulsive gamblers," reports a spokesperson for Compulsive Gamblers Anonymous. Indian tribes establishing casinos on their reservations in states where gambling is otherwise illegal have been astute in cashing in on this trend. Las Vegas—a single industry town—is one of the most rapidly growing cities in the nation. Gambling on sports events proliferates wildly, and gambling web sites are even accessible on the Internet.

An innocuous or harmless façade has allowed gambling to become a recognized institution and a huge industry. It is the fastest growing legal business in the United States. More than $410 billion were wagered in casinos in 1995, more than 20 times what Americans spent on movies and videos. Casinos are legal today in over half the states, and that number is expected to increase. Through state lotteries governments participate most lucratively in the gambling industry. Lottery earnings are growing at an average of 17.5 percent annually. The Coalition Against Gambling describes this trend as government cannibalizing its own citizens. And finally, there is the stock market, a pivotal tool of capitalism. The number of Americans day trading and otherwise gambling on the stock market (as opposed to investing for the long term) is also steadily increasing.

## The Meaning of the Drug Epidemic

Like a glass of wine at dinner, most things in moderation are healthy. It is quite human and natural to seek a peak experience or an emotional high. Compulsion and addiction, however, are another matter. Any attempt to solve the problem of substance abuse, the nation's leading and most destructive behavioral addiction, without addressing our imbalance in seeking peak experiences, will be futile. To "just say no" will not work because one is saying no to a symptom without understanding the motivation behind the compulsion and addiction. Little attention has been paid to the meaning of the drug epidemic in America. This epidemic is so commonplace now that people take it for granted and forget that it had an origin, a distinct piece of cultural soil it sprang from if not a specific starting point. By looking at that source we may discern what it is about drugs that is so appealing to Americans, and what purpose they serve in the national psyche.

Drugs have been with us for a long time, cutting across civilizations and national borders. Still today one can travel in India and discover opium dens hidden in its inner cities, and the plenitude of opium dens in China up until the Communist ascendancy was a well-known fact. However, in these settings drugs were largely used as an escape from the drudgery and oppressiveness of life. They were not acts that in themselves made a social comment about anything other than the facts that life was hard and full of suffering and that people sought relief. Working class people frequented opium dens as well as the affluent, and in colonial days, drugs were given to laborers—"coolies," as they were often derogatorily called—to ease their pain and increase their indifference.

In America, it's a different story. The proliferation of drugs here is a phenomenon with roots other than the usual hardships of life. It is true that there has been a strong undercurrent of alcoholism in many Western cultures in recent centuries, and that alcohol has served the same purpose that opium did in the East (it was additionally used by soldiers going into battle). Likewise, the use of heroin was for some an equivalent to the opium of the East. Many disenfranchised blacks whose lives were marginalized in the ghettos of America's cities resorted to heroin addiction and, in order to support it, crime. Malcolm X's autobiography paints a gritty picture of the despair that drove such African-Americans to this addiction. But even in their case, their use of drugs was not exclusively of the type that can be described as a search for relief from suffering. It already had a distinctly American character and was not unrelated to the kind of drug use that was going on with writers and artists in the Beat movement. Indeed, the bridge between these two groups were the black musicians—particularly the jazz musicians—who regularly used marijuana and made it "hip." Some of course also used heroin.

The reason I am focusing here on the era before the 1960s is because this period, the 1950s, ushered in the counterculture and hippie movements that made marijuana and other drugs part of the cultural mainstream. In fact, the Beat generation very much launched the 1960s and christened them with their values, particularly those in connection with drug use. These values have since become obscured, forgotten, and even irrelevant in light of the more conservative values that supplanted them during the 1970s and thereafter. What now exists is the current widespread use of drugs but without any cognizance of the social statement originally intended in their usage. Listen to a description of the Beat movement in *Benet's Reader's Encyclopedia:*

> Although they never had a stated manifesto or program, the beats' creative efforts and lifestyles bespoke a vehement rejection of middle-class life and values. With a few exceptions, they were not considered respectable by the literary or social establishment until the 1970s. But the ideas they championed—pacifism; reverence for nature at the expense of sophisticated technological pursuits; and stress on enhancing one's consciousness, whatever the methods employed—became ideas much of the nation championed as well. They came to be venerably regarded as descendents of American

Transcendentalism, Thoreauvian in their distrust of the machine and Whitmanesque in their faith in America and the individual. . . . The nomenclature *beat* was coined by Kerouac from *beatific*. . . . The three most sensational volumes to appear were Ginsberg's *Howl,* a long, incantatory poem, which depicts America as a horrifying wasteland; Kerouac's *On the Road,* a novel about a rootless individual who wanders around America in search of an unshaped life; and Burroughs's *Naked Lunch* (1957), a hallucinatory novel about a faceless addict living in a sick, institutional society.

Jack Kerouac and William Burroughs very much lived the life they wrote about: Kerouac died of alcoholism at age 47 and Burroughs was an alcoholic and heroin addict.

The above passage alludes to the underpinnings of the current drug epidemic in an unstated but telling way. The American love affair with drug intoxication did not begin as a relief from the toil of life but rather from the spoil of life as the American century was reaching *its* peak. Tracking the origins of today's drug epidemic leads less to Harlem and Watts than to Greenwich Village and the universities, where a disenchanted intelligentsia was feeling increasingly alienated and marginalized by the mushrooming cults of modernity. The widespread recreational and mind-expanding use of drugs that took off with such figures in the 1960s as Timothy Leary and Carlos Castaneda really had its beginnings with the Beat movement as an expression of heroic disillusionment and malaise. The "vehement rejection of middle-class life and values," the "reverence for nature at the expense of sophisticated technological pursuits," the "stress on enhancing one's consciousness," the Thoreauvian "distrust of the machine," and the Whitmanesque "faith in America and the individual," were all assertions of humanity and liberty that were intended to strike against the tyranny of modern culture. The progression from Ginsberg's *Howl* to Kerouac's *On the Road* to Burroughs's *Naked Lunch* were but the most recent Stations of the Cross in America's trip up the Golgotha of contemporary culture. They were portraits of the undoing of the American heroic ideal, and included in their arc the heroic disempowerment of not only the intellectuals or those in Harlem and Watts, but all Americans. "Beatific" was the right word for the Beat movement's aspiration to rise above it all and reach for the heavenly. Their forerunners were indeed the Transcendentalists, who also underwent a revulsion against modernity, modernity experienced then as the early effects of the Industrial Revolution.

After the 1960s, drug use became dissociated from this cultural backdrop that endowed it with its original intent or significance. People today no longer connect their use of drugs with *why* they are using them. But the discontent and the impulse to rise above discontent are the same. What now thrives is a cult of passion without direction, a cult that does not know what drives it other than "it feels good." It does not make a difference whether one is speaking about the drug epidemic, the gambling boom, the profitable opening of eating disorder clinics across the nation, or the explosion of sexuality in all its forms, be it pornography or simply the great importance it has assumed in the media and in our relationships. All these things have come together as mutual developments of a culture passionately seeking peak experiences of release and unification because the traditional ways of attaining these no longer work or are just not enough.

The sexual revolution that began in the 1960s coincided with the mass use of drugs in the same period. Many people like to think that the sexual revolution was a release of the repressed sexuality that was still hanging on from the Victorian era, but this is not quite right. As history shows, there were many Victorians who were replete with a seething sexuality that thrived behind closed doors. The cultural persona was one of dispassion, but there was plenty of passion in understated ways, much of it sublimated as Freud showed, but also much that was expressed secretly *as it should be* in a culture that still considered the sexual as sacred. All traditional cultures provide a place where the erotic can be treated casually (indeed, prostitution *is* one of the oldest professions in the world), but they also provide a very clearly defined place in which it is seen as embodying the sacred or divine. The Victorians were no exception. Sexuality today has burst out of its old container, but in doing so has lost its sacred quality and become a purely casual affair. However, not that casual: as the American preoccupation with it shows, it carries the charge of a peak experience, but without the recognition of the innermost meaning and secret nature of this charge.

In discussing the behavioral addictions of Americans, one can move back and forth between them and still always be discussing the same thing, for they *are* all aspects of the same thing, the same cult of passion. Americans treat sex like a drug, drugs like sex, relationships like a gamble, gambling like a relationship with one's beloved, and so on. The cult of passion—and it needs to be emphasized that I am here speaking of the *cult* of passion and not passion itself—is a compensation for heroic disillusionment and failure. It is no coincidence that the word "heroin" is derived from the Greek *heros*, or hero. Heroin, first developed in Germany in 1898, was given this name for the feelings of power and euphoria it engendered.

Of all the drugs one can become addicted to, heroin is the drug of choice for many who feel the natural need for the heroic in order to give their lives meaning, but cannot satisfy this need through natural means; it is a quick way to feel like a hero. This is why heroin has always appealed to the socially and economically disenfranchised. In having become a drug that cuts across class distinctions, its appeal continues to be its ability to simulate a seductively satisfying, heroic state of mind. The numbers of those to whom it appeals are indeed many: in 1997 the government estimated that there were 600,000 hard-core heroin addicts in the United States.

That heroin use is really a way to access the heroic dimension is borne out by the particular cult—let's call it a cult of specialization—that has grown up around it. When President Clinton criticized Calvin Klein for advertisements that displayed teenagers who had the "heroin look," advertisements that gave the impression that heroin is chic, he was not in effect deterring heroin use, as if young people would because of these ads automatically go out and buy heroin instead of jeans. Rather, he was, intentionally or not, condemning a warped and self-destructive form of heroism. He was condemning the very idea that heroism could be attained merely by injecting a chemical substance and going into an altered state, or by bonding with fellow addicts around the rituals of the needle that accompany heroin use. Heroin use is motivated by the same thwarted hunger for heroism that lies behind the drug epidemic at large, though with heroin use it is observable in a concentrated form. What else can explain the phenomenon that occurred when Jonathan Melvoin, the keyboardist of the rock band, the Smashing Pumpkins, died from an overdose of heroin in 1996? The announcement that his death was caused by a certain strain of heroin created a rush among heroin users in New York City to find that strain, rather than, as one might think, a panic to avoid it. The peak experience sought here was not just ecstasy, but a flirtation with and conquest of death. These users were on a heroic mission. It is no different with drug use at large in America; the drug may be different and the peak experience may not be about death, but the unconscious aim is almost always to fill a heroic vacuum.

Of course, if drug use is a way to access the heroic dimension, it also tends to be a way to escape it. Insofar as its aim is unconscious and it is symptom-oriented rather than problem-oriented, it does not provide a real solution. It just becomes part of the problem. The same is true for other behavioral addictions as well. George Will had this to say about gambling:

> Gambling fever reflects and exacerbates what has been called the "fatalism of the multitude." The more people believe in the importance

of luck, chance, randomness, fate, the less they believe in the importance of stern virtues such as industriousness, thrift, deferral of gratification, diligence, studiousness. It is drearily understandable why lotteries—skill-less gambling; gambling for the lazy—are booming at a time when the nation's productivity, competitiveness, savings rate and academic performance are poor.

Will wrote this in 1989 when America was in the throes of a recession. But the economic recovery that came in the 1990s did little to change the nation's gambling fever, suggesting that the problem is larger than economics. Certainly, America's crisis in heroism is not prone to the same cycles as the economy and needs more assiduous remedies. The "stern virtues" Will mentions are all heroic virtues, at least from a Franklinian point of view. These, however, no longer seem to define what is a meaningful and valuable way to live. The avoidance of a genuinely heroic fate inevitably results in a fatalism of the multitude. In other words, the reverse of Will's premise is also true: the belief in the importance of luck, chance, and randomness not only makes people believe less in the heroic virtues, but the decline in these virtues makes people embrace luck, chance, and randomness more desperately and zealously. One is reminded of those Publishers Clearing House commercials where the winners are portrayed in a state of mania, heroes in their own right.

# Chapter 10

## The Metaphor of Depth

*The descent into the world may be painful and costly. . . . The heights seek the depths; one way or another they want to come down. . . .*

—James Hillman

### The Heart of the Matter

When his wife died, Thomas Jefferson was so stricken with grief that he did not leave his room for three weeks. He couldn't talk without breaking down in tears. He was so inconsolable that friends worried that he was losing his mind. He paced in his room, his daughter wrote, "almost incessantly night and day, only lying down when nature was completely exhausted on a pallet that had been brought in during his long fainting fit. When at last he left his room, he rode out, and from that time he was incessantly on horseback rambling about the mountain in the least frequented roads and just as often through the woods." Then and again—for tragedy had not ceased to visit him with this one episode—Jefferson openly pondered the purpose of human suffering. However, in spite of never finding a satisfactory answer, he accepted his own suffering. He did not seek to escape or minimize it. He did not hide his vulnerability or take false refuge in frenzied activity, in amassing a fortune (indeed, he died practically bankrupt), in indulgences of food and drink, or in religious platitudes. The excess that characterizes all the cults of height he knew in the end would only make his suffering worse.

Jefferson was of a breed that had a hygiene of intelligent living, a practiced understanding that the mind and will need to be developed and disciplined for a life that is in harmony with nature and the order of things. He particularly struggled with his passions. On one occasion, having fallen deeply in love with a married woman four years after his wife's death, he wrote a letter to her that later became famous for its meditative "dialogue between my Head and my Heart":

> *Head.* Well, friend, you seem to be in a pretty trim.
>
> *Heart.* I am indeed the most wretched of all earthly beings. Overwhelmed with grief, every fibre of my frame distended beyond its natural powers to bear, I would willingly meet whatever catastrophe should leave me no more to feel, or to fear.
>
> *Head.* These are the eternal consequences of your warmth and precipitation. This is one of the scrapes into which you are ever leading us. . . . To avoid those eternal distresses. . . you must learn to look forward, before you take a step which may interest our peace. . . . Do not bite at the bait of pleasure, till you know there is no hook beneath it. The art of life is the art of avoiding pain; and he is the best pilot, who steers clearest of the rocks and shoals with which it is beset. Pleasure is always before us; but misfortune is at our side: while running after that, this arrests us. The most effectual means of being secure against pain, is to retire within ourselves, and to suffice for our own happiness. Those which depend on ourselves, are the only pleasures a wise man will count on: for nothing is ours, which another may deprive us of. . . .
>
> *Heart.* Let the gloomy monk, sequestered from the world, seek unsocial pleasures in the bottom of his cell! Let the sublimated philosopher grasp visionary happiness, while pursuing phantoms dressed in the garb of truth! Their supreme wisdom is supreme folly; and they mistake for happiness the mere absence of pain. Had they ever felt the solid pleasure of one generous spasm of the heart, they would exchange for it all the frigid speculations of their lives, which you have been vaunting in such elevated terms. . . . We are not immortal ourselves, my friend; how can we expect our enjoyments to be so? We have no rose without its thorn; no pleasure without alloy. It is the law of our existence; and we must acquiesce.

As it turns out, in this dialogue the heart has the final word. In Jefferson's later years, the head would win out.

This dichotomy between the head and the heart is, of course, an ancient theme. It roughly corresponds to the archetypal split between the spirit and the soul, between man's higher, heavenly, spiritual nature and his lower, earthy, emotional nature. Nietzsche understood this polarity as the "Apollonian" and "Dionysian" approaches to life, and others have described it in terms of a "Classical" and "Romantic" typology. It is a recurring theme in literature; for example, Hermann Hesse's *Narcissus and Goldmund* makes it its central theme. In the American literary tradition, one could say that Emerson and Thoreau traveled the high road, and Hawthorne and Melville the low road. These are temperamental differences that reflect, among other things, how the divine is experienced. The high road aspires to reach toward the heavenly heights and, using the noble gifts of the mind or spirit, help man lift himself up by his bootstraps; it sees the transcendent as above or beyond and wishes to orient man towards its high ideals. Jefferson summed this orientation up nicely as the Head's appreciation of the "inestimable value of intellectual pleasures. Ever in our power, always leading us to something new, never cloying, we ride serene and sublime above the concerns of this mortal world, contemplating truth and nature, matter and motion, the laws which bind up their existence, and that Eternal Being who made and bound them up by those laws." The low road, on the other hand, sees the divine manifesting in the nitty-gritty details of man's life on earth, in his tormented heart and body, in his daily conflicts and challenges; it sees the transcendent as immanent in the here-and-now, and wishes to help man discover it through the experience of his darkness, suffering, love, and earthly joys. The low road seeks man's redemption in the world, as opposed to seeking it in the transcendence of the world. Lincoln was more familiar with this path.

Of course, these are not separate realities, but related types of experience. In fact, what we are discussing here are the metaphors of height and depth, which are relative to and need each other for their contrasting definition. Sooner or later, the metaphor of height must meet and come to grips with its opposite, the metaphor of depth. Depth complements and completes height, and vice versa; the two together give human experience its full range. Depth as a metaphor is as widely diffused in American culture as height, although not as appreciated in its possibilities. We speak of a deep friendship, a deep conversation, a deep conviction, deep feelings. Depth implies meaningfulness that is rich, layered, and profound. It is a movement down from the pristine heights of the mountain peaks to the fertile lushness of the valleys. Depth is earthy and grounded in the stuff of life. It has a viewpoint that is, if not as all-seeing as height's, more penetrating. It sees into the *under*lying nature of things. It probes and digests things, whereas height envelops and conquers them, gaining a great command over them. Depth tends to be patient and slow in its reflection upon things, whereas height, being unencumbered by time and space, tends to grasp things immediately and in their totality. Height is quicker, freer, and more agile. One hurries *up,* but one slows *down.* Thus is the cult of motion and speed, as one example, antithetical to depth. Depth and height are not youth-authority distinctions. Though both pairs represent ways in which humans experience and define the world, they operate on different axes. These axes, however, intersect and qualify each other. Thus can one speak of a high authority or the deep passions of youth as easily as of youth's lofty ambitions or seniority's deep wisdom.

The interplay of height and depth in the various myths of the hero's journey tells us something about what America, a nation whose character is predicated on the heroic ideal, can expect from its own heroic, historical journey. It is the nature of the hero to aspire to great heights; that is what makes him immortal and great. He must cross great distances, climb mountains, fight dragons, and save damsels in distress. But it is also in his nature and in the nature of his journey to fall to great depths, for that is where his humanity is tested and his character forged; that is where he comes to terms not with his immortality but his mortality. This is how he discovers not the secrets of his higher, spiritual nature but the secrets of his heart. This includes not only his hidden passions and talents, but the wisdom of the heart, as some traditions speak of it. It is a wisdom distinct from the wisdom of the mind or spirit. The philosopher Blaise Pascal alluded to it poignantly: "The heart has its reasons which reason knows nothing of." When Emerson said, "Heroism feels and never reasons and therefore is always right," he meant that heroism prevails by the reason and wisdom that can only be known in the heart, in the depth of one's being.

This reason or wisdom is, firstly, rooted in common sense, in the demands of life and the everyday, physical world. The heart knows how to live the good life because it knows what *feels* right on a sound, instinctual level. This is the wisdom of Benjamin Franklin, to cite one example. He speaks to the man on the ground, and to how he should keep his feet on the ground. He teaches about the art of living with the passions, which he rightly calls the art of virtue. The cult of passion is actually a cult without heart and virtue. The passions here are dissociated from the heart and are not in relationship with anything "other" that gives them meaning or relevance; other persons or objects are used narcissistically as a means to provide pleasure and gratification. Secondly, this reason or wisdom is rooted in the mysteries of why we are placed on this earth. It is rooted in our innermost calling, which only the heart can fathom. The depths—what modern psychology calls the unconscious—thus contain not only knowledge that has to do with our fate, but, by virtue of this, our fate itself. The ancients, who understood the unconscious in terms of the secrets of the heart, knew this well, and that is why they looked to the heart—which they also saw as the seat of the soul—to learn what their calling or fate was.

The hero falls or descends into the depths of his soul in order to both recover his common sense and to discover his fate. Again we may think of Moses and Jonah, the first in an oppressive desert and the second in the bowels of a whale. In Greece, Orpheus' descent into the underworld to retrieve Persephone served a similar transformative function, and Plato's use of the Myth of Er, a story of the workings of fate as discovered by a soldier during his descent into the underworld, also was intended to provide a deepened perspective on life. In the Middle Ages, St. John of the Cross coined his now-famous term, the "dark night of the soul," to describe the soul's confusion and depression as it undergoes such a journey of reorientation, of death and rebirth. This dark or depressive state is not to be confused with modern clinical depression. It is rather to be thought of as a creative depression or what the sociologist Émile Durkheim understood as anomie, a lack or uprooting of purpose, identity, and ethical values that can grip a society as easily as an individual. Certainly, Lincoln's bouts of depression and the darkness that the nation fell into during the Civil War were at least to some degree this kind of descent into the depths.

More than anything, the dark or depressive aspect comes in response to inflation or false security in one's direction, or indeed, from an altogether false direction. But dark or not, a descent into the depths is natural and necessary. And if it is necessary, then the errors that lead to it are also necessary. All are part of the hero's journey. Plato implies as much when he connects the Goddess of Necessity, *Ananke*—who sits at the center of the universe and whose three daughters govern the fate of every soul—with the principle of errancy. Although this errancy and error do not mean exactly the same thing, Hillman makes the observation that they are related insofar as they both involve itinerant wandering and shifting about in one's course. He cites the Platonic scholars Francis Cornford and Paul Friedlander, the former of whom describes *ananke* as rambling, aimless, and irresponsible, and the latter of whom describes it as the principle of indefiniteness, unreason, and chaos. Do not these terms also describe the cults of height? The heroic tradition of the Arthurian Round Table makes the same connection between these qualities and necessity: the knight-errant develops his insight and character in an indirect, irrational, peripatetic way, unearthing his fate by trial and error as he goes along. Deviation is one of the ways Necessity becomes known.

In other words, what I am suggesting here, based on the various myths of the hero's journey, is not only that America has deviated from its course and needs to descend into the depths in order to return to this course. I am also suggesting that this deviation may itself be a necessary part of the course; that, for all one may conjecture about the mysterious ways history and the human psyche operate, this deviation may be a natural occurrence in a larger pattern of digression, regression, and progression. Biological evolution, too, does not proceed in a straight line; it inches forward in a seemingly experimental mode, taking different twists and turns in order to find the right adaptation. Deviation, when its distressing effects are confronted, may be the factor that compels the nation to descend into the depths of its character so that it can deepen or advance its civilization. This would not be the first time history has served such a deviant-looking and devious challenge to a society or civilization in order to move it forward by first moving it downward to the roots of its character and heritage, to what is important or necessary.

The stakes in such a challenge are high. If America fails to meet this challenge, the result could be a repetition of history. In the worst possible scenario, it would not be the first time that a nation-state would have been consumed by its addiction to height and turned into a history lesson for some future nation-state. Americans who believe that this could never happen to America might wish to examine history more carefully: the nations that were gripped and crippled by this addiction were always in strong, influential positions in the world, and their demise often came suddenly and unexpectedly. Macedonia, Rome, and, to a large extent, the Soviet Union are examples. It is true that in most instances such nation-states fell because the tyranny they imposed upon other nations was not tolerated and their own expansionism undermined them; in this their addiction to height was different than America's. But in fact this tyranny usually originated *inside* these states, and was played out to its extreme in an international setting. Tyranny is tyranny, and sooner or later its effects take their toll one way or another. The tyranny America is at risk of, as Governor Huey Long first intimated, should not be thought of in terms of a military tyranny with the external trappings of fascism, such as a dictator, secret police, concentration camps, and special judges. Nor for that matter should it be thought of as a social tyranny, that is, as an oligarchy or plutocracy (though no one can deny that elitism is alive and well in America). The tyranny America is most at risk of is a *cultural* tyranny, an oppression that comes from the people themselves, from their culture or way of living. This would be a subtler

tyranny and hard to pinpoint precisely because there would be no one social body that would be visibly imposing itself upon another. The insidious
cults that have arisen from America's addiction to height provide the perfect medium for such a tyranny. Their encroaching effects upon society—
material insatiability; excessiveness; rapid, ungrounding movement; empty
celebrity worship; narrow religious thinking; and numbing intoxication in
one form or another—threaten both democracy and the moral health of the
nation.

Understanding deviation as the call of Necessity gives the former
meaning and purpose. This is similar to the way Freud understood symptoms. As he saw it, a symptom is a compromise between the disease and its
cure. It attempts to correct the disease but in the wrong way. If the disease
goes untreated, the symptoms may exacerbate until they cause a crisis of
catastrophic proportions or just slowly eat the organism up. Toynbee
showed the same principle at work in societies and civilizations that decay
and disintegrate. The various symptoms of America's disease of height
"seek" to bring the nation's attention *down* to their underlying, core meaning and purpose. Viewing these symptoms in this way provides a sense of
optimism and hope together with a sense of grave concern. There is a magnetic pull in the symptoms that gives cause to embrace them. If freedom is
the recognition of necessity, then it must also include a recognition of the
meaning and purpose of the deviation that serves necessity.

The heart that has reasons which reason knows nothing of is the hero's
heart. Cultivating this heart and its wisdom harks back to the heroism of
the founders of America and *their* heroes. America has a strong heritage
and rests upon a deep tradition of which it today has little cognizance. The
deviations in America today point to what is necessary. A return to the
roots, a descent into the depths, a reacquaintance with heritage and tradition, bring the hero to his senses and help him through his impasse. He
needs the wisdom of common sense and the vision of his fate to guide him.
Certainly, education in America today needs to orient itself according to
this project: the learning of what is necessary for a good life; the art of
virtue; and the duties or responsibilities of the citizen to society. Allan
Bloom and others are probably correct in their belief that if education, from
the lower levels to the higher, does not become infused with democratic
values, in a few generations Americans may no longer be living in a democracy, at least not as the Founding Fathers conceived it. The spiritual heritage, the intellectual tradition, and the political and humanistic vision of
the latter will be lost.

Of course, as these educators argue, American education must return to the study of not only the founders themselves, but the wellsprings that nourished them: the classics, including the myths and stories that reveal the truths of human nature and of what is humanly important, philosophy and ethics, history, literature, and the study of religion but in a democratic spirit. These are chief among the sources of the wisdom of the Founding Fathers. Today's education is so enamored with the mastery of science and technology in order to guarantee students jobs and keep America abreast in the Information Age, that students are ill-equipped to even ask the right questions about what is wrong with the quality of contemporary life. Needless to say, this is not the failing of science but of education itself, which has allowed science to be pursued one-sidedly and myopically. As the saying goes, specialization trains one to see more and more of less and less, until he sees nothing at all. Young people today are not being taught how to think about, much less deal with, the problems of living—the problems of love and human relationships, the problems of evil and suffering, and the ethical issues that are attached to important and commonplace decisions alike. In catering to the cults of prosperity, technology and progress, and motion and speed, American education accomodates the trend toward a Hobbesian society instead of a genuinely civilized and free society. Not only does modern education not create freethinkers, informed by such traditions as the Enlightenment, the Renaissance, and ancient Greece and Israel, but it does not create thinkers at all. The emphasis is on doing, not thinking and critical reflection.

But it is useless to tout the benefits of a traditional education and attempt to implement educational programs that draw upon the deeper roots of Western civilization when this is just a gesture of lip service to some noble ideal. If the actual ideals of such education are not *lived*, of what value are they? Education that ends with the repetition of ideas, even the dynamic ideas of the Great Books, is merely a cerebral exercise. As Santayana said, "The great difficulty in education is to get experience out of ideas." The books and their ideas have to become contemporary, that is, in sync with the times, alive in the here-and-now. The fact that such old books and ideas speak to all times is what makes them great and deep, and the art of education lies in making the relevant connections between their ageless wisdom and the current age we live in.

Moreover, as Jung and others point out, education that is disconnected from the life of the society that is going on around it is doomed to fail. People do not learn only from books but from other people. What benefits can we hope to gain from providing a liberal education to young people when all around them the only living examples who can demonstrate the moral and other lessons of that liberal education are parents, teachers, and other role models who are themselves swept up in the cults of prosperity, technology and progress, motion and speed, celebrity, and passion? Young people tend to do as they see, not as they are told. Words, intellectual discourses, and admonitions are of little social consequence when they are not supported by the world outside the school's walls. To teach the Great Books in a social vacuum would not go far toward fostering a great or enlightened society. It is illusory to believe that educational reform can be brought about in a purely institutional manner, that wisdom and character can be cultivated by one generation simply passing the responsibility of knowledge on to the next. The task of true education or learning is not a buck that can be passed.

The problem is difficult. Where does one begin? One may suppose that that is itself the beginning question. Education, in the sense it is being discussed here, must become a social process, and not merely a phase of preparation for employment in the life of the citizen. The cultivation of character and wisdom, the descent into the depths, must become a matter of public discourse, particularly at a time when it has become so eclipsed. And reflection upon the problems of modernity in America must become an item on the agenda of America if the latter is not to become arrested in or undermined by its current addiction to height. There must develop an awareness in the culture that it is alright for the eagle to descend from flight and settle for a while on some perch, a perch from which it can take stock and plan its next move. American Indians chose the eagle as one of their totem animals because of its shrewdness and alertness, and not just because of its fantastic abilities of flight and hunting. Indeed, even the eagle needs to descend, rest, and reflect. It is not only alright but necessary to permit what Maslow called a plateau experience, namely, a lowering of intensity in order to evaluate the peak experience and its impact on ordinary, everyday life.

But today we live in what is being called the postmodern age. This is just a euphemism for modernity that is in a permanent state of peak experience. Whereas modernism could look back to the Victorian Age or the Enlightenment or premodernism for some repose and a sense of where it came from, the postmodern age with its inbred forgetfulness has only modernity as its compass. There is no way to compare one historical mode of existence to another, with the result that the current age is, for all the explosion of information, cocooned in an insulated consciousness. There is no other point of view from which to examine the question so well put by Bob Dylan: "Are birds free from the chains of the skyway?" The very question, What does freedom or democracy mean?, is obscured in a postmodern age where height is blindly accepted as man's essential and total condition. Even a Transcendentalist like Thoreau early on saw the coming dangers and pleaded for depth: "Men think that it is essential that the *Nation* have commerce, and export ice, and talk through a telegraph, and ride thirty miles an hour, without a doubt, whether *they* do or not; but whether we should live like baboons or like men, is a little uncertain. . . . Let us settle ourselves, and work and wedge our feet downward through the mud and slush of opinion, and prejudice, and tradition, and delusion, and appearance . . . till we come to a hard bottom and rocks in place, which we can call *reality. . . .*"

In the end, the reality of gravity cannot be ignored. America needs to come to terms with this fact, and recognize that the high life and the good life are not necessarily the same.

# Part III

## The Underside of Innocence

*Then the Lord God said, "Behold, the man has become like one of us, knowing good and evil; and now, lest he put forth his hand and take also of the tree of life, and eat, and live forever"—therefore the Lord God sent him forth from the garden of Eden, to till the ground from which he was taken. He drove out the man; and at the east of the garden of Eden he placed the cherubim, and a flaming sword which turned every way, to guard the way to the tree of life.*

—Genesis 3:22–24

*If there is any major addiction that the United States of America has, it is the addiction of innocence, to keep ourselves unknowing, just new, putting it all behind us, and to have the wide open eyes and mouths of the child.*

—James Hillman

*It may well be that a society's greatest madness seems normal to itself.*

—Allan Bloom

# ★ Prelude: The Style of Innocence ★

If the addiction to height poses a growing threat to democracy in America, then the addiction to innocence already has a formidable grasp not only on the nation's understanding and practice of democracy, but its soul. Freedom itself has acquired a special meaning from having been filtered through the lens of innocence, so that it has become difficult to distinguish which social beliefs and practices genuinely express freedom, and which innocence. Innocence is a kind of freedom too, but it does not understand the importance of the recognition of necessity. Given this, even the addiction to height is hinged upon the addiction to innocence, since the culture exhibits a complete innocence about the former and does not recognize the need to set limits and come down from the heights.

Innocence, in the sense I am referring to it here, is an epistemic style, a way of knowing. It operates according to the principle or assumption that the world is what it appears to be, that is, that the nature of things is as the things themselves suggest by their appearance. Appearance is the criterion that determines what is meaningful and real. The philosopher Bertrand Russell called this principle "naive realism," and saw it as the root condition of man: "We all start from 'naive realism,' i.e., the doctrine that things are what they seem." In other words, human beings, like animals, are born naturally believing that things are what they seem. Innocence is the original condition of all living creatures.

As an account of the beginnings of humanity, the Book of Genesis clearly highlights the primacy of innocence and the latter's significance in the drama of human existence and suffering. It is tempting and comforting to see the serpent, who was later associated with the devil, as the culprit responsible for man's expulsion from the Garden of Eden. But this temptation is just an avoidance of responsibility, exactly the sort that got Adam and Eve into trouble in the first place. Eve blamed the serpent, and Adam blamed Eve. The truth behind this allegory of the beginning of humanity is that Adam and Eve were tempted because they were *able* to be tempted. Original sin occurred as a corollary to the condition of original innocence, indeed, as a consequence of it. It is even possible that innocence *was* the original sin, and not pride, as most biblical authorities contend.

God said to Adam, "Do not eat from the tree of the knowledge of good and evil." Things being what they seem, and with this rule seeming fairly straightforward, Adam did not think to eat from the tree. But then the serpent said to Eve, "God does not want you to eat from the tree only because you will become like him. Eat from it and you too will have special knowledge." Things again being what they seem, now the situation was different. Now it seemed like a good idea to eat from the tree. So they ate. But the special knowledge that the tree gave was precisely derived from the shattering of innocence. Now man knew good and evil, sacred and sacrilegious, and all the other pairs of opposites that riddle human nature. And he knew guilt and shame. He was ashamed of his innocent nakedness, and felt compelled to cover himself. There's a price for this knowledge. One cannot stay in paradise without innocence or purity. As the Talmud points out, God did not banish man from the Garden of Eden in anger or vengeance; he did it matter-of-factly and for man's own good. Having the freedom and power this knowledge brings without really knowing how to live with it would be far more injurious to man than to be sent out from the garden. A particular injury and danger, the Bible tells us, would be that man, after having eaten from the tree of the knowledge of good and evil, would then eat from the tree of (eternal) life and live forever. (There were, according to the oral tradition of the Talmud, many trees in the garden.) With no suffering and finality to his condition, he would then never be motivated to learn how to live with good and evil and manage his condition. In fact, it was in exiling man that God assured that man could eventually find his way to eternal life, but with the knowledge that he now had of good and evil.

Genesis is the story of man's emergence from his original condition of youth. Adam and Eve before the Fall lived as children: carefree, cared for, spontaneously living in the moment, uninhibited, and innocent. Psychologically, they *were* children, and the part they played in the Bible is analogous in human history to man's childhood. After Adam and Eve's exile from the garden, man had to work in order to live, childbirth and life thereafter became difficult, and suffering and death became part of the human condition. These are undoubtedly the realities that a discerning, maturing consciousness must face.

Of course, *Homo sapiens* always had to struggle to survive and eke out an existence in the world. Allegories such as Genesis use parables to speak about psychological and social differentiation or complexity. The exile from the Garden of Eden represents the fact that man cannot live in a paradisaic condition of eternal youth and innocence, though he may want to. He must leave this condition in order to become not only more fully human, but more fully aware of his divine nature. One might take note that the tree of the knowledge of good and evil is a tree of *knowledge* and *awareness* that would, Genesis tells us, make man become like God; and one might then ask: why did God plant this tree in the garden in the first place if he really didn't want man to eat from it? Did not God, who according to the Talmud has foreknowledge of all events in the future, know that man would eat from it?

A more explicit occasion in which the Bible uses childhood as a paradigm of consciousness is Christ's admonition that unless one becomes like a little child one cannot enter the kingdom of heaven. But even here, the reference is to being child*like* and not literally, psychologically, a child. The innocence alluded to in the Christian paradigm is the innocence of a wise man or woman who has the simplicity of a child but the discerning consciousness of a mature person. Thus did Christ admonish his followers to be as gentle as the dove but as cunning as the serpent. Innocence here reflects a conscious attitude, a purity of heart, and not a static condition, either psychologically or socially.

Likewise, with Christ, whom Paul describes as the second or "last Adam," there is a redemption of the exiled condition and a restoration of Adam's connection with God in that the kingdom of God can now be attained through a life of faith, love, and righteousness. This, however, points to an evolution of consciousness and not a regression to an original condition of puerile innocence. In Judaism, too, this evolution is evident in the idea of the *tzaddik* or "righteous one" who has lost his sense of individuality in attaining union with God. The *tzaddik,* as the tales of the Hasidim illustrate, is a wise person who may be childlike yet is anything but a child.

The paradigm on which America is founded does not make clear this distinction between the first Adam and the second Adam. Consequently, there is to this day a profound and profoundly unconscious confusion about the meaning of innocence. In fact, America was very much founded on the paradigm of the first Adam. The literary critic R.W.B. Lewis has traced the development of the theme of an American paradise from the inception of the nation through the nineteenth century, demonstrating how this theme has shaped the outlook of such influential writers as Emerson, Thoreau, Hawthorne, Melville, and Henry James. Lewis writes that the new American Adam was

> an individual emancipated from history, happily bereft of ancestry, untouched and undefiled by the usual inheritances of family and race; an individual standing alone, self-reliant and self-propelling, ready to confront whatever awaited him with the aid of his own unique and inherent resources. It was not surprising, in a Bible-reading generation, that the new hero (in praise or disapproval)

was most easily identified with Adam before the Fall. Adam was the first, the archetypal, man. His moral position was prior to experience, and in his very newness he was fundamentally innocent.

Adam is a favorite American archetypal hero. As Lewis adds, he appears as Hawkeye in James Fenimore Cooper's *The Deerslayer,* Huck Finn in Mark Twain's classic *Adventures of Huckleberry Finn,* Donatello in Hawthorne's *The Marble Faun,* and Billy Budd in Melville's *Billy Budd.* In twentieth-century literature he surfaces as Fitzgerald's Gatsby, Faulkner's Isaac McCaslin in *The Bear,* the "invisible man" in Ellison's novel with that title, Salinger's "Catcher in the Rye," and Saul Bellow's Augie March. He also continues to be an appealing figure in American films. One may think of Gary Cooper's character in "Meet John Doe," Robert De Niro's character in "Taxidriver," Chauncey Gardner in "Being There," Dustin Hoffman's character in "Rain Man," and, of course, Forrest Gump. The fact that some of these characters are developmentally delayed is merely a creative device, but is apt: even the term "developmentally delayed" speaks to the condition of Adam before the Fall.

A nation's heroic ideal and its national character are formed from the same mold. Thus, in having found a "fundamentally innocent" hero, America had also founded itself upon his psychology. As Emerson said, "Here's for the plain old Adam, the simple genuine self against the whole world." This position, of course, inevitably sets in motion some drama or tragedy that brings about the necessary departure from innocence. The Genesis story, as is the case with all mythic allegory, didn't happen once-upon-a-time a long time ago; it happens again and again as a regular occurrence in human experience. The Civil War was just such a tragic departure or fall from innocence, as the psychologist Guilford Dudley argues. An innocence that believed that slavery was justified by virtue of the needs it fulfilled—this was naive realism operating in an economic and racial framework—was bound to result in cataclysm. A similar innocence or belief in the virtue of appearances was preponderant in the Vietnam War and Watergate. On the other side of innocence is its lesson, that, as Henry James, Sr. wrote, "nothing can indeed be more remote . . . from distinctively *human* attributes . . . than this sleek and comely Adamic condition." Emerson, too, in the final analysis recognized the two sides of the equation, calling the side of Adam before the Fall the "party of Hope" (or the "party of the Future"), and the side after the Fall, the "party of Memory" (or the "party of the Past"). Do these not also correspond, respectively, to the spirit of youth and the spirit of authority?

# Chapter 11

## The Historical Roots of American Innocence

*Ye are the light of the world. A city that is set on an hill cannot be hid. Neither do men light a candle, and put it under a bushel, but on a candlestick; and it giveth light unto all that are in the house.*

—Matthew 5:14–15

*O America! Because you build for mankind I build for you.*

—Walt Whitman

### The American Vision

American innocence takes many forms, some of which we shall be discussing in some detail. If there exists a single historical source for them, it is probably the vision upon which America was founded. This vision consists of the nation's understanding of its mission on earth, its raison d'être or purpose in history. Not all nations have a vision or heroic mission as part of their constitution or national endowment. England, France, Russia, and China are among the modern nations that can claim such a heritage, and of course, the visions of each are different from the other. The American vision is especially distinct, not only in its aims, but in how explicitly it was conceived and promoted. Indeed, in spite of the innocent assumptions and consequential shortcomings of this vision, it continues to be explicitly promoted by politicians, as if simply touting a belief in the vision has superseded any need to revise and revive it in a matured, sobered form.

If money talks, the American dollar bill boldly proclaims the American vision. The seal of the United States, first put on the backside of the dollar by FDR to express his view that the New Deal was a step toward creating a new order in the world, is the equivalent of what a personal signature is to the individual; it is a symbol of identity. As such, the Great Seal is the alpha and omega of American symbols: it extols the basic premises and goals with which the nation was conceived. Its imagery, the design of which in the initial stages involved the efforts of Franklin, Jefferson, and Adams, speaks to the heart of the American enterprise. It tells how both the Founding Fathers and the Puritans before them viewed America and what they had in mind for it.

The American bald eagle, of course, is universally associated with liberty and democracy. It represents not only the idea of natural rights, that all men are equal, but the norms of political organization that keep this idea alive and strong. With its escutcheon or shield, the eagle signifies the American scheme for the practice and preservation of democracy. This scheme or system checks the tendency toward inordinate power by a few on the one hand and the confusion of the multitude on the other by making every center of power responsible to the people. It prevents injustice by balancing subordinate centers of power with other centers. And it assures freedom by denying to any source of prestige or authority immunity from criticism. In its mouth the eagle holds a scroll upon which is inscribed *E Pluribus Unum,* or "Out of many, one." Although this motto largely alludes to the union of the thirteen colonies into one nation, it also points to the idea of the brotherhood of man that was conveyed in the biblical phrase, "Ye are brethren," and that was central to both the Puritan and Jeffersonian plans for America. Jefferson saw the democratic principle of equality as the primary means that would advance the brotherhood of man.

If the eagle represents the heart of the American vision, it is the reverse side of the seal, the pyramid, that represents its significance in the greater scheme of things. The pyramid of course is an Egyptian motif. It here implies strength and duration, as the Egyptian pyramids are among the most ancient manmade structures still intact. There was, during the eighteenth century when the seal was designed, a general fascination with Egypt and things Egyptian. Like the Great Pyramid of Giza, the oldest and largest in the world and probably the one upon which the seal is modeled, the new American republic was seen as a monumental achievement in human innovation. At the base of the pyramid is the scroll that expresses the importance of this achievement; upon it is inscribed, *Novus Ordo Seclorum,* or

"New Order of the Ages." This was intended to announce the beginning of a new era in history, an era in which democracy and the republican form of government were to establish the brotherhood of man. This was to be the American era. Naturally, the Puritan ideal of a new order was the precursor to the ideal held by the Founding Fathers; the former was predominantly religious in character and predemocratic, while the latter was conceived in political terms and was to be achieved through the principles and practice of democracy. Yet both had this in common as their most important defining quality: the new order was to reinstate a morally mindful direction for humanity.

The Puritans and Founding Fathers alike believed America to be the stage for the next scene in the drama of God's plan for humanity. Both felt the inspiration of the Prophets to be their own: "Prepare ye in the wilderness the way of the Lord, make straight in the desert a highway for our God" (Isaiah 40:3). The Puritans, as everyone knows, overtly expressed the view and hope that America would be a godly nation. In particular, it would reestablish and continue the theocratic tradition of ancient Israel, a nation believed to have been founded by the will of God and meant to live according to the will of God. The Puritans saw themselves as a latter-day "Chosen People," led out of the House of Bondage into the wilderness and the Promised Land with the mission to create a righteous nation. They wished to establish America as the "new Jerusalem" or heavenly city on earth; it would be, as Yale University's president Ezra Stiles said a century later, "God's American Israel." Americans for generations would continue to feel this special calling. "We Americans," Melville remarked in 1850, "are the peculiar, chosen people—the Israel of our time." To the Puritans, the implications of this were of course seen in the context of their particular odyssey: there would be a new and purer church, and the order of the land would be defined by a clean break from the sin, injustice, aristocratic exploitation, and religious persecution of Europe. America would be a new beginning for humanity, a place concerned with moral as well as material improvement. This work of transforming or redeeming the human condition, Cotton Mather insisted, was not merely part of America's identity, but essential to its unfolding. As Richard Hofstadter put it, America began with a "belief in perfection," the signpost of innocence.

The ideal of the Founding Fathers was, of course, the one that has prevailed upon the nation. Their vision of a new order was partial in what it borrowed from Israel. It disregarded the idea of a theocracy and focused on the idea of establishing a moral nation whose citizens would conduct their affairs with virtue, virtue here understood not as devout purity or holiness but as the integrity that constitutes a life of well-being. There are some scholars who believe that Israel had a political influence on the Founding Fathers other than suggesting the model of a theocracy: within the framework of its theocracy, Israel had a chief judge who served in the capacity of a commander-in-chief and chief executive, a kind of senate (eventually known as the Sanhedrin), and a popular assembly whose functions corresponded, respectively, to the U.S. Senate and House of Representatives. But it is not likely that the Founding Fathers drew much inspiration in their political thinking from this, in spite of their familiarity with the Bible. They didn't need to draw on this source. The main political sources that informed their vision of a new order were the democracy of Greece, Roman republicanism, and the political philosophy of the Enlightenment. Jefferson was additionally inspired by what he learned about idealistic, egalitarian societies in the forests of prefeudal Saxony, in England before the Norman Conquest, and in the American colonies before the French and Indian Wars. (The societies in the colonies consisted of the Indian tribes and the independent yeoman farmers on the edge of the frontier.) Even though much of what he gleaned from the history of these prepolitical orders appears to have been glorified by his imagination, one cannot dismiss their influence upon him.

A word about the moral nature of the new order as conceived by the Founding Fathers may be of interest here. This morality was seen as grounded in what the Enlightenment philosopher Francis Hutcheson described as the moral sense or faculty that is inherent in all human beings. For the people to effectively rule themselves, there needed to be an enlightened citizenry that could engage itself in benevolent, mild-mannered government. For Jefferson, this would be attainable because the evils of the old European order, the evils of monarchy and aristocracy, would no longer interfere with the people's ability to access their natural, God-given moral sense. The slate had been wiped clean with the new beginning in America. Again we encounter the innocent belief in perfection. In fact, Jefferson believed that a large measure of moral enlightenment had already been attained at the outset of the American enterprise: "If all the sovereigns of Europe were to set themselves to work to emancipate the minds of their subjects from their present ignorance and prejudice and that as zealously as they now attempt the contrary, a thousand years would not place them on that high ground from which our common people are now setting out." Needless to say, history would soon prove Jefferson wrong not only by spilling the blood from the Civil War on this "high ground," but by transforming Western Europe's absolute monarchies into constitutional monarchies and parliamentary democracies.

Morality, however, is not the sole or even the primary feature of the new order envisioned by the Founding Fathers. Above all, the new order would be what Jefferson called an "empire for liberty" (this is implied by the obverse side of the seal, the eagle). Again, it was liberty that made the moral sense accessible. Liberty was seen as the first and last principle that circumscribed all the other attributes of the new order. In the words of Daniel Boorstin, "America was where the equal destiny of the human species might be realized and attested, where the adaptability and pioneering talents of man might be given superlative expression, where morality would have the reward of health and prosperity, and prosperity would prove the rightness of morality, where the political self-governing possibilities of the species would be demonstrated." All this would be possible for the first time in modern history because of liberty.

The empire of liberty that would establish the egalitarian brotherhood of man was to be realized first in America, but being a New Order of the Ages, it was not to be confined there. All humanity was to benefit from this. As Washington declared in his first inaugural speech, "the preservation of the sacred fire of liberty and the destiny of the republican model of government are justly considered, perhaps as deeply, as finally staked on the experiment intrusted to the hands of the American people." America's purpose in the scheme of things was to exemplify and spearhead the empire of liberty. This was believed to be decreed by destiny, by the will of God. The doctrine of Manifest Destiny and the justification of American expansionism were in no small measure derived from this belief.

This brings us to the top of the pyramid, to the eye in the triangle. This is the all-seeing, omnipresent eye of God, an image that goes back to the seven eyes of Yahweh that "range through the whole earth" (Zechariah 4:10) and the single but all-observing eye of the god Horus in ancient Egyptian religion. In the American context, the eye of God signifies not only God's watchfulness but his will, otherwise known as Providence. God watches over America with a specific aim or plan, and bestows his care, provision, and guidance in order to realize this plan. The notion of Providence was so intimately related to the idea of a new beginning and order, that one of the first settlements in America was named after it. The Puritans' idea that America was the place for a new beginning in the history of mankind was, to them, not merely a hope, but a conviction borne out by the evidence of their survival. Escape from religious oppression in England, a false start at a new life in Holland, perilous journeys across a vast ocean, harsh winters in the wilderness of an unknown continent, all reinforced their impression that their exodus was second in history only to that of the Israelites, and that God must be willing it, too. Similarly, the Founding Fathers, although religiously a different breed than the Puritans, were compelled to recognize a less-than-vague sense of destiny at work in events. Remember, history tells us that they did not set out to be revolutionaries but were, as Edmund Burke put it, conservatives fighting for the traditional rights of Englishmen. To have been cornered into the risky undertaking of a revolution, and to have undertaken it successfully, was living proof to them that a divine authority was mysteriously involved and had blessed their actions.

The Latin motto *Annuit Coeptis*—"He favors our undertakings"—puts into words the sense of Providence with which the Puritans and Founding Fathers were imbued. Arched like an umbrella over the pyramid, this motto reflects the view that the entire building process of the American enterprise occurs and must occur under the auspices of Providence and divine grace. Everything is before God's eye. In the final analysis, the American venture was seen not only as a material project, but a moral and spiritual one. The apex of the pyramid, the high point of the American experiment, is not a material but a spiritual pinnacle. The fact that the capstone is not firmly placed on the rest of the pyramid is intended to suggest that the pyramid is not finished; the American experiment is a work in progress.

## The American Vision as a Paradigm of Innocence

With its idea that the founding of America was a new beginning for humanity, the American vision was predicated on the notion that some original condition of innocence or purity, some virginal way of being that man had deviated from, could be recaptured. This notion was quite explicit and by no means merely implied. The Puritan Edward Johnson spoke of New England as the place "where the Lord would create a new heaven and a new earth, new churches and a new commonwealth together." Jefferson's view on the high ground upon which America launched humanity's new beginning has already been cited. Thomas Paine captured the sentiment of the Founding Fathers and their entire generation more succinctly: "We have it in our power to begin the world over again." Even the seal boasted a conviction in America's purity and innocence. One of the Department of State's official publications on the history of the seal states that the colors of the pales or bands in the shield of the eagle are those used in the flag, and that the white signifies purity and innocence.

Of course, it would not be fair to claim that the founders of America were altogether innocent in their assumptions. In spite of their ideal of a new social order, the Puritans were not blinded by naive innocence. Theirs was not a naive realism that believed things are how they appear; or at least, given how things appeared *to them,* they did not perceive the world in a naive fashion. The pessimistic Calvinist view of human nature as fundamentally sinful and flawed grounded the Puritans in a sober realism. The cosmic forces of good and evil were seen to meet in the world as if upon a battlefield, and the human struggle, a struggle against human nature itself, was to beat a virtuous path through this battlefield. Righteousness was not given as a natural gift or blessing, but earned. Likewise, Jefferson was not unaware of the human propensity toward corruption, and he knew that a vigilant eye must be kept on the tendency of government to deteriorate and itself become corrupt: "In every government on earth is some trace of human weakness, some germ of corruption and degeneracy, which cunning will discover, and wickedness insensibly open, cultivate and improve." In any event, Jefferson had John Adams standing over his shoulder, balancing his optimism with a sober realism equal to that of any Puritan.

Nevertheless, any wish for a new world order was bound to be colored by innocence, by the imagination's longing for paradise. It was bound to be Edenlike, for there has *never* been a new order in the world that was peaceful and harmonious for very long. Even the Israelites didn't have the kind of order that the early Americans aspired toward. Strife and disharmony plagued the Kingdom of Israel from its inception, until the nation was finally divided into two and then conquered by the Babylonians, resulting in the exile of the Jews and their eventual worldwide dispersion. Given this kind of historical experience, some modern-day Orthodox Jews do not place great stock in the idea of a new order or even a modern state of Israel; only an apocalyptic and messianic event can bring about a truly alternative order. Whether in the form of a Christian, communist, or utopian state, ideas of a new social or world order have always been illusory and thereby often the cause of even greater disorder and suffering in the world. As the theologian Reinhold Niebuhr observed, "One interesting aspect of these illusions of 'new beginnings' in history is that they are never quite as new as is assumed, and never remain quite as pure as when they are new."

Even in their conception, their purity is questionable. The existential philosopher Nikolai Berdyaev had this to say about this subject (and it should be noted beforehand that his use of the adjective "world" is intended to mean "worldly" rather than "international"):

> World harmony is a false and an enslaving idea. One must get free from it for the sake of the dignity of personality. World harmony is also disharmony and disorder. The realm of world reason is also the world of the irrational and senseless. It is a false aestheticism which sees a world harmony. . . . Optimism about the world order is the servitude of man. Freedom from servitude is freedom from the crushing idea of world order which is the outcome of objectivization, that is to say, of the fall. The good news of the approach of the Kingdom of God is set in opposition to the world order. It means the end of the false harmony which is founded upon the realm of the common. The problem of theodicy is not solved by objectivizing thought in an objectivized world order. It is only solved on the existential plane where God reveals himself as freedom, love and sacrifice, where He suffers for man and strives together with man against the falsity and wrong of the world, against the intolerable suffering of the world.

Said otherwise, freedom cannot be confined to or defined by the idea of a worldly order, no matter how harmonious and peaceful the latter may aspire to be. Freedom that finds its ultimate expression in the social or collective order, in an object, rather than in the spiritual condition of the person, the subject, is not a complete freedom. Jesus and Buddha, for example, demonstrated their spiritual liberation by living among the poor and the suffering; the Buddha even died from food poisoning. The truly free person finds freedom amidst worldly conditions, and is not dependent upon them or upon their alteration or eradication.

If the idea of a new world order smacks of the innocence of the Garden of Eden, then Providence—a most mysterious and mystical idea when it is not used to explain every whim of nature or history as divine intervention—also easily lends itself to innocent pretensions. This invariably occurs when it is allied with the desire for a new order. It becomes the grounds for justifying any and all deeds that are deemed necessary in order to establish the new order. As the psychologist Rollo May said, the hallmark of innocence is to "always identify your self-interest with the design of Providence." We may add to the category of self-interest the interest of a cause one strongly believes in, regardless of the merit that that cause may have in and of itself. Using the idea of Providence to promote such interests has justified countless atrocities in history. The Crusades, the Inquisition, and the religious wars from 1550 to 1648 were just a few that preceded the American demonstrations of this tendency. In more recent times, Hitler proclaimed in a 1936 speech that "I go the way that Providence dictates for me with all the assurance of a sleepwalker."

America's examples of course begin with the genocide of the Indians, which the early generations of Americans believed was ordained by God in order to make way for the new inhabitants. Even Benjamin Franklin, who was known as a friend to the Indians, could not help but innocently wonder if God's hand were behind man's deeds: ". . . if it be the design of Providence to extirpate these savages in order to make room for cultivators of the earth, it seems not improbable that rum may be the appointed means. It has already annihilated all the tribes who formerly inhabited the sea-coast." (Franklin wrote this in connection with a commission that he was part of and that had given rum to the Indians in exchange for signing a treaty.) Providence and its natural corollary, Manifest Destiny, were blatantly used to justify the Mexican War, a war clearly provoked by the Americans in order to annex Mexican territories. In his protest song, "With God on Our Side," Bob Dylan sings with pathos about how confidently Americans enlisted God not only in the campaign against the Indians but in other wars bridging from the Spanish-American War to the Cold War. Indeed, in the Civil War, *both* sides claimed to have had God on their side.

The recruitment of the idea of Providence in such episodes shows how evil can disguise itself in and operate through innocence. One wills or resigns to stay innocent or is simply engulfed—as Hitler insinuated, asleep—in the innocence of his viewpoint, so that he does not or cannot see that something evil is being propagated. Often this type of innocence is the naive realism of *desire:* things appear the way one *wants* them to appear. Given the deceptive and seductive nature of this naive realism, the second of Buddha's Four Noble Truths teaches that desire is the cause of suffering. Certainly, it can easily and dangerously inspire us to use great ideas in the service of great lies. At other times, however, such innocence simply defies explanation. "Perhaps innocence is a greater mystery than evil," Hillman concludes.

The misuse of the idea of Providence is a practice that psychologically and spiritually enslaves man. It enslaves him to false ideas of God and the world. Berdyaev again had this to say about this problem:

> The world is not in such a state as justifies an optimistic doctrine of the action of divine providence in it. If everything is from God, and everything is directed by God towards happiness, if God acts in the

plague and in cholera and in tortures, in wars and enslavements, alike, the consequence, when thought out, must be to lead to the denial of the existence of evil and injustice in the world. The providence of God in the world, which in any case we admit only as an inexplicable mystery, is rationalized by theological doctrines, and that is always an affront both to the honour of God and to the dignity of man. It makes God appear always as an autocratic monarch, making use of every part of the world, of every individuality, for the establishment of the common world order, for the administration of the whole to the glory of God. This is held to be a justification of every injustice, every evil, every sorrow, of the parts of the world.

Precisely because Providence can be admitted "only as an inexplicable mystery," St. Augustine took great care in framing his thoughts on this subject. He wished to remove from history the element of irrational capriciousness, but at the same time he did not wish to eliminate the mystery of history or turn the idea of Providence into a device that explained history with perfect human hindsight, justifying every evil in the world. That God is active in history as the redeemer does not mean that he is the executor of a bureaucratic master plan. As the theologian W.H. Vanstone wrote, "The activity of God in creation must be precarious. It must proceed by no assured programme. Its progress, like every progress of love, must be an angular progress—in which each step is a precarious step into the unknown; in which each triumph contains a new potential of tragedy." The potential for tragedy, for wrong turns, for evil is part and parcel of the process of history, and a notion of Providence that removes this potential gives a false impression not only of history but of the mysterious ways God works in history. Vanstone adds that it is in the concrete and individual crises of human existence that we see the workings of God, that is, the "ever precarious creativity of the love of God." Because man's response to these crises and that love must be one of freedom, there can be no predetermined goal of Providence, be it "the good society," "the caring society," "the fulfillment of humanity," "personal development," or "happiness." There is thus nothing about Providence that manifests in a general, solid pattern or that one can predict, other than that it appears to be the expression of divine love.

In his first inaugural address, Jefferson famously described America as a nation dedicated to "acknowledging and adoring an overruling Providence, which by all its dispensations proves that it delights in the happiness of man here and his greater happiness hereafter. . . ." Clearly, this reflects the belief in a Providence that had solid proofs and that proceeded according to an assigned program or predetermined goal of human happiness. This belief had difficulty holding together the opposites of God and the evil in the world. The Calvinist sense of evil had been emptied from the Jeffersonian universe, and Providence in the latter indeed had an "overruling" quality in a way that it didn't quite have in the Puritan universe. To the Puritans, Providence stood over and against evil; to the Jeffersonians, there wasn't even a need for it to take such a position. One could argue that in the end Jefferson used Providence much the way absolute monarchs did, that is, to bolster the authority of the political order. The fact that he used it in favor of democracy and not autocracy simply made it more palatable.

And certainly, the clever way he wove it together with natural philosophy made it especially palatable. The incentive for this piece of fine stitchery Jefferson owed largely to his mentor, John Locke. Locke saw natural rights as derived from the law of nature, which in turn he saw as the will or "voice of God." Jefferson's idea of this is basically identical. To Jefferson, God primarily was, although not other than the God of Judaism and Christianity, the "Author of Nature." (In the Declaration of Independence, Jefferson referred to him as "Nature's God.") He was the Creator who made the earth. In the Jeffersonian cosmology, divine order manifested in and as natural order. Every fact of natural history and the natural environment revealed the Creator; to Jefferson, nature itself was revelation. It was the context of his faith, providing ample testimony of Providence and the purpose of the Creator. Providence here revolved around the notion of God as Provider through the gifts of nature and the splendors of the earth. The laws of nature were themselves the guiding hand of Providence, and thus to live in accord with these laws was to live by the will of God. Among these laws was the one that all men are created equal. Nature deemed this so because equality and freedom enable men to find their optimal place in its economy.

A hundred years before Darwin, Jefferson believed that the forces motivating human beings are natural, and that the society that promotes the fittest adaptation to these forces will be the healthiest. The principles of nature are a society's surest guide to attaining the good life—good not just materially, but morally. Nature is consummately skillful and balanced. It is complex but aesthetically pleasing and harmoniously ordered. It is efficient in its economy, making room for all its creatures and benevolently promoting their sustenance and well-being. "All the great laws of society," Thomas Paine said in Jeffersonian fashion, "are laws of nature." It was in no small measure for this reason that Jefferson was opposed to America departing from an agrarian way of life. To live removed from nature would obscure the experience of nature's overruling Providence. As for the larger purpose or design of the Creator, it was for man to energetically develop the resources of nature for his advancement in "Life, Liberty and the pursuit of Happiness." God's purpose for mankind was thus also naturally oriented. Needless to say, these ideas of divinity were well-suited to the continental task of the early American, and it has been said that Jefferson recast the image of God to suit this purpose.

Nevertheless, the Jeffersonian synthesis of natural philosophy and creationism can hardly be dismissed on the grounds of being merely utilitarian or even just the minority view of a few of the more philosophically-minded Founding Fathers. It may not have been a view unanimously held by all the Founding Fathers, but certainly it was the view that gave the Declaration of Independence its spiritual authority and set the tone of the American vision as the Founding Fathers saw it. It did so because it linked what was natural or "self-evident" to what was divinely willed. The Declaration of Independence states it to be self-evident that men are "endowed by their Creator with certain unalienable Rights." In an earlier draft of the Declaration, Jefferson asserts as "sacred & undeniable . . . that all men are created equal and independent." In other words, God's will for natural rights was as self-evident to the Founding Fathers as were the natural laws themselves. Democracy and Providence had been wed.

All this, of course, underscores Jefferson's legacy as one of history's great innovators of democracy. If there is an innocence in his use (or misuse) of the idea of Providence and in his grafting it together with nature, there is at least something to be said for the way this gave democracy a spiritual value. At least in the eyes of God, all men are created equal. In fact, everybody knows that men are *not* created equal. Some are more intelligent, others more gifted in diverse ways, and still others stronger and healthier. But in the eyes of God and the economy of nature, these are differences of no real consequence and only serve God's purpose in making nature more diverse and bountiful. Jefferson's genius was in reconciling thorny contradictions and making them appear nonexistent. The visible world as it appears, the world of nature, is much more conducive to the egalitarian spirit of democracy than the artificial, hierarchical world man creates based on his desires and vices. Boorstin has identified the basic feature of Jeffersonian thought as "an attempt to capture naiveté; to divest individual minds of their peculiarities that each might sense the visible universe with childish innocence. The large purpose was to save men from ideas and systems: to take them out of the cave where they saw nothing but the puppets of their own brains, into the open air where they could see the sensible objects which alone were real." This is as good a description of naive realism as one gets.

Jefferson's vision of a morally directed, new order of democracy buttressed by Providence is perhaps the most idealistic national vision in history. Only Marxism-Leninism, which has since passed into history because of its untenable idealism and assessment of human nature, is comparable in the degree and quality, if not the content, of the idealism. This may partly explain why the United States and the Soviet Union were at such great odds with each other: both were driven by intensely idealistic, messianic visions that were ideologically opposed to each other. The Soviet vision had an extremely idealistic core or foundation which could not hold up the weight of the pragmatic needs of the nation and the people. This is why it ultimately failed. The communist credo misjudged the factor of human motivation, failing to recognize that personal ambition not only outweighs ideals to serve the collectivity, but, if organized in a more or less moral, life-enhancing manner, is the *best way* to serve the collectivity. On the other hand, the American vision has an essentially pragmatic foundation with an idealistic overlay; this is, in spite of any overly optimistic illusions in its idealism, eminently more manageable.

This pragmatic foundation, the idea of natural rights, had its beginnings with the Greeks, but the particular theory of natural rights that the American vision is built upon comes from John Locke. The idealistic overlay upon this, the actual visionary component of the American vision, comes largely from Thomas Jefferson. Joseph Ellis writes:

[Jefferson's] several arguments for American independence all were shaped around a central motif, in which the imperfect and inadequate present was contrasted with a perfect and pure future, achievable once the sources of corruption were eliminated. . . .

The vision he projected in the natural rights section of the Declaration, then, represented yet another formulation of the Jeffersonian imagination. The specific form of the vision undoubtedly drew upon language Locke had used to describe the putative conditions of society before governments were established. But the urge to embrace such an ideal society came from deep inside Jefferson himself. It was the vision of a young man projecting his personal cravings for a world in which all behavior was voluntary and therefore all coercion unnecessary, where independence and equality never collided, where the sources of all authority were invisible because they had already been internalized. . . .

Though indebted to Locke, Jefferson's political vision was more radical than liberal, driven as it was by a youthful romanticism unwilling to negotiate its high standards with an imperfect world. . . . The American dream, then, is just that, the Jeffersonian dream writ large.

It seems that any way we turn the discussion, we find ourselves on the doorsteps of the spirit of youth.

## The Innocence of Humanism

I have already defined humanism as that tradition that, originally taking form through the Renaissance and the Enlightenment, expressed a rational faith that man is capable of self-fulfillment and ethical conduct without recourse to supernatural forces. Here I'd like to focus on the ways humanism shaped the thinking and the values of the Founding Fathers, particularly Thomas Jefferson. As Ellis pointed out, American idealism is Jefferson's idealism writ large. While it is true that the development of America was influenced by the views and temperaments of the Founding Fathers acting *together* in a creative tension and balance, it was Jefferson who most made an impression on the nation's idealistic vision and character. The influences on *him* in turn were very much those of the tradition of humanism.

The rise of humanism was a crucial chapter in Western intellectual history. The inquiry into man, nature, God, and the relationships between them was freed from the dogma of religion and theology and from prescientific, superstitious thinking. Reason replaced faith as the primary way of knowing, and the Age of Reason (or the Enlightenment) was born. With this, the modern era began. In the words of Kant, the Enlightenment represented "man's exodus from his self-imposed tutelage," that is, from his reliance upon external authority. Or, as the sociologist C. Wright Mills more recently said, the "central goal of Western humanism [was] . . . the audacious control by reason of man's fate." Man as opposed to God or the church became the source of authority on questions of truth and meaning; from this did humanism derive its name. With Auguste Comte, humanism even became a new religion of humanity, and humanity an object of devotion.

Given this departure from religious tradition, one of the first things to be thrown out the window by humanism was the doctrine of original sin. Man is born as a *tabula rasa* or blank slate. Innocent at birth, it is society that corrupts him. Rousseau's "Noble Savage" embodied the new original condition, and Voltaire's "Candide," the modern prototype of all Forrest

Gumps to come, exemplified the prelapsarian innocence which many people now wished to recapture. (It should be noted, however, that Voltaire was parodying this innocent's condition, not idealizing it.) The idea of the "natural man"—the ideal man who lives a balanced, harmonious existence—arose side by side with natural philosophy, itself an offshoot of the Enlightenment. This idea became alloyed in America with the notion of the rugged individualist, though individualism per se can also be traced to European humanism. Morality was removed from the fears of divine retribution and recast according to ethics such as those of Spinoza or to empirical principles such as Kant's categorical imperative. Man became the author of his moral code. This was not only liberating but, many now argue, too liberating, eventually resulting in complete moral relativism. This trend reached a critical point with Nietzsche, who insisted that man is ultimately free— "God is dead"—and that there is no absolute standard of truth outside human experience; truth is relative to the changing experience of man.

We are today the direct heirs of the humanist tradition. Jung believed that modern man's exclusive reliance on his power of reason has split him off from his instinctual, irrational side, leading to a psychic dissociation and such catastrophes as our two World Wars. The instinctual, irrational side that was once let in through the front door under the auspices of faith has now been forced to sneak around and break in through the back door with a vengeance. Pointing out our deviant use of rationalism and designating us today as "Voltaire's bastards," John Ralston Saul says much the same. The gift of reason that originally liberated us from the shackles of ignorance has now become a new form of tyranny. In becoming a closed system of methods and dictates that are devoid of values and common sense, reason has launched us into "headless abstraction" and "unending, meaningless battles."

The extermination of the Jews by the Nazis, as the extreme example of this, was conducted *systematically*, with cold, rational precision. What the political scientist Hannah Arendt described in that situation as the "banality of evil" was an evil that was *made* banal because, aided by the technology of the death camps, it was mechanized and sanitized of human contact, contact between the perpetrators and their victims. The architects of the "final solution" did not have to see the consequences of their designs. Thus, by defining the human being as a rational creature and making his relationship to the universe one-sidedly rational and abstract, the humanist tradition has ironically led to the exact opposite of what it wished for. Instead of a humanism, the world has, in the twentieth century, demonstrated an inhumanity and cruelty unparalleled in scope and kind at any other time. The

Austrian poet and playwright Franz Grillparzer said it well 150 years ago: "The ways of modern erudition: From humanism/through nationalism/ to brutalism." This progression—or rather, regression—goes *through* nationalism because the latter has, of course, been a vital source of identity and meaning since humankind first banded together in large groups. Although one might expect that with the rise of humanism, nationalism and the wars it fuels would have been assuaged, evidently the opposite is true. Nationalism now has the onus of supplying all by itself a meaning to existence that faith formerly supplied. However, in the final analysis, humanism makes catastrophes such as those of the twentieth century possible not because it breeds nationalism, or for that matter secularism or even moral relativity. Humanism makes possible every crime of humanity against humanity because it promotes the full development of the human being and his powers but with an innocence about his fullness, about his primitive, irrational side and his capacity for evil.

The soil from which the flower of modern civilization sprouted is the same soil in which the American nation has its foundational roots. Certainly, the liberal—or as Ellis points out, radical—vision of Jefferson was a humanistic vision. "The Enlightenment for Thomas Jefferson," explains the historian Andrew Burstein, "was a spirit of intellectual optimism. The Enlightenment thinkers saw the good in the human spirit, and Jefferson was most intoxicated by the idea that human beings possessed the potential to do remarkable good and that a government could be created which would tap into this spirit, into this impulse to do good." The vocabulary of Jefferson, like that of Voltaire and Locke before him, was inclined toward a simple, ungraded scale of good and evil. An evil leader was believed to be one who knowingly and intentionally used his power abusively. But this view did not take into account the way most evil acts would in fact occur in the humanist age, that is, innocently and with the naive realism that they *appeared* to be serving good causes. The road to hell that is paved with good intentions is by definition a humanist road.

Humanism's ideal of man as a "natural man" had strong repercussions on Jefferson's thinking, as did natural philosophy as a whole. It has been argued that Jefferson was seduced by natural philosophy. His apotheosis of the natural had two notable effects. Firstly, it limited his view of society, a view which, like his idealism in general, became very much America's own. His sense of community was less concerned with traditions, institutions, and values than with instincts, needs, and physical health. Again, the continental task and the nation's spirit of youth were served well with this. Secondly, Jefferson's emphasis on the natural clearly responded to the question of natural rights, but it shed no light on the question of social duties. As Boorstin writes, "His 'natural rights' theory of government left all men naturally free from duties to their neighbors: no claims could be validated except by the Creator's plan, and the Creator seemed to have made no duties but only rights." Boorstin adds that slavery was an example of how Jefferson's political theory faltered when society had to affirm positive moral values. The theory made it explicit that slavery was a violation of God-given rights, but it could not articulate the appropriate, dutiful response "because it had left the moral ends of the human community vaguely implicit in nature." One sees the same shortcoming regarding the articulation of social responsibilities in Locke's thought as well. He asserted that natural law would enable man to develop "a body of ethics . . . teaching all the duties of life," yet he never made a serious effort to elaborate such a code.

Jefferson's idealism was permeated with the innocence of humanism. The principles of "Life, Liberty and the pursuit of Happiness" are at the core of the American creed. Every American believes in them. However, so much of what makes them believable is not only that they appeal to our human innocence but that they appeal in a charming, innocent way. Jefferson, in the Declaration of Independence, articulated these principles at a sufficiently abstract level and with a rhapsodic, inspirational quality so that no one would notice that they are unattainable and mutually exclusive or contradictory. "Perfect freedom," Ellis asserts, "doesn't lead to perfect equality; it usually leads to inequality." He adds that the truths of the Declaration of Independence are "in some sense nice representations of Jefferson's personality, wishing to be above it all and concealing the contradictions." This may be true but should not be allowed to detract from the fact that Jefferson's personality was informed by the times he lived in just as he himself informed those times. The principles he glorified and the way he glorified them were, in hindsight, typically humanistic. To be above it all and to conceal contradictions were also prevailing tendencies of the humanism blossoming in Jefferson's day.

# Chapter 12

## Jefferson's Bastards

*Nothing can indeed be more remote (except in pure imagery) from distinctively* human *attributes, or from the spontaneous life of man, than this sleek and comely Adamic condition, provided it should turn out an abiding one: because man in that case would prove a mere dimpled nursling of the skies, without ever rising into the slightest Divine communion or fellowship, without ever realising a truly Divine manhood and dignity.*

—Henry James, Sr.

### The Diffusion of the American Vision

On the occasion of his visit to America in the last quarter of the nineteenth century, Thomas Huxley addressed a group of Americans as follows: "I cannot say that I am in the slightest degree impressed by your bigness, or your material resources, as such. Size is not grandeur, and territory does not make a nation. The great issue, about which hangs a true sublimity, and the terror of overhanging fate, is what are you going to do with all these things? What is to be the end to which these are to be the means? . . . Truly America has a great future before her; great in toil, in care, and in responsibility; great in true glory if she be guided in wisdom and righteousness; great in shame if she fail." Huxley, coming from England, a nation with a strong sense of destiny, understood how important these questions and concerns are for the fate of America. Evidently, he had his doubts about how well Americans understood their importance.

In the practical sphere, the American vision has a long way to go to realize those possibilities which are attainable. Certainly, by historical standards, the institutional practice of democracy in America reads like a success story, and inasmuch as America has spearheaded the cause of democracy in the world, it has helped to promote a more egalitarian way for humans to govern themselves. But the larger and spiritual ramifications of the American vision remain as elusive today as they did in the days of the founders, if not more so. The founders were hoping to create a society and civilization on the level of Israel, Greece, and Rome—a great society and civilization. Their ideas about a New Order of the Ages and Providence may have been innocent, but the cultural and moral advancement of humanity as exemplified by these ancient civilizations should not be deemed an improper or unrealistic goal in and of itself. Of course, it is an idealistic goal, but striving toward great ideals is what made the founders the heroic figures that they were.

The diffusion of the American vision has occurred hand-in-hand with the diffusion of the American heroic ideal at large. Both the vision and the heroic ideal have become diluted in the culture and distorted from their original conceptions. Today the national vision is still given much lip service, but most of the direct focus upon it takes place in the sphere of international politics, where America can exercise its role as a world leader and advocate of democracy. It is easier to crusade abroad than to implement genuine advancement at home.

The diffusion of the American vision can be observed in the various ways it has fallen out of focus in the mindset of the nation. It has become peripheral and sublimated in the culture. If one imagines the vision to be a vehicle such as a car, it is as if the axle has been removed and the wheels have gone off in directions of their own. The *themes* of the American vision continue with a life of their own, but disconnected from a structure that unifies them and mobilizes them in a direction that has purpose. Not only has the cohesion of the vision been lost in this process, but the themes have become transformed, indeed, transmogrified, so that they no longer mean what they originally meant. A kind of fundamentalism has developed as these dissociated wheels or themes have given rise to cults in their own right; the themes have become idealized in a reductive, simplistic manner that was not intended in the original context of the vision, and yet they continue to exert a major influence on the culture. Eric Voegelin has studied the process that occurs when the vision of a society, as originally represented in the symbols of its political tradition, goes off-track; he has appropriately called this process "derailment." Since the vision is a vital constituting factor of the society's identity and character, its derailment can lead to the disintegration of the society. This chapter will look at how such a derailment is happening today in America.

## The Cult of Novelty

The idea that newness means renewal or regeneration is an age-old motif known by all civilizations and cultures dependent upon the seasonal cycles of winter and spring. These cycles signaled the death and rebirth of not only the earth's fertility but, it was believed, the earth itself. Newness here, however, was predictable because it regularly repeated. The specific idea of newness as change or progress, that is, that tomorrow can be completely new and different from today, seems to have originated, in Western civilization, with the Hebrews. It is upon this latter and rather radical idea of newness that America was founded. America was conceived as a clean break from the past, a paean to progress. "Our national birth," the *Democratic Review* boldly stated in 1839, "was the beginning of a new history . . . which separates us from the past and connects us with the future only." Or, as D.H. Lawrence poetically put it, America "starts old, old, wrinkled and writhing in an old skin. And there is a gradual sloughing off of the old skin, towards a new youth." The movement from the old European consciousness towards golden youth, Lawrence suggests, is the "true myth of America."

From its very beginnings, the American venture was permeated with *adventure,* with the challenge and conquest of the unknown. Everything was new. Even the continent was new in that nature was perceived as operating with a freshness that was unknown in Europe. New races, new species, and new foods and consumable items (for example, corn and tobacco) were evidence that America was indeed an altogether New World, and not only in the social and political sense. Socially and politically, of course, places with names like New England, New Hampshire, and New York signified a new beginning for the human race. America was to be the land of de Crèvecoeur's "new man" and of the New Order of the Ages. In declaring the United States a new nation with new grounds for existence (i.e., natural rights), Jefferson merely formalized the already deep-seated conviction that the American enterprise was not only novel, but *about* novelty. The idea that everything in America is to be new is thus part of the genesis and character of the nation.

The formalization of novelty as an integral part of the American experience has made it a regular cultural fixture, a perennial style, as opposed to merely an appreciation for new things that eventually mature, settle, and age, as most new things do. Novelty has become a value esteemed for its own sake, a cult of permanent potential. In this regard, the cult of novelty is closely related to the cult of motion and speed: constant change and newness are common to both, so that one might be inclined to conclude that the two cults are really one and the same. Certainly, they feed off and exacerbate each other, but they are different tendencies with different origins. The cult of novelty is not dependent upon technology nor connected with the rise of industry. It is more concerned with the freshness of things and the youthful innocence of optimism than with excitement, movement, and the thrill of attaining great heights.

One sees the glorification of novelty where motion and speed are held in no special regard and are even suspect, as in the case of Jefferson himself, for example. He more than once insinuated that a new revolution may be needed to oust the Federalists, whom, because of their monarchial, centralist approach to government, he came to believe had betrayed the American Revolution. When he finally defeated them after much struggle in the presidential election of 1800, he conceived of his victory as the second American Revolution: "The revolution of 1800 was as real a revolution in the principles of our government as that of 1776 was in its form. We can no longer say there is nothing new under the sun. For this whole chapter in the history of man is new. The great extent of our republic is new. Its sparse habitation is new. The mighty wave of public opinion which has rolled over it is new." Novelty in Jefferson's mind was an indication of authenticity because it was not only a departure from old, static forms but an initiator of the future. If the first Revolution had failed to complete the transition from the old and the past to the new and the future, then Jefferson's loyalties would be to a second revolution. His famous remark about wanting to see "a little rebellion now and then" was also an exaltation of novelty and a goad to keep the spirit of democracy fresh.

Because Jefferson judged men more by their destiny than by their history, the novelty of the future was more important to him than the knowledge or deeds of the past. "I like the dreams of the future," he confessed in a letter to John Adams, "better than the history of the past." His belief in the rights of the current generation over the binding laws, traditions, and institutions of former generations amounted to a pronouncement that the earth was for the living and not the dead, and that claims to property and the wealth of the land should not be an inherited right. (Madison, though very much the protégé of Jefferson, made sure that such socially unenforceable views never found their way into the Constitution; a nation, he believed, could not redefine its institutions with each new generation.)

Jefferson's preference for the new was also reflected in his approach to education, which emphasized knowledge that is of immediate use in the practical spheres of life and in the mastery of the new continental task. Even the value he placed on the ancient classics was more aimed at preparing the student for civil and active life than at enriching his interior life or personal consciousness. Jefferson faced the future in a thoroughly modern way, curiously unaffected by the ancients whose wisdom had so nourished him. The Greeks did not anticipate the novelty of the future with the same eagerness as modern man, since they did not see themselves as facing the future. Rather, they saw the future as coming upon them from behind their backs, with the past receding away before their eyes. This is as plausible a metaphor for the human experience of time as ours, since the past is visible and the future is not. Of course, we moderns prefer the forward view of the future because we feel it positions and prepares us for the unknown and allows us to engage our free will in an active-creative manner. But in truth, our ability to respond to the future in modern times has not been any more enhanced by this position. Perhaps this position has even handicapped us, for if anything, it has made us forgetful of the past and thus more innocent.

New beginnings in American politics have occurred with some regularity since Jefferson's time. Novelty has become a style whose appeal to the American imagination politicians can count on if the timing is right. Schlesinger's cycles of American history show that a national mood favoring novelty or change comes and goes in an almost predictable pattern. The Jacksonian revolution, the Reconstruction, Roosevelt's New Deal, Kennedy's New Frontier and his call for a new generation of leadership, Bush's new world order, and Clinton's New Covenant were all new beginnings that offered new dreams of the future and that occurred when this mood was ripe. American culture, too, is continually upgraded with new products, new technologies, new movements, new ages, new science-fiction futures, new religions and ways of life, and new hobbies and adventures; as long as they're new, they're good. Today we even have a "new economy" and "new media"—among the latter, the sensationalist entertainment media that, in contrast to the established newspapers and networks, specialize in inventing news regardless of how false or superficial. The infatuation with novelty goes with the condition of innocence; it is innocence in quest of identity. But as soon as innocence finds or creates some sense of identity, it moves on to something new in order to preserve its basic condition of innocence or freshness. "Americans," Melville said, "are still engaged in inventing what it is to be an American. That is at once an exhilarating and a painful occupation." His observation is as true today as it was in the nineteenth century.

The perpetual consumption of novelty may feed the spirit of eternal youth, but its effect on the nation is not without a high cost. Because nothing human can in fact stay young forever, including nations and civilizations, this form of addiction to youth forces an awkward aging process upon the nation. An individual who refuses to age gracefully and tries too hard to look younger than his years actually looks older because he draws attention to his age in an unbecoming way. If he also acts in ways that are too young for his years, his immaturity will be increasingly apparent. Again, there is a difference between being youthful and being too young: the former invigorates, the latter arrests. This irony of individual behavior may be observed in collective behavior as well. America suffers from a kind of cultural progeria in which oldness and tiredness are actually amplified because of the fixation with youth and novelty. Progeria is a genetic disorder characterized by premature and rapid aging. Children with this disorder look like old men and women and often die in their adolescence.

Nothing exemplifies cultural progeria more clearly than American cities. Cities evolve differently in America than in Europe. Too often buildings come to have an ugly appearance in a few generations, rarely acquiring that elegant, antique quality that they have in European cities. Modern architecture can be aesthetically pleasing, though too often it is either obsessed with erecting glass boxes or is compromised by the bottom line of functionality and cost-effectiveness. The continuous thrust of novelty without foresight or planning has left many American cities overdeveloped and without charm. Some have not been well maintained, since the emphasis has been more on new developments than on keeping up or improving what already exists. The infrastructures of these cities—their streets, transportation systems, parks, etc.—have been allowed to decay to a point that makes their use unpleasant. To cite but one example, New York City, for all its beauty in many regards, has huge spreads of urban terrain that look and feel old, gray, and decayed. The recent decline in the quality of American urban life has pushed people to the suburbs, but here too the cult of novelty has suppressed the gradual sculpting of environments that has given residential neighborhoods elsewhere in the world and even in former times in America their special character. The cookie-cutter homes and strip malls of modern suburbs make the latter all look opulently but drearily alike.

The cult of novelty does not allow things to ferment and simmer, to take root and grow in a slow, complex, textured way. It does not allow the culture to cultivate and become refined. Only the new carries value and the conviction of identity, and thus, when the culture periodically gets saturated with novelty, it turns to nostalgia and makes *it* a new fad and form of identity. This is observable in films like *American Graffiti*, in the love of old automobiles that become collector's items, and in political trends such as the one during the Reagan years, when the nation yearned to return to an earlier America and looked to that president for familiar reassurances. Fads shape the culture in America more than anywhere else. Adam Gopnik of *The New Yorker* points out how things in France have staying power. Chez Luis in Paris is the same restaurant today with the same food as it was 50 years ago. But Chez Luis in New York will only last as long as its patrons support it, and that may not be very long at all.

Novelty may be alluring, but is so mercurial and transient that what it creates gives only a fleeting satisfaction. America has developed few great artisanal traditions like those of other cultures. There is little that is comparable to fine French and Belgian tapestry, Oriental carpets, Persian tiles and illuminated books, Venetian glass, Arabian marquetry, Spanish leatherwork, Chinese porcelain and embroidery, Japanese lacquer, Viennese brocade, or West African masks and bronze castings. America's predilection for novelty has enabled it to excel at technology and such new art forms as jazz, filmmaking, and modern art and architecture, but for the most part, its aesthetic sensibilities remain too young and are sorely lacking in imagination, exuberance, and magic.

## The Cult of Freedom

In America, "freedom" is a holy word that has come to mean all things to all people. It is regarded as the core principle upon which the nation was founded, the raison d'être of the American Revolution and republic. Americans have fought and died for this principle, used it to justify their role as policeman of the world, and generally paraded it before disempowered peoples and totalitarian regimes as the *summum bonum* of political and social life. In the Civil War, Americans even fought and killed each other over this principle. However, as discussed in an earlier chapter, the United States was founded on a much narrower concept of freedom than many people think. The kind of freedom the Founding Fathers initially sought consisted of basic liberties in connection with the ownership and protection of property. The freedom of religion, of speech and press, and of the other early amendments to the Constitution were *amendments* precisely because the concept and practice of freedom needed to be broadened. Even then, these freedoms were not extended to slaves and indentured servants.

Given this original starting point, the broadening of the concept of freedom to the status it has today, where it means practically nothing because it means everything, has been quite a leap. Although the innocence and freedom of the 1960s did not survive beyond that decade per se, they have infiltrated the culture in other ways. An excessive sense of entitlement or privilege has become pervasive. People say "it's a free country" not to express their belief in a practice of democracy in which they define and meet their obligations to society as conscious, self-determined citizens, but to express their belief in the primacy of self-gratification. Indeed, they seem to feel that society and life itself are obliged *to them,* to help *them* in their pursuit of self-gratification. One can observe this not only in the corruption of the social welfare system, but in all areas of society. Education in America has been almost totally derailed by catering to this impulse. Not only does society give unprecedented prestige to university degrees that guarantee large incomes as opposed to knowledge, but the fields that are deemed as worthy of large incomes are all too often not those that enhance the democratic quality of society. Why, for all the lip service given to the needs of children and the importance of building a strong America for the future, do high school teachers with 20 years of experience earn less than recent MBA or law school graduates? Are the services they provide less valuable, or the skills needed for their jobs less demanding?

People today believe that they are free to do whatever they like, as long as they are not harming anybody. But there is a huge gulf between the obligation to not harm anybody and the obligation of meaningful service to society or to other human beings. In Greece, the height of personal freedom was seen as the voluntary pursuit of social duty or responsibility, namely, philanthropy, understood here not in the modern sense of charity but in its original sense as "love of man" (*philanthropia*). Today there are two kinds of freedom that are predominant in America: one is political freedom or liberty, which supposedly has an ethical dimension, and the other is a prelapsarian or paradisaic freedom, a make-believe condition in which things require no effort or have no cost. The latter is characterized by the mentality that life should be easy and gratifying, that the way of least effort is the best way, that getting a free ride or something for nothing is a good deal. If anything, this kind of freedom is defined by negation—by what it is *not*, by what you *don't* have to do and what *isn't* expected from you. Indeed, it is so passive that it is practiced with utter unconsciousness and goes unrecognized for the regression to the Adamic condition that it is. It places no ethical demands or responsibilities upon citizens. Thus, political freedom and paradisaic freedom are contradictory, or at least, they should be. The first represents the original starting point of the American venture, and the second a subsequent point at which contemporary American culture has arrived. How did this transition happen, and how is it that these contradictory freedoms can coexist?

The truth of the matter is that if paradisaic freedom wasn't prevalent at the outset of the American enterprise, the factors that made it an eventual certainty were. When Jefferson and the framers of the Constitution established the American model of political freedom almost exactly upon the precepts of Locke's liberalism, they could not foresee that these precepts would play out in history in a way that would insidiously promote paradisaic freedom. Locke's doctrine of property—the central and most characteristic part of his teaching—is like a rock thrown into a pond: its effects permeate the body politic like rippling waves. According to this doctrine, the innate, natural rights to self-preservation and happiness are contingent upon the ownership of property; property assures self-preservation and happiness. In fastening self-preservation and happiness to the ownership of property, Locke has materially and quantitatively qualified the meaning of well-being. Furthermore, because people "must be allowed to pursue their happiness, nay, cannot be hindered," it also goes to say that the ownership of an unlimited amount of property is a natural right. With the invention of money, the concept of property was revolutionized, so that man may now "rightfully and without injury, possess more than he himself can make use of." This framework defines the purpose of freedom in very narrow yet radical terms. The political philosopher Leo Strauss writes:

> Locke's teaching on property, and therewith his whole political philosophy, are revolutionary not only with regard to the biblical tradition but with regard to the philosophic tradition as well. Through the shift of emphasis from natural duties or obligations to natural rights, the individual, the ego, had become the center and origin of the moral world, since man—as distinguished from man's end—had become that center or origin. . . .
>
> Locke is a hedonist: "That which is properly good or bad, is nothing but barely pleasure or pain." But his is a peculiar hedonism: "The greatest happiness consists" not in enjoying the greatest pleasures but "in the having those things which produce the greatest pleasures". . . . Since there are therefore no pure pleasures,

there is no necessary tension between civil society as the mighty leviathan or coercive society, on the one hand, and the good life, on the other: hedonism becomes utilitarianism or political hedonism. The painful relief of pain culminates not so much in the greatest pleasures as "in the having those things which produce the greatest pleasures." Life is the joyless quest for joy.

In other words, Locke's liberalism, by making the right to acquire property—"those things which produce the greatest pleasures"—the cornerstone of happiness, has set as the chief goal of freedom the exercise of that right. Jefferson made that even more explicit when in the Declaration of Independence he used the phrase "the pursuit of happiness" to connote the conventional third right—the right to acquire property—that Locke memorialized in his *Second Treatise on Government.*

It is not hard to see how this liberalism has made possible the rise of a hedonistic culture. Not only did it leave social responsibilities undefined and nurture an idealistic belief that political freedom would alone be sufficient for establishing a sound national character, but then this political freedom was defined in a rigid way that made natural rights practically a religious creed. As Strauss indicated, the individual, the ego, became the center and origin of the moral world, and the purpose of human existence became service to this individual ego. Natural philosophy apotheosized natural rights, and humanism apotheosized the individual and the individual's rights. In such a worldview, the urge toward happiness and the pursuit of happiness assume the character of an absolute right, and the well-being of the individual can easily be pursued at the expense of the well-being of the people, that is, public happiness or the common good. Certainly, this absolute right to happiness leaves the individual unrelated to the concerns of society at large.

There is nothing new in this claim that, in America, the freedom of natural rights is rigid, or that this freedom has been conducive to the rise of a culture of self-gratification. Murray Levin writes:

> With conservatism and socialism absent, with aristocrats and proletarians absent, America developed a political ethos unique to the West—a unanimous Lockean liberalism, a liberal way of life, a massive middle class society—bourgeois to the core—which has never been seriously threatened by extremist political movements of any magnitude. Facing no serious opposition, this liberalism could only become unanimous. It could only become the totality of our political consciousness—a unanimity—strengthened over time

and reinforced by generations who knew of no other tradition. This Lockean liberalism could *only* become an enormously powerful nationalism—an American way of life and unconquerable giant—which, like most totalisms, became over time, dogmatic, compulsive, rigid, visceral, aggressive, unconquerable domestically, and militant abroad.

And then there is the political scientist Louis Hartz, who fingered Lockean liberalism as the source of what Tocqueville first observed as the venturous conservatism and unidimensionality of the American. These traits are not only the results of what Tocqueville feared as democracy's dangerous tendency of promulgating enslavement to public opinion. When a prosperity-oriented, Lockean liberalism becomes fulfilled, it flips into an opposite orientation of conservatism. John Kenneth Galbraith commented that "One of the reasons that liberals in our time have been reduced in power . . . is that government, through social security, through public services, through one benefit or another, has made a very large number of people comfortable, happy, and conservative." But it is not only liberal government that has done this. It is liberal democracy as a whole. "Surely then," Hartz ponders, "it is a remarkable force, this fixed, dogmatic liberalism of a liberal way of life. It is the secret root from which have sprung many of the most puzzling of American cultural phenomena."

The cult of freedom is a fundamentalism of Locke's liberalism on the one hand and the individualistic libertarianism that it has fostered on the other. Of course, it is not Locke's thought per se that is fundamentalist—after all, it provided the blueprint for one of the finest systems of government in the world—but rather the canonization of and narrow subscription to it. There are many illustrations of how this has created a social environment that allows indulgent liberties, that is, liberties that do not recognize necessity and limits. One that is especially telling occurred in 1996 when a New York judge threw out evidence that police had seized when they searched an African-American man who had behaved suspiciously when they approached. They found drugs in his car. The judge claimed that the police searched without due cause, since it is entirely normal for a black man to fear and flee from white police officers in that particular neighborhood. The case caused a national uproar, and both New York State Governor Pataki and President Clinton responded with harsh criticism, the former threatening to remove the judge from the judicial circuit. Civil libertarians in turn responded with alarm that the freedom of judges will be infringed upon if they fear governmental interference in their decision-making.

A similar case six months later and in the same city involved a high school student who was suspended for going to school with a loaded gun. The suspension was overturned by the court. A safety officer at the school had found the gun after spotting a bulge in the student's jacket, and the judge ruled that the bulge was not a probable cause to search and threw out the evidence. The Parents Coalition for Education and Mayor Giuliani protested the decision, but of course, to no avail. Listen to the logic of this decision as explained by the student's attorney: "The fact is, the school security guard did not have a reasonable basis to search the student. The fact that he found a gun after the fact does not mean that he had at the time he observed the student a reasonable basis to stop the student."

Such incidents show how a rigid interpretation of natural rights perverts freedom so that those with criminal behaviors can go free under the guidelines of the Constitution. The recurring use of the word "fact" in the attorney's explanation is not just legal double talk. It speaks to a naive realism that places greater value on the *appearance* of things—the bulge in the student's jacket or, in the first case, the black man's suspicious behavior in a white neighborhood—than on the *meaning* or *value* of things. Strauss has appropriately made the distinction between facts and values a launch point for his study, *Natural Right and History*. We can gather from his treatment of this subject why there exists today a confusion around what constitutes "common sense." Is "common sense" a scientific understanding of facts (the appearance of things), or is it the interpretation of what these facts mean according to value judgments on truth, justice, the good life, and so forth? Cases such as the above hinge upon this question. Attacking the notion of value-free relativism in Weber's thought and its influence on the twentieth-century approach to social reality, Strauss states: "The rejection of value judgments endangers historical [and we may add, all social] objectivity. In the first place, it prevents one from calling a spade a spade. In the second place, it endangers that kind of objectivity which legitimately requires the forgoing of [subjective] evaluations, namely, the objectivity of interpretation." In other words, objective truth is a picture that must be *ascertained,* and is not always self-evident in the facts that comprise that picture. Certainly, the above cases show that when truth or common sense is confined to legal categories based on facts alone, morality, authority, and freedom are undermined.

Of course, the freedom that is undermined is the freedom or natural rights of the people, of the commonwealth. Society as a whole suffers while the individual in such cases gets off scot-free. It is in response to this issue of balancing the individual's right with the people's right that judges like Harold Rothwax are advocating a change in America's criminal justice system. At what point does society determine that the individual's rights must be limited because the preservation of those rights is exacting an unfair toll on the well-being of other people or society at large? This is precisely the question at the heart of the stormy debate around the Religious Freedom Restoration Act (RFRA), to cite a final example of the abuse of freedom. This piece of legislation was aimed at assuring that the government shall not burden the individual's exercise of religion. Specifically, its purpose was to restore the individual's constitutional right to practice his or her religious beliefs when this right had been infringed upon by the government. The situations in which this had occurred and which had prompted this legislation were mostly employment-related. Prior to its passage in 1993, there was some debate on preventing prison inmates from using this law inappropriately, but somehow there was nothing incorporated into the language of the act that addressed this issue.

Of course, once it was passed, the prison population jumped on this law as if it were a bandwagon. Prisoners all across the nation began to insist on their right, for example, to have overnight visits by their spouses with special provisions for them to have sex because their religions obligated them to procreate. Prisons saw a mushrooming of cult practices with all kinds of official liturgies because prisoners demanded these as their natural right. The courts became backlogged with litigation cases brought by prisoners against the government, all at the taxpayer's expense. Those in favor of RFRA defended it on the grounds that religion is not only a right but is rehabilitative for prisoners and thus good for society. Of course, who could argue against that? However, when the individual uses that right to manipulate society in costly ways there is another issue at stake. Even Locke would have agreed that individual rights should not violate common sense or the common good; there are not only natural rights, but natural limits, including to tolerance. In this situation, this would probably mean that the freedom of prisoners to express their religious preferences would not be the same as that of employees; prison by definition is a restriction of freedom. Needless to say, this argument is not to be used in support of returning to the formerly conventional practice of denying prisoners some semblance of decency within prison walls; it is merely to state the obvious, to state what is common sense.

Freedom is a complex problem, and as society itself becomes increasingly complex, the complexity of this problem will magnify. Freedom that is thought of as a simple, absolute principle that need not be adapted to changing times and circumstances will inevitably find itself in a quagmire when confronted with issues that are not black and white. The bioethical questions raised not only by abortion but also euthanasia and genetic engineering are just one example. Another is gun control. Americans in key regards still conceive of natural rights in the framework of the eighteenth century, but today's world and its problems are far removed from that time. Even a conservative like President Nixon privately expressed the view that the right to bear arms is absurd today because what was deemed a vital liberty in revolutionary America is not a vital liberty in modern America. Indeed, the restriction of firearms that would have been an infringement upon liberty 225 years ago may be a necessity for liberty in today's crime-infested society. Here again, a doctrine of natural rights without a doctrine of social responsibilities can hinder freedom more than help it.

When the individual's rights are considered in a vacuum without the larger social context to which they pertain, without a measure of that individual's responsibilities to and effects upon others, freedom loses that moral ingredient that makes a democracy work and hold together. The same may be said about corporate rights and responsibilities. The excessive liberties extended to corporations to protect their rights or "special interests" take no less a toll upon society than the excessive liberties extended to individuals; in fact, they take a far greater toll. Corporate abuses occur in a wide range of categories, spanning from the environment and public health to business practices like profiteering and tax evasion through special investments, write-offs, and shelters, so-called "corporate welfare." Many of the liberties granted to corporations in the name of economic productivity undermine democracy by promoting antisocial freedoms, that is, the freedom to act irresponsibly. What Diderot said in regard to the individual is just as applicable in the case of the corporation: "The means for enriching oneself may be criminally immoral, although permitted by the law."

Freedom that is disconnected from the moral world that raises human passions and ambitions to some level of dignity leads to a Hobbesian or Machiavellian world. We end up living like animals in the jungle or like soldiers of fortune for whom only conquest counts and the ends justify the means. These two types of freedom—Hobbesian and Machiavellian—merge together at some point, so similar are their basic orientations. An enlightened citizenry capable of self-government requires a different type of freedom, a dignified freedom that is not a cult of purely instinctual and self-serving behaviors but a disciplined practice. Democracy, as the political thinker Michael Sandel writes, requires the individual to be related to the civic realm as a "situated self," obligated by and fulfilled through a web of meaningful social relations and activities. America, Sandel argues, has gotten away from this original conception of democracy and has become a "procedural republic" as opposed to one of substance. Individual choices have been vastly expanded, but without regard for the moral character of the particular choices individuals make in how they lead their lives. Society engages in little or no reflection upon itself, and political discourse is more concerned with the private vices of public officials than with public issues. And, with its basis in the acquisition of property or material goods, the American economy is bound to be morally neutral and oriented toward self-gratification, that is, at odds with the civic conception of freedom. Keynes expressed its formative principle well: "Consumption . . . is the sole end and object of all economic activity."

Freedom, in the end, is itself a great responsibility. Rights may be natural, but democracy has to be created and nurtured. The demands placed upon citizens in a democracy are much greater than those in a monarchy or any other form of government. As the journalist P.J. O'Rourke said, "Freedom is its own punishment."

## The Cult of Happiness

I have already stated that what Jefferson had in mind when he advocated the "pursuit of happiness" was different than the meaning it has acquired today. The intent of Locke—from whom Jefferson directly borrowed this idea in formulating the Declaration of Independence—was the pursuit of public happiness or well-being, that is, the creation of a republic which enables humans to thrive. Other Enlightenment thinkers such as Montesquieu and Voltaire also spoke of happiness in terms of general, social well-being. Later Jeffersonian language such as "the happiness of the species" or "the happiness of mankind" referred to material prosperity and survival power. The word "happiness" was not by and large used in the humanistic sense to connote the individual's happiness or well-being, and certainly it was not used in the simple, hedonistic sense that signifies the individual's attainment of pleasure.

Nevertheless, the purely political and the purely collective were not the sole measures by which Jefferson understood happiness. As aptly pointed out by Clay Jenkinson, a performance artist who impersonates Jefferson, the latter appreciated happiness in a much broader sense than this. Happiness to Jefferson implied "a life of friendship, a life of love and family, grandchildren, gardening, good food, good wine, good conversation, correspondence with absent friends, a love of the arts, music, architecture, dance, literature. In a sense, happiness for Jefferson means finding the art of living without intrusions by institutions that might get in the way of that." So happiness to Jefferson was connected not only to self-preservation but to self-improvement. It was a type of personal fulfillment in the form of a meaningful, healthy life of culture and character. Jefferson implicitly understood this to be the good life, and saw it as the basis of public happiness or well-being. It had the added if unintended benefit of serving as a social nexus, of placing the individual as a "situated self" in a social context. And as far as this personal fulfillment went, Jefferson was not under the modern-day illusion that it was either an entitlement or permanently maintainable: "Perfect happiness, I believe, was never intended by the Deity to be the lot of any one of his creatures in this world. The most fortunate of us frequently meet with calamities which may greatly afflict us, and to fortify our minds against the attacks of these misfortunes should be one of the principal studies and endeavors of our lives." In other words, inner reflection and a philosophical disposition were more enduring and reliable to Jefferson than the fleeting fortunes of life.

The cults of happiness, freedom, and prosperity all give rise to and guarantee the existence of each other. The most basic and historically influential in this American trinity is prosperity, since the ownership of property and material goods—the index of prosperity—was and still is the defining principle of the American dream. It thus defines, in the American scheme, what constitutes freedom and happiness. Accordingly, the pursuit of happiness originally meant, to a large extent, the pursuit of material comfort. This drive was reinforced by the experience of conquering the wild American continent and frontier. The struggle against the harshness of life fueled the desire for material comforts. As a result, Americans today still seek to defend themselves against the suffering of life by imposing upon it a buffer of physical comforts. This they vaguely define as "happiness."

Of course, there is nothing wrong with making life comfortable and with eliminating needless suffering. But as with all cults, the cult of comfort-seeking has taken on a life of its own and has created an impression that life should be all comfort and no pain. The gist of this cult is a denial and avoidance of the inherent suffering of life—suffering that is inescapable because it is existential, that is, built into the structure of the universe as humans experience it. This suffering includes not only illness, tragedy, and death but all the undermining and annoying, minor frustrations of life, what Buddha described as *duhkha* and referred to in his First Noble Truth when he said, "Life is suffering." Existential suffering at heart is the suffering of meaninglessness and of the struggle to find meaning in the face of illness, tragedy, death, and the frustrations of life. The drive to avoid this suffering amounts to an effort to cheat life. This explains the illegitimate suffering that secretly underlies the pseudo-happiness of Americans and takes form in the variety of neuroses that sends them in increasing numbers to the psychotherapist's office. Too many Americans lead comfortable but quiet lives of desperation. The sociologist Philip Slater comments on "the contrast between the sullen faces of real people and the vision of happiness television offers: men and women ecstatically engaged in stereotyped symbols of fun—running through fields, strolling on beaches, dancing and singing. Americans know from an early age how they are supposed to look when happy and what they are supposed to do or buy to be happy. But for some reason their fantasies are unrealizable and leave them disappointed and embittered." Tocqueville made a similar observation over a century earlier, well before the invention of TV.

The cult of happiness is also closely related, if not now identical, to the cult of passion, which has come into play as the pursuit of happiness progressively became a pursuit of diminishing returns. As the cultural understanding of happiness gradually shifted from the kind of personal fulfillment Jefferson valued to the self-gratification of modern times, the libido also shifted from the more refined passions of the soul to the more basic. Eros, the creative life force that inspires not only love but the love of life and the art of living, is now exclusively experienced in the form of sexual and other pleasures. These have become addictions that swallow us in their concretism precisely because Eros has been raped and robbed of its mythopoetic, divine attributes. America has opted for the Freudian version of Eros as opposed to the original and full-bodied version of the Greeks.

In the same way that a freedom conceived in terms of the ownership and protection of property and the natural rights that ensure these is bound to result in a narrow, fundamentalist experience of freedom, so too a happiness conceived in terms of self-preservation without due consideration to self-improvement is bound to result in a fundamentalist and hedonistic experience of happiness. Is it any wonder then that the nation that has enshrined the pursuit of happiness as a sacred value is today ironically so disturbed in matters pertaining to happiness? The nation's youth illustrates this disturbance most dramatically. Juvenile shooting sprees have steadily increased, and though the profound sadness etched in the faces of the young criminals responsible for them is apparent to all, authorities are at a loss as to how to address this problem before it manifests so destructively. Less explosive illustrations are just as condemning. In 1995 the organization

Kidspeace conducted a poll of children, finding that 40 to 50 percent had fears of becoming single parents, drug addicts, or crime victims. The same number stated that they do not expect to find happiness in their futures. A 1996 government survey stated that 8.8 percent of high school students had attempted suicide. It is evident that the art of living has become a lost art. Schools do not even think of this as a necessary subject in the curriculum, nor do families think of it as something at the heart of family life.

In Greece, the happy life, or *eudaimonia*, was a life in which one lived in accord with the forces that inspired creativity and a meaningful connection to life. The highest form of happiness was to be blessed by one's *daimon*, guardian angel, or muse and to have discovered the art of living, but in a personal way and not some collective formula dictated by the mass culture or society. Bob Dylan is one among many modern voices that have expressed this ancient value: ". . . these are yuppie words, *happiness* and *unhappiness*. . . . Knowing that you are the person you were put on this earth to be—that's much more important than just being happy." Indeed, self-knowledge of this kind may have no connection at all with what we mean by "happiness" today. The Greeks knew that to search for one's calling in the depths of one's being and to then follow it to the best of one's abilities—to be the person one was put on this earth to be—did not necessarily guarantee happiness in the sense of pleasure and self-gratification. Throughout history, artists and others who have faithfully served their inner calling were known to have had especially difficult lives, often living and dying in poverty and obscurity. But they knew happiness in the sense of self-transcendence and joy, and as the American Trappist monk Thomas Merton said, "if you do not know the difference between pleasure and joy you have not yet begun to live." When Tocqueville said Americans are "serious and almost sad, even in their pleasures," he was in part alluding to this discrepancy in their experience of happiness. Pursuing happiness as if it were an object to be captured and subdued is like chasing the reflection of the moon on the water: the more you chase it, the more it recedes.

## The Idolization of an Ephemeral Self

When Jefferson and the Founding Fathers envisioned America as a new order in which freedom was the governing principle and the pursuit of happiness the prerogative of all citizens, they of course could not foresee the cults that would evolve from this. The vision they had has not been modified or adapted to the unfolding trends of history, to the changing circumstances of the nation. To a large extent, the cults of novelty, freedom, and happiness developed because the aspects of novelty, freedom, and happiness in the American vision became frozen and inflexible. Certainly, the kinds of novelty, freedom, and happiness that are the obsessions of the nation today were not what the founders had in mind. These are partial, limited notions derived from an original vision that wasn't further refined in order to keep up with the changing demands of history. As such, they are notions that are currently arrested rather than visionary in their outlook.

When a nation or civilization gets fixated on notions that are frozen or arrested in time, it can develop what Toynbee called an idolization of an ephemeral self. In attempting to stay forever young by clinging to those notions, it fails to meet the oncoming challenges of history. It thus fails to evolve and mature. Its selfhood—that is, its identity vis-à-vis culture, character, and ethics—becomes, instead of something solidly grounded, ephemeral or miragelike. Though perhaps having solid roots in the past, its selfhood now becomes transient and short-lived because it is not being actively and appropriately adapted to the present. This is only half the problem. The other half is that this frozen or arrested sense of selfhood is glorified as something wonderful, as the best possible way to be. It is idolized, so that the problem cannot be recognized for what it is. Toynbee writes:

> Idolatry may be defined as an intellectually and morally purblind worship of the part instead of the whole, of the creature instead of the Creator, of time instead of eternity. It is an abuse of the highest faculties of the human spirit, and its effect is to transform one of 'the ineffably sublime works' of God into an 'abomination of desolation.' In practical life this moral aberration may take the comprehensive form of an idolization of the idolator's own personality, or own society, in some ephemeral phase of the ceaseless movement which is growth; or . . . it may take the limited form of an idolization of some particular institution or technique which has once stood its devotee in good stead.

Toynbee cites the later periods in Athens and Venice as examples of the idolization of an ephemeral self. These were periods during which these societies were flush with opulance and riding high on the laurels of earlier achievements, or as Toynbee says, resting on their oars. They were characterized by self-adulation, egoism, and in the case of Venice, indulgent pleasure-seeking. The film "Dangerous Beauty" nicely portrays what life was like—at least for the intelligentsia and noble class—in sixteenth-century Venice, about 100 years after the Venetian Empire had reached its cultural zenith. But, Toynbee tells us, because this city-state "failed to make any fresh creative contribution to the life of the society in which she managed to survive," it basically carried on from the sixteenth to the nineteenth century much the way it had in the fifteenth. It was thus ill-equipped to respond to the challenges that came in the nineteenth century, namely, annexation by the Austrians and the *Risorgimento,* or Italian liberation and unification movement. The Venetians "were striving to restore an obsolete Venetian Republic and not to create a new Italian nationalist state; for this reason their enterprise was a forlorn hope. . . ."

In contemporary America the idolization of an ephemeral self does not occur exactly the way it did in Athens or Venice. It is not an old and high culture that is idolized, but an old and highly idealized "institution and technique which has once stood its devotee in good stead." The "institution" of Lockean liberalism and the "techniques" of novelty, freedom, and the pursuit of happiness have become fixed forms. Indeed, even the novelty is hardly ever new: the change that comes with every passing fad and whim does not amount to real, substantial change when the formula for freedom and happiness that underlies it is so limited and always the same.

America's idolization of an ephemeral self is most evident in the sense of selfhood, individually and collectively, created by this institution and these techniques. The individual of the new American order has no connection to history or tradition, is free to pursue wealth and self-gratification as he or she wishes without regard to social duties, and shows no appreciation for freedom in its deeper significance, as it was understood, for example, by the Greeks, by the mystics and sages of Judaism and Christianity, or by the medieval and existential philosophers. Collectively, as a civilization, America does not give much reflection to the burning questions which were at the center of the great civilizations of both the West and the East. The Greek tragic plays revealed what was on the minds of the citizens of Athens just as American movies reveal what's on the minds of America's citizens. Of course, there was violence, betrayal, and vice of every kind in classical Greece, but the Greeks looked at these with an eye to fathoming their meaning or purpose in the human drama. Americans seem to vicariously enjoy these on the screen for the base pleasures they provide. A radio advertisement for the Broadway musical "Chicago" in 1998 said it well: "Welcome to violence, adultery, and treachery—all those things we hold close to our hearts." The Greeks approached "those things" soberly; the American approach reeks of innocence, which at least in part is why those things are so rampant in the society at large.

It is no wonder that Christopher Lasch speaks of American culture as the "culture of narcissism." The idolization of an ephemeral self is always narcissistic. Everybody naturally has some measure of narcissism, but narcissism as a psychological disorder occurs when certain processes in an individual's development are thwarted and arrested. It is a disorder rooted in childhood. Likewise, the collective idolization of an ephemeral self occurs when a culture gets arrested in the spirit of youth or in some phase or aspect of its youth—in Toynbee's words above, "in some ephemeral phase of the ceaseless movement which is growth." Elsewhere Toynbee describes this historical phenomenon as the "infatuation with a dead self." This indeed is what narcissism is, and American culture is rife with it. The leading television show of the 1990s, "Seinfeld," captured this with uncensored precision. With its juvenile humor and emphasis on nothing, it epitomized the infatuation with a dead self. Jerry Seinfeld pinpointed this dead self in his cynical fashion in a 1993 episode: "No matter how desperate we are that someday a better self will emerge . . . we know it's not to be. That for the rest of our sad, wretched, pathetic lives, this is who we are to the bitter end." Of course, the characters of "Seinfeld" continued to indulge in their sad, wretched, pathetic lives for another five years, and with unbeatable ratings.

# Chapter 13

## The Land of the Overrated Child

*For thine is unending youth, eternal boyhood: thou art the most lovely in the lofty sky; thy face is virgin-seeming, if without horns thou stand before us.*

—Ovid, addressing the child-god Iacchus

*Concern for children can mask a multitude of sins.*

—Richard Stengel

### The Cult of Childhood

Of all the things idolized in America today, few exude a greater shimmer of holiness than the appearance and fact of youth. Youth is seen as something entirely innocent, instead of the teeming profusion of chaos that it really is. The innocence inherent in this attitude breeds a profusion of chaos of its own. America is in service to a cult of youth as no other nation or civilization has ever been.

The obsession with youth is by now a familiar fact of American life. Nobody wants to look their age today. We say "age before beauty," but really mean the reverse. The cosmetics industry makes a fortune from the desire for eternal youth. The bias toward youth in the job market is also well-known. The cultural critic Neil Postman concludes that, as the culture increasingly promotes youthfulness as the single standard for behavior and appearance, "the differences between adults and children are disappearing." In a culture where everybody is always young, we all become, as one

12-step program would put it, "adult children." The special esteem reserved for older people in traditional cultures is based on a value long lost to Americans. No longer are the old considered the wise elders of the community or the tribe; instead they are separated from the integral life of the community and shuffled off to "old people's homes" or "retirement communities." Their invisibility protects the rest of society from sickness and death, painful reminders that no one can stay young forever.

The cult of youth, needless to say, is unaffected by the fact that the average age in America is increasing. It is increasing as a result of three factors: the aging of the large generation of baby boomers; extended life spans due to modern medicine, health education, improved diet, and better housing; and a decrease in the size of the average family, yielding a less youthful population. However, even if the largest age group in America were to be octogenarians, it is doubtful that the bias toward youth would change. "America," Emerson wrote in his reflections on old age, "is a country of young men." He meant that it is a country that is not only literally young, but psychologically young.

Within the cult of youth there thrives a specific cult of childhood, to which America is in particular service. This cult confuses the spirit or principle of youth with the concrete image of the child, and glorifies children and childhood without recognizing why it is doing so. Nor does it recognize that this glorification, although widely practiced and by now taken for granted, is a distinct and questionable trend within the larger current of Western cultural history. This trend is especially strong in America, but its roots stretch back to medieval Europe and earlier. The historian George Boas has traced the development of our *ideas* of childhood, showing how certain *fantasies* about childhood have been *projected* onto children, whose actual world, in fact, most of us know and remember very little of. These fantasies are expressions of what Boas calls "cultural primitivism," the belief that earlier states of consciousness are better or purer because they are more innocent. We may add here that they are also expressions of that part of our psyche or experience that *remains* in an earlier state of consciousness—in what Russell called our naive realism, Lewis our Adamic condition, and Jung the child complex or archetype. These fantasies actively express the spirit of youth, and that is why they are so preoccupied with innocence and are themselves full of innocent assumptions. In other words, what we as adults say about children tells us more about ourselves than it does about children.

As Boas informs us, fantasy ideas about the child began as early as with Herodotus and Cicero. In the Bible, the wisdom and innocence of the child are extolled in such famous passages as "Out of the mouths of babes and sucklings hast thou ordained strength. . . ." (Psalm 8:2) and "Except ye be converted, and become as little children, ye shall not enter into the kingdom of heaven" (Matthew 18:3). (Boas humorously notes that the authors of the Gospels probably did not have in mind Freud's perception of the child as polymorphously perverse.) Also significant is that Jesus' relationship to God is as Son to Father, suggesting the idea that we are all God's children. Veneration and visions of the Child Jesus were common in the Middle Ages, during which time the child came to further represent moral and psychological innocence. By the fifteenth century painters began to portray angels as *putti*—cherubs or little children—because they thought of children as being closer to angelic purity than adults. Cultural primitivism then took shape and burgeoned as a distinctive trend—beginning in the sixteenth century—with the rise of philosophical scepticism, humanism, the Renaissance, and such concepts as the "Noble Savage" and the "ideal man." The American vision with its premise of fostering a "new man" and a "new beginning" fit right in here, like a hand into a glove. The child came to symbolize Paradise Lost. Nietzsche in the late nineteenth century captured this well: "The child is innocence and forgetfulness, a new beginning, a sport, a self-propelling wheel, a first motion, a sacred Yes."

Alongside this, paradoxically, the reality of childhood through the centuries was, to say the least, stark. Children in the world of everyday life (as opposed to the world of human imagination and fantasy) had lives no different and no less difficult than their parents. From the way they were dressed to the way their inner psychology was understood, they were considered to be small adults. They did not have special books, games, and toys, and their birthdays were not celebrated as special events. They did not see special doctors and certainly they did not have special immunity from the law. Only their size and their need to be taught about the ways of life set them apart from adults. Education, however, was for the privileged, and most children worked long hours in the fields and later in the mines and factories. The wheels of the Industrial Revolution were in no small measure turned with the steam of child labor. Children were not perceived as pure and innocent, and in fact, in many cultures they were treated as innately bad and empty, needing strict education to improve them. The aim of child-rearing was not, as it is today, to produce a "happy" child. What held value was a child who was industrious and useful, obedient and mannerly, and adapted to the demands of parents, church, and society—very much a child seen but not heard. This split between the fantasy image of the innocent, archetypal child and the actual treatment of real children speaks to the fact that the former was *always a symbol* for something ethereal and paradisaic inside man, and not a statement about real children.

In America, there is a great unconsciousness of this split, of this difference between the paradisaic and innocent fantasies about childhood and real childhood. The cult of childhood occurs as a function of this unconsciousness. The more people are unconscious of these fantasies, the more they project them onto living children. In America, Boas writes, the cult of childhood "has reached amazing proportions." One finds it not only in the love of "cuteness" and other qualities associated today with children, but, more importantly, in the general philosophy of life and in education.

> If adults are urged to retain their youth, to 'think young,' to act and dress like youngsters, it is because the Child has been held up to them as a paradigm of the ideal man. It has often been pointed out that in the United States children are indulged in all their desires. . . . Discipline in schools [not to mention the family] has become greatly relaxed—indeed there was room for relaxation—and it has been suggested that the child's interests should alone determine the curriculum that he would pursue. Self-expression was the aim sought by all, though few ever raised the question of what the self was or whether there were good and bad ways of expressing it. In the arts the teaching of any technique was deplored, for the very fact that what a child made was childlike sufficed to justify him.

The transformation of children into beings of special status was aided in America by the nation's particular history. America, like most other nations of the world, depended to a significant extent on child labor, especially during its period of industrial development. In 1880, 1.1 million children under 16—one out of six—worked. At the beginning of the twentieth century, 284,000 children between the ages of 10 and 15 worked in mines, mills, and factories, often in appalling conditions. As the century unfolded, the value of children became inextricably linked to the American dream of fulfillment for reasons other than the need for cheap labor. Hardship dictated that improvement of the average citizen's lot in life be viewed generationally. Rarely could a typical immigrant family in America raise itself by its bootstraps within a single generation. The ethic of sacrifice, of working selflessly to insure that the lives of one's children will be better than one's own, became part of the American way of life. Americans found their redemption and purpose for living through their children.

With the subsequent advent of the affluent society, the special significance of children continued, but with the benefits of affluence now becoming part of the equation. Childhood was elevated as a sacred time that must be nurtured and unperturbed by life's harsher demands. Children came to be seen as special citizens, deserving unlimited benefits and exceptional privileges right up to and even past the threshold of adulthood. Canadians remark upon the luxury of the American tradition of sending teenagers to out-of-state colleges and universities rather than having them live more modestly at home until they have earned their independence themselves. One should hardly be surprised why so many young people today have difficulty assuming the responsibilities of adulthood when they have been so indulged throughout childhood. The special status afforded to children is not even a consideration for Americans; they simply take it for granted. As Germany's Count Hermann Keyserling said in 1930, "America is fundamentally the land of the overrated child."

And yet, again paradoxically, in the real world, America behaves in key respects as if it were indifferent to the real needs of real children. In spite of the accentuated value it places on children, its record in practical matters of childcare and education establishes it, by international standards, as a land that undervalues children. America lags behind most other developed nations in both economic and spiritual investment in the concerns of the young. In an international study on this subject in 1994, Noam Chomsky found that the market economies of America and England provided considerably fewer social services for child-raising and family support than did the market economies of continental Europe and Japan. He even went so far as to accuse America of harboring an anti-child, anti-family attitude that amounted to a war against children and families.

There are some sad statistics to support this position. Different studies estimate that 20 to 25 percent of America's 70 million children live in poverty. By contrast, two percent of Japanese and four percent of German children live in poverty. These figures reflect only the amount of poverty, not the degree. Qualitatively speaking, America is a nation of extremes, producing both the wealthiest adults and the poorest children in the Western world. It ranks close to Iran and Romania in the percentage of babies born below normal standards of birth weight. No other industrialized nation permits a third of its mothers to have babies without prenatal care.

Child immunization rates are also shamefully low. Only 14 percent of the day care in the United States is considered high quality. About half the children in America live in single parent households in which the parents never married, are separated, or are divorced. One of every six children is a stepchild, and half a million live in residential treatment centers and foster homes. One out of every 11 high school students has attempted suicide. More children actually die from suicide than from cancer, AIDS, birth defects, influenza, heart disease, and pneumonia *combined.* Whether diagnostic skills have improved or the actual numbers are increasing, the amount of children in treatment for attention-deficit disorder, hyperactivity, defiance, obesity, bulimia, and depression is staggering. Addiction and teenage pregnancy are increasing. At least one million "latchkey children" return everyday to a home that has a gun. As of 1995, 50,000 children had been gunned down in America, almost as many as the 58,000 Americans killed in Vietnam. Thousands of students of all ages bring guns to school everyday—270,000 according to one study. Each year 2.5 million children are arrested. The majority of them have documented histories of neglect and abuse. At least 2,000 children, most of them age 4 or younger, die each year from neglect, abuse, and homocide. These are astounding statistics for a nation supposedly so devoted to children.

How does one explain this contradiction and hypocrisy? One can only conclude that Americans are really not interested in children very much at all. What they are interested in is the Idea of the Child, an *image* of the spirit of youth. The cult of childhood is the concretization of this Idea and spirit. This concretization, and the unconscious manner in which it occurs, have led to a variety of syndromes that basically reflect the nation's fixation upon youth. Their destructive effects upon both children and adults are the symptoms of a nation stuck in the madness of childhood.

## The Madness of Child Abuse

When the philosopher-historian Michel Foucault said, "Madness is childhood," he was referring to the huge dependency needs of children. In particular, he was talking about the comparison of the insane in nineteenth-century asylums with children: both were absolutely dependent on the care and judgment of the one in possession of reason—in the case of the child, the adult.

The dependent condition of childhood speaks to the child's extreme vulnerability and neediness: the human child is dependent upon its mother for its survival far longer and in more fundamental ways than are the off-spring of other species of the animal kingdom. This condition of extreme neediness exerts great demands upon others. Consequently, through those demands, the *child* is the one in the position of control. As Erik Erikson said, the child raises the parents. The process of learning and discovery involved in parenthood can foster tremendous adult growth, and naturally, the child raises the parents in this sense too; but the child's extreme dependency needs are the primary determinants that shape the child-rearing experience. Furthermore, the child knows no reason, as parents who are up all night with their crying baby or have to deal with their older child's tantrums can attest. This dependent condition qualifies childhood, indeed, as a cultural primitivism, but in the least attractive sense of the meaning. There is no noble savagery here. Irrational and driven by impulse, it is savage in the most primitive way. The neediness of human children exerts a tyranny because of its paradisaic expectation: *"You will take care of me and my needs, no matter what."* This tyranny, of course, is not only imposed upon the parent; it also grips the child. The garden of Eden has a dark side for both.

As a parent, one should naturally anticipate this situation. Because children *are* primitive savages, when we choose to have and love them, we choose to accept this situation. We *choose* to accept the tyranny or madness of childhood. However, in the syndromes that characterize the cult of childhood, there is no such choice because the *adult* is in the condition of childhood—a psychological condition one can only be aware of when one has, at least in some measure, been removed from it. Again, the fish is the last to know that it is in water. In psychological childhood, the adult is in the demanding position and is unconsciously compelled to be there. He or she is, indeed, an adult child.

Nothing illustrates this more dramatically than the epidemic of child abuse. Whether or not America suffers more from this problem than other nations and whether it is more prevalent today or is simply being reported more, are unclear. No doubt, it is a problem that transcends national boundaries and has existed throughout history. But at least it *seems* more rampant today and no one can deny that it has been discovered in every corner of American society. *Time* had the following item in its section on "Milestones" in a 1997 issue:

SENTENCED. DANIEL CARLETON GAJDUSEK, 73, Nobel Prize-winning scientist, to up to a year in prison; on two counts of child abuse, for molesting a 16-year-old boy. Beginning in the 1960s, Gajdusek ferried 56 children from the Pacific islands to the U.S., allegedly to educate them, but journals of the scientist's research trips to the South Pacific contain graphic descriptions of sex between men and boys.

Particularly in the form of sexual abuse and incest, child abuse clearly demonstrates the adult's regression to a position of needing to be taken care of and satisfied by the child. Or at least it clearly demonstrates the adult's regression to a psychological level coequal with the child's. Child sex abuse—and we may here add child pornography as well as the use of child-like models in racy ads in fashion magazines—is as much a fixation with the child as with sex, if not more. Men sexually abuse children more out of a need for power and control than for sexual gratification. Power and control issues for the child sex abuser tend to be rooted in his own childhood experience. His frustration and "stuckness" in his own "inner child" compel him to seek comfort with a complementary if inappropriate partner, his unfortunate outer child (or, as the case may be, somebody else's). Similarly, studies of pedophiles reveal that many of them had been abused as children or had developed a sexualized orientation toward children in their teenage years, sometimes as early as age 12.

But to focus just on the perpetrators of sex crimes is to stop short of seeing the wide scope of the problem we are here discussing. One does not have to be an offender to participate in the madness of this regression to the childish. This madness has spread through the culture like a wildfire, evoking mass excitement. We all seem to love to watch and condemn this madness from a comfortable, superior position, but is the source that motivates this excitement and fascination outside of us in others or within ourselves? In a *Time* essay appropriately entitled "Who's Bad?," Richard Corliss had this to say about the Michael Jackson child abuse scandal:

The allegations also speak to the modern preoccupation with child abuse. In an age when lurid lyrics, sniggering sitcoms and trash-talking stars work hard to rob children of innocence, the sexually abusive parent, guardian or family friend is not only a predator in his own right but also a stand-in for all the gaudy malevolence of pop culture. "There's a social hysteria about child abuse," says Professor Melvin Guyer, a psychologist and lawyer who teaches at the University of Michigan. "It began with the McMartin Pre-School case and continued with Woody Allen. There has been a feeding frenzy, in which the ordinary presumptions of innocence are not applied. The allegations are treated as evidence." And the public reacts with wide eyes and a bit of drool at the corner of the mouth.

"The public gets to be puritanical and voyeuristic at the same time. Their attitude is basically, 'This food is terrible, and there's not enough of it.' "

Thus, society itself regresses to the childish and behaves abusively.

The madness of child abuse may be understood as a symptom of society's damaged condition due to its cult of childhood. Sex has always been on people's minds, in ancient cultures as well as modern. (Witness, for example, the ancient, erotic temple sculptures of Khajuraho, India.) The sex drive may have periodically led to a loosening of sexual mores, but rarely with enough force to cause a violation of incest and pedophilic taboos in the epidemic proportions that seem to be occurring in contemporary America. Even the relief afforded today to the excessive repression of the Victorian Age does not explain the sexualization of children that is going on in America. It seems that the Eros in this instance is, again, concentrated in the image of youth as much as in the pleasure of sex, if not more. If the culture sees youth as a heavenly elixir and panacea, is it really so surprising that adults will turn to children for their sexual gratification? Society's infatuation with the spirit of youth and the Idea of the Child in particular is symbolically acted out in the adult act of sexual union with children. This is, surely, a metaphorical way of thinking, but symptoms are often metaphors.

That child abuse is a concrete metaphor for a madness of society's, and only secondarily and manifestly of its individual members, is amply borne out by repressed memory syndrome. This is another symptom of America's perverse cult of childhood. What else can explain the high numbers of people across the nation reporting recovered memories of having been sexually abused by their parents when they were children? Some also report that they were ritually abused by their parents and such pillars of the community as the mayor, the police chief, and the school principal. These accounts include lurid details of being sequentially raped by all the above, blood-drinking, and the sacrifice of fetuses in the worship of Satan. Monarch Resources, a California referral service for incest survivors, receives more than 5,000 calls annually from people who claim to have been victims of satanic abuse. Philadelphia's False Memory Syndrome Foundation acknowledges that 16 percent of the calls it receives similarly involve reports of ritual abuse. However, there appears to be no substantial evidence to support such claims, especially in such large numbers. "If you look at the alleged number of deaths that would [have to] be accounted for," says trauma specialist Lorraine Stanek, "there should be bodies in all our backyards."

Repressed memory syndrome is a public fantasy generated by the cult of childhood. Fantasies, whether we are speaking of those about childhood in general or of repressed memory syndrome in particular, are not to be scorned and summarily dismissed as illusions or hallucinations of the mind. Rather, they are to be appreciated as an activity of the human imagination that is full of meaning in its own right, much like dreams or myths. In fact, Jung argued that fantasy is the root activity of the mind, underlying not only dreaming and daydreaming, but directed thinking and creativity as well. The fantasy of repressed memory syndrome symbolically conveys the madness of society's ambivalence toward children, the fact that it loves the Idea of the Child but in reality treats children poorly. Furthermore, by loving this Idea so *concretely* in children, the spirit of eternal youth is treated *abstractly*. Instead of being appreciated as a powerful force whose origins are divine or preternatural—remember, in former times this spirit was always revered as a god or divinely inspired hero—it is now idolized in humans and in the human sphere. Society seeks something eternal where the eternal cannot be found. It is the *human spirit* that is being abused by this attitude and behavior.

Ultimately, this is what syndromes such as child abuse and repressed memory are about. Rampant child abuse and incest can only be symptoms of a civilization unaware of its violations against the human spirit. The bizarre if infrequent demonic element in repressed memory syndrome, with its satanic rituals, aptly portrays this: something evil is being perpetrated. It should not be surprising that a nation so innocently convinced that it is the advocate of the child and so unconsciously glorifying the innocence of the child, is going to have large numbers of people carrying a dark fantasy that compensates that fantasy of innocence. The fact that parents, mayors, and police chiefs are the villains in this dark fantasy points to the breakdown of authority. A one-sided identification with the spirit of youth tends to be accompanied by a breakdown or perversion of authority. Jung had this to say about understanding the larger, collective forces at work in individual disturbances:

> A collective problem, if not recognized as such, always appears as a personal problem, and in individual cases may give the impression that something is out of order in the realm of the personal psyche. The personal sphere is indeed disturbed, but such disturbances need not be primary; they may well be secondary, the consequence of an insupportable change in the social atmosphere. The cause of disturbance is, therefore, not to be sought in the personal surround-

ings, but rather in the collective situation. Psychotherapy has hitherto taken this matter far too little into account.

If repressed memory syndrome is indeed the manifestation of a collective problem, to seek the cause of it in the psyches of the individuals whom it afflicts—as many mental health professionals have been inclined to do—is to put the cart before the horse.

## Divorce and the Long Reach of Childhood

If child abuse is the most striking manifestation of the madness of childhood, then the current American model of marriage and family life is the most obscure. From the beginning of courtship to the court of law at the end, the American style of intimacy is a reflection of unresolved issues of childhood and of childhood's dreams. There is nothing unusual or novel about the fact that intimacy is influenced by childhood, except that in America there is little tolerance for working through the issues on the one hand and for disappointment of the dreams on the other. "Working through" is a cultivation and discipline that requires a healthy dose of the spirit of authority. The same may be said for enduring the disappointment of dreams. This spirit is sorely lacking in America today. Those who do espouse its virtues in matters of marriage and family life, such as religious fundamentalists, unfortunately do so in a puritanical, formulaic style; they wish to impose authority on people externally rather than educate them so they can develop wisdom from within.

To begin with, Americans choose their life partners according to a factor that traditional cultures have always regarded as suspect, namely, romantic love. Americans place great value on the experience of falling in love. Almost any Hollywood movie can attest to this. Certainly, romantic love is a strong force. From Shakespeare back through the Bible and even earlier, love stories have captured the human imagination. But as Rollo May, M. Scott Peck, and many others have pointed out, falling in love is an experience that happens *to us;* it is not an act of will. There is not much voluntary choice involved, and we can just as easily fall in love with a person who is ill-suited for us as one with whom we are compatible. This is one of the reasons why traditional cultures have not put great stock in romantic love and its use as a gauge for finding a suitable marriage partner: they anticipated the likelihood of the experience so many Americans today have, of falling out of love and becoming disillusioned with one's spouse and marriage.

The breakdown of traditional cultural norms has left a vacuum in which there is no mentoring or guidance around the difficult problem of choosing a good partner. The film "Crossing Delancey" wonderfully illustrates how the wisdom of an elder could help steer a confused young person through the folly of his or her poor choices, eventually finding a well-suited if not romantically glamorous partner. But with the vacuum left in place of the traditional cultural norms, the powerful experience of falling in love has rushed in as the sole means of helping people decide who would make a good partner.

This powerful experience, as affirming as it is, is actually a matter quite separate from practical, conjugal concerns. This is why the troubadours of the tradition of courtly love that emerged in medieval Europe kept a clear dividing line between the women they romantically idealized and worshiped and the flesh-and-blood women they married and had children with. The ecstasy and surrender of falling in love is, together with mystical experience, probably the closest we can come to experiencing the garden of Eden while in this world. But unlike mystical experience, falling in love is shrouded in the flawed innocence of that tyrannical, paradisaic expectation, "You will take care of me and my needs." If this is not foisted upon the person we fall in love with, then certainly we expect the bliss of this experience—which we innocently believe will last forever—to take care of us. When we are one with our beloved, and everything is so perfect and wonderful, we are nurtured by the universe as if it were a Great Mother and we its divine child. Many psychologists have likened the fusion that occurs with the other in romantic love to the fusion of the infant with its mother.

Marriages made exclusively on the altar of this experience are bound to sooner or later lead to disappointment because this experience never lasts, certainly at least with the degree of intensity it has during courtship. The honeymoon always ends. The marriages may be *made* in heaven, but they must be *lived* on earth. After we have fallen out of the state of being in love, or find that it is no longer all-enveloping, we are faced with the challenge of growing in love, of growing or evolving together, which requires an act of will. Then we find out if we really love the person we claimed to love, or if we only love the idea of love and the image of that person, that is, a fantasy. This is, all too often, when the tyranny of the paradisaic expectation makes its force known (up to now it was camouflaged behind the bliss). This is when the child in us comes up and has a tantrum: "No! I will not leave the garden!" This moment can come three months after the wedding, or three years. Or disillusionment can linger, and people can decide to divorce much later. But whenever a couple attributes the reason for divorce to no longer being in love and having consequently drifted apart—a common reason for divorce among Americans—one can assume that the marriage never evolved beyond the fantasies of childhood. To such people, nothing is more defeating than having the adolescent fantasy of being forever in love unfulfilled. They divorce their spouses, only to start the search for and cycle of romantic love all over again. This seems to be a pattern more prevalent with men than women.

Other typical reasons for divorce also reveal that too many marriages are made under the auspices of childhood without an awareness that the problems this brings will need to be patiently and lovingly worked on. Early marriage often offers one or another of the partners a sanctuary from the home of the parents. The psychological effects of the problems of that home, if not the actual problems themselves, are brought into the new home. Alcoholism, abusiveness, abnormal neediness (such as "codependency"), and other destructive patterns have been demonstrated to travel across generational lines. Often a parent who has been neglected and beaten by his parents will beat his children; he has become their rival for their mother's affection. The unresolved issues of childhood are replayed. These issues can manifest subtly as well; people do not have to overtly neglect or beat their children in order to slight them. But whether the problems manifest overtly or subtly, marital therapy in such instances tends to be, as Hillman indicates, a therapy of the abandoned child within the adult, that is, of the condition of psychological childhood that is still alive and acting up through the problems in question.

Marriage provides an opportunity for personal development and for realizing heroic possibilities in a down-to-earth, day-to-day context. The disturbances of childhood, such as having had an alcoholic, abusive, or neglectful parent, present a truly heroic challenge to the victim when he decides to become a partner and a parent himself. As the psychologist Meredith Mitchell points out, finding the heroic urge and consciously seizing it is essential for the victimized adult child, for only this can empower him and help him redress his victimization so that he doesn't wreak its havoc upon his partner or *his* child. Divorce and family breakdown that result from generational patterns are thus, in the end, results of personal, heroic failure.

America has one of the highest divorce rates in the world. It was steady during the 1950s and early 1960s, but doubled between 1968 and 1978, reaching its current level. In 1995, 2.4 million couples took marriage vows, and half as many renounced them. Undoubtedly, some divorces are necessary, not only for the benefit of the couple, but also the children. But in too many cases, divorce not only reflects problems of childhood; in one form or another, it forces the next generation to deal once again with these same problems. One study that followed children over a 25-year period found that the impact of divorce lasted well into adulthood and affected the adult children's work lives, marriages, and the raising of their own children. Trust, openness, a willingness to depend on another, are often significantly impaired. Teachers and therapists also agree that children from divorced families have a greater degree of insecurity and self-doubt than other children; the chaos or disturbances in their family experiences predispose them toward having a less sure footing in the world. Thus, divorce is both a function and a furnisher of the darker elements of childhood.

## The Pro-Life Movement and the Cult of Childhood

In 1994, a former minister named Paul Hill gunned down and killed a doctor in Pensacola, Florida in front of the abortion clinic where the doctor worked. His hardened, unpenitent attitude brought the trial much publicity, but it was only one case in a multitude that occurred around the same time. From 1993–95, five medical professionals were killed and seven others injured as over 40 abortion clinics across the nation were targeted for shootings, arson, and bombings. Evidently, the militant activists responsible for such deadly assaults believe that the life of an unborn fetus is more sacred than that of the people performing the abortions; they argue that the fetus is unprotected and the medical professionals are murderers and should be treated as such. Fortunately, most people in the pro-life movement have the common and moral sense not to subscribe to this viewpoint.

The belief that life is sacred from the moment of conception is a religious value that of course predates the pro-life movement. This core idea of Christianity can be traced to Scripture, and Catholic countries have always as a matter of public policy been opposed to abortion. However, the fanaticism and emotionalism displayed by individuals like Paul Hill, who know full well that their actions will in fact not save any unborn lives—the person seeking the abortion will just go to another clinic, and the doctor they have killed will eventually be replaced by another—suggest there is another factor involved beyond religious conviction. Or rather, an emotional factor has been blended with the religious one and has come to assume the character of a religious conviction. This emotional factor is expressed with all the vigor and imagery that generally accompanies the cult of childhood. It is not only that they are protecting an unborn *life*; they are protecting an unborn *child*. And the fact that this life is a *child's* seems to automatically make it more sacred and worth preserving than a doctor's, even though that doctor may also have children waiting for him at home.

The child being unborn seems to add to its lovability, suggesting even more that what we are dealing with is the Idea of the Child, an idea that by definition is about the unborn possibilities of youth. This is not to deny that many people are genuinely conflicted about the taking of a life, however early or potential its status. Any way one turns it, abortion raises moral questions. But in the case of individuals who hold extreme, militant views, there again seems to be something at play beyond moral considerations. As one critic remarked, if such individuals were really concerned about life, wouldn't they focus their energies more on life *after* birth, for example, on disadvantaged children in the inner city or the homeless (who are most certainly society's orphans or abandoned adult children)? Or wouldn't they be more concerned with the conditions that prompt so many young women to get abortions in the first place?

Incidents such as the one in Pensacola reflect not only the general confrontation of religious fundamentalism with liberalism; they reflect the subtle influence of the cult of childhood on pro-life values. Such incidents furthermore illustrate a principle discussed in the first chapter, namely, that when the spirits of youth and authority become dissociated from each other and polarized, they become identical but in a negative way. Immaturity prevails. The spirit of authority animates the pro-life movement with a moral sense of right and wrong, but it succumbs to archaic thinking and primitive, barbaric measures when it approves the murder of living people so that unborn fetuses may potentially survive.

## The Cry for Initiation

In 1993, the news media carried the story of a group of teenage girls in California undergoing initiation rites into gangs: they had to sleep with men who had AIDS without catching the HIV virus. Naturally, this sounds insanely suicidal. However, the underlying significance of this behavior, if not the behavior itself, begins to makes sense when we understand suicide psychologically and symbolically.

In the initiation rites of all traditional cultures, it is not at all literal death or suicide that is aimed for, but psychological and spiritual death and rebirth. The adolescent must separate from the world of childhood and be initiated into the world of adulthood. In primitive cultures, this transformation has always been accompanied by ritual violence because the separation or transformation is itself a violent act, psychologically speaking. It is painful to grow up. Initiation rituals reenact this violence and celebrate the endurance of pain as a mark of the youth's readiness to join the adults. The psychiatrist Karl Menninger writes:

> The rites vary among different peoples. In some instances a tooth is knocked out, amid much noise and ceremony; more frequently the prinicipal initiatory rite consists of circumcision performed with a sharp stone or piece of glass or with a knife; sometimes an incision is made in the penis and the blood is mixed with water which the boys and men drink. Following and preceding the circumcision the boys are compelled to go through various forms of torture. They are made to fast for many days, "feigned attacks are made upon them," so-called spirits appear to them in masks of animals and threaten to eat them; occasionally an actual fight takes place between the men and their sons. Among the Karesau islanders black ants are allowed to bite the novices. The Mandan Indians thrust a knife with a saw-edge through the youth's arm, forearm, thigh, knee, calves, chest and shoulder and then push pointed pieces of wood into the wounds. All of these methods seem to carry the significance of death for the candidate, followed by rebirth. This rebirth drama is also enacted by the novices after the ceremony when they appear to have forgotten all about their previous existence, do not recognize their relatives, and cannot eat or speak or even sit down without being shown how. If they do not adhere to this formality they must go through a second and much more severe ceremony which may result in actual death.

In a word, initiation rites are humankind's age-old ways of formally introducing the heroic ideal into the lives of young people at the time they are believed to be mature enough to begin to live up to it. To be an adult is tantamount to being a fully dimensional human being, which in turn, according to certain North American Indian tribes, is tantamount to being someone who knows how to live in harmony with the spirits or gods. Initiation rites are fundamentally religious rites; they are initiation not only into the social order, but the mysteries of the cosmic order. Native American initiation rites are therefore often accompanied by vision quests and visionary experiences.

Thus, in essence, initiation rites are social celebrations of the individual entering into a new relationship with the cosmos. By conducting such initiations with its individual members, society itself, person by person, becomes transformed and initiated into the larger mysteries of life. All social initiations have this purpose to some extent: baptism, circumcision, confirmation, the bar mitzvah, college graduation, marriage. But modern society has stripped much of the meaning from these functions. The significance of dying to one's narrow ways and being reborn into a broader and deeper relationship with the cosmos, into the company of fellow men and women and God, is no longer understood. Nor is there any longer a real belief in the symbolic rituals that can convey this meaning and make it come alive. However, instincts being what they are, young people are searching, whether consciously or unconsciously, for such initiation. Their souls yearn for this age-old experience, but our society has become spiritually bankrupt and deaf to their cries.

The high rate of suicide and suicide attempts by young people today can be seen as directly correlated with the decline of initiation rites as practiced in traditional cultures. Suicide is a preoccupation of many adolescents, as adolescence is a time of great confusion and upheaval. The libido turns in upon itself in an intense, all-consuming way, and often there is no outlet and no one who seems to understand. The disappointments and darkness of this period are simply too much for many youths. But the care and mentoring that should be provided to young people as they prepare for initiation can help them contain their suicidal impulses within a larger framework that then rechannels their interest in death in a meaningful and ultimately life-enhancing way. The interest in death is appropriate as a drive for inner death that leads to rebirth. Today this drive is neither addressed nor acknowledged, and there is a dearth of skilled mentors or guides to help young people identify and deal with it. America's high suicide rate among adolescents is in large part a concrete manifestation of society's failure to grasp the inner meaning of the suicidal impulse and channel it appropriately through an initiation process of some kind or another. Suicide of this sort is thus another form of heroic failure.

Many youths today avert death by attempting to initiate themselves. But, unfortunately, this does not work. The angry gestures of rap and alternative music and all the ear and nose rings and tattoos that are now worn by young people from all social classes cannot provide the rebirth they secretly long for. Young people cannot initiate young people, and the more this is denied, the more concrete and violent are the efforts to implement such initiation. The example of the teenage girls mentioned above is just one of many. Gang initiation can be extremely dangerous, painful, and humiliating, ranging from participating in robberies or drive-by shootings to receiving beatings by bona fide gang members. Female gang members are often multiply raped by male gang members. If the violence of this strikes the reader as something alien and purely restricted to the inner city, one need only recall the incidents of military hazing that received so much media attention in the late 1990s.

Such initiations do not work because, as the poet Robert Bly argues, young people need to be initiated by mentor-figures who are older and wiser and can impart some of their wisdom through the initiation process. They do not work because the initiating trial of strength or ordeal must involve more than merely enduring violence; they must mold character and bring the youth into contact with things eternal. Such contact is the catalyst for death and rebirth, and without it, initiation loses its meaning. One can see why in America, as in other countries that have lost their traditions of initiation, young people have such difficulty making the transition from adolescence to adulthood. Gangs emerge in response to this difficulty; they are sibling societies of the uninitiated. A 1995 study reported that the United States has 9,000 gangs with 400,000 members. These are not exclusively black or ethnically defined, and include motorcycle gangs and the like. And they are not gender-limited; both males and females may be found in many gangs.

But gangs are only the most visible form of the lack of initiation, as Bly indicates. Schools are run by the students, and adolescence, instead of lasting the traditional three or four years, now often stretches until age 35. Young people may be versatile on the Internet, but they are deficient in literacy and the emotional demands of human relationships. The creative spark of adolescence usually ends in social conformity because there is no initiation or mentorship that helps young people nurse that spark into a fire of real achievement that offers light and warmth. Too many settle for mindless jobs and those that go on to university all too often stretch their abilities not through the classics but through drinking binges. When they graduate and get jobs in the corporate world they have no sense of their individual uniqueness or calling, so they hunt for their pot of gold at the end of the rainbow with a cutthroat competitiveness and an unconsciousness of the emptiness which underlies it.

## The Puerile Society

As young people who have never matured through an initiation process or mastered the basic vicissitudes of adulthood increasingly become the adult children who run society, society itself becomes more and more childish and adolescent in character. Adults in a childhood-dominated society become perpetual adolescents, seeking little more from life than self-gratification; indeed, the cults of novelty, freedom, and happiness are collective pursuits of the things most dear to the adolescent heart. Recent decades have witnessed the rise of a parentless culture in which fathers are "deadbeat dads" and kids go on shooting sprees with automatic weapons. Parents use their children to fulfill their own fantasies, as in the case of 6-year-old JonBenet Ramsey or 7-year-old Jessica Dubroff. The former, a child beauty pageant queen, was mysteriously murdered in 1997, and the latter, egged on by her parents, attempted in 1996 to break a record by flying across America, crashing and killing herself, her father, and her flight instructor. Such tragedies illustrate the extreme consequences of parental narcissism. Parentified children—that is, children who have become the caretakers of their parents' emotional needs or of the other siblings in the family whom the parents have neglected—have become the strongholds of the new American family. But there are no strong winners in the land of the overrated child. In their search for initiation and love, teenagers become parents well before they have reached their own psychological maturity and ability to provide care and to give of themselves. The rate of teenage births in America, though declining in recent years, is still significantly higher than in the other industrialized nations of the world, costing the American taxpayer $7 billion a year in welfare, healthcare, and other services. One can imagine that the impoverished conditions, physically and psychologically, that these teenagers raise their children in will have long-range effects not only upon the children but the rest of society as well.

The parentification of the child and the infantilization of the adult are, of course, two sides of the same coin. Both can exist only in a culture that has sanctioned the spirit of youth and the cult of childhood in particular as an authoritative principle in the conduct of human affairs. There is in America a widespread sense of entitlement: people expect that problems should be resolved magically even though they scream at government to get out of their affairs. The *Washington Post* journalist Paul Taylor wrote that the American populace has become accustomed to a habit of "whining" and of having politicians pander to it. People blame their discontents upon the wealthy, the corporations, the politicians themselves, the PACs, welfare recepients, immigrants, everyone but themseves. In his appropriately entitled book, *Big Babies,* Michael Kinsley accuses the American public of wanting to have its cake and eat it too. It wants a balanced budget, but also tax cuts. It wants Medicare and welfare to be more effective, but to cost less. The American public, Kinsley argues, is self-indulgent yet full of self-pity. Are these not the characteristics of a society dominated by a mentality and cult of childhood? The assumption is, "You will take care of me and my needs, no matter what."

In its more overt forms too, the society exhibits puerility, and with uncensored exhibitionism. Television audiences thrive on a number of Jerry Springer-type shows in which the most private parts of peoples' lives are paraded without any sense of dignity or shame whatsoever. The participants speak, fight, and generally behave like poorly raised children, and the host and live audience egg them on like spectators at the Roman Colosseum—a demonstration of cultural primitivism at its worst. Howard Stern likewise continues to be a big hit. His appeal is largely sexual, but at the expense of Eros rather than through its cultivation. David Deneau describes Stern as the "id of the airwaves" (and fundamentalist talk radio, Stern's opposite, as the "superego of the airwaves"). "Naturally," Freud writes, "the id knows no values, no good and evil, no morality."

However, even the more morally motivated adherents of the New Age can appear childishly regressed as they sit with teddy bears on their laps at the "wounded inner child" workshops of John Bradshaw. The cultural critic Robert Hughes laments that "the pursuit of the Inner Child has taken over just at the moment when Americans ought to be figuring out where their Inner Adult is, and how that disregarded oldster got buried under the rubble of pop psychology and specious short-term gratification." Certainly, when Jung developed his theory of the child archetype and its important function in the human psyche, he did not have in mind this complaint-ridden, literalized version of an inner child which pop psychology has made into a dogma and icon; this inner child is full of rage rather than creative and spiritual possibilities. Given the madness of child abuse, the prevalence of divorce, the breakdown of the family, and the failure to be initiated, could one expect otherwise?

In a puerile society, authority and order are undermined by childish innocence and indulgence. At the 1997 U.N. Earth Summit Conference, the Chairman of the Conference said: "We continue to consume resources and pollute as if we were the last generation on earth." Although America is by no means the sole culprit of unrestricted consumption and pollution, it is, as mentioned in an earlier chapter, not only a leader of it but, hypocritically, a leader of advocacy against it. This environmental disorder is akin to the messy room of a child who has not been disciplined to clean up and plays with no regard for the consequences of his play. America's ecological behavior reflects a childlike or primitive animism, a belief that things will somehow fix themselves and just "work out." Al Gore has likened the world's ecological problems to the kind of mess that gets created in a dysfunctional family. Can America expect to lead the "dysfunctional family" of the world if it is itself in such disarray and so arrested in childhood thinking?

In other domestic and international affairs, too, the puerile society makes a mockery of authority and order. The tyranny of the paradisaic expectation to have all one's needs automatically cared for is here, as in the matter of ecology, overshadowed by that other great tyranny and madness of childhood, namely, solipsism and the belief that the world is one's self or at least one's oyster. As Lawrence Kohlberg and Carol Gilligan explain, "adolescent thought entertains solipsism or at least the Cartesian cogito, the notion that the only thing real is the self. [We] asked a fifteen-year-old girl: 'What is the most real thing to you?' Her unhestitating reply was 'myself.' " This attitude was especially prevalent in America's policy in the Vietnam War. As Robert McNamara's own retrospective study revealed, the only thing real for America's policymakers in that war was their own agenda, regardless of the emerging facts that told them that the war could not be won.

The pioneer explorer and ethnologist John Wesley Powell has put his finger on a mechanism that is closely related to solipsism and adds to that form of tyranny and madness: "The confusion of confusions is that universal habit of savagery—the confusion of the objective with the subjective." This confusion is intrinsic to the epistemic style of innocence, and it, too, colors American public affairs. If it is not the Cartesian *cogito*, "I think, therefore I am," then it is "I am, therefore I think the world is the way I am." Whatever personal, characterological flaws and foibles were at play in the scandals that have scarred the stronger and more effective presidencies of recent decades, this confusion was at the heart of them all. The indiscretions of Watergate, Iran-contra, and the Monica Lewinsky affair were rooted in the tendency to blur the boundary between subjective wishes and objective limitations. In each of these fiascos, the value of wish fulfillment gained ascendancy over the value of the recognition of necessity. Impulsiveness obscured judgment and common sense, and lust of one kind or another triumphed over the ability to sacrifice untenable wishes and to accept ordinariness in the course of one's dealings. In the Lewinsky case, the entire nation was awash in the merging of the subjective with the objective—or the private with the public—as a president's sexual indiscretions were broadcast in graphic detail for all to be privy to; limitations were as lacking in the treatment of the problem as in the problem itself.

Arriving at a more or less clear awareness of the boundary between the subjective and objective is a lifelong struggle that defines the transition from psychological childhood to maturity. A proper alignment of the subjective to the objective signals a balanced relationship between the spirit of youth and the spirit of authority. *True freedom is to wish for and voluntarily accept what is necessary* (or as Jung said, "Freedom of will is the ability to do gladly that which I must do"). Until American leaders and the public who elects them can come to terms with this fact, power will continue to be abused in one embarassing and morally defeating episode after another.

"The 'eternal child' in man," Jung wrote, "is an indescribable experience, an incongruity, a handicap, and a divine prerogative; an imponderable that determines the ultimate worth or worthlessness of a personality." And we may here add that it determines the ultimate worth or worthlessness of a society, too. To be childlike is to have a gifted disposition, but to remain in childhood as a literal, psychological condition stifles the human maturation process in a cloud of innocence and infantilism. Childishness is then mistaken for childlikeness, and the society, like the person, becomes arrested in a self-satisfied state of youthful stupor.

# Chapter 14

## The Metaphor of the Eternally Young Hero

> *Metaphor is a way of knowing—one of the oldest, most deeply embedded, even indispensable ways of knowing in the history of human consciousness. It is, at its simplest, a way of proceeding from the known to the unknown. . . . Metaphor is our means of effecting instantaneous fusion of two separated realms of experience into one illuminating, iconic, encapsulating image.*
>
> —Robert A. Nisbet

> *I shouted out, "Who killed the Kennedys?," when after all, it was you and me.*
>
> —Lucifer, in Mick Jagger and Keith Richards'
> "Sympathy for the Devil"

### The Language of Images and the Imagination

In almost all the ancient myths of young gods and in so many of the world's stories of heroes, death comes early. Even in the instance of Jesus, his death was prefigured into his drama: he knew that in order to fulfill prophecy, he would need to be sacrificed. Of course, at one level this makes perfect sense: the eternally young god or hero must, in order to stay young, die young. In his classic study of magic and religion, *The Golden Bough*, Sir James Frazer revealed that primitive peoples

> sometimes believe that their safety and even that of the world is bound up with the life of one of these god-men or human incarnations

of the divinity. Naturally, therefore, they take the utmost care of his life, out of a regard for their own. But no amount of care and precaution will prevent the man-god from growing old and feeble and at last dying. . . . There is only one way of averting these dangers. The man-god must be killed as soon as he shows symptoms that his powers are beginning to fail, and his soul must be transferred to a vigorous successor before it has been seriously impaired by the threatened decay.

Eternal youth and its magical qualities must be maintained at all costs.

The hero's death makes sense on another level, too. A psychological and spiritual transformation that so completely marks a departure from one's common, known condition can perhaps only be alluded to by that great, unknown thing we call death. Death is here a symbol for inner death and rebirth. The death and resurrection of Christ speaks to such transformation and the Christian mystics always knew that "death" and "resurrection" were intended to be experienced while one was living and not just when one literally died. The goal of the mystic was to imitate the heroic journey of Christ and internalize it as his or her own.

The eternally young hero who has attained immortal status because he or she has died young is a major source of fascination and fantasy for the American psyche. History and imagination merge together here to create new myths of the hero, or at least to recast old, perennial myths with new hero figures that make the myths contemporary. These reveal not only the American preoccupation with eternal youth. They also cast a light upon the difficult juncture America appears to be at vis-à-vis a collective death-and-rebirth experience of its own. This would naturally seem to revolve around the heroic ideal itself. Thus, the eternally young hero is a metaphor for a particular drama going on within the American soul or psyche, a drama that, because of its spiritual nature, *must* be told in the language of images and the imagination as well as the more factual language of historical and current events. The metaphor and the underlying drama are always consistent; merely the faces of the heroes and the particular facts and details of their lives change according to circumstance.

## The Myth of JFK and the Conspiracy Theory

Few figures in American history have assumed so large a place in the American imagination as John Kennedy. He continues to be a magnetic personality who inspires curiosity, political idealism, and an all-round sense of the extraordinary. He is one of the most beloved presidents of recent times, in spite of the fact that new material about his shadier characteristics and dealings keeps coming out. Much has been written and accepted as historical fact concerning Kennedy's sexual escapades, his connections to people in organized crime, and his father's illegitimate use of money and influence to advance the young politician's career. Yet Americans find a way to hold such information together with what they know as his better qualities and with what they love about him. Perhaps in this regard—in the fact that his is a heroic image of extremes—he is a perfect embodiment of the American character itself. On the surface, he radiates the possibilities of greatness, youth, and innocence, but underneath there lurks an underside which one prefers not to look at too closely.

The Kennedy myth has evolved with such ebullience that *Time*'s Richard Lacayo has charted seven periods that reflect the types of books that have been written about this man and his life. (By 1997, the number of books hovered around 265.) The seven periods, some of them overlapping with each other, include the Golden Era of books that tended to be sentimental and celebratory (1964–69); the Assassination books that tried to reconstruct the events around Kennedy's death (1965–68); the Conspiracy Era (1965–93) in which dozens of titles as well as Oliver Stone's film "JFK" explored the possibility of a conspiracy; the First Revisionist Era which presented a cooler and more realistic view of Kennedy as a person and a politician (1971–79); the Second Revisionist Era in which more books exposed Kennedy's character and private indulgences (1988–present); the books of the Analysts who focused on how President Kennedy made policy (1992–present); and finally, the period of Nostalgia for Kennedy and the Camelot era (1995–present). The latter was provoked by the death of Jacqueline Onassis. Clearly, this history of the public's interest in Kennedy concludes where it began; Americans have completed a full cycle and returned to a sentimental and celebratory view of Kennedy. This speaks to the power of what historian Mircea Eliade called the "mythicization" of historical personages, that is, the "metamorphosis of a historical figure into a mythical hero."

What can explain this enduring fascination with Kennedy? As Elizabeth Gleick wrote, even "the desire to own third-rate objects that Kennedy and his wife Jackie once merely touched can set off a frenzied auction. . . ." Indeed, Kennedy is revered as the eternally young man-god and hero. His mythicization, one might suggest, began with Jackie Kennedy herself. The journalist Theodore H. White interviewed Jacqueline Kennedy days after the assassination. It was in his subsequent article in *Life* that the term "Camelot" was first used to describe the Kennedy years. "For one brief shining moment there was Camelot," was its memorable conclusion. Camelot was of course the town where King Arthur held his court and the Round Table. It was a magical time of glamorous heroes and brilliant young men, a time of grace, good taste, and courage. In his posthumously published notes, White documented how the First Lady thought of using this analogy and even insisted upon it. She was, he says, obsessed with her husband's place in history and worried that the "bitter old men who write history" would not do him justice. Kennedy's image was purposely cast as a noble young hero so that the cynical authority figures who write history would not tarnish his image.

It is doubtful that this image of Camelot would have stuck the way it did had Kennedy not been killed. The nation's grief and the painful fact that Kennedy had been cut off in his prime created a void that only the human heart and imagination could fill, with no less than an image that would immortalize him. His tragic, early death guaranteed him the status of eternal youth. Strangely enough, this mythic pattern of great promise cut short was dramatically reenacted with the deaths of his brother RFK and his son, JFK, Jr. Millions lined the railway tracks to watch RFK's memorial train travel across the nation, so bereaved was the public. The national out-pouring of grief for JFK, Jr. also strongly resembled the anguish people felt when the president was assassinated, and there can be no doubt that their father-son relationship contributed to this. Just as JFK, Sr. became the fallen king of America's Camelot, JFK, Jr. now evoked the image of America's fallen prince. Tragedy and early death tend to go hand-in-hand with the mythicization of a person. The same process may also be observed in the case of Lincoln. Lincoln, as the historian Michael Burlingame points out, was mythicized as the quintessential figure of authority, that is, a wise old man. This is quite the opposite of Kennedy. Yet because of his tragic death, also from assassination, he was immortalized in the American imagination much the way Kennedy was later on.

The fascination with Lincoln and Kennedy cannot be separated from the fascination with Thanatos, the principle of death. As much as their life accomplishments, the tragic way they fell into the hands of Thanatos is the stuff that their myths are made of; Thanatos has raised their lives and deaths to heroic stature. The fascination with Thanatos here is really no dif-ferent than the kind that compels a crowd to gather around an accident or ambulance scene. Partly this involves the feeling of "There but for the grace of God go I," but mostly, it is curiosity about the inexplicable mystery of death and how death can suddenly seize us and remove us from life. There is no way to tell when it will strike, and when it strikes a figure like Lincoln or Kennedy, our awe of that figure becomes mixed with our awe of death. In the same way that one who courageously risks death is glorified as a hero, a person who is already a hero, for whatever reason, is glorified even more if death prematurely claims him. The person did not go gently into the night in his old age; death descended and took him, making something of a martyr out of him.

It is therefore not unlikely that conspiracy theories would evolve around a figure like Kennedy. The fact that he died the way he did is an endless source of mystification. As Shakespeare illustrated, conspiracy is as much a universal motif in the imagination as the death of the hero, and often the two go together. Something has to explain the evil which would cause death to come in this unseemly way, and if explanations of a higher, otherworldly kind are no longer sufficient as they once might have been, worldly ones will do just as well. They have the advantage that they can be attached to concrete persons or parties, but curiously, they are so slippery that in the end they seem as out-of-this-world as the otherworldly explanations. No doubt, it is difficult to explain in any fashion how two bullets could have caused eight wounds between JFK and John Connally. Even President Johnson admitted on his White House tapes that he did not believe in the lone gunman theory. Yet astute investigators like Gerald Posner, Vincent Bugliosi, and Walter Cronkite continue to express the view that there is little or no basis for the conspiracy theory.

But to pursue a discussion of the conspiracy theory based on its pros and cons is not of relevance here. For our purposes it makes little difference whether there was a conspiracy or not. Our interest in the conspiracy theory is in its significance as a public fantasy and in what this fantasy says about the American psyche. The conspiracy theory is another metaphor, a statement of something other than the occurrence of an actual conspiracy. It is a "fable in brief," to use the philosopher Giambattista Vico's definition of metaphor. If the conspiracy theory continues to thrive in the American imagination with such wide support—over 60 percent of Americans believe in it, according to one poll—then its significance lies as much in the belief, in the fable, as in any facts related to its possible occurrence or verity. It is already *as if* the "conspiracy" were a real occurrence. As the philosopher Hans Vaihinger explained, fictitious inventions of the mind that operate on an as-if basis, *as if* they were true, express "fundamental psychic forces." If the fictions do not tell us anything real about the world, they at least tell us something very real about those psychic forces. Just as important as any possible conspiracy "out there" is the conspiracy "in there." This may not be a comfortable way to think about this matter. Indeed, as Hillman said, "It is easier to bear the truth of facts than the truth of fantasies."

What is the truth of the fantasy behind the JFK conspiracy theory? In one regard, as indicated above, the conspiracy theory makes a martyr out of Kennedy and assures that he will be forever revered in the American imagination. But in another regard, it functions as a counterweight to bring the pendulum of that imagination back to an equilibrium from its tendency toward extreme innocence. If Kennedy carries America's projections of innocence, then the conspiracy theory offsets those projections by seizing upon the dark side of human nature. The perpetual fascination with the conspiracy theory seems to be the psyche's way of balancing the excessive innocence Americans attach to Kennedy. In this way the theory functions in the culture very much like those revisionist books that show the dark side of Camelot, to borrow Seymour Hersh's phrase. If the glorified Kennedy is Adam before the Fall, then the revised Kennedy is Adam after the Fall. Similarly, if Kennedy and his administration (which launched conspiracies of its own against Cuba and North Vietnam) are perceived as having a halo, then the conspiracy theory reflects some other part or parts of the government as the complementary, shadowy underside of this innocence. The conspiracy theory appears to be the collective psyche's mechanism for regulating its own overblown innocence. It is because the conspiracy theory assaults the American psyche's basic presumptions of innocence that it is accepted so ambivalently by the population. As Guilford Dudley wrote about the film "JFK," "No wonder the film has been excoriated in the media, for it reaches right to the root of the nation's mythic nerve."

The fantasy of the conspiracy theory does indeed seize upon the dark side of human nature. By saying that the government cannot be trusted, it is saying that *authority* cannot be trusted. That authority is the focus of such profound distrust is to be expected. A culture under the spell of innocence is dominated by the spirit of youth, and therefore it will also be subject to a split between the spirits of youth and authority. Fragmentation and extreme polarization will occur. If youth is all-innocent, then authority will, either in perception or fact, tend to be all-malevolent, that is, evil. The conspiracy theory is usually dependent upon an evil authority structure for its story line. Certainly, in the film "JFK," everyone was "in" on the conspiracy: the Mafia, right-wing extremists and Cuban exiles against Castro, the CIA, the FBI, the U.S. Army, the Dallas Police Department, the Secret Service, the Warren Commission, and even Lyndon Johnson. Oliver Stone, one might think, had Shakespeare's words in mind when he made this film: "Hell's empty. The devils are all here."

The paranoid style of this film, however, can be observed elsewhere today in the media and the culture. Conspiracy theories have become a television and film genre, and are integral to the ideology of certain cults and militia groups. This further suggests that what we are dealing with here is a widespread metaphor and not a phenomenon isolated to JFK. Government conspiracies are portrayed as being responsible for anything and everything that has gone awry in the nation. As one character on "The X-Files" said in regard to how much suspicion should be harbored about covert government activity, "You're not paranoid enough until you're paranoid too much."

A culture insulated by innocence will be prone to outbursts of paranoia and hysteria not only in its attitude toward authority but also, as the McCarthy hearings and Nixon's "enemy list" demonstrated, in the exercise of authority. When the innocently paranoid come into power, they merely do to the public what the public already fears they will do. The public fantasy about conspiracies becomes a public fact, and paranoia becomes a natural part of the culture. This only intensifies the phenomenon of a divided society and its divided heroic ideal. The society does not recognize that, in its innocence, *it* is its own worst enemy, and as such either projects its dark side *onto* its authority structure or, indeed, lives its dark side out *through* its authority structure.

## Why Elvis Presley Won't Die

After John Kennedy, Elvis Presley is in recent times perhaps the most beloved and immortalized figure who tragically died young. In fact, one could argue that the quality of Presley's immortalization surpasses even that of Kennedy. There has been something almost divine about Elvis Presley from the beginning. As Paul McCartney said about what the youth of his day felt when Presley first appeared on the music scene, "the Messiah has arrived." Indeed, Presley is treated by his fans like a divine monarch— he is called "the King"—or like a saint who has left the earth and been canonized. There are, worldwide, some 480 Elvis fan clubs. Public tours of Graceland, Presley's mansion in Memphis, draw approximately 750,000 visitors a year and generate over $20 million in revenues per year. This is more than the number of people who visit Jefferson's home at Monticello or Washington's home at Mount Vernon. Before "Trekkies," there was an Elvis cult that claimed innumerable devout followers. And Presley's fans are not limited to the "wanna-bes." Shortly after he made the cover of

*Newsweek* in 1975, Bruce Springsteen climbed over the walls of a highly guarded Graceland in an effort to meet the King himself (Presley died in 1977). Also without limit are the absurd forms of fan worship. In the 1970s, vials supposedly containing Presley's sweat were marketed, and shortly thereafter a British retailer called "Elvisly Yours" was selling edible Elvis panties.

Clearly, if Elvis is treated as a saint, it is as a Dionysian saint. As a man-god, Elvis Presley was the incarnation of Dionysus, the Greek god of vegetation, fertility, wine, ecstasy, and sexuality. Along with Marilyn Monroe, another tragic figure who died young and became a sex idol for millions, Presley tapped into the primitive, Dionysian elements in the Western psyche that were resurfacing after the long hibernation they underwent during the Victorian period. As the journalist David Halberstam wrote about Presley and Monroe, "Each radiated a powerful, almost magnetic, sexual force, made far greater by the fact that they arrived in the mid-Fifties . . . [in] an America still capable of being shocked." The ancient cult of Dionysus partook in orgiastic festivities whose aim was mystical communion with Dionysus and whose religious frenzy was induced by wine, music, and dance. These celebrations were of particular importance at the beginning of spring, when they marked the return of life after winter. They were thus death-and-rebirth celebrations, and it is in light of this that Dionysus was a god who died young but always rose again. In this there is a parallel to Christ, who also rose at springtime, as celebrated during the Easter holiday.

From this it should be apparent what inspired the hysterical screaming of young women attending the concerts of not only Elvis, but Frank Sinatra before him and the Beatles and Rolling Stones after. These concerts were modern Dionysian rites. The singing gods had to fear for their lives should they fall into the hands of their entranced worshipers. Their clothing would be torn off and their hair pulled out as these possessed young women attempted as nearly as possible to cannibalize them. Of course, we are not speaking here of possession in the way the prophets of the Hebrew Bible were gripped by visions of God, but rather of a merging with the forces of nature such as what occurred in the pagan mystery religions well before the emergence of Judaism and Christianity. Elvis was in fact a very ancient god.

Also apparent should be the reason for the erotic cult that has mushroomed around Presley. Men and women alike have a romantic kind of relationship with him in their imaginations; that is, his significance is charged with romantic meaning. He is a great purveyor of love—the love of music, the love of women, the love of life. He is as popular after his death as before, if not more. Professional and amateur Elvis impersonators compete in regional and national contests and conventions and earn their livelihood in Las Vegas officiating at weddings. So powerful is Presley's impact on American culture that the University of Mississippi held a symposium in 1995 to study it. Paraphernalia connected with his image has become such a booming business that his former wife registered a trademark to regulate his family's right. Even the U.S. Postal Service cashed in on his appeal with a stamp that is among the most popular of all time. One sees Elvis' image everywhere in the culture, and it even seems to take precedence over his music. Like Dionysus, he has risen. Accordingly, it is no wonder that people claim to have had "Elvis sightings"—at the corner grocery store late at night, hitchhiking at a truck stop, fishing at a lake. Like UFO reports or repressed memory syndrome, these apparitions are a contagion myth, or what Jung called a visionary rumor: they have spread through the culture like wildfire, seemingly leaping from person to person on the level of the collective unconscious. Elvis won't die because his death has made him an eternally young god, a hero who lives on in the imagination and culture forever and who moves people's souls so powerfully that he appears to them in visions as real as anything in their physical world.

## Rock 'n' Roll and the Dionysian Death

Dionysus died from dismemberment, and, in a manner of speaking, so did Elvis. Drugs, insomnia, exhaustion, the struggle to force his body to stay forever young and trim, and an insatiable appetite for adulation but a debilitating emptiness within, all contributed to his depression and falling apart. A Dionysian death raises the hero's demise to dramatic proportions as unequivocally as would an assassination, thereby also assuring his immortality in the public's memory. The hero who dies from having surrendered to the passions would in olden times have been looked upon as having made the ultimate self-sacrifice to the gods, or at least to the god Dionysus. In modern times, although such an act is condemned as a waste, it is, paradoxically, still held in awe. This is because a life that is so engulfed in passion that it leads to death is one that for many is secretly attractive. So naturally, the hero who has lived and died in this way attains a special mythic status. Kennedy's image, though tarnished, is simultaneously enhanced by the sexual passion and indulgences the revisionist books claim gripped him. Marilyn Monroe needs no introduction as a goddess who, at least in the public's imagination, lived and died according to the Dionysian code. James Dean, the object of an entire generation's fantasies of dark brooding passion, could for all intents and purposes be considered as having been dismembered in a fatal car accident. And of course, we should not forget the host of other Hollywood stars, ranging from Rudolph Valentino to River Phoenix, who were tragic young hero figures.

The escalating number of such deaths among young American culture-heroes since Kennedy is truly remarkable. Rock 'n' roll offers a litany of fallen young heroes and heroines. This should not be surprising: rock is a return to Dionysian roots par excellence, and the Dionysian life has a greater likelihood of ending prematurely because of the inherent difficulty of moderating the excesses to which it is prone. Jazz too is an original American art form that has for the same reason numerous dead Dionysian heroes—Billie Holiday, Charlie Parker, and Chet Baker to mention just a few. But nothing quite surpasses rock 'n' roll. In addition to Elvis, we may include the following among the many who died young: Buddy Holly; Bill Haley; Ritchie Valens; Rick Nelson; Phil Ochs; Otis Redding; Jackie Wilson; "Mama" Cass Elliot; Jimi Hendrix; Janis Joplin; Jim Morrison; Brian Jones; Keith Moon; John Bonham; John Lennon; Dennis Wilson; Duane Allman; Bob Marley; Marvin Gaye; Andy Gibb; Harry Chapin; Jim Croce; Stevie Ray Vaughn; John Denver; and Kurt Cobain. Of course, not all of these died a Dionysian death, a few were not American, and others were only on the fringes of what is considered rock. However, by popular standards, all were talented people, and they compel us to wonder about the adage that "only the good die young."

Of those above, Jim Morrison is of particular interest. Characterized as a satyr and notorious for his alcoholism, he epitomized the Dionysian life. As illustrated in Oliver Stone's film, "The Doors," he had a consuming obsession with Thanatos, seeking it out as an escape from ordinariness and toying with it in repeated acts of defiance and inflation. Eventually, his alcoholism and love affair with Thanatos caught up with him, and he died a Dionysian death. Like many other rock stars, his was not a sudden, violent suicide, but one prolonged through self-indulgence and -neglect. (It is curious how Stone picks tragic and eternally young heroes as subjects for his films; even his film "Nixon" was about a man who, like Kennedy, could not complete his heroic mission and became immortalized for the tragic way he was stopped short.) What makes Morrison noteworthy, however, is the fact that he became considerably more popular after his death than he was before it. He has even become a cult figure, which he most likely would not have become had he lived. Not even John Lennon, whose music almost consistently had a timeless quality and who was assassinated, became a cult idol after he died. The factor that has catapulted Morrison to a cult status seems to be his Dionysian death. It is *as if* the youth culture itself has glorified the principle of Dionysian death *through* Jim Morrison, as it has made not only a hero out of him, nor just a death-hero, but a Dionysian death-hero. This marriage between the cult of passion and the cult of celebrity is steeped in the innocent belief that a life and death ruled by passion is noble because it is instinctual and pure. The glorification of the hero who lives the life and dies the death of Dionysus is an extreme form of cultural primitivism.

## Death-Heroes and the Wish for Transformation

The culture's awe of young heroes who have died tragically was captured comically but truthfully in a 1986 episode of the television show "Saturday Night Live." In a skit involving a rock musician and his manager, a meeting is arranged with a business consultant because the musician's career has been in a steady decline. At the meeting, the manager and consultant, using a chart with a bell curve, try to convince the musician that the record sales of Buddy Holly, Jimi Hendrix, and Jim Morrison had soared since their deaths. The punch line, of course, was that for the musician to pull his career out of its slump, he should kill himself.

On a more serious note, this worship of death-heroes begins to make sense when we understand it in light of the suicide impulse. This is essentially what has motivated most death-heroes as well as the culture's fascination with them. It is basically the same as what Freud called the death wish. But the death wish is not always a wish for literal death, though it may appear that way. It is often, as discussed in the last chapter, a wish for psychological death and rebirth. It is a wish for spiritual transformation. Even as early as with the ancient Ionian tale of Amor and Psyche in Apuleius' *The Golden Ass,* such transformation is connected with suicide: every time Psyche—with whom the idea of the psyche or soul is obviously connected—was faced with a transformation, she went into a suicidal frenzy. Inner transformation and death are closely related. Something old must die before something new can be born, or as Picasso said, "Every act of creation is first an act of destruction." Psychological death is usually a painful experience in which something of the self must be destroyed or abandoned.

Adolescents often mistake the pain they are going through and the impulse behind it—an impulse aimed essentially at growth and only incidentally at destruction—as an impetus to annihilate themselves. Instead of destroying *something* of the self, they destroy the self. The experience of inner death becomes concretized as literal, physical death. To the extent that

American culture worships heroes like Jim Morrison who concretize the death wish in a glorified act of suicide, it exhibits this adolescent mentality and mistake. However, we must not fall prey to the tendency of becoming too literal ourselves. Perhaps the culture's fascination with young and innocent thanatotic heroes is less an identification with them per se than an expression of the death wish for its own heroic ideal, of which the heroes are merely symbols. Could this death wish be a necessary first step in a larger death-and-rebirth process which our culture is about to undertake? Similarly, one may wonder whether rock groups with names like "Arrested Development," the "Dead Kennedys," and "Suicide," or the nihilistic, violent features of punk and rap music, merely glorify destruction and death, or if they also point to this larger process.

However, transformation is always dependent upon consciousness. A society's critical reflection upon its own need to change is a crucial ingredient for such change. America seems to be largely unconscious of the dynamic behind its fascination with eternally young and innocent death-heroes. This dynamic consists of the society's own youthful innocence and a death wish that would quite appropriately end that innocence. America must face the end of its innocence in order for there to emerge a heroic ideal that is more suitable for a maturing nation.

Unfortunately, the American heroic ideal remains hinged upon the notion of innocence. It is true that the JFK myth in its revised versions and the conspiracy theories attempt to unhinge this notion. However, most public fantasies revolving around eternally young heroes—whether Elvis Presley, Marilyn Monroe, or Jim Morrison—are idealizations and idolizations of people who were actually very troubled. Each of these people mirrored society's problems and then suffered as its scapegoat—"scapegoat" not in the modern sense of being blamed for society's problems, but in the ancient, sacrificial sense of carrying the sins of society and, supposedly, relieving it of them. They became victims of the same adoring society that had idolized them insofar as they became, willingly or not, the objects of that society's innocent but thanatotic fantasies. To make matters worse, their woundedness has also been glorified, and thus there is now an all-enveloping shroud of innocence from which the culture has almost hopelessly left no way out for itself. A wound, Hillman tells us, usually marks the end of a consciousness that is too young. It kills innocence with reality. But America will not accept the wounds of its heroes or its own wounds for very long; these too it converts into the high drama and innocence of eternal youth.

# Chapter 15

## The Explosion of Innocence

*When innocence has been deprived of its entitlement, it becomes a diabolical spirit.*

—James Grotstein

### War and Imperialism, American Style

No wound to American heroic idealism compares with that of the Vietnam War. Certainly the Confederacy suffered a fatal wound when it was defeated, but that was less a defeat to American heroic idealism or America's sense of itself than a struggle to define what these should be. The Vietnam War struck a debilitating blow to America's idealism and self-concept not only because it was the nation's first defeat, but because of the bewildered condition in which the war was fought and lost. Few could foresee that America's heroic ideal—particularly its simple differentiation between good and evil—would not stand up to the complex realities that riddled this war. Many Americans at home and in the jungles in which they fought had no real convictions about why they were fighting, or at least they lost those convictions if they had them in the beginning. And they could not understand why the war was not being won in spite of the great investment of men, weapons, and other resources. America was defeated on the front lines of its innocence well before it retreated from those of Vietnam.

James Thomson, Jr., a National Security Council staff member in the Johnson administration, nicely summed up the innocent mindset of America during the Vietnam War: "There was a strong sense that Americans were can-do people, and anything we put our mind to we could accomplish. And the kind of rural, jungle warfare that the Communists were inflicting on us in the Third World, we could adapt to, and we could win at it because we were smarter, we had more technology, we had billions of dollars, and we would prevail." The innocence of course was not only in the sense that Americans could overcome all odds but, again, that they had God on their side, that they were undoubtedly the righteous ones in this conflict.

Thus did the TV images of young American soldiers in a state of confusion about their heroic mission and, moreover, appearing as losers rather than winners, so upset American viewers back home. This was probably chief among the factors that turned the tide of public opinion against the war. A schism between the public and its leadership developed in a way that was itself warlike, and the relationship between the public and the young soldiers fighting the nation's war similarly became warped. That relationship came to resemble the one between a critical, rejecting parent and an abandoned child. As General Norman Schwarzkopf commented, "We soldiers, sailors, airmen, and Marines were literally the sons and daughters of America, and to lose public support was akin to being rejected by our own parents." The despair of America's soldiers fighting a war whose purpose and rules of engagement they could not understand has yet to be fully assessed. It has been estimated that of the 58,000 servicemen who died in Vietnam, 8,000 were suicides. Frederick Hart's statue of three soldiers at the Vietnam Veterans Memorial in Washington, D.C. is revealing. When erected it caused controversy because the soldiers look so haggard and defeated. But this precisely is its significance: it reflects America's admission of defeat, moral and otherwise.

Carl Jung once said that self-realization is always experienced as a defeat for the ego. The greater part of our personality can only come into the foreground when the lesser part and its will to dominate have been frustrated. The same principle applies to collective psychology: the greater possibilities of a nation's character can only come into play when old, familiar modes have been frustrated and outgrown. Defeat in a war has often been an incentive for nations to set off in new directions and launch new eras in their histories. The aphorism commonly repeated in regard to Japan and Germany—that they lost World War II and won the peace—is often used by Americans to ironically convey the twentieth century's best examples of this. Of course, the Marshall Plan helped Western Europe get back on its feet, but this alone was not the sole cause of Germany's postwar success. Defeat compels a nation to re-vision its orientation. Another example of this that is less economic in nature is Egypt's defeat by Israel in the Yom Kippur War. Finally convinced that it could not prevail over Israel's military superiority, Egypt under Sadat's leadership embarked on a new course of peace and cooperation with Israel, the first Arab nation to do so.

Defeat in the Vietnam War introduced a sobering-up process through which America began to examine some of the innocent assumptions of its foreign policy. In particular, its image of itself as the policeman of the world—a notion first articulated by Theodore Roosevelt but which is rooted in the larger bedrock of its messianic complex and desire to be an empire— has come under review and revision. But this revision is a slow process and is characterized by the kind of ambivalence that one might expect in con- nection with defeat. Barely 20 years after the end of the Vietnam War, George Bush was proudly boasting, on the eve of victory in the Persian Gulf War, that "we have finally kicked the Vietnam syndrome." Of course, one might argue that sometimes the world does need America to be its po- liceman. The prospect of America not intervening in Bosnia-Herzogovina and Serbia, for example, would have suggested an innocence with frighten- ingly dark consequences. As it was, the crimes committed in that area were already hauntingly reminiscent of those of the Holocaust.

The issue then is not whether America acts as policeman of the world, but whether it does so out of the innocence of its messianic complex and de- sire to be an empire as opposed to a genuine consideration of moral imper- atives. Policing that is not really concerned with justice ends up being impe- rialistic and exploitative, traits America has often been accused of by Third World countries. The slogans one hears and placards one sees in mass demonstrations in Third World capitals are grounded in this impression of America. In his illuminating study, *Empire as a Way of Life,* the historian William Appleman Williams traces the development of American expan- sionism, beginning with the effort to drive Native Americans further and further westward and off their lands, through the consolidation of the sub- continent by means of civil and international war, to the achievement of an economic empire with interests all over the world. He shows how "America as an empire required a coordinated government program to integrate fi- nance, agriculture, manufacturing, and commerce through a continental transportation system and a systematic effort to acquire land and markets." To this purpose, American interventionism from 1787 to 1941 consisted of over 150 military incursions or acts of aggression (excluding declared wars) in almost every continent of the world.

American empire-building differed from the traditional style of empire- building; it was, and continues to be, an economic imperialism. The acquisi- tion and protection of markets and the development of industries abroad have been integral to the flourishing of prosperity at home. As Williams adds, "the United States never embarked upon a program of acquiring colonies, or even spheres of influence, in the classic European way of empire. The map of the world has never been splashed with a color keyed to the continental United States in the way that it has been washed with the hues used for Great Britain, France, or Germany . . . [Yet] a map colored to show primary or major economic, political, and military *power and influence* would reveal the United States as a global empire." This distinction between classical and economic imperialism is important. America *never had to* militarily and permanently occupy other nations, even if it had been inclined to do so, because it could obtain the same results of power, influence, and affluence from its penetration of foreign markets across the globe. With globalization and the emergence of America's strategic control of the global economy, this model has served America better than the nation's early empire-builders could have ever imagined.

A number of prominent figures have understood that if America must be an empire, it must at least be true to its own democratic principles and be, as Jefferson conceived, an empire of liberty. Herbert Hoover clearly recognized that an imperialism that harms the nations upon which it depends—that exploits them through unilaterally beneficial trade agreements and exacerbates inequities by dividing their political economies into rich and poor—would not only lead to social unrest, revolutionary nationalism, and a need for American intervention escalating into wars; it would also lead to the eventual end of the American empire. But Hoover and his kind were a minority. For the large part, American imperialism has been exclusively self-serving, either innocent in its understanding of its evil effects or actively complicit in generating them. When, for example, America went to war with Spain in order to "liberate" Cuba, little did the Cubans realize that their self-government would be limited to serving American interests. The Platt Amendment, passed by Congress in 1901 and incorporated into the new Cuban Constitution, gave the United States the right to intervene in Cuban domestic affairs and get coaling or naval stations at specified locations. Philip Foner, in his extensive study *The Spanish-Cuban-American War and the Birth of American Imperialism,* describes how American merchants, real estate agents, stock speculators, and promoters of all kinds flocked to Cuba by the thousands, and how railroad, mine, and sugar properties were taken over by Americans at unbelievably low prices. Although it would be sixty years until Fidel Castro would emerge on the scene, the seeds of the current, conflict-prone relationship between Cuba and the United States had been planted, and the events of the two periods cannot be seen as unrelated. America had, as Cubans complained, merely replaced Spain as their imperial overlord.

The Philippines provide an even more clear-cut example of how America asserted its power in an underdeveloped nation, promising to improve the quality of political and economic life but instead imposing tyranny and destruction. After acquiring these islands from Spain in the same Spanish-American War that involved Cuba, America rejected a proposal for Filipino independence as a U.S. protectorate. In 1899, the Filipinos revolted against American rule, resulting in a three-year conflict that involved 70,000 American troops and cost hundreds of thousands of Filipinos their lives, either through combat, famine, or disease. The Manila correspondent of the Philadelphia *Ledger* reported in 1901:

> The present war is no bloodless, opera bouffe engagement; our men have been relentless, have killed to exterminate men, women, children, prisoners and captives, active insurgents and suspected people from lads of ten up, the idea prevailing that the Filipino as such was little better than a dog. . . . Our soldiers have pumped salt water into men to make them talk, and have taken prisoners people who held up their hands and peacefully surrendered, and an hour later, without an atom of evidence to show that they were even *insurrectos,* stood them on a bridge and shot them down one by one, to drop into the water below and float down, as examples to those who found their bullet-loaded corpses.

The carnage and widespread leveling of villages—much of it, as Howard Zinn points out, race-related—aroused some protest on the home front. The philosopher and psychologist William James angrily proclaimed: "God damn the U.S. for its vile conduct in the Philippine Isles." Mark Twain commented:

> We have pacified some thousands of the islanders and buried them; destroyed their fields; burned their villages, and turned their widows and orphans out-of-doors; furnished heartbreak by exile to some dozens of disagreeable patriots; subjugated the remaining ten millions by Benevolent Assimilation, which is the pious new name of the musket; we have acquired property in the three hundred concubines and other slaves of our business partner, the Sultan of Sulu, and hoisted our protecting flag over that swag.
>
> And so, by these Providences of God—and the phrase is the government's, not mine—we are a World Power.

Evidently, the innocent self-assuredness and barbaric My Lai-type massacres that made the Vietnam War so toxic and brutal had manifest as early as the war against the Filipinos. Although these wars had different origins and objectives, they were both manifestations of the same kind of imperial power-wielding.

## America's Messianic Complex

As Thayer Greene remarked and as history shows, such imperial muscle-flexing is typical of young, adolescent nations that are reaching the peak of their prowess. Empire-building goes hand-in-hand with the spirit of youth. The many corporate empires that Americans created domestically and multinationally reflect this spirit too, and are the economic components of a single great, global empire. The desire for empire is basic to the American enterprise, and although many Americans today may not like to use the word "empire" to describe this enterprise, this word was common in the vocabulary of the Founding Fathers. Again, the Founding Fathers were very much inspired by the Greeks and Romans, particularly the latter. Empire, which is but the object and substance of imperialism, was not a derogatory term for them but something they explicitly sought. To them, empire-building or imperialism was the manifest form of the American vision of the brotherhood of man and the heavenly city on the hill, of the *Novus Ordo Seclorum* or New Order of the Ages. One did not go without the other.

Given this heritage, it should come as no surprise that there is a great sense of entitlement, of a special calling, that colors American empire-building. This is no doubt connected to that other vital component of the American vision, Providence. As Mark Twain indicated above, Providence was seen as a justification for the war in the Philippines. Similarly, it can be demonstrated that Providence has been recruited in every war America has fought, starting with the war against the Indians and including the conflict in Vietnam. That America has been specially chosen by God to bring its vision to the rest of the world renders this vision messianic, a term that has been widely and loosely bandied about but requiring some clarification.

The messianic idea goes back to ancient Israel, the first messianic nation. In the Israelite scheme of things, the people of Israel were chosen to be a godly nation and thus a light unto the other nations of the world. But the messianic idea here was rooted as much in Israel's own need to be saved as in its calling to serve as a beacon for others. Beginning with the crises that characterized the period of the Judges, the disparate tribes of Israel came to believe that God would unite them and, in each crisis, send an inspired leader who would deliver them from evil. With such "deliverers" as Deborah, Samson, and Ruth (notice the strong role of the feminine in Hebrew heroism), one sees elements of the later concept of the "Messiah"— literally, the "Anointed One." With the Prophets, there then emerged the specific idea that there would one day come a divinely appointed, enlightened ruler who would lead the world to righteousness and peace. This was not a simple idea to begin with, and as Judaism evolved it became even more complex. By Jesus' time it became clearly associated with political liberation from the Romans and restoration of the Jewish state, though this was always understood in a theological or religious framework and not a secular one: occupation and emancipation were connected, respectively, to the nation's sinfulness and divine forgiveness. (Indeed, Jesus' mission must be seen in this context, a context that gave rise to a host of messianic figures who preached across the land and died at the hands of the Romans.) Hopes of deliverance similarly fueled the messianic idea from the thirteenth to the eighteenth centuries, when the Jews suffered recurrently from persecution and oppression in foreign lands and produced a series of spectacular messianic heroes. Of course, these were all eventually disclosed to be false messiahs and more or less delusional. Partly as a consequence of this, modern Judaism has moved toward a less concrete and fixed understanding of what the coming of the Messiah means.

The merging of the messianic idea with the heroic ideal, with the aspiration toward greatness, results in a messianic complex. This can occur on both the individual and collective levels. It consists of a deeply ingrained belief that one or one's social group has a special if not divinely appointed mission to bring redemption to the world, in whatever form this may be conceived. A number of nations since ancient Israel have believed that they have had messianic missions. Condorcet wrote about the perfect world that was coming as a result of the pairing of the French Enlightenment and the American Revolution. Comte a century later asserted that France alone would be the leader in this new world order, and hoped that French would become the universal language. Lionel Curtis' *Civitas Dei* outlines the British version of this regeneration of mankind. Mazzini advocated Italy's future contribution to the development of humanity. Fichte envisioned Germany becoming a *Menschheitsnation* ("humanistic nation"), and Emanuel Geibel boasted that "the German spirit will be the world's salvation." This was well before Germany embarked on the dark mission of its Third Reich or empire, namely, to establish Germans as the *Herrenrasse* (the "sovereign race"), to exterminate the Jews, and to make Eastern Europe—and probably after that the entire world—its *Lebensraum*, or "living space." As for Russia, it has always had messianic impulses, with the Marxist-Leninist, Soviet state being a culmination of them. Almost every great nation has had some form of messianism, some conviction that it would save the world by leading the way in showing how humanity could be the master of its destiny.

Having sketched the larger backdrop against which to view America's messianic complex, let us turn to the latter. Following are some presidential pronouncements that speak to this complex. Notice how seamlessly these connect to the prospect of empire-building and maintenance:

> George Washington: ". . . the preservation of the sacred fire of liberty and the destiny of the republican model of government are justly considered, perhaps as deeply, as finally staked on the experiment intrusted to the hands of the American people."
>
> Thomas Jefferson: "I am persuaded no constitution was never before as well calculated as ours for extensive empire and self-government."
>
> James Madison: "This form of government [constitutional democracy], in order to effect its purposes, must operate not within a small but an extensive sphere."
>
> James Monroe: ". . . the greater the expansion [of the Union], within practical limits, and it is not easy to say what are not so, the greater the advantage which the States individually will derive from it. . . . Extent of territory, whether it be great or small, gives to a nation many of its characteristics. It marks the extent of its resources, of its population, of its physical force. It marks, in short, the difference between a great and a small power."
>
> John Quincy Adams: "[The United States is] a nation, coextensive with the North American Continent, destined by God and nature to be the most populous and most powerful people ever combined under one social compact." (Adams eventually came to question the conventional wisdom of the practices of American empire-building.)
>
> James K. Polk: "Our system may be safely extended to the utmost bounds of our territorial limits and . . . as it shall be extended the bonds of our Union, so far from being weakened, will be stronger."
>
> Abraham Lincoln: "In giving freedom to the slave, we assure freedom to the free—honorable alike in what we give and what we preserve. We shall nobly save or meanly lose the last, best hope of earth."

William McKinley: ". . . there was nothing left for us to do but to take them all [the Philippines] and to educate the Filipinos, and uplift and civilize and Christianize them, and by God's grace do the very best we could by them, as our fellow men for whom Christ also died."

Theodore Roosevelt: "Chronic wrongdoing, or an impotence which results in a general loosening of the ties of civilized society, may . . . in the Western Hemisphere . . . force the United States, however reluctantly . . . to the exercise of an international police power."

William Howard Taft: "The diplomacy of the present administration . . . is an effort frankly directed to the increase of American trade . . . [as a part of our] international philanthropy."

Woodrow Wilson: "The stage is set, the destiny disclosed. It has come about by no plan of our conceiving, but by the hand of God who led us into this way. We cannot turn back. We can only go forward, with lifted eyes and freshened spirit, to follow the vision. It was of this that we dreamed at our birth. America shall in truth show the way."

Franklin Delano Roosevelt: "It would be particularly unwise from political and psychological standpoints to permit limitation of our action to be imposed by any other nation than our own."

Harry Truman: "[It is necessary for the United States to police the world:] in order to carry out a just decision the court must have marshals; in order to collect monies for county governments it has been found necessary to employ a sheriff."

John F. Kennedy: "[America has] obligations which stretch ten thousand miles across the Pacific, and three and four thousand miles across the Atlantic, and thousands of miles to the south. Only the United States—and we are only six percent of the world's population—bears this kind of burden."

Ronald Reagan: ". . . I believe there was a divine plan to place this great continent here between the two oceans to be found by peoples from every corner of the Earth. I believe we were preordained to carry the torch of freedom for the world."

As one can gather, the particular trademark that distinguishes the American messianic complex from that of other nations is the method by which it wishes to show humanity how it could be the master of its destiny. This method is democracy, the instrument that will bring about the empire of liberty. But this is only one prong in a two-pronged approach; the other prong, as one can also gather, is quite typically the darker side of this complex: imperialism, or empire for the sake of empire. This prong of America's messianic complex is in fact less concerned with showing humanity how the latter could be the master of its destiny than in showing how *America* could be the master of humanity's destiny. Such has been the inherent message of most empires in history, no matter how beneficial or well-meaning have been the gifts of civilization that they have bestowed upon their subject-nations. America in particular wishes to deny to the world *and* to itself that it is indeed an empire, for that appears to be contradictory to its mission of advancing liberty and democracy. But whether overtly or covertly, this messianic self-validation, too, is typical of young, adolescent nations reaching the peak of their prowess. Messianism goes with youth, even in individual psychology. Jean Piaget writes that the synthesis of social cooperation and high self-valuation characteristic in adolescent development "often appears as a form of Messianism. The adolescent in all modesty attributes to himself an essential role in the salvation of humanity and organizes his life plan accordingly. . . . The adolescent makes a pact with his God, promising to serve him without return, but, by the same token, he counts on playing a decisive role in the cause he has undertaken to defend."

The apparent contradiction between the two prongs of American messianism, democracy and imperialism, is resolved ideologically in the American mind. Again, the Founding Fathers saw no contradiction between them. The connecting point that brings them together so that they may coexist is prosperity. This connection makes sense as soon as one recalls that the purpose of liberal democracy is, *à la* Locke, the acquisition of property and the attainment of prosperity (the "happiness of man"). If democracy assures prosperity, then imperialism begets it. One can deduce from Locke's own words the justification for empire: "Riches do not consist in having more Gold and Silver, but in having more in proportion than the rest of the World, or than our Neighbours, whereby we are enabled to procure to ourselves a greater Plenty of the Conveniences of Life than comes within the reach of Neighbouring Kingdoms and States." That this Lockean worldview inevitably creates problems in a world that has a highly interrelated and sensitive global economy and that, as we now know, has limited resources was naturally not considered by such advocates of empire. How this will affect the American empire in the future remains to be seen, and is a problem of critical concern. Indeed, how will America reconcile its messianic mission with the rapidly changing contours of the world? How will a nation that presently has 5 percent of the world's population continue to consume 25 percent of the earth's natural resources—a disparity which could never exist without the practice of imperialism—when the rest of the world's increasing population will need more and more of the earth's resources for its own sustenance?

Defeat in the Vietnam War was the first strong signal to America that it is going to have to adapt its mission if it wishes this mission to be relevant and acceptable in the modern world. Reinhold Niebuhr and Alan Heimert have described two moral hazards that typically plague a nation with a strong sense of mission. Firstly, it tends to regard its mission as proof of its superior virtue—a pretension that can be very dangerous when allowed to fashion foreign policy. Secondly, it tends to slavishly "interpret its mission in a rapidly changing history in terms of the original content and substance of its messianic dream. . . . The content of the messianic commitment must be constantly amended and adjusted to the emerging unpredictable contingencies of history. . . ." It can be argued that the first of these hazards led to the war in the Philippines, and the second to the war in Vietnam. Ironically, the war in the Philippines demonstrated how lacking in virtue America could be, and the Vietnam War showed Americans completely confused about their mission or at least touting a mission that was completely maladapted to the world of the Vietnamese. That America still touts its mission in a maladaptive way is evident when its policy of pressuring Third World nations to democratize becomes so rigid and forceful that it creates crises in diplomacy and trade. Henry Kissinger warns against the alienating effects of this stance of playing the colonial missionary who passes judgment and exerts coercion on the domestic human rights policies of countries like China. Should the smaller Asian countries ever have to choose to ally with only one nation or the other—China or the United States—it is wrong to assume that they will hands down choose the United States.

The messianic complex is the aspect of the American heroic ideal that extends the nation's heroic idealism into the international theater and serves as the compass that guides the nation in its global activities. Whether in the form of a missionary, policeman, or all-round superpower and "political Messiah," to use Melville's phrase, America has been driven by this complex. Many of its wars and much of its imperialism are rooted in it, illustrating Rollo May's assertion that "It is not by its history that the mythology of a nation is determined, but, conversely, its history is determined by its mythology." A messianic complex, vision, and mission always consist of a kind of mythology. In America's case this is so strong that the psychologist Adolf Guggenbühl-Craig claimed that "The United States is not really a nation but a religion. From the beginning the United States has had a messianic-religious outlook." There may be a separation between formal, institutional religion and the state in America, but the nation is permeated by the informal religion of its messianic outlook.

The problem in all of this is not necessarily with the complex itself. After all, as Jung pointed out, complexes are a natural part of the human constitution. They seem to be characterological and to serve a purpose in human development (if not the purpose they literally promote in their mythology or religious outlook). What is a grave problem and danger is the innocence or naive realism with which nations act upon them. In that case, the nation does not have the complex; the complex has *it*. The violence and destruction this reaps have been repeatedly demonstrated by history. The messianism of Nazi Germany, for instance, was part of a complex that Jung argued had existed long before the rise of the Third Reich and that once had even produced a variety of cultural benefits. Every complex has both constructive and destructive elements. However, the violent, destructive features of this complex became dominant when the Germans became gripped by the complex in an unconscious, inflated manner. It is not a complex that wages wars and destroys lives, but people who unquestioningly submit to the complex's force and its distorted, godlike way of thinking.

## Violence as the Fist of Innocence

To turn from America's violence in international affairs to the violence on its own streets involves a shift only in focus. In significance, both behaviors are explosions or eruptions of innocence. Violence as an acting-out of innocence, Rollo May notes, is characterized by the quest for power or identity. It compensates for how impotent or confused in identity the perpetrator of the violence really is, but of course, it only deceives the perpetrator into believing he has some real power—other than brute power—or a sense of identity. The innocence rests in his lack of awareness about any of this. He is innocent about his need *and capacity* to genuinely empower himself and find or create a meaning to his life that will give him a sense of identity. And of course, like with the nation that resorts to violence to empower itself or establish its identity, so too with the individual: there is an innocence in the false entitlement and justification he feels in being violent. One always sees oneself as innocent and the other as meriting the violence; always the other is the evil one. The fact that so much of the violence in the history of the world falls into this category only goes to show how closely allied innocence is with evil.

Violence has always been part of the human condition. There has never been a society that did not have violence. Primitive tribes and archaic cultures that were not warlike often had some form of ritualized violence in their religious rites, such as human sacrifice, and even among the supposedly peace-loving Tibetan Buddhists there has for centuries been an often violent struggle for power between the two main sects, the Yellow Hats and the Red Hats. Any good English or French novel of the eighteenth or nineteenth century—when the novelist functioned very much in the role of society's faithful witness—can plainly show that one put his life in others' hands when he traveled between cities. However, the increase of violence in America in the last half of the twentieth century is of concern because it goes against the trend of increasingly widespread civility that emerged, in all Western nations, with industrialization, higher standards of living, education, and cosmopolitanism. (This is in contrast to the rarefied civility that before modern times could only be enjoyed by the privileged few in the courts and the noble class.) Violence in America today clearly indicates a deterioration of this civility.

The statistics, though they vary depending on which source is used, confirm this as well as the fact that America is the most violent of the industrialized nations (excluding those engaged in civil war). America's homicide rate is twice that of Spain, which has the second highest homicide rate in the industrialized world, and four times that of Canada. In 1999 there were 15,500 murders in the United States—approximately 8,000 less than the number five years earlier; the declining rate is believed to be largely due to the decreasing number of 18- to 34-year-olds—the most likely group to commit murder—and only secondarily to the increased amount of police patrolling the streets where many of these murders take place as a result of gang warfare and the like. Homicide is a leading cause of death among young people aged 13 to 24, second only to car accidents (4,000 people in this age group were murdered in 1999); for black men aged 15 to 24, it *is* the leading cause. The homicide rate for children and adolescents has more than doubled since 1965, and it goes without saying that the juvenile rate for committing homicide has also dramatically increased (55 percent from 1985 to 1995).

In addition to homicide, there are approximately 1.5 million assaults every year and 12 million property crimes, including 8,800 hate crimes. In 1999, the number of women who reported that they had been raped was 89,100. However, at least 550,000 unreported rapes or rape attempts are estimated to occur every year. A staggering 2 million women are beaten by their partners each year, and 8 to 11 percent of pregnant women are assaulted. A national survey of schools in 1991 found that 26 percent of high school students reported carrying a weapon at least once during the prior month, a problem compelling many schools to employ metal detectors at their entrances. Of the 46.8 million elementary and high school students in America, it has been estimated that 270,000 bring guns to school every day and 160,000 stay home from fear of violence. One in nine teachers has been assaulted at school, and 95 percent of these assaults were committed by students. For those who like to think that there is a correlation between violence in society and violence on TV, the average child witnesses 40,000 televised murders and 200,000 violent acts by the age of 18; the rate of incidents of violence in prime time is five per hour.

One can only conclude from all this that Americans have a strange love affair with violence, even seeking it out on TV and in the movie theaters during their hours of leisure. Rollo May points out that violence has an ecstatic quality—a phenomenon also reported in many memoirs of soldiers in combat—which would mean that it can be a form of addiction not only to innocence but to height. It is charged with passion and provides a peak experience, however destructive this may be. Though modern times have seen an alarming increase in violence, it is evident that this love of violence has been in the American psyche since its birth. Trends of greater or lesser violence may come and go but the basic inclination towards it remains constant. As the Black Panther H. Rap Brown said, "Violence is as American as cherry pie." Even Jefferson recognized that the violent origins of the United States were a vital part of the nation's mythology and would continue to influence its history for no other reason than that the people were proud of these origins. "The blood of the people is become an inheritance," he wrote. Moreover, this basic inclination is rooted in the frontier experience which, as Boorstin so eloquently stated, forced the European settler "to relive the childhood of the race, to confront once again the primitive and intractable wilderness of his cave-dwelling ancestors." Primal youth *is* violent.

Modern times have recreated a frontier environment insofar as the individual has become lost in a consumer culture and information age that generate a mass mindset and identity. Finding himself at odds with something very huge—indeed, without recognizable boundaries and with a tendency to swallow him—he must do everything he can to survive and just keep up. Life today is a psychological and cultural frontier that assaults the individual with the forever new and overwhelming demands of the cults of technology, prosperity, and novelty. It is not surprising that this frontier assaults the development of the individual's identity and integrity. And so, modern times *again* force the American into a frontier mode that compels him to confront, if not the primitive and intractable *wilderness* of his cave-dwelling ancestors, then the primitive and intractable *wildness* of these ancestors. "On the frontier," McLuhan informs us, "everybody is a nobody, and therefore the frontier manifests the patterns of toughness and vigorous action on the part of those trying to find out who they are." Like Rollo May, McLuhan believes that

> This is where the violence [in America today] comes from. This meaningless slaying around our streets is the work of people who have lost all identity, and who have to kill in order to know if they're real or if the other guy's real. . . . Violence as a form of quest for identity is something the people who have been ripped off feel the need of. He's going to show who he is, what his credentials are, that he's tough. So anybody on a psychic frontier tends to get tough or violent and it's happening to us on a mass scale today.

Violence in America today is a Hobbesian reaction to an increasingly Hobbesian world.

Thus, the basic inclination toward violence, originally expressed through America's heroic ideals of the revolutionary, frontiersman, and outlaw, continues to thrive in new but similar ways in modern America. The way that heroes in the movies and now kids on the street tote their weapons about and riddle people with bullets shows that violence is still idealized. The psychologists Franz Alexander and William Healy wrote in 1935 that this adolescent hero-worship of criminality, combined with modern civilization's mechanization and tendency to strangle individuality, has made criminality one of the few outlets through which the individual can express sovereignty. Their observations are as relevant to the rise of organized crime in America as to the increase of violence. Although organized crime does not tend to be as overtly violent as random crime, it too is a violation against society that can only exist because society tolerates it. The argument that society cannot be brought to bear down upon organized crime because the latter is so cleverly camouflaged and uses democratic laws and procedures to protect itself is nonsense. Recently increased efforts by the FBI to clamp down on Mafia bosses have shown that they can be caught even when they play society's game, for in the final analysis, they are *somehow* breaking the law. But the fight against violence and crime cannot be won solely by focusing on reactive strategies to catch perpetrators. The root causes must be addressed. As long as America's heroic ideal does not evolve beyond the traditional frontier mode to one that can creatively respond to the mechanization and strangulation of individuality induced by the modern "psychic frontier," as McLuhan calls it, violence and crime will continue. For those who are on the outer fringes of society, they will remain the only available methods for dealing with the problems of modernity.

Community leaders who advocate after-school programs that keep violence-prone kids off the street recognize that society must provide an alternative that helps these kids gain not only a sense of mastery in life but of meaning and identity. Of course, additional police and interdiction of the drugs and drug trafficking that generate violence are important. But such after-school programs provide something more than mere prevention. They build character. In fact, much more of this kind of applied authority, involving parents as well as teachers and community role models, is needed in order to offset the current explosion of primal youth that would of course so naturally erupt in young people. Children are always the most vulnerable members of society and on its fringes because their personhood is still forming. America's raging children vent the nation's impotence in managing the social and spiritual imbalances wrought by the strange new psychic frontier of modernity that beseiges everyone alike.

Undoubtedly, those children who suddenly explode and go on murderous shooting sprees seem to be gripped by an evil so heinous that it is otherworldly, yet are we so innocent as to deny it has anything to do with the rest of us? Do we not have a responsibility to teach children about the problem of evil and help them manage it as well as other problems of modern life? If we teach them about the private parts of the human body for the purposes of sex education, why wouldn't we teach them about the hidden parts of the human spirit for the purposes of moral education? This need not and should not be done in a sectarian manner that violates the principle of separation of church and state. A resourceful educator can find many ways to sensitively and sensibly approach the mystery of evil so that children of different ages can begin to wrestle with it instead of act it out in and upon society. For example, the animated telling of fairy and folk tales has been one of the chief ways societies in former times prepared children to deal with such core problems of the human condition.

Television has replaced these age-old methods of conveying meaningful stories about the human condition. Today kids acquire their knowledge about the human condition (if indeed they acquire any at all) from MTV and shows like "South Park." Or worse: they get a steady diet of violence from the many other shows that fill prime time. However, it is naive to believe that violence in the media causes violence on the street, or that restricting it will by itself substantially lessen the violence in society (though the restriction of gratuitous violence, one must conclude, is long overdue). The belief in such simplistic, band-aid solutions is just part of the wider innocence that masks the problems underlying violence. If violence is the expression of impotence, as Hannah Arendt first observed, this impotence must be genuinely confronted before the violence can abate. The communications theorist George Gerbner insists that violence on TV only further promotes impotence, and that

> people who watch more television are not more aggressive; in fact, they *lack* aggressiveness. The major effects of exposure to TV violence are insecurity, dependence, and emotional vulnerability. If people were *more* aggressive, they would stand up for their rights [to have more diverse views and content presented on television]. . . . The notion that exposure to violence incites violence is itself media-driven. Exposure actually does something much worse than incite violence. . . . [It] cultivates passivity, withdrawal, and insecurity.

Gerbner concludes that "we are headed in the direction of an upsurge in neofascism in a very entertaining and . . . amusing form." The kind of fascism Gerbner speaks of here and to which I alluded earlier when I spoke of cultural tyranny can only occur with a population lulled into the somnambulism of innocence and impotence.

Of all the forms of violence in America, the one that has been the most innocent, and that brought together into a single focus the violence of empire-building and violence on American soil, was slavery. Nothing could be more innocent than the belief that one race is entitled to enslave another simply because it thinks it is superior and because it is economically profitable to do so. The innocence that originally made this possible has continued well past the abolition of slavery, as observable in the attitudes and practices that have maintained the status of African-Americans as second-class citizens. Racism is still the greatest testament to America's innocence. This topic, however, is so complex that it deserves a separate chapter.

★

# Chapter Sixteen

## The Metaphor of America's Darkness

*The history of the Negro in America is the history of America written in vivid and bloody terms; it is the history of Western Man writ small. It is the history of men who tried to adjust themselves to a world whose laws, customs, and instruments of force were leveled against them. The Negro is America's metaphor.*

—Richard Wright

*Even in our sleep, pain which cannot forget, falls drop by drop upon the heart, until in our own deep despair, against our will, comes wisdom through the awful grace of God.*

—Aeschylus, as quoted by Robert F. Kennedy the evening Martin Luther King, Jr. was assassinated

### The Roots of American Racism

The issue of race in America today is perhaps more complex than ever before. When the Kerner Commission concluded in 1968 that the United States was "moving toward two societies, one black, one white—separate and unequal," the gulf between these two races was patently unmistakable. But today the economic disparity between the races has been decreased due to the rising numbers of blacks who have attained middle class status, and the tensions between them have been somewhat dissipated in response to certain changes in the social fabric. Blacks have been eclipsed by Hispanics as the dominant minority, and according to demographic trends, the ratio of Caucasians to colored peoples is steadily decreasing. America today is not moving toward two societies, but is already a plurality of societies, or at least racial and ethnic groups. White Americans are increasingly being forced to accept America's racial diversity, a phenomenon that can no longer be limited to just a few groups consisting of a comparatively small number of people. All this tends to level or open the racial playing field that blacks and whites once so uniquely dominated as polar opposites locked in conflict.

However, underneath these surface changes, race relations between blacks and whites remain psychologically much the same as always. Overt racism is less tolerated, but the feelings and attitudes of each group toward the other are still strongly conditioned by old habits. History is far more entrenched than the conditions affecting economics or demographics. The current psychology of black-white relations is embedded in their prior history. It may thus be well worth our while to look at this history with a view to fathoming this psychology. Although this chapter will focus almost exclusively upon black-white relations, it is good to keep in mind that the principles discussed here apply in varying degrees to the relations between whites and other races as well. The black-white relationship offers a yardstick against which to measure other relations because it so intensely constellates the forces of the psyche.

It would also be helpful to keep in mind that the argument here will follow a rather traditional line of inquiry as to the ways racial inequality is imposed, namely, discrimination. This is not to dismiss or diminish the value of more recent approaches taken by such authors as William Julius Wilson, who in *The Declining Significance of Race* argues that inequality and black poverty today persist not so much by means of discrimination in the usual sense but through the vulnerability of blacks to structural changes in the economy; race still shapes the fate of many African-Americans, but systemic factors such as socioeconomic class crucially affect their situation. We will take the more traditional tack (though from a distinct perspective) because it strikes at the heart of the psychological and spiritual dimension of the problem of race in America. Although this may not provide a complete understanding of this problem, it does offer an insight into the essential undercurrent that runs through its history.

To begin, it should come as no surprise that the psychological and spiritual dimension of this problem is riddled by a volatile conflict between the spirits of youth and authority. If the South during the Civil War was driven by the spirit of youth and rebellion in its relationship to the North, it certainly assumed the role of authority—authoritarian authority—in regard to its slaves. Since the Civil War, the African-American has increasingly taken up the cry of youth—the cry for change and progress—stirring within his soul. Martin Luther King's plea to let freedom ring from every hill and mountain in America resounds with the spirit of youth, as does every voice in the civil rights movement, be it black or white. And of course, the more revolutionary figures advocating black nationalism and empowerment, such as Malcolm X, the Black Panthers, and Louis Farrakhan, have clearly expressed the spirit of youth opposing authority.

That the African-American carries the calling card of youth is, needless to say, not an easy role in a society that has historically viewed him through the eyes of racial authority and in an inferior, subordinate position to that authority. Blacks were brought to America for the sole purpose of supporting a plantation economy. Though their role as slaves ended, the underlying, unconscious factors on the white man's part that made him feel justified in shackling them into that role still persist. Some of these factors are distinctly youth-related and others only vaguely, yet all have merged together to generate a perception of blacks that has impelled whites to act with the harshest authority and control. All these factors are fueled by fear and ignorance. Their persistence on a subliminal level suggests that the fundamental psychological relationship of whites to blacks has not changed all that significantly from the days of slavery, in spite of what many white Americans may feel.

Considering that it was the European who colonized America, it is curious that racism during the first two centuries of American history became dramatically more pervasive and severe than the racism practiced in Europe during that time. The Indians, as we now finally admit, suffered a genocide on an enormous scale. Estimates on the number of Native Americans living north of the Rio Grande River when Columbus first arrived on the continent range from 850,000 to 15 million, with a general consensus of about 1.3 million. Whatever the actual number, only 250,000 were left by 1900, the rest perishing through exposure to European diseases and warfare. Those that survived were largely restricted to reservations. (The population since 1900 has risen significantly, now numbering 1.4 million.) The same rationale that permitted all this also permitted the importation and slavery of up to 500,000 Africans by one account, an event whose institutionalized brutality was depicted in such popular films as "Roots" and

Steven Spielberg's "Amistad." Aboard ships whose conditions have been likened to slaughterhouses, as many as one-third of the slaves died en route from Africa. By the time of the Civil War, there were approximately 4,000,000 slaves in America. Historians unanimously acknowledge that American slavery was among the cruelest in history. In contrast to the African and European slavery that existed at the same time, Americans treated their slaves as if they were subhumans, crushing their dignity as human beings, destroying their families, and forcing them into submission through such legal punishments as whipping, burning, mutilation, and death.

One has to wonder what it was about the black man that provoked such profound contempt and inhumanity on the part of the white American. Differences among groups of people were not new to the colonies. James Baldwin points out that before black people were brought to America, there were the Dutch, the English, the French, and the Germans, but when the Africans arrived, all the others suddenly became "white." A sharp division was cultivated as the white man vehemently kept the black man at arm's length and under his thumb. However, the color line, as W.E.B. Du Bois called it, served as a marker for differences—or rather, supposed differences—far more subtle than purely physical ones. To understand this we are led yet again to Boorstin's observation that the early American experience involved a regression to the childhood of the species. With this in view, white American racism begins to make sense.

A regression to the childhood of the species meant that the American was compelled to drop down into the "Africa within," as Conrad described this primitive, barbaric level of experience that is humanity's root condition. Again, this is our primal youth, the natural, instinctive state out of which we evolved and from which we had to separate with the aid of taboos, laws, and moral codes. Always existing within us, but for the large part repressed into the unconscious, it can be a troublesome part of our nature—especially when it surfaces unexpectedly and unwantedly. Such was the situation in which the early American found himself. The wilderness of the continent evoked this side of his nature. And there can be no doubt that the African, like the Indian before him, also stirred it up, as their cultures lived closer to the instincts than European civilization did. This elicited fear because of the capacity of the instinctual life to overwhelm and extinguish the other aspects of human life. It elicited fear because 2,000 years of Christian teaching, reinforced by the separation of body and mind that Western man inherited from the Greeks, had warned against the corrupting dangers of the senses and instincts. The Puritans of course incorporated this attitude into their way of life. To be chaste in body and mind was central to what made them pure or puritan.

The African and Indian, however, also inspired envy, which can be just as unsettling as fear. The instinctual life, being our root condition, is something most desirable (a fact prodigiously illustrated by the twentieth century's rebellion against the Victorian ethic). The intricate relationship tribal societies forged between the world of the senses and the world of the spirit was outside the experience of the American, and it both attracted and threatened him. As McLuhan said, "The cultural aggression of white America against Negroes and Indians is not based on skin color and belief in racial superiority. . . . the Negro arouses hostility in whites precisely because they subliminally recognize that he is closest to that tribal depth involvement and simultaneity and harmony that is the richest and most highly developed expression of human consciousness." This expression included the instincts in a way which the American deep down longed for even though he knew it could only disrupt the order he was attempting to impose upon his own instincts and upon nature at large. Given both the fear and the envy, it was more comfortable for the white American to project the "Africa within" onto the African outside, and to then hold him in contempt for reminding him of it. This was a side of human nature that the white man had for a long time not seen due to the camouflage of European civilization, and he did not wish to see it staring him in the face once again. It was ostensibly to feel in control of this unpleasant reminder that so many heinous acts of colonial, plantation, and frontier history were condoned.

If this sounds like too simple an explanation for the special character of American racism, we need only probe a little deeper into its implications. The return to primal youth unleashes the threat of spiritual darkness, a threat and a darkness that have also been projected upon the black man. It would seem that "black" and "dark" have unconsciously become equated in the white American psyche. But they are not by any means the same. The tendency to confuse the two is, of course, not a uniquely American trait. The Oxford English Dictionary of sixteenth-century England defined black as: "Deeply stained with dirt; soiled, dirty, foul. Having dark or deadly purposes, malignant; pertaining to or involving death, deadly; baneful, disastrous, sinister. Foul, iniquitous, atrocious, horribly wicked. Indicating disgrace, censure, liability to punishment, etc." In America, however, this tainting of the color black with the qualities of spiritual darkness has had drastic social consequences.

Spiritual darkness is basically the blackness of night and Thanatos, or death. It is, very literally, the darkness we must face every night, surpassed only by what we fear as the eternal darkness of death. The nighttime is the time of sleep and unconsciousness, of the "loss of soul," as primitive cultures perceived it. This harks back to the primordial night, the long span of time before the dawn of consciousness, when humankind lived in a state of unconsciousness—that is, un-*self*-consciousness—like all the other creatures in the animal kingdom. Much of our primal youth or childhood as a species was spent in this state. "The coming of consciousness," Jung writes, "was probably the most tremendous experience of primeval times, for with it a world came into being whose existence no one had suspected before." He adds that God's proclamation in the Book of Genesis, "Let there be light," marks the "immemorial experience of the separation of the conscious from the unconscious." Inevitably, the darkness of night is associated with the unconscious itself, with our original condition, and evokes the fear of falling back into it.

Even more substantially, night is a time of terror, as the behavior of primitive tribes and children famously demonstrates. The night harbors the irrational, the supernatural, the unknown. Deadly things can happen at night, and in death, one supposedly goes into the night forever. Fear of death, as Ernest Becker elucidated in *The Denial of Death*, is universal, and secretly underlies the motives for many of our otherwise inexplicable behaviors. Death is perhaps the most ominous of all things unknown because it is a sure thing. Unlike God or life *after* death or other such mysteries, we know for certain that we will eventually come face to face with that great void we call death.

The intense fear and hatred that many white Americans have had, and continue to have, of blacks seems to be charged with the terror of Thanatos and the night. At a very basic, preconscious level, the white American has mixed up African blackness with the blackness of Thanatos and night. But the latter blackness is a transcultural phenomenon, as the psychologist Robert Bosnak has noted. It is, he states, "another kind of black than the racial black. There will be thanatic black figures in the dreams of people from all kinds of different races." Likewise, the symbolism of the color white is also transcultural, signifying the light of consciousness, purity, holiness, and wisdom, whether in Christianity, Islam, Hinduism, or the religious traditions of Africa. The unconscious blurring of spiritual whiteness and racial whiteness in the white man's psyche seems to accompany the same blurring around the color black, and is probably a consequence of it.

From here it is easy to see how the problem of evil is also projected onto the African-American. This age-old problem takes into its scope the dark, evil side of human nature and the dark side of the God-image. The latter consists, in every religion, of the human experience of the wrathful side of the divine. The benevolent, positive side is of course easier to understand; the destructive side appears contradictory and tends to be incomprehensible to the rational mind.

The evil in human nature and the corresponding agent of God that is seen as responsible for it are merged in Judaism and Christianity in the figure of the devil. Satan is a figure of darkness, as the name Lucifer implies: "Lucifer" in Latin means "to bear light." When Lucifer, an angel of light, revolted against God in an epic fit of youth, he was cast into hell. In his fall from grace, he became both the opposer and opposite of light. His darkness is explicitly evil, and it too has become confused with African blackness in the white American's imagination. The crusades of the Ku Klux Klan, fully staged in white attire with burning crosses, reveal the religious dimension of white racism. Most deep-seated racism can be seen, in the final analysis, to occur on the level of the mythic and religious imagination.

## The Infantilization of the African-American

The dynamic that is set in motion when primal youth is projected by one group onto another is infantilization. Its form is different than the infantilization we spoke of earlier in the context of the puerile society, but the end result of arrested or curtailed development is the same. The group in the authority position projects its own unconscious primitivity and spiritual darkness onto another group that serves as a hook for this projection, and then insists that this group needs to be tamed, civilized, and reared from its childhood condition. This has been the thrust behind all white-supremacist forms of racism, whether in the Americas, Africa, India, or Australia.

In the United States, slavery reduced its subjects to a degree of infantilization and subordination rarely equaled in the practice of slavery elsewhere in the world. To be a slave in the South meant remaining a permanent child, dependent forever. Slaves were considered material property, to be bought, sold, bequeathed, and inherited like any other property. They had no legal rights. Children could be separated from parents and parents from each other upon the master's whim. Reading and writing were forbidden, and a slave caught with a book could be executed. Submission was enforced in a way that was absolute. One historical study estimates that half of all slaves were whipped.

The oppressive plight of the African-American of course did not end with slavery. One of its spinoffs, segregation, continued to categorically impose a second-class, "less-than" status upon black people. In its 1896 ruling in the case of *Plessy vs. Ferguson*, the U.S. Supreme Court established the policy of "separate but equal" public facilities for blacks and whites. The decision provided a mandate for widespread segregation in the South for over 50 years. Within living memory, many beaches, parks, and other public facilities were off-limits to blacks, strictly *verboten*. In practice, public facilities for blacks were inferior and in short supply, and consequently, separateness amounted to inequality. Black residents and taxpayers in Southern communities that had only one public library or swimming pool could never borrow a book or go for a swim. "Indeed," Andrew Hacker reminds us in *Two Nations*, "black youths were even forbidden to stroll past the pool, lest they catch a glimpse of white girls in their bathing suits."

The fear behind such infantilizing legal strictures was fueled by the fantasy that the black man's primal youth could dangerously explode at any moment. Even worse, what if it were contagious? How would this affect innocent white girls? The Swedish sociologist, economist, and Nobel laureate Gunnar Myrdal correctly intuited that the underpinnings of segregation were the same as those of lynchings and the castrations that often preceded them. White women needed to be protected from the advances of black men. Stereotypical images of the black's lasciviousness and sexual prowess also figure in in the condemnation of interracial relationships and marriage: white people wonder, what do black people have and do that they don't? If one side of the strong reaction white supremacists have against intermarriage is the fear of it impoverishing the white gene pool and racial standard, then the other, perhaps more secret side of this reaction is the envy they have of the benefits it might bring. Again, envy is as threatening and unsettling as fear because it points to one's shortcomings and to desires one cannot admit to or fulfill. The strange way white people are compelled to stare at interracial couples suggests this ambivalence.

Desegregation laws promoted integration in schools, public facilities, and employment settings, but when it comes to residential neighborhoods they have had about as much impact as laws against racism would. Everybody knows that if too many black families move into a white neighborhood, the value of properties drops because white families begin to move out and no longer move in; within a matter of time, the neighborhood becomes entirely black. Statistics reveal that although blacks constitute 13 percent of the population—and thus an integrated neighborhood should reflect at least this figure—if they exceed 8 percent in a given neighborhood, white residents will eventually leave and no longer move in. The threshold of tolerance does not match the demands of the situation. Neighborhoods consequently tend to be either all black or all white.

Of course, the argument has been made that blacks prefer to live among their own kind no less than whites. In the economic arena, the continuing disparity between many blacks and whites cannot be papered over by such arguments. In his work as an attorney, the novelist Scott Turow made the observation that a significant portion of black America does not live in the Third World, but the "Fourth World." This is a condition of poverty amidst plenty, a condition in which one watches the rest of the society flourish but without having access to its abundance. The facts amply bear this out. Job opportunities and upward mobility are simply not as available to black people. Their unemployment rate is twice as high as that of whites—a significantly narrower gap than earlier times, but still high. Whereas approximately 10 percent of the white population lives in poverty, 24 percent of the black population does—also a significantly narrower gap than earlier times. Full-time black workers earn less than their white counterparts. Even with a college degree, black males tend to earn substantially less than white males. Black infant mortality, disease burden, and longevity all compare poorly with whites. One can make such comparisons endlessly. They only prove that racial inequality in America is still a prevalent problem.

As mentioned, the traditional argument about the cause of this problem has focused on discrimination, on how blacks have been treated differently than whites. That discriminatory practices have been widespread is now commonly accepted. Blacks and now even whites know too well that blacks have often not been treated the same as whites in restaurants, stores, and hotels, and that in many workplaces there has appeared to be a glass ceiling in place just for black employees. Black men, regardless of socioeconomic class, still fear for their safety when they are pulled aside in their cars at night by the police. And still, whites do not, as a general rule, appreciate the pressures blacks have suffered from by having to prove their self-worth each day anew and to continually fall short of expectations; whites cannot easily imagine how a lifetime of this has for many led to rage and despair, or why, with no suitable outlet, the risk for hypertension is higher for blacks than whites.

Doctors, psychiatrists, psychologists, and social workers are acquainted on a firsthand basis with how race affects blacks. They know that many of the problems that African-American patients present cannot be understood independently of their sine qua non condition of simply being born black. Whether they suffer from poverty or unemployment, alcohol or drug addiction, anxiety or depression, domestic violence, sexual abuse, criminal behavior, or even fear and sabotaging of success once success has been attained, almost always the problem has been staged and compounded by racially determined life circumstances. Although it can hardly be argued that white people do not suffer from the same problems, the ratio and predisposition to them are considerably greater among blacks, particularly in large urban areas.

The effects of infantilization are so pervasive and yet subtle that even black people themselves are often unaware of them. Psychologically speaking, one can discern significant differences between blacks who grew up before the civil rights era and those who grew up in its wake. There has been a change, if not in the general impact of the infantilization, then in the ways it operates and is expressed. In *Black Rage,* William Grier and Price Cobbs, both black psychiatrists, provide a portrait of African-American psychology that was by and large the norm up until the civil rights era. Much has undoubtedly changed since then, yet their penetrating study reveals how the dynamic of infantilization was for generations internalized within the African-American family and psyche. Because of the very real danger of being killed or hurt if he showed aggression, the black male child was reared to be submissive in order to survive. This was a holdover from the days of slavery, when black people were confronted daily with two clear choices, to submit or die. Thus, the enslaved mother herself "had to take the role of slave master, treat the child with capricious cruelty, hurt him physically and emotionally, and demand that he respond in an obsequious helpless manner—a manner she knew would enhance his chances of survival." Defiant, aggressive traits had to be crushed, and maturity and independence disallowed. Along with fear and exaltation of the master, self-hatred was instilled. This unfortunate role fell more upon the mother not only because child-rearing was traditionally the woman's responsibility but because the father's authority had been undermined by forces outside the home. The status of the head of the household was naturally assumed by the mother.

Inasmuch as the African-American parent-child dynamic mirrored the master-slave relationship it was infantilizing and toxic. The mother, Grier and Cobbs write, was experienced in a sharply contradictory way—one moment gentle, the next cruel—as if she were purposely preparing her child with "the polarities of ambivalence so that he could understand his later role in a white society." Her son grew up depending upon her for nurturance but at the same time with an unconscious rage toward her for emotionally and developmentally inhibiting him. Bound up with this were feelings of profound sadness—also largely unconscious—over opportunities that were lost due to her inhibiting influence. The rage of course was against white society but was displaced onto the mother as the mediator between the child and society.

African-American women, by contrast, tended to displace their rage and sadness onto themselves. Grier and Cobbs cite as a typical example women suffering from chronic depression. An unconscious feeling that they did not and could not measure up to the white American ideal of a woman had predisposed them to a loss of interest and esteem in themselves. They often "let themselves go" in matters of appearance and feminine attractiveness, aging well before their time. Their source of self-worth was predominantly in their roles as mothers and householders. When professional advancement was possible, the black woman found that her appeal to black men and her chances to have a satisfying relationship suffered. The kind of men she now attracted tended to be opportunistic and were attracted to her because she appeared closer to the white ideal and not because of her personal merit or character. Her professional success had a high cost.

Again, many elements of these patterns with respect to both men and women have significantly changed. The civil rights movement had a dramatic effect not only in vocalizing African-American concerns and in initiating social improvements, but upon the internal self-perceptions African-Americans had of themselves. Underlying civil rights were the basic right to be black—"black is beautiful"—and the right to think of oneself as possessing the same human dignity that is accorded other citizens. If white Americans would not grant these rights, African-Americans would take them for themselves. The only real militancy this required was an act of pride.

With this, the dynamic of infantilization also underwent a change. No longer would the mother rear her child with a parent-child dynamic that mirrored the master-slave relationship. No longer would a man's rage be displaced upon his mother as the mediator between himself and society. No longer would a woman have to compete so blatantly with a white feminine ideal. The essential change this spelled for the dynamic of infantilization was that it would no longer occur in the internalized way of quiet desperation that corresponded to the old orders of slavery and segregation. But this does not mean that it disappeared any more than racism and social inequality disappeared. Rather, it would occur in a new way that met the new order, an order that tells many African-Americans that they have the right to be equal but in fact cannot be equal. The right is there but the social reality is not. The consequence is that the sting of infantilization is now acted out externally in contrast to being exclusively turned inward. A greater sense of entitlement to equality has brought to many African-Americans, if anything at all, a freer sense of self-expression.

The effects of this are manifold. To begin with, it needs to be underscored that just because the infantilization has shifted from being inwardly directed to being socially expressed does not mean that its basic unconscious character has changed. As long as the African-American's rage remains raw and unfocused, and his disenfranchisement is not authentically addressed, he is still engulfed in his infantilization. However, now it victimizes not only himself but whites too. One might argue that this victimization of the white man is the point. But generally it is not. As shall be discussed in the following section, much of the current rage and disenfranchisement is acted out within the black community and in what whites comfortably designate as the "inner city." (Indeed, in expounding the effects of infantilization, we are speaking mostly about the inner city populace, and not those who have gained entry into the middle class.) Yet there can be little doubt, given recent events and trends, that the rage of the inner city is well capable of spilling over into society at large. And whether intended or not, it makes its point.

## The Rage of the Disesteemed

The dynamic of infantilization is particularly evident in the image whites unconsciously have of blacks. In the minds of many white Americans, the African-American has become a sort of *enfant terrible*. Perceived as angry, primitive, and unpredictable, the black man evokes the fear that he will take his revenge upon the white man for the deeds of the past. The eruption of black rage as a formidable force on the American scene cannot be denied. The nationwide riots in the 1960s and the Los Angeles riots in 1992 were demonstrations of this, and there are others. However, all show that the social effects of this rage tend to fall back upon the African-American, further exacerbating his sense of infantilization and explosive frustration and hostility.

The most obvious proof of this were the riots. The mayhem they let loose was largely limited to the black communities where they took place. Enraged blacks destroyed *their own* businesses, public facilities, and, in some instances, even their own homes. Although it has been argued that rioters also destroyed white-owned businesses and government facilities that represented white authority, their destruction in the long run only served to deprive black communities. In the midst of the mindless fury that consumed people there may have been some instinct of self-preservation or self-protection at work here. Blacks know only too well that white America would not tolerate the spread of mass violence into its own neighborhoods and business districts, and would be severely punitive for such a transgression.

But this is hardly the main reason why blacks inflicted such destruction upon themselves. Self-destructiveness as a response to infantilization has been observed in situations other than the African-American's. As Frantz Fanon noted before the close of the colonial era over a generation ago, natives in colonized societies periodically turned against themselves, beating each other in "astonishing waves of crime." And then of course there is the behavior of children, with whom the term "infantilization" is obviously connected and who are known to destroy their rooms and toys when they feel unjustly punished. In their powerlessness and overwhelming rage, they cannot distinguish between what is self-destructive and what is destructive to the other. This lack of discrimination appears to be a key factor behind the self-destructiveness that is incurred by infantilization. Such a comparison is not to reduce the psychology of African-Americans to that of children, a gesture that would have a shaming quality and would of course be further infantilizing. Rather, its purpose is to show how power in its most basic, elemental form—the power to be and to express oneself—can be thwarted with a large population as easily as with a child. In both cases, the psyche is crippled before it finds its sea legs. John Bradshaw, the popular spokesperson for the "inner child," commented on how the Los Angeles riots were an expression of the same "preverbal powerlessness" experienced by the child who is unseen, unheard, and unappreciated. Feelings that were never validated came out the only way they could.

Riots in fact are few and far between. The rage of the disesteemed, as James Baldwin called it, surfaces in America on a daily basis in ways that, though perhaps spreading the rage thinner, cover far more territory. The dramatic increase in crime in recent decades, much of it drug-related, goes hand-in-hand with the disillusionment and despondency of inner city life.

While African-Americans comprise, again, 13 percent of the nation's population, they comprise 47 percent of the prison population. This means that over a million blacks are in jail or can be returned there for violating probation or parole. One out of every three black males aged 20 to 29 is under some form of criminal justice supervision. The correlation with violent crime is also high. Of the prisoners sentenced to death, 40 percent are black. The black share for all arrests for murder and manslaughter is 55 percent; for robbery, 61 percent; and for rape, 43 percent. However, one has to take into account the disparity that suggests that assaults by whites are either less frequently reported to the police or are less likely to lead to arrests: for example, although the black share for rape arrests is 43 percent, only 33 percent of the women who said they had been raped identified their attackers as black. If there is a bias toward what whites call "black crime," there is evidently a bias also in the criminal justice system. It was a blatant demonstration of this latter bias, after all, that ignited the Los Angeles riots of 1992.

Again, much of the crime reflected in the above figures is enacted within the black community. Most violence perpetrated by blacks is black on black. Three-quarters of the black men who perpetrate rapes choose black women as their victims, and similarly, more blacks than whites are victimized by black muggers. It is widely accepted that men do not rape for sexual pleasure. They rape because they feel disempowered in their manhood, most often in their roles as social achievers and financial providers. Rape as a psychological statement says: I have been raped, now I will rape you. The loss of power and self-esteem experienced by black men is in turn inflicted upon those who most immediately threaten them and are available, namely, black women.

The same aggression toward women is evident in the language of the ghetto, which as Christopher Lasch observed now pervades American society as a whole: "It is symptomatic of the underlying tenor of American life that vulgar terms for sexual intercourse also convey the sense of getting the better of someone, working him over, taking him in, imposing your will through guile, deception, or superior force." In the ghetto, however, "the violence associated with sexual intercourse is directed with special intensity by men against women, specifically against their mothers." Sexual intercourse has thus become a metaphor for rage and exploitation. The language depicting it is used as if it is intended to divest oneself of his sense of infantilization; motherhood and what it symbolizes accordingly become a target for insult. But where there is infantilization, dependence is not far off, and the merging of sex, rage, and exploitation, as Lasch also points out, is translated among some men in the ghetto into a lifestyle of depending on women and pimping for a living. In this, the women of course also become infantilized, enraged, and exploitive.

Nowhere are the raging effects of infantilization more evident in the black community than in the preponderance of guns and gang violence. The gang is closely allied to the gun, and as a cultural phenomenon even preceded the proliferation of gun violence. The gang is the quest for power and identity in numbers; it is the army or the tribe. Gang violence is largely the result of hostilities between one gang and another. The Cryps and the Bloods, two large African-American gangs in Los Angeles, illustrate how the turf over which gangs fight—be it drug turf or whatever—is almost always commonly shared territory in the inner city. The Cryps and the Bloods kill some 380 of their own every year. The infantilization of the black American is again acted out within the black community.

But studies of gang members show that the key factor motivating them to join gangs is not so much rage as despair, the rage being something that vents once the gang congeals and gives voice to the grievances of its members. Young people join gangs not because they are angry but because they have nowhere else to turn. As McLuhan wrote, "the teenager, compelled to share the life of a city that cannot accept him as an adult, collapses into 'rebellion without a cause.' " The absence or failure of role models is endemic to the inner city. Large numbers of an entire generation of men who might otherwise have served as father figures or mentors are unemployed, underemployed, employed in illegal activities, drug addicted, or incarcerated in prison. Fathers do not keep their commitments to their children either as providers or as teachers about life, often having three or four children with as many women. The vacuum left by a fatherless household is filled by the gang, but the gang only mimics partiarchy. As discussed earlier, it is a sibling society, which is why the infighting between gangs resembles sibling rivalry.

Like the gang, the gun compensates for the void of genuine authority and initiation in the lives of black youths. It provides a way to feel adultlike and important. The gun is a quick fix for "preverbal powerlessness," a fact which has made gun violence in schools a national concern. A large proportion of the 270,000 children who are estimated to bring guns to school everyday live in the inner city. In one study, two percent of all students reported being victims of some sort of violence, whereas 23 percent of inner-city students reported being victims of gun-related violence. Most of the homicides that are now the leading cause of death among young black males are the result of black-on-black gun violence. Largely because of the latter, a black man has a seven times greater chance of being murdered than a white man.

As a psychological statement, the gun of course is no ordinary phallic symbol. Because it is so deadly it is as much a symbol of Thanatos as *phallos*, if not more. In inner-city life, the painful reminders of death are continuous. Everybody knows somebody, or of somebody, who has died "before their time"—if not violently, then from drugs or some other ill-fated event spawned by the disadvantages of being black in a white society. The killing or decimation of black youth, however, occurs in the sphere of morale and identity well before it manifests physically. One rap singer summed it up thus: "If you strip away the identity of a child, he is left with nothing. That vacuum is filled by the surrounding environment. If his environment is cold-blooded, negative and violent, he becomes cold-blooded, negative and violent." (It is no coincidence that rap music, too, is as a rule cold, negative, and violent.) This statement of self is actually what the gun as a symbol is loaded with in the young African-American's psyche. The gun in modern times is no less an extension of the cultural and psychological environment than it was in frontier times. A broken family and chaotic home life, the degradation caused by poverty (51 percent of black children live in poverty), a drug- and crime-infested neighborhood, the poor quality of education in many inner-city schools, the irrelevance of the curriculum to the cultural history, experience, and needs of African-Americans, and the limited prospects of continuing on to higher education and obtaining gainful employment—in spite of affirmative action—are the chief factors contributing to the demoralized state of inner-city kids.

An environment such as described above, imposed upon a child from birth, leads not only to a deficiency in morale but an impairment in morality. The direction inner-city kids are heading in has chilling implications when one considers that the most criminal of them may represent the leading edge of current trends. Criminal justice experts inform us that the quality of crime has become increasingly violent and cold-blooded in recent decades. A series of tourist murders in Miami in 1993 provide an example of this. European tourists were targeted for their valuables, and though these were reportedly surrendered without resistance, the tourists were shot to death in their cars. The inner-city teenagers apprehended and charged with the crimes were diagnosed as sociopaths, meaning, among other things, that they lacked the capacity for conscience. Conscience is a socializing principle that to a large extent is itself socially instilled and that enables a person to become a productive, interactive member of society. It is a function of what Freud called the superego. It is an internalized aspect of the spirit of authority. The ability to discern right from wrong and to weigh the moral consequences of given actions is essential not only for the development of personality but of civilization. Dostoevsky said that without God everything is permitted. This is not entirely true. Many atheists behave more ethically than certain professed believers in God. It is without conscience that all is permitted.

Police, justice, and juvenile specialists confirm that such teenage murderers are devoid of conscience. They are not person-related; people are mere objects for their pleasure or use. "When you look into their eyes," one police officer said, "you can see a light, but nobody is home." Thus, there is a deficiency in ego development as well as conscience. These adolescents live perpetually in the original, precivilized condition of primal youth. They live not in the land of the overrated child but the underrated child who can depend only upon himself to take care of his needs. Thus the Darwinian mentality: survival of the fittest is the law that rules.

But these adolescents are not only social products of their dysfunctional families and neighborhoods, but a pocket of society into which is stuffed all the displaced primitive and spiritual darkness from which the rest of society has dissociated itself. This particular pocket of society, whose members populate the nation's inner cities, prisons, and now its schools, is the part of America where nobody is home. It is the displaced part of us that is sociopathic or without conscience. Charles Manson was not altogether crazy when he reminded us at every opportunity he could that he is us. The homeless also represent, very literally, the part of society where nobody is home, but they are the more harmless members of this subclass. As is often the case, they tend to be more mentally disturbed than sociopathic and thus more harmful to themselves than to others. By contrast, America's disenfranchised youth have both the sanity and the means to direct their energies outwardly. Unless society brings this split-off part of itself back home and conscientiously owns and embraces it under the roof of a single society, it will continue to produce teenagers who shamelessly murder tourists—or each other, as they do in their gang wars and street shootings.

## The Infatuation with the African-American

It is ironic, in view of the low esteem in which the white American has held the African-American, how the latter has become a culture-hero, that is, a cultural icon. There is among white people in America a curious infatuation with things African-American. This was clearly captured as early as with George Gershwin. In the words of the jazz musician Warner Carr, Gershwin "depicted the American Negro in an enigmatic, spiritual, and beautiful way." In more recent times, the African-American has become the embodiment of all that is "cool." He often speaks in a "cool" vernacular and frequently looks and behaves in a "cool" manner. In films and elsewhere he conveys a laid-back, easygoing demeanor. The imitation of the African-American that one typically sees now in the language, clothing style, and musical taste of white suburban teenagers across the nation is just one form of this infatuation.

It is important to recognize what drives this attraction. One can suspect that it has a great deal to do with the very thing that makes the white man so hateful and fearful of the black man: namely, the deep, natural connection to the instinctual life, or as McLuhan earlier described it, "that tribal depth involvement and simultaneity and harmony that is the richest and most highly developed expression of human consciousness." Here in this attraction the coin of hatred and fear again flips over onto its other side, envy and desire. The black's connection to the primal depths, to primal youth, long ago buried by Western civilization, becomes now the white's way to reconnect to the same—but he does so *through* the black man. The black carries not only the split-off, sociopathic part of the white man, but the split-off, instinctual part; not only the part that is pathologically void of superego, but the part that is imbued with the vital energies of the id. The African-American is a culture-hero for *all* Americans because he carries a particular kind of Eros that the majority culture cannot. It is thus a special role that the black man plays in connection to the white man: he has to be the white's conduit for Thanatos *and* Eros. What a great burden he carries, and what a great service he provides.

The evidence of the African-American's Eros is everywhere, and it has been suggested that, of all the strains of Eros in American culture, the African-American's is the richest. Its roots go back to the Bantu cultures of Africa. Michael Ortiz Hill explains:

> The roots of the African American psyche are in Western Bantu village culture, from the estuaries of the Zaire River as far inland as the Zambesi basin in central Africa. Western Bantu people—Kongo, Luba, Lunda, Chewa, Ovimbundu and others—account for perhaps half of the slaves imported to the American colonies. Unlike slaves taken from other parts of West Africa, who were ethnically diverse,

Western Bantu people had mutually comprehensible languages and cultural sensibilities. The classical African American culture in the rural South is replete with "bantuisms" in language, place names, proverbs, stories, traditional medicine—even the religious imagery of old spirituals.

These cultural sensibilities and "bantuisms" are more pervasive in America than one might think. They have had a profound influence on the shaping of American culture at large. Jung understood this influence as a kind of boomerang effect of the African upon the white American: ". . . whenever you affect somebody so profoundly [as when you enslave him], then, in a mysterious way, something comes back from him to yourself." This boomerang effect also occurred with the Indian, as discussed in Chapter Three. It is the effect of two collective psyches merging on an unconscious level.

What came back to the white man, what was internalized in an unconscious way, Jung felt, was the basic temperament and behavioral style of the African. The movement of American culture away from European culture was markedly a movement toward African culture. This was stronger in the Southern than the Northern states because of the different quality and degree of interdependence of blacks and whites. Jung believed that the openness and great ease of expression typical to Americans are probably an African influence. This style is more emotional and free with laughter—and boisterous laughter—than most European styles. "America as a nation can laugh," Jung says, "and that means a lot." The rapport between people, the remarkable vivacity of self-expression ("Americans are great talkers," he adds), the slang and aliveness of language, the gossip and chattering of even the newspapers, the boundless publicity of American life that diminishes the distance between people, all are more characteristic of an African village than a European city. McLuhan decades later independently reached the same conclusion when he said that America is more like an oral, tribal culture in Africa than a European one.

Jung also thought that the easygoing and demonstrative way the American physically carries himself, in his walk and other movements, is an imitation of African behavior. American jazz, he noted, "is most obviously pervaded by the African rhythm and the African melody." American dance, with its swinging shoulder and hip movements, reminded him of the African n'goma dance he observed on his travels in Africa. And finally, Jung thought, American behavior incarnates the African soul through the expression of religious feeling. Revival meetings, the Holy Rollers, and other forms of charismatic religion were strongly influenced by the African-

American and his animated faith and gospel music. This kind of religious awe and worship didn't just spring up spontaneously on American soil, according to Michael Ortiz Hill. Contrary to the popular assumption that Africans first encountered Christianity when they were brought to America, many of the slaves were already Christians, bringing with them a Christianity that had a distinctly African flavor. Those from the Western Bantu cultures of central Africa practiced Bantu Christianity, known for its rich emotional expression.

These aspects of temperament and behavior are facets of Eros, or what African-Americans refer to as "soul." They have been subtly taken over by the majority culture, their origins quickly forgotten. Who would guess, for example, that the Nashville recording company that first signed Elvis Presley was originally established to record black musicians of the South? When it was discovered that Presley could perform the sound of the black South with conviction, the career of the "King of Rock 'n' Roll" was launched. Presley eventually received three Grammys for gospel, and inspirational music was the category in which he earned the most awards. The so-called "British invasion," too, was really an introduction of the African-American via a white, Anglo-Saxon package: the Beatles were obviously inspired by black artists, in particular, Chuck Berry and Little Richard, and the Rolling Stones acknowledge among their primary influences, in addition to the aforementioned, Howlin' Wolf, Muddy Waters, and Jimmy Reed—three blues artists. Like jazz, much of rock 'n' roll has its origins in that distinctly African-American art form, the blues. Of course, who could better sing the blues than a black man or woman who has lived them everyday in no small measure because of his or her color and place in society? Eros here manifests as the dark passion of pathos.

This brings us to another factor responsible for the emergence of the African-American as a culture-hero: his suffering. He is attractive and admirable because he is, in accordance with the paradigm of Christ himself, a suffering servant and an outcast. Steven Spielberg nicely makes this connection in "Amistad," but one can see this theme beginning to crystallize as early as Stanley Kramer's film "The Defiant Ones," in which a black convict, played by Sidney Poitier, is portrayed in an admirable, empathic way. Of course, there is nothing new about African-Americans being figures worthy of admiration. Long before film became a venue for them, history recorded their heroic deeds in the Revolutionary War, the Civil War, and every war since. What is new is the white American's growing recognition of this and his own process of identifying the African-American as a culture-hero.

The African-American culture-hero wears a variety of masks, and it goes without saying that he is not always a hero to both blacks and whites. He can be a basketball player, a musician, a lawyer, or a gang leader. He can be Martin Luther King or Colin Powell, or he can be O.J. Simpson or Tupac Shakur. Often, he or she is a figure who had to overcome great odds to achieve success. In addition to whatever field had to be mastered, the African-American hero had to contend with the color barrier. As a general rule, something more or extra special has been expected from the African-American, as he had to become distinguished not only among his own people, but also among his white professional counterparts and skeptics. Think of Frederick Douglass, George Washington Carver, Paul Robeson, Louis Armstrong, Thurgood Marshall, Jackie Robinson, Muhammad Ali, Maya Angelou, Toni Morrison, Alice Walker. Indeed, much of African-American excellence is intimately connected with the struggle for freedom, equality, and self-mastery.

## The Meaning of Integration

The white American has probably always had a secret curiosity about, if not an overt infatuation with, the black man. The fact that this curiosity is now increasingly becoming part and parcel of mainstream American culture bodes well for relations between the two races. Yet this in itself cannot heal a wound which, as many have pointed out, is so divisive and poisonous that it is one of the most serious threats to America's future as a great nation. As Erik Erikson writes, "nations, as well as individuals, are not only defined by their highest point of civilized achievement, but also by the weakest one in their collective identity: they are, in fact, defined by the distance, and the quality of the distance, between these points." The wide gulf between the races that is the result of racism not only brings *both* races down to their lowest or weakest point; it brings America's contribution as a civilization down with them. Integration of blacks and whites into a single society is a moral imperative that, in the long run, will define the mettle of American civilization. Integration here implies a spiritual and psychological partnership and not just economic parity. It implies a genuine sense of shared community and not just paranoid togetherness. Can America truly be a model of a refined, democratic civilization in the absence of such integration?

But such integration, to begin with, requires an acknowledgment of race as a problem at the center of American life, a problem that poses a heroic challenge in the profoundest sense. The jazz musician Wynton Marsalis has aptly described this challenge:

> Race for this country is like the thing in the story, in mythology, that you have to do for the kingdom to be well, and it's always something you don't want to do. It's always that thing that is about you confronting yourself and that is tailor-made for you to fail. And the question of your heroism, courage, and success at dealing with this trial is, can you confront it with honesty and with energy to sustain an attack on it? . . . . The more we run from [race] the more we run into it. It's an age-old story. If it's not race, it's something else. But in this particular instance, in this nation, it is race.

In most of the myths, legends, and folk tales of the hero, there is a confrontation between the hero and a "wholly other," some monster, evil figure, or antagonist who threatens him or tests his worth and abilities. From a psychological point of view, the "wholly other" is really within the hero himself; it is the unrealized or unconscious part of his own personality. Perhaps it is his fear, or his untapped strengths, or, not unlikely, it is the monstrous, evil part of himself. The outer battle or conquest is a symbol for the inner one. The truth of such tales is universal, and Marsalis is correct in appraising the heroic challenge of race relations in America as a confrontation with oneself.

On an experiential level, fundamental changes must take place within both races before the gulf between them can be really bridged. Each race must confront the "wholly other" within itself before it can reach across the racial divide to the other. Each race must confront its dissociated part and integrate it into *itself* before it can integrate with the other race into a single society under a common roof. It was to these dissociated parts that Jung was referring when he said, "every [American] Negro has a white complex and every [white] American a Negro complex." Herein lies one of the mechanisms that make racism the destructive form of innocence that it is: when a complex such as one of these takes hold of us, we act it out unknowingly, unconsciously, seeing both others and ourselves in a distorted way through the lens of the complex.

The white complex is, figuratively speaking, the white man inside the black man's psyche, as the black complex is the black man inside the white man's psyche. The white complex operates in the African-American psyche as a judgmental and alienating authority principle, and compels the African-American to displace onto the white man his inner authority and the measuring rod of his own goodness. The black complex operates in the white American psyche as a paganizing primal-youth principle, compelling the white American to displace onto the black man his animal nature, dark fears, and evil impulses. The white complex of the black American is grounded in a very real history of oppression, suffering, and injustice, leading on the one hand to the black's deep resentment and mistrust of the white American, and on the other to a profound longing to be accepted by him. The black complex of the white American is not grounded in a historical experience; rather, it is loaded with dark, thanatotic material of a fundamentally irrational and mythic, religious nature. This casts the black man into the position of somebody or something "wholly other" than the white man.

On the one side then, integration would require the white American to become conscious of his black complex and assimilate it into his being. For this, he must come to terms with what makes the African-American an enemy at the same time as a culture-hero: his deeply tabooed but deeply desirable connection to the instinctual side of the psyche. This includes the "wholly other" darkness he so dreads to face. *By having unconsciously projected all this upon the black man, the white man has in fact become what he most fears in the black man: barbaric and diabolically dark.* And yet, the more the white man condemns and pushes this side of his psyche away, the more it is forced to live itself out through the African-American. The latter thus becomes the white American's unconscious connection to this side. The more it is scorned, the more it is forced to manifest in a shadowy, menacing form. The problems from which African-Americans suffer and which invariably affect the rest of society—poverty, unemployment, drug abuse, violence and crime—are basically symptoms or ways through which the dissociated part of the white American psyche returns to obtain recognition and redemption. What is not let in through the front door sneaks around and breaks in through the back door. Unfortunately, in this way the white American's worst fantasies of the black American become a self-fulfilling prophecy, and American society remains polarized and divided by racial animosity.

One could add to this black complex a guilt complex that the white man has for what he has done to the black man. Because one can hardly claim that this complex haunts him, it exists more as an unconscious guilty condition than as a guilt complex in the usual sense of the meaning. Unlike the black complex, this condition *is* grounded in history as the counterpart to the black man's complex. Though one may deny its existence, it has a palpability and pervasiveness that affect even immigrants and others who have no connection to the enslavement or segregation of blacks in their personal or family history. Commenting on a similar condition that has affected Germany since the end of the Second World War, Jung wrote: "Psychological collective guilt is a *tragic fate*. It hits everybody, just and unjust alike, everybody who was anywhere near the place where the terrible thing happened. . . . Therefore, although collective guilt, viewed on the archaic and primitive level, is a state of *magical uncleanness,* yet precisely because of the general unreasonableness it is a very real fact, which no European outside Europe and no German outside Germany can leave out of account. If the German intends to live on good terms with Europe, he must be conscious that in the eyes of Europeans he is a guilty man." The same goes for the American case: if the white American intends to live on good terms with the black American, he must be conscious that in the eyes of the black American he is a guilty man. Of course, the argument made by the Nobel laureate Elie Wiesel in regard to Germans can be made in regard to white Americans too: it is unfair to hold current and future generations responsible for the deeds of past generations. Rather than to blame and punish, the existence of collective guilt as a "very real fact" seems to have the purpose of making sure that the abominable transgressions of the past are not forgotten; it seems to be history's way of living on in the present, seeking redemption through our acknowledgement of it.

But is this enough? To be conscious of guilt in a way that produces meaningful results must involve more than merely acknowledging the past deeds that merit the guilt. In 1998 there was discussion in the media about whether the government should issue a formal apology to African-Americans for the slavery under which their ancestors suffered. Such a public acknowledgment of collective guilt might have been a nice gesture, but to believe that this alone would have really amounted to anything more than pure emotionalism is as innocent as the beliefs that permitted this injustice in the first place. Guilt cannot be absolved simply by saying "I'm sorry." As McLuhan writes, without some redeeming act of expiation or creative renewal, guilt and remorse are just forms of despair and sloth.

In recent years, affirmative action has been one form of attempting to expiate guilt and create new possibilities for African-Americans, and through this, American society as a whole. Of course, this program is not without its flaws; many whites *and* blacks believe that it perpetuates the infantilization of blacks by giving them special breaks that have not been squarely earned. But any compensatory measure that makes amends by singling out one group and favoring it is bound to be seen by some as indulging that group or as reverse discrimination against other groups. The need thus far for social interventions that operate by strict quotas only speaks to the fact that expiation and creative renewal will not occur spontaneously. Indeed, the resistance to change is so strong that the past deeds meriting guilt and giving rise to such interventions are by no means ancient history. They are in tow to their present versions. Institutional racism is *still* rampant. For example, in the same year that there was discussion about a government apology for slavery, the U.S. Department of Agriculture admitted to discriminatory loan practices that, while enabling white farmers to save their farms, led to the bankruptcy of many black farmers. The situation was so overtly racist that the Department of Agriculture was compelled to offer a settlement the following year to those affected by these practices. Yet even with this acknowledgment of guilt, the very fact that this case occurred goes to show that the white American treats his general condition of guilt like he treats his black complex: he is still too dissociated from it and still too innocent.

On the other side of the equation of what integration would require, there is the work the African-American must undertake to integrate his white complex into his being. Any examination of race relations in America must take into account the role of both parties in collective infantilization. This, again, is the dynamic that occurs when one group projects the childhood aspects of the psyche onto another. To the extent that this latter group then "buys into" or internalizes this dynamic, it indeed becomes infantilized. Too many African-Americans are still in the grip of infantilization, defeated in their outlook and ragefully exploiting and hurting their own people. *By not assimilating their own white complex, blacks unconsciously act out the role of the white exploiter, but upon themselves.* They believe they have no power to help themselves, that all the power rests with the white man. No doubt, inasmuch as money or ownership of resources is power, the facts show that much of the power in America does reside in white hands. But people with a sense of peoplehood are powerful too, and as civil rights leaders have pointed out, integrity of self is the most important power one can have. Hopefully the rest of society will recognize that the inner city needs more in the way of education and opportunities than just promises and good will, but waiting for this to happen cannot be an excuse for the people who live there to waste their energies and lives away. Psychological integration of their infantilizing white complex is the first and most critical step toward their empowerment.

The only real solution to America's race problems, as Jung repeatedly emphasized in regard to social issues, is consciousness of the shadow, of the disowned, projected parts of the personality and of one's own propensity toward evil. But this can only be practiced by individuals, as it is a matter of learning to live with awareness. Such learning can surely be fostered by good education—education that has depth—but by and large, it is not something that can be enforced collectively or top-down from the government through social programs. The solution to America's race problems is a matter of the individual's efforts to achieve integration within himself, and of many such efforts by many individuals. In the end, a nation can only be as conscious, integrated, and moral as its individual citizens.

# Chapter 17

## The Implosion of Innocence

*The blood-dimmed tide is loosed, and everywhere*
*The ceremony of innocence is drowned;*
*The best lack all conviction, while the worst*
*Are full of passionate intensity.*

—W.B. Yeats

### The Ossification of Authority

Innocence left to its own vices and increasing over time instead of diminishing is bound to eventually explode in some act of physical violence, like war or the nationwide epidemics of gun violence and racism. However, it is also bound to implode in acts of nonphysical violence that seem more permissible because they are subtle and do not break laws. The implosion of innocence is like the implosion of a star, or what is known in astronomy as a black hole: it is innocence that has collapsed in upon itself. Its gravity or force is so strong, and it is so dense or convoluted, that nothing in its field can escape it. Everything that comes near it is sucked in. And because it is like a black hole, one does not see or recognize it for what it is.

The implosion of innocence is a growing problem in American culture. It begins with the ossification of authority. This occurs when the culture is so addicted to innocence that not only is the spirit of youth engulfed in innocent thinking, but the spirit of authority as well. This illustrates the dynamic described in the first chapter, that when youth predominates, authority follows suit. Both become agents of innocence, but in different ways. If the overly innocent spirit of youth leads society down a path of puerility, then the overly innocent spirit of authority leads society down the path of senility. That these two paths simultaneously coexist in the culture indicates the degree of dissociation and polarization of the two spirits. Authority here asserts itself in its most reactionary, controlling, and saturnine aspects. Although its preoccupation may be with the effort to contain the innocence and folly of youth, because it too is swept up in the same innocence and naive realism that dominate the culture, it has no access to the wisdom and principled thinking that could help it in its containing role. In the mutual dissociation that occurs between youth and authority, the latter furthermore loses contact with that revitalizing force of youth that is needed to bring ageless wisdom and principles into the current context and make them relevant. Once again, when youth and authority become dissociated, in the long run, youth wins and both lose.

The word "ossification" is derived from the Greek *osteon,* which means "bone." When authority becomes hard as a bone, it has ossified, or, synonymously with this, it has petrified or calcified. It has become rigidly settled or fixed. Because it has become hard and rigid, it can also easily splinter into many fragments; that is, it is prone to highly compartmentalized thinking and hairsplitting over minutiae. This is no ordinary appreciation for the natural complexity of details, but a glorification of the method of reason in itself because it rules absolutely and, supposedly, rules out human error.

The fact that America prides itself on being a nation ruled by law and not individuals makes it especially subject to the compartmentalized thinking, hairsplitting, and overdone ratiocination that come with the legal mentality. When its deep admiration for law, order, and justice falls into the hands of an ossified spirit of authority, America gets caught up in what many foreign observers feel are peculiar indulgences. A recent illustration of this was Kenneth Starr's five-year investigation of the Clintons, which of course, with its relentless pursuit of all kinds of details in the name of truth, resulted in the Lewinsky scandal and the impeachment proceedings against Clinton. Not only did Starr's style of investigation and the very partisan Congressional debate on impeachment smack of the ossification of authority, but so did Clinton's legalistic way of handling the Lewinsky matter from the beginning. Clinton's loss of moral authority, together with the prying, paternalistic authority of Starr, demonstrated how authority that lacks integrity can quickly turn into youthful folly. With its details blasted across the Internet, the Lewinsky affair became a national and international spectacle. Alan Dershowitz's reference to this episode as "sexual McCarthyism" was apt: the McCarthy trials were the acme of ossified authority in America.

Even by itself, without the ossification of authority, America's admiration for law, order, and justice, as the historian Perry Miller has shown, makes the American mind or spirit legalistic. On a popular level, this amounts to the belief in fair play that Americans widely hold. On a governmental level, this takes the form of the Supreme Court's painstaking efforts to find the correct practical applications of the principles embodied in the Constitution. As William H. Kennedy said, the Supreme Court "has spent the last couple of hundred years, or nearly, in an effort to do for justice what the Church Fathers and the scholastics did for faith by a careful elaboration of their theological doctrine. We are in the process of a careful elaboration of legal doctrine in our quest for justice." Of course, state courts are also subject to this process, as was demonstrated, for example, in the Florida Supreme Court proceedings in the presidential race between George W. Bush and Al Gore. In matters of law, order, and justice, the American psyche is driven by a passion to "get it right," even if, as alleged with regard to both federal and state proceedings in the Bush-vs.-Gore case, this passion may not be the only one at play.

But certainly, when the ossification of authority takes hold of this passion, the elaboration of legal doctrine also becomes ossified. Because common sense is replaced by a legalistic but naive realism—what is just or right is defined in purely legal terms—the quest for justice becomes a farce. What puzzles foreigners is not only the farce, but how seriously and to what extremes Americans will take it. Jefferson, in his concern about this tendency to mistake the finger that points to the moon for the moon, warned that "to lose our country by a scrupulous adherence to written laws, would be to lose the law itself. . . ."

I have, in the discussion on the cult of freedom, given some examples of how lawfulness can be lost by a scrupulous adherence to written laws. Those examples illustrated that the ossification of authority in the defense of freedom actually diminishes freedom. An example that is especially revealing in this context was an episode in 1996 that fortunately even Americans were able to laugh at, no doubt encouraging its quick resolution. School authorities in Lexington, North Carolina, had charged Johnathan Prevette for breaking the written rules against sexual harassment. When the media brought this event to national attention, they backed off, saying he had only broken a general school rule prohibiting unwelcome touching of one student by another. Johnathan Prevette was a six-year-old boy who had kissed a girl in his first-grade class. In similar cases that year, at least three children were expelled from schools for having in their possession over-the-counter drugs such as flu or cold medicines. The authorities argued that the rules did not make a distinction between these and illegal drugs.

More commonly, the problem of ossified authority colors the American quest for justice through the complex legal system erected by the nation. The law has become a force in itself rather than a clear set of guidelines to enable decision-making. No doubt, the swelling mass of legislation passed by the government reflects the complexity of implementing social policy in a democracy of widely varying and often competing interests. But the sheer weight and technical Catch-22s of the laws make actual governing nearly impossible. Often, neither elected officials nor citizens understand the legal system. Sonny Bono, when attempting to negotiate the maze of health inspection requirements to open his restaurant in Palm Springs, became so frustrated that he ran for mayor so that he could, in his own words, "get even" with the health inspectors.

John Ralston Saul has sketched the historical process by which the legal structures of all Western countries, not just America, mushroomed. He explains that the understanding of justice laid out in the seventeenth and eighteenth centuries was perfectly clear, but with the proliferating effects of the method of reason, legal language obscured the principles of justice and these principles became divorced from their application. Further laws were required to compensate for the inadequacies or holes in the legal system that now appeared, and then these laws created even more holes. By the 1950s the legal profession had grown by leaps and bounds in order to both plug and exploit these proliferating legal holes. As a result, by 1998 there were 951,000 lawyers (including 39,000 judges) in the United States. Of course, unmitigated deregulation, which would undo the Gordian knots of the modern legal system but at the same time throw out the concern for principle, is not a solution. One would not wish to replace the law with lawlessness. In the final analysis, laws must be rooted in genuine authority, serving humans rather than the other way around. The great American judge Learned Hand joined figures like Rousseau and Edmund Burke in believing that the law must be subservient to a moral center within man himself. "I often wonder," he said, "whether we do not rest our hopes too much upon constitutions, upon laws and upon courts. These are false hopes; believe me, these are false hopes. Liberty lies in the hearts of men and women; when it dies there no constitution, no law, no court can save it."

The innocent absence of a moral center guiding the legal process has given rise to a litigious society—a society steeped in the "sue me, sue you blues," to borrow George Harrison's term from his song of the same title. Aside from the thousands of petty suits that fill up the courts, and the lengthy delays these cause for those who really need the courts to help them, there are other serious consequences. Entrepreneurs today know that they have to take special legal and financial precautions against competitors who hire lawyers to research any possible excuse to launch lawsuits against them purely in an effort to destroy or acquire their businesses. Litigation has thus become a way to earn a living not just for the lawyers. Even when litigation clearly is required, the absence of an inner moral center that distinguishes common sense from nonsense or from naive legal realism makes it increasingly difficult for the law to serve justice. Again, one may think of the cases cited in the discussion on the cult of freedom: the law was interpreted so narrowly that the guilty parties could not be punished.

And then of course one may cite the O.J. Simpson trial, which many feel was an illustration of the same dynamic. The Simpson trial, however, was more a dilution or watering-down of authority than an ossification or hardening of it, but the effects were similar. As Vincent Bugliosi argued, the use of authority in this trial was so loose that it led to misuse or abuse. From the defense team to the prosecuting team to the judge, there was a failure to properly and conscientiously exercise authority in one instance after another. In the aftermath of the verdict, the legal experts asserted that the system's failure here to obtain a guilty verdict in light of the overwhelming evidence supporting one was an exception and not the rule. Certainly, the data on successfully prosecuted trials in the United States shows that it was an exception. But the *degree* to which authority was undermined in such a highly publicized case, where one would imagine that special care would be taken to prove the rule and not the exception, suggests that it can happen in any case.

Litigiousness, at root, is only one manifestation of the splitting of American heroic idealism into two camps, "us" and "them." Perhaps the greatest damage caused by the ossification of authority in the United States is the extreme polarization of "We the People" into two camps, liberal and conservative. As Jefferson pointed out, polarization is a natural part of the political process and the polity. However, when the polarization becomes so divisive and the camps so rigid that the polity is fractured, no middle ground can be found and society cannot debate its problems in a civil manner, much less find solutions to them. Ross Perot with his straight-talking style of authority made his bid for the presidency in 1992 on the grounds that the argumentative politics of the two major parties had stifled public discourse and made effective policymaking impossible. But not long after the election that year, "politics as usual" had reasserted itself and congressional gridlock was the order of the day. Each party accused the other of being ossified. However, neither could legitimately claim innocence in this matter, though both tried.

The issue of health care reform—one on which Clinton very much ran his 1992 campaign and had acquired a mandate for change—clearly exemplified the ossification of authority in the White House, the Congress, and the polity at large. The Clinton administration did not democratically open up the reform process to the public—for example, through Clinton's customary, televised town hall meetings—but instead kept its task force meetings private. It did not enlist the public in the debate and use its support to set and drive an agenda. As a result, Clinton's plan not only failed but almost ruined his first term. The insurance companies and the Republicans took control of the debate, going directly to the people with negative TV ads; the task force members—511 policy analysts—argued over principles, values, and economic theories, finally conceiving a 1,342-page plan that was excessively complex and bureaucratic; the two parties could not reach a consensus on a proposal; and more than 1100 special interest groups had attacked every reform package proposed. The media, reacting to the circus that the debate had turned into, treated it in terms of which side was doing better and which not, instead of accurately reflecting the public mood and desire for genuine reform. In the end, the need for health *payment* reform— for a payment system that guarantees that services would be fairly priced (what most people were at heart concerned about)—was obscured by the hard-to-define concept of health *care* reform, causing the debate to get bogged down on the issue of universal coverage. The fact that over 40 million Americans do not have health insurance is of course a most serious problem, but instead of gaining momentum with reforms that could have been more easily agreed upon and then taking on the most difficult problem, the debate became preoccupied with the complexities of the latter. Naturally, by that time, the public was lost in confusion, questioning whether reform was viable or even beneficial. The entire process had become fragmented and frayed. The ossification of authority inevitably constellates not only fierce animosity between differing viewpoints, but self-dividedness; one corners oneself in too narrowly. This general condition of ossified authority all across the social and policy spectrum fueled the Republican "Contract with America," a campaign whose success gave the Republicans a majority in both houses of Congress for the first time since 1955. But of course, the condition of ossified authority hardly disappeared.

The ossification of authority is a threat to democracy. It masquerades not only as the voice of freedom but the voice of truth. It is not something that occurs just in isolated legal cases or the legal profession or the legislative bodies of the nation. It reflects an attitude that exists in the culture at large inasmuch as the population expects and supports it. One finds the ossification of authority in the mechanized management style of corporations, in the materialistically oriented approach to education at all levels, and in the narrow parameters of how the media decide what makes good news. It would be a misconception to assume that the ossification of authority occurs only in the domain of law and order or, as one might imagine, in the Christian fundamentalist or right wing agenda for America. The ossification of authority is a problem that has not so much to do with right vs. left or right vs. wrong as with what makes good sense vs. what doesn't. As Jung said, "The pendulum of the mind oscillates between sense and nonsense, not between right and wrong." The McCarthy hearings, for instance, did not end because Americans suddenly realized they were wrong or evil, although they undoubtedly were; the hearings ended when people finally saw that they were grounded in nonsense.

The ossification of authority is a condition that lacks common sense and knowledge but wears the guise of them. Because human beings so desperately want the appearance of being knowledgeable and the comfort of certitude that being knowledgeable supposedly brings, they get sucked into the empty pretense of ossified authority. In their innocence they cannot tell the difference between authentic knowledge and pseudoknowledge. They do not recognize that the Socratic notion of authority, upon which the Western method of inquiry and knowledge is based, assumes that doubt is a natural part of the search for truth. A Socratic dialogue does not rigidly close off the inquiry with hard answers. Every answer raises a new question. Socratic authority is akin to what the modern management theorist T.T. Paterson has called "sapiential authority," an authority based on wisdom and experience, and not just title, position, or legal recourse. Grounded in a discriminating moral center and a willingness to tolerate and pursue the unknown, such authority can be trusted to find its way without getting clamped down in its own vices.

## The Cult of Cynicism

The cult of cynicism that is so prevalent in America today is a direct effect of and response to the ossification of authority. When authority becomes brittle and ineffectual, people no longer trust it. Yet because a society cannot function without authority, it is embraced, but only halfheartedly and with mistrust. An ambivalence develops in the form of cynicism. The cynic actually wants to trust authority, but, finding it impossible to do so, becomes disillusioned and reacts with anger and criticism. More than that would require revolution, or at least taking charge of things oneself, which most modern cynics do not wish to do. This is very different from the ancient and original Cynics, the Greek philosophers who held virtue to be the only good and stressed independence from worldly needs and pleasures. Their criticism of society rested upon their inner authority and their willingness to abandon the world in order to create a better one. Their cynicism was heroic and not purely reactive. They didn't just criticize society's lack of vision; they offered an alternative vision, one that they demonstrated by the way they lived.

By contrast, the cynicism in America today is reactive and pseudo-heroic. It is not the directed response of the ancient philosophers, nor, for that matter, is it the engaging irony of humanist philosophers and writers of more recent times. It is at worst an off-putting, sloganeering cynicism, and at best a quietly festering, insidious attitude that pervades society. Granted, the ossification of authority is an insidious problem that is difficult to respond to, but the lack of critical thinking that characterizes it is also intrinsic to our current cynical response to it. As a result, while the cynicism is critical it shows little critical awareness of what the problem is behind the symptom it is criticizing, and it offers little critical reflection on what might be viable alternatives. This is not conducive to positive social change.

A cross-sectional view of the American population amply illustrates its cynicism. The lack of trust in institutions and others in general is remarkably high, as is the level of disillusionment. Polls show that 75 percent of Americans do not believe their government can be trusted. Ninety percent of American parents would not want their children to become president. In a 1995 poll, 25 percent of respondents believed that the O.J. Simpson trial demonstrated that there is no justice in the United States; 85 percent believed that justice depends on the defendant's wealth or race. Another poll showed that 65 percent of Americans believe that most people cannot be trusted, a belief that goes hand-in-hand with the collapse of trust in institutions. This latter poll indicates not only a deterioration of authority and integrity, but the isolated individualism of modern American life. As the political philosopher Jean Bethke Elshtain points out, public discourse is bound to break down as society is atomized: people give in to that democratic cultural credo, "You are entitled to your opinion and I'm entitled to mine," and then just walk away from each other. Tocqueville's fear of democratic despotism is rooted precisely in this free reign of the "me-principle." This principle has difficulty accepting that any authority has the right or worthiness to limit the individual's actions or define his social obligations. For Tocqueville, authority and liberty are not opposites, but partners. Without one, the other cannot exist. Our contemporary distrust of and disdain for authority promote a free-for-all rather than greater freedom.

Without principles to guide it, cynicism falls victim to the Machiavellian mentality. It becomes prone to the same duplicity, craftiness, and amorality it denounces when it lashes out without principled thinking. It innocently attempts to criticize ossified authority with ossified authority. As many have observed, the Vietnam War, the secret war in Cambodia, and Watergate set the precedents for this. These events made the uncovering of the hidden and illicit necessary, but that imperative to search for truth has degenerated into a general tendency to expose and undermine. This is done by investigating the sex lives of political leaders or other incidents that cast light upon their flaws and foibles—anything that focuses on embarassing moments from their past. Clinton has accurately described this as the "politics of personal destruction." The social thinker Jonathan Lear argues that such politics are a form of attacking idealizations of authority, idealizations that invariably arise from society's own innocence. "In general," Lear says, "we do not understand how active we are in constructing our sense of political disillusionment." The Machiavellian way the media, as well as the politicians themselves, tear down individuals without really addressing these idealizations, speaks to society's unprincipled, unthinking cynicism. This cynicism is as steeped in innocence as the idealizations to which it is a reaction.

As in other matters, with cynicism one may see similar patterns on both collective and individual levels. Probably everyone has known at least a few people who are terribly cynical or bitter. The psychologist Marie-Louise von Franz writes that such people have not really worked out their childish illusions but have just cut them off. On the surface, they are very realistic, disillusioned, self-contained, and independent, but underneath they secretly harbor a childish longing for the nurturing parent they may have never had or for an idyllic happiness. A brittle sense of authority has been superimposed upon a childishly idealistic condition of youth. For such individuals, innocence is the foundation of both the youth and authority principles, ultimately engulfing both. The cynicism may appear to be a sophisticated denouncement of innocence, but it is only sophistry that is innocent underneath, unconsciously.

The same holds true collectively. The disillusionment of modern American cynicism is not really a *dis*-illusionment in the sense of a necessary sacrifice of illusions—one of the more crucial ways the recognition of necessity makes people free. Disillusionment today does not imply, for example, the sacrifice of the illusion that political leaders are superhuman, parentlike authorities, people who are somehow immune to the vices and shortcomings shared by the people who elected them. Even the illusion that the people themselves are without these vices and shortcomings has yet to be addressed. Rather, disillusionment today is merely disappointment in and resentment of our political leaders because they have turned out to be different than we innocently anticipated. Such disillusionment is preferable for many, for it puts the focus upon the other rather than upon themselves and allows them to maintain their innocence. It is also preferable because of the satisfaction or pleasure it provides in its superior, cynical stance. The feeding frenzy that occurs when the media goes on a rampage of character assassination reveals this pleasure on the parts of both the media and the public.

The media's role in fueling cynicism about politicians and the political process is not new by any means. Jefferson himself was publicly humiliated when the press spread a rumor that he had had a sexual relationship with his slave Sally Hemings (a relationship recently corroborated by DNA analysis that linked some of Hemings' descendents to Jefferson). This experience led him to conclude that the newspapers tend to present "only the charicatures of disaffected minds," and that their abuses of freedom had generated a scatological political culture "never before known or borne by any civilized nation." This situation, however, has become even worse today. The journalist James Fallows has correctly surmised that the cynicism of the media—whose accepted news format is "If it bleeds, it leads"—has spread to the populace and is undermining democracy. With respect to the populace, this has resulted in a loss of faith in government and in the participatory democratic process. The percentage of those voting in general elections is lower today than ever before. With respect to the government, the constant attacks by the media have forced it to adopt a siege mentality that is mostly defensive and too preoccupied with scandal to be genuinely innovative. As the communication theorists Edwin Diamond and Robert Silverman remarked, the current environment of conflict makes it "all but impossible for even the best organized, most adept White House to govern effectively." One journalist joked that a presidential candidate today is not even taken seriously unless he has an independent counsel investigating him. The cult of cynicism has become a regular feature of the political landscape.

The innocence that insists that leaders be flawless and then punishes them when they fail to be so creates a shadow effect that is the exact opposite of what it ostensibly wants. This too undermines democracy. As John Ralston Saul explains, leaders must give a false public impression of what their character is in order to get elected and survive. Thus, falsification "becomes an essential talent for the elected, and eagerness to be duped a characteristic for the citizen. This also suggests that only people with severely deformed characters will be able to rise to high office. The system can't help but reward those whose prime talents are acting and punish those who are straightforward." The hypocrisy of the innocence that undergirds this system becomes evident whenever a leading figure is indeed straightforward. When the Harvard Law School professor Douglas Ginsburg, for instance, admitted during his confirmation hearings that he had used marijuana on a few occasions, his nomination for the Supreme Court died. There was, however, no indication of regret on the part of the citizenry either for his disqualification or for the use of marijuana— whether occasional or not—among its own ranks. Political correctness won out over truthfulness. Warren Beatty's satirical film "Bulworth" reveals the hypocrisy of America's innocence in this regard in an outrageously funny way.

It is no surprise that almost every American presidency in the last four decades began with high, optimistic hopes on the part of the people (the post-election "honeymoon" period), and ended in disappointment and pessimism. From the innocent assumptions with which it begins, where else can the political process go? Again, as Jonathan Lear noted, people do not understand their role in creating their own disillusionment; that when they idealize the government or a president, they are displacing their own innocence. Nor do they realize that when they hate the government, they hate themselves, since in a democracy "We the People" and the government are, theoretically at least, one and the same.

And while all this innocence, cynicism, and self-destructiveness march on, so does the rest of the world. It is a serious problem when the nation that the world looks to for leadership becomes so puritanically concerned with its internal leadership that it fails to take notice of all the dark and impure things going on around it. Americans, for example, were hardly able to see that while they were obsessing over Bill Clinton's sexual and ethical foibles during the Lewinsky escapade, Russia was breaking down and at risk of reversing its course toward democracy and capitalism; Islamic terrorism against Americans abroad was increasing; the economy of Japan was coming apart at the seams; North Korea was starving its own people while exporting advanced missile technology and continuing its nuclear blackmail of the United States and South Korea; India and Pakistan were headily escalating their nuclear arms race against each other; Rwanda's people were starving in the wake of that nation's ruthless genocidal war; the world's financial crisis was threatening to spread to Latin America; and, last but not least, the hole in the ozone layer above the Antarctic had, according to NASA scientists, reached a size larger than the North American continent. These facts should have raised serious concerns about the condition of our global village.

All told, the cost of innocence is great.

# Chapter 18

## The Sacrifice of Innocence

*The truth was obscure, too profound and too
pure, to live it you had to explode.
In that last hour of need, we entirely agreed,
sacrifice was the code of the road.*

—Bob Dylan

### The Journey of the Hero and Beyond

Given all that has been said about the addiction to innocence and its threats
to American democracy, it is important to appreciate the critical juncture at
which we find our nation. Living under Roman rule during the first century
A.D., the Greek historian Plutarch noted that immature spirituality is characteristic of republics in their final stage before they devolve into tyrannies. In
modern times, tyranny needs to be understood, again, in its wider and subtler sense as cultural and not just political tyranny. When Jefferson said, "I
have sworn upon the altar of God eternal hostility against every form of
tyranny over the mind of man," he probably was not referring to the kind
of tyranny that arises imperceptibly from the mind itself, from its original
condition of innocence. Jefferson was enamored by America's fresh start in
history and its supposed innocence and purity. Yet were he to have known
how prevalent immature spirituality and its threat of tyranny would become in America, would not his pledge still have held? As Hillman informs
us, the ancients had less of an infatuation with the innocence of youth.
Plato, whom Jefferson incidentally detested (most expressly for his ab-
struseness but possibly also for his antidemocratic views), recognized the
two sides of youth: a more evolved side, as exemplified with the child of

the *Meno*, and a less evolved side, as illustrated with the undifferentiated child of the *Lysis*, *The Republic*, and the *Laws*. St. Paul, too, in a Christian vein, praises childlikeness of heart but has little tolerance for childishness of the mind (I Cor. 14:20); St. Augustine commented on this distinction as follows: "Childhood is proposed to us as a model of humility which we should imitate, but it is equally proposed as a type of folly to be avoided."

The folly of youth rests in its naive realism. A nation or civilization gripped by this will not be able to tell the difference between what is naively real and genuinely real; that is, it will not be able to tell the difference between illusion and reality. This inability is the benchmark of the spiritual immaturity that in turn sets the stage for tyranny, and ultimately the decline of that nation or civilization. As Hannah Arendt said, "The ideal subject of totalitarian rule is not the convinced Nazi or the convinced Communist, but people for whom the distinction between fact and fiction (*i.e.,* the reality of experience) and the distinction between true and false (*i.e.,* the standards of thought) no longer exist." The loss of this distinction is also connected to what John Wesley Powell called "that universal habit of savagery—the confusion of the objective with the subjective"; from the universal habit of savagery to the particular savagery of totalitarianism or tyranny is just a baby step. America has demonstrated significant steps in this direction already in its history of tyranny against indigenous peoples and blacks. It now likes to pride itself on being a free society, but the tyranny of innocence is an invisible totalitarianism that can exist freely underneath the institutional structures of democracy.

Just as educational reform and an open, inquisitive public discourse are required in order for the nation to examine its addiction to height, so the same are required for it to examine its addiction to innocence. The Fourth Step of the 12-Step Program of Alcoholics Anonymous is a guideline that is as good for one addiction as for another: we need to make "a searching and fearless moral inventory of ourselves." Innocence begs for critical examination; if it does not get this, it will opt for evil. With its naive realism and capacity for denial, it will use beliefs of every kind to maintain a hold on the American psyche. Not only will racism continue, but the other evils of innocence as well: perpetual novelty; unrestrained freedom; the pursuit of a happiness that is hedonistic and self-centered; the idolization of an ephemeral self; the epidemic of child abuse; widespread social puerility; national and international violence; the ossification of authority; and bitter cynicism.

These are not obscure and abstract phenomena that are impossible to understand. Even high school students can grasp the effects of innocence acting upon them, upon their families, and upon the society all around them when these effects are explained to them in a practical, commonsense way. Education here, once again, is more a matter of becoming aware or awake than of reading books or becoming technically proficient in a specific field. It is more a matter of discovery that, as McLuhan says, "comes from dialogue that starts with the sharing of ignorance." Indeed, it is ignorance—the condition of not knowing—that makes innocence or naive realism so acceptable. As Americans do not know of their addiction to height, so they do not know of their addiction to innocence. They do not know of the threats these pose to their survival as a nation, particularly to the survival of their democracy. Hillman aptly describes this condition, itself the epitome of innocence, as America's "mystical cloud of unknowing": "We are forgiven simply by virtue of not knowing what we do."

Education thus must return to its original meaning in order to become truly effective in the Information Age: the Latin root of the word "education" is *educere*, which means *to lead out*, as in to lead out from ignorance and not knowing, or from innocence and naive realism. This is very different from the kind of education prevalent today in our institutions, which aim *to put information into* the minds of our children and young people (as if they were mere extensions of the computer that they now need to master to become "educated"). But of course, in advocating a return to Roman and Greek notions of education, the question arises, who will educate the educators? Who will design curricula or authorize educators to design curricula that address in a less-than-innocent way the real problems of living—that is, the problems of finding meaning in life; of social duty; of relationships, marriage, and parenting; of suffering and evil? Who will take the lead in asking, as every civilization must do afresh with each generation, what does it mean to lead the good life?

Reflection on these questions seem to be above all what history is demanding of America right now. This—and this alone—can shatter America's innocence. The Vietnam War alone was not enough, nor were the assassinations of the Kennedys and Martin Luther King in the 1960s, nor Watergate. It is not catastrophe alone that wakes a nation up, but also introspection. I am not suggesting that America's heroic ideal must necessarily become a philosophic ideal, but it must begin to move toward the wisdom and the love of wisdom—of knowing as opposed to not knowing—that are at the root of philosophy. America's heroic ideal has fixed the aspiration toward greatness upon the pursuit of height and the cultivation of innocence. This is a very young heroism that is suitable for a young nation. But America is not exactly the young nation it was when this ideal was imprinted upon its character. Nor is it living in a young world.

Indeed, the bitterness that underlies cynicism and that also tends to characterize ossified authority reflects the current status of America with regard to its heroic and historic journey. It is a symptom of heroic failure not in the sense that there is a failure to live up to the heroic ideal, but in the sense that the heroic ideal is *itself* failing. That is essentially why people are bitter, whether they recognize it or not. And it also seems to be why people are depressed in such large numbers. Studies by the psychologist Martin Seligman show that depression today is occurring at a rate ten times greater than before World War II. The world is changing, but people's understanding of what constitutes the good life has either failed to change with it or has been altogether lost. The heroic idealism of the frontiersman-soldier-world conqueror who defines success purely in terms of what he has won; the heroic idealism of commercialism and wealth without limitation; the heroic idealism of flying higher and higher, whether through motion and speed, celebrity worship, or sex, drugs, and gambling; the heroic idealism that gives rise to the cults of novelty, freedom, happiness, and childhood; all are attempts to attain the good life based on the assumption that these things are just what they appear to be, that they will satisfy the human spirit. They generate an excitement that is appropriate in adolescence—the adolescence of a nation as well as an individual—but if unduly prolonged, they lead to the dreariness that typically sets in upon adolescence as the latter in turn also becomes too prolonged. With its metaphor of suicide, the fixation upon eternally young death-heroes speaks to adolescence's own wish for transformation. Sooner or later, the human spirit needs a life that is balanced with the wisdom of authority and not one-sidedly driven by the passion and innocence of youth. It needs this in order to become whole and to be well-grounded in itself and in the world.

In many hero myths and legends of the world, the hero becomes disillusioned at some point in his journey. He is tricked or in some way mistreated so that he loses his naive realism. There is some ordeal he must undergo, a trial of strength that tests his character and worthiness. In this process, his old self must die so that there can be a rebirth. His fall from innocence is integral to his becoming a hero; it is this that compels him to develop himself through effort and mastery. Like the phoenix who dies and is reborn, he falls and rises to his calling. Disillusionment is thus a necessary part of the hero's journey. He experiences this not only as a sacrifice of illusions, but as deeply disheartening and confusing. Disillusionment, like foolishness, is not the opposite of wisdom. (Indeed, these three very much go together, or as William Blake famously quipped, the fool who persists in his folly eventually finds wisdom. The road that goes from folly to wisdom indubitably passes through disillusionment.) No, the opposite of wisdom, Jung tells us, is bitterness. Bitterness is what one is left with when he fails to extract the wisdom from disillusionment, or from any painful experience. Bitterness is what remains when the death-and-rebirth experience stops short with death—that is, psychological death—and there is no rebirth into wisdom. Collectively as well as individually, bitterness is a sign of failing to age wisely and gracefully. It is a sign of stagnation.

The sacrifice of innocence is so central to the hero's journey that there are specific symbols that universally capture this motif. "In many of the dragon legends," the psychologist M. Esther Harding writes, "when it is a question of rescuing the maiden, the sacrifice of a lamb is demanded. This means that the childish innocence within man must be voluntarily relinquished. If he is to become a conscious being, he cannot remain innocent like the animals." Because it is a lesser evolved or younger version of the hero that needs to be sacrificed in order for a more highly evolved, mature version to be born, we see sometimes an even greater sacrifice than a lamb. Thus was Abraham called by God to sacrifice his son, Isaac. The torment a man must suffer in sacrificing his son is a good analogue for what is involved in sacrificing the young, immature part of oneself. Innocence causes suffering, but, because of the attachment we have to innocence, the sacrifice of it causes even deeper suffering. As Marie-Louise von Franz notes, it is suffering that forces a person who is caught in his childish inner core to mature. Hillman, too, concludes that the childish wound that makes adaptation so difficult also makes possible a new fate. Accordingly, in the end God let Isaac live, but only because Abraham, in accepting the sacrifice demanded of him, on an inner level *did* go through with the sacrifice. He was spared the outer pain, so to speak, because he had submitted to the inner pain. And Isaac eventually became the father of Jacob, whose offspring became the children and nation of Israel. In other words, Abraham's submission or surrender led to redemption and, indeed, a new fate. Job also went through a similar ordeal, as did Jesus. For all, sacrifice was the key to transformation. The psychologist Robert Johnson explains: "Sacrifice really involves the art of drawing energy from one level and reinvesting it at another level to produce a higher form of consciousness."

The transformation induced by the sacrifice of innocence is a process so mysterious that one can never tell where it will lead. As the novelist Robertson Davies wrote, "One always learns one's mystery at the price of one's innocence." Fate—one's new fate, that is—may conceivably demand a sacrifice not only of the childish, but of the heroic ideal itself. For this too there are illustrations in the folk literature of the world. In *Beyond the Hero*, the psychiatrist Allan Chinen analyzes a series of folk stories of just this kind from different cultures. The central figures in these timeless tales are healers rather than heroes, communicators rather than conquerors, explorers rather than exploiters. They are fierce but avoid violence; they are strong-willed and independent but relate to their emotions and the feminine; they are wild and instinctual but also tender and nurturing. Such folk stories are a culture's ways of teaching its individuals about the possibilities of human character, but the principles they shed light on have just as much relevance to the culture itself and *its* possibilities. In his autobiography, Jung tells of a dream he had in 1913 whose folk tale imagery and drama simultaneously had personal and collective implications. In his dream, he had murdered the legendary Germanic hero and dragonslayer, Siegfried.

> . . . suddenly the meaning of the dream dawned on me. "Why, that is the problem that is being played out in the world." Siegfried, I thought, represents what the Germans want to achieve, heroically to impose their will, have their own way. "Where there is a will there is a way!" I had wanted to do the same. But now that was no longer possible. The dream showed that the attitude embodied by Siegfried, the hero, no longer suited me. Therefore it had to be killed.
>
> After the deed I felt an overpowering compassion, as though I myself had been shot: a sign of my secret identity with Siegfried, as well as of the grief a man feels when he is forced to sacrifice his ideal and his conscious attitudes. This identity and my heroic idealism had to be abandoned, for there are higher things than the ego's will, and to these one must bow.

Jung evidently understood the need here to shift to values beyond the hero's. The German nation did not, as witnessed by the First World War that broke out the year after Jung had this dream and by the Second World War that came almost 30 years later.

Probably one of the best recent examples of a nation that successfully shifted to values beyond the hero's, that let go of its investment in heroically imposing its will to have its way, is Great Britain. History will undoubtedly record the fall of the British Empire as one of the most significant events of the twentieth century, certainly comparable to the collapse of the

Soviet Union. One can argue that Britain was compelled to make this sacrifice, that it had no choice. Its resources spent in the Second World War, it could not prevent the subject-nations of the Empire from gaining independence one by one. Britain's era as master of the globe had come and gone. But one could say the same about Abraham's sacrifice, too—that God commanded him and he had no choice. Perhaps it is in the *way* the sacrifice is made. In the end, England did not fight its destiny, but surrendered to it with dignity and grace. It is today still a thriving nation, one that the rest of Europe often looks to for moral leadership. England succeeded in drawing energy from one level and reinvesting it at another.

In the end, a nation's only viable alternative if it wishes to survive may be to leave behind its heroic ideal, itself a truly heroic and courageous act. Indeed, youth itself, if not youthfulness, has to eventually be sacrificed. The ideals, attitudes, and vision of a nation must mature—as must the nation—or else all become stagnant. As Toynbee showed, a nation or civilization may be in a state of stagnation and even decline even though there is a profusion of social, economic, and other activities, and it may therefore not even recognize that it is in a state of stagnation or decline. The civilizations most blessed by history—in the form of longevity, a lasting legacy, or both—have been those that developed strong traditions of wisdom (albeit high achievements in aesthetics have also been rewarded). Israel, Greece, Rome, India, and China are foremost in the league of civilizations that developed such traditions, though civilizations such as Persia and Tibet must also be included as exemplars of spiritual authority. Within all these civilizations, there was a maturation process that occurred in a timely fashion and that was suited to their intrinsic characters.

America, of course, is in a completely different situation. It is far more extroverted than any of the above civilizations, and had its beginnings with the Enlightenment and the rise of the secular worldview. While one might anticipate that America's wisdom would build on that of the great ancient civilizations, one could also anticipate that it would somehow be different—probably exercised in the context of its political-spiritual vision rather than in the context of a religious or philosophic one. But whether in the Old World or the New, the challenges of history still demand a clear choice between creative movement and movement that is only a mask for stagnation.

★

# Part IV

## The Fate of America

*All great changes are irksome to the human mind, especially those which are attended with great dangers and uncertain effects.*

—John Adams

*The dogmas of the quiet past are inadequate to the stormy present. The occasion is piled high with difficulty, and we must rise—with the occasion. As our case is new, so we must think anew, and act anew. We must disenthrall ourselves, and then we shall save our country.*

—Abraham Lincoln

*Fate avoided becomes one's nemesis.*

—Unknown

# ★ Prelude: The Unpredictable Nature of History ★

Humans have a special need to know what the future will bring. We believe that if we can know the future, we will find relief from our anxieties around the fact that we have only a moderate degree of control over our destinies. This need to know the future is as strong in the collective arena as in the individual arena: for example, how comforting it is to learn from the political and economic pundits that America's future looks good, that we can look forward to more of the success and rewards that we have reaped in the past. Such news is always welcome, yet one cannot help but wonder about the fears that are masked by its frequent repetition.

In fact, history rarely unfolds in precisely the way that its prognosticators anticipate. This is not to say that educated guesses about the future have no value; guesses that are even approximately accurate can help a society and its policymakers plan ahead. But in general, the more precise the predictions, the more likely will they be foiled by the complexities of history. In the mid–1980s, for instance, Arthur Schlesinger, Jr., a fine historian, had predicted that during the 1990s the two-party system in America would become deadlocked and a three-party system would emerge. He was, of course, right in the first part of his prediction, but he had no way of knowing how the particular developments and personalities of that time would prevent the second part of his prediction from fully materializing. While Ross Perot and Ralph Nader profoundly influenced the outcomes of two presidential elections nearly a decade apart, their third-party initiatives hardly amounted to three-party governance. Schlesinger's keen instinct picked up the scent of a trail, a general pattern of forces and factors influencing history, but how human nature would interact with these forces and factors and mold them into a specific form, he could not accurately predict. Above all, it is human nature that makes history unpredictable.

The fate or destiny of America can only be considered with this in mind. A student of the history of civilization pondering the phenomena discussed in this book would conclude that the course America is currently on, the forces and factors shaping its unfolding history, are troublesome at best, dangerous at worst. He or she would conclude that the optimism of the pundits is an expression of dizziness from the heights and of naive realism, that is, of tendencies that are part of the problem of the nation's addiction to youth; such optimism is thus not an objective reflection of the nation's condition and its future. Yet, in speculating about the nation's future, he or she would also have to allow room for that single most unpredictable element of history, human nature. To this, one could furthermore add particular traits of the American character, making any prediction of the nation's future especially tentative. America's character is more fluid and adaptable than that of most nations—in no small measure due to a history of adapting to a wild frontier and to the rapid changes that came after the frontier era. One can only hope that America, with its creativity, resilience, passionate desire to thrive, and practical, can-do mentality, will find a way to deal with its current condition. Curiously, these are all qualities of the spirit of youth. But perhaps this should not be surprising. As an ancient Greek proverb says, "The god that wounds, heals." It may be that the opposite spirit heals by complementing, balancing, and completing. But even in such a case, it is still the spirit most natural to one's orientation that heals by inspiring, by moving towards that opposite spirit, and most importantly, by coming to terms with it in some way. Only then can there be a synthesis of spirits, and can the relationship to the wounding god be transformed.

# Chapter 19

## America in the Third Millennium

*For what nation is there so great, who hath God so nigh unto them, as the Lord our God is in all things that we call upon him for? And what nation is there so great, that hath statutes and judgments so righteous as all this law, which I set before you this day? Only take heed to thyself, and keep thy soul diligently, lest thou forget the things which thine eyes have seen, and lest they depart from thy heart all the days of thy life: but teach them thy sons, and thy sons's sons.*

—Deuteronomy 4:7–9

### Opportunity Repeats, History Knocks

When the king of the Persian Empire appointed Nehemiah and Ezra, respectively, governor and administrator of Judah, the two were faced with a formidable challenge. The Jewish nation had been in a state of decline for four centuries—first from its division into Israel and Judah, and then from its subjugation under the Assyrians, the Babylonians, and now the Persians. The Jews lived in exile, and those that remained in Judah were rapidly assimilating with neighboring peoples. Jerusalem was underpopulated and in ruins. Even more to their detriment, the Jews were losing their national vision or sense of purpose, namely, to be a righteous nation that lived in accord with the will of God as prescribed by the laws of Moses. This vision was their founding and guiding principle, their raison d'être. To become disconnected from it would have made their survival as a people questionable.

To redress these problems, Nehemiah and Ezra, both prominent Jews in the Persian king's court, engineered a major restoration of Judah. This the king approved under his liberal policy of improving conditions in the nations of his empire. Nehemiah implemented social and economic reforms and rebuilt the walls around Jerusalem, an action taken not only to safeguard the city but to signal the rejuvenation of Jewish nationhood. Ezra led a large exodus of exiled Jews to Judah in order to repopulate the country, and then with Nehemiah introduced a host of measures to insure the preservation and continuity of Jewish identity. It was these two who fused together the diverse Mosaic documents into the first five books of the Bible and canonized them (assuming here, of course, that this was not done by God, as orthodox faith asserts). It was they who established the liturgy of reading these books publicly, a practice continued in synagogues today.

If Moses was the father of the Hebrew religion, then Ezra, a priest and scribe, was the father of Judaism. Known as the "second Moses," he reinstituted the observance of the Mosaic Law with its accompanying festivals as the centerpiece of Jewish life. He gave new meaning to the concept of the Jews as a people chosen to serve God in a special way. Indeed, he did not merely return to the original vision of the Jews in his effort to revitalize them; he took that vision *to another level* in order to give it even greater breadth and depth. He took the next practical step in integrating its ideal into the daily lives of the people. By making the vision more central and accessible, he assured the survival of the Jews not only in their homeland but in their exile, transforming the traditional idea of nationhood into the possibility of nationhood without geographical boundaries. Without this broadening and deepening of the national vision, the Jews may very likely have disappeared from the stage of history, as all the empires that conquered them and all the Middle Eastern nations that fought with them soon enough did.

This episode from history pointedly illustrates Toynbee's premise that if a nation or civilization responds creatively to history's challenges, it can turn crisis into growth. It also illustrates that the creative response may demand a return to the nation's original conception or vision, but not for the sake of recapturing it as it once was. As the French say, *il faut reculer pour mieux sauter en avant* (one must back up in order to leap forward). It is a *re*-visioning or renaissance of the vision that in such instances provides the nation with the morale and motivation to regenerate itself. In times of crisis there is a tendency to react with piecemeal solutions—such as economic initiatives—that deal with the nation's problems in a mechanistic, nuts-and-bolts manner. But what is often missing is a larger, unifying vision that connects these solutions to an overarching purpose. A clear vision that is invigorated—or reinvigorated—with the purpose of transformation may not always be a wrench for the nuts and bolts of the nation's problems, but is still a most valuable and practical asset. As in the case of Judah, it may mean the difference between survival and extinction. How well the filmmaker Federico Fellini understood the practical value of visionary thinking when he said, "The visionary is the only true realist."

The United States today is in a remarkably similar position to that of Judah in the time of Nehemiah and Ezra. This is of course not in regard to the external features of its social and political situation, but to the internal workings of its visionary inheritance and disposition. Cotton Mather was the first to draw an analogy between America and Judah in Nehemiah and Ezra's time, emphasizing the theme of reestablishing a nation with a distinct spiritual vision. A Puritan, Mather saw America as the proper beneficiary of Israel's legacy, picking up where Israel left off. Historically, however, it is more accurate to say that the founding of America by the sojourning Pilgrims paralleled the establishment of Israel after the Exodus, and the restoration by Nehemiah and Ezra is a theme more resonant with America's situation today.

Like Judah of old, contemporary America is at a critical historical junction, a crossroads with two possibilities, or rather, two choices. The first choice—hardly a choice, since it would be made so unconsciously—is that it can continue on its present course. To what end its outdated heroic ideal and addictions to height and innocence will lead, only time will tell. Conceivably, the current diffusion of the American vision, as observable in the cults of novelty, freedom, and happiness and in the idolization of an ephemeral self, could lead to its complete derailment and the eventual disintegration of American society. History has shown that this is what happened when other great nations failed to keep their visions alive or failed to live up to them. As Voegelin, Strauss, and others have noted, a society which has been accustomed to understanding itself in terms of a universal purpose cannot lose its orientation toward that purpose without, naturally, becoming seriously disoriented. For example, Rome was a great republic until its vision of republicanism became thoroughly derailed with the civil wars that concluded in 27 B.C. Though the empire emerged and Rome basked in glory and prosperity for another 400 years, the tyranny that replaced this republican vision was sooner or later bound to lead to Rome's demise. Will America, with its different type of empire and a different kind of tyranny, follow in Rome's footsteps?

The second choice America has is to attempt what Judah accomplished, namely, a spiritual revitalization and deepening of its vision. Of course, this would take a very different form for America than it did for Judah, for this crossroads is where the similarities between the two nations end. Although their visions share certain key elements due to a common religious tradition, the two nations represent very different societies existing in very different eras. Nevertheless, as was the case with Judah, America would need to take its vision to another level, one in which it is integrated into the daily lives of the people. It would need to seize its vision with a fresh understanding that would equip it to face its problems and its fate. Most certainly, vision is about *fate*, about meeting an inner calling. "In everything that matters," the writer G.K. Chesterton said, "the inside is much larger than the outside." It seems that contemporary America is completely dissociated from the inside—the spiritual side or calling—of its vision. Part of the problem here is with the vision itself, or rather, with its innocent aspects. Lacking clarity about social responsibility, and with an extroverted emphasis on a new world order orchestrated by Providence, the vision is one-sided and unadapted to people's spiritual and ethical needs. As long as the American vision continues to be lauded in history books, news magazines, and political speeches without any sense of its inner meaning, that meaning will never become a living truth in the minds and hearts of the people and the practical affairs of society.

## The American Vision as a Paradigm of Integrity

The vision of a free people spearheading an empire of liberty leads to a number of difficult if interesting problems when one pares it down to its inner core. One must, in the final analysis, conclude that it is an idea that has consistency only when freedom is understood as an expression of personal integrity. Any other understanding of freedom tends to lead to a kind of freedom that in the long run is good neither for the individual nor for society.

From its Puritan beginnings, the American vision was about integrity, moral integrity and the integrity of good, balanced living. As the Puritans saw it, America's special calling was to become a righteous nation, a land where nationhood and virtue were to be combined. In a world corrupted by ecclesiastical politics, monarchies, and other sordid forms of tyranny and human vice, this was a rather novel idea. In significant ways it represented a departure from Israel. It presumed that every individual in the nation must attain a moral probity that is genuinely free. Ideally, such morality would not be forcefully imposed from outside by some social authority, but would be an expression of individual integrity and conscience. This kind of morality or virtue is what the early Puritan founders were thinking of when they envisioned America as a "nation of saints."

That moral authority should rest within the individual is a principle that can be traced back from the Puritans to Martin Luther and earlier. (Of course, with their own ecclesiastical politics, the Puritans didn't always practice this principle purely either.) Luther's teaching that every man is his own priest with his own relationship to God was a building block of American democracy. By honoring the individual, it advocated his right to govern himself. It held the view that the individual holds the key to what is common ethical sense, not the collectivity. It also goes without saying that the establishment of this kind of freedom in America, a freedom of the spiritual and not just political realm, was to be the fulfillment of the Protestant Reformation. Almost every Puritan tract expressed the view that the Reformation had reached its final culmination in America.

The Founding Fathers of course had their own version of this moral venture. We have already spoken of the influence of the Scottish philosopher Francis Hutcheson upon Jefferson. Hutcheson's idea of the moral sense or faculty innate to all human beings was seen by Jefferson as a guarantee that the American, once freed from the institutional shackles that weighed down the European, could develop his energies fully while still being a moral citizen. In fact, it was largely because of this idea that Jefferson was so confident in his belief that the less government interfered in the citizen's affairs, the better. Jefferson's enduring trust in what he called "the will of the people" rested on this idea. The will of the public was essentially benign and would not behave despotically because democracy, having eliminated the corrupting institutions of monarchy, would allow people to act freely in accord with their moral instincts.

With his Puritan heritage and conservative streak, Adams was not so optimistic. His differences with Jefferson often revolved around such concerns, and it was because of these differences that Benjamin Rush dubbed Adams and Jefferson "the North and South Poles of the American Revolution." Adams feared that misguided majorities—"the people"—could be every bit as tyrannical as a king or pope. This was why he opposed a single-chambered system of representation. For Adams, integrity was not given to humankind as a natural disposition, but had to be earned the hard way. If Jefferson spent much time studying the ethics of the ancients in an effort to educate his moral faculty, Adams thoroughly went to school on this matter. He believed that personal integrity is the bridge that connects the psychological freedom attained by the individual with the democratic freedom of society. It is the inner integrity and freedom of the individual that serve as the cornerstone of the freedom of society. Joseph Ellis writes:

> Virtually all of [Adams'] political convictions, especially his most piercing political insights, derived from introspection, or what we would call psychology. . . . [If] Madison is the master sociologist of American political theory, Adams is the master psychologist. Virtue was not an abstract concept he learned about simply by reading Montesquieu, David Hume, or the writers of the English Commonwealth tradition. It was a principle of self-denial he harbored in his heart and kept preaching to himself in his diary. A state constitution was not just an agreed-upon framework of social customs and laws. It was a public replica of one's internal order or constitution. The very idea of government itself was the act of implementing in the world the lessons learned in dealing with one's own internal demons.

And:

> . . . Adams was obsessed with interior integrity, not with the exterior rewards that the mastery of appearances could bring. Humility, piety, self-denial, and other habits of the heart were not just means to an end for him, but the ends themselves. . . . Politics for him remained psychology writ large, a heaving collection of irrational urges that moved across the social landscape like the ambitions and vanities he felt surging through his own soul. More than any member of the revolutionary generation, Adams thought of statecraft as a public application of the skills required for self-management, regarded political analysis as a public version of introspection.

Integrity to Adams was not a state of purity acquired through having permanently exorcised one's demons; he did not believe, given human nature, that this was possible. Rather, integrity was characterized by an honest effort to confront one's demons and at least keep them plainly in view and under a modicum of control. The control came more from understanding them than dominating them. Similarly, freedom did not necessarily come from being free of them, but from knowing that they existed and making wise decisions on how to act. Thus did he believe in the importance of introspection as the basis for action, including public action. Adams was not a moralist; he did not adhere to a prescribed system of right and wrong conduct and did not seek to impose his personal morals on others. Though perhaps conservative, he was unlike the advocates of virtue so popular in America today, such as William Bennett, who with his politically partisan and aggressive moralism has been fittingly described by James Hillman as a "thug of virtue." The ethical sensibility of Adams was much more willing, in matters demanding moral consideration, to openly question which actions would be helpful, which harmful, and which simply meaningless. Though his most inviolable ethical principle was at heart Christian—"Do unto others as you would have them do unto you"—his was largely an ethics of common sense.

John Beebe has described this kind of integrity as "a commitment to serving the process as a whole." It is wholesome not because it has attained purity but because it acknowledges and is willing to struggle with that which is impure but unavoidably part of the picture—one's vulnerabilities, one's flaws, one's demons and evil propensities. It aims to own and understand these dark realities within oneself before focusing on them in others. The psychologist Erich Neumann referred to this kind of integrity as a new ethic of wholeness replacing the old ethic of perfection that has prevailed throughout most of Western history. Writing shortly after the end of World War II, Neumann concluded that "The old ethic of the Judeo-Christian epoch has proved itself incapable of mastering the destructive forces in man. . . . The new ethic is based on an attempt to become conscious of both the positive and the negative forces in the human organism and to relate these forces consciously to the life of the individual and the community." Similar to Adams' approach to integrity, "the individual must work through his own basic moral problem before he is in a position to play a responsible part in the collective."

The great difference between Adams' ethic and the new ethic of which Neumann speaks is that the latter is rooted in modern psychology. It understands the problem of objectivity that arises when the object of introspection is the same as the instrument—the psyche—and it recognizes the existence of an autonomous, unconscious part of the psyche that by its very nature changes the parameters of discussion about things dark and evil. It is true that thinkers like Jefferson and Adams knew the unconscious as the secretive will and pleasures of the heart, and they knew of its depth and passions and could poetically speak of these in the language of the heart. And it is true that they were writing and thinking at the beginning of the psychological age, whose dawn was the Enlightenment. After all, Jefferson and Adams were contemporaries of Kant. The investigation of the psyche or mind was not unheard of. Nevertheless, because their ways of introspection predated

Freud, Adler, and Jung, the gaze of their introspection saw different things or saw the same things we do but very differently.

It is curious how much of Jefferson's personality was imprinted upon the American vision and how little of Adams', especially in view of the fact that in their day they were considered equally important fathers of the American Revolution. Adams was a classical political theorist and strangely out of sync with the modern political theory of republicanism that had in his day come to play a central role for leaders such as Jefferson and Madison. And he was simply not as inspiring a figure as Jefferson. Yet it would be interesting to fantasize how Adams' outlook and the introspection and ethic it was based on might have influenced the American vision—indeed, American history as a whole—had his impact been different. In going back to a nation's original vision in order to reconceive or re-vision it, it is helpful to sift through all its original possibilities and its less well-known strands, especially those which are introspective and thus more intimately entwined with the vision's inner core. As the Chinese sage and founder of Taoism, Lao-tzu, said, "Let your wheels run along old ruts."

Historians have only recently begun to reclaim Adams' importance both as a thinker and an actor on the stage of events. The polarity of spirits that runs through American history, including the unfolding of the national vision, reach a uniquely balanced equilibrium in the political thought of John Adams. His sagacity fell somewhere between the pessimism and strict moral calculus of the Puritans and the idealism of Jefferson. The Puritan vision was a vehicle of authority steered by a rare sense of youth. The vision of the Founding Fathers, by contrast, was a vehicle of youth steered by the common sense of authority. Among the Founding Fathers, John Adams' voice was the one that most resounded with the call for common sense.

In hindsight, it is evident that Adams' particular gift of common sense did not steer the revolutionary vision nearly enough on matters where it may have been of benefit. Adams' vision for America is conspicuously devoid of the innocent assumptions that colored Jefferson's and that, among other things, provided a charter for the cults of novelty, freedom, and happiness. Adams did not believe that Americans had special access to the moral faculty or that they were an elevated people simply because they broke from Europe. He did not believe in the unfaltering benevolence of "the will of the people." Nor did he believe that America had a mandate rooted in divine Providence; in his view, God's grace would render Americans immune from the ravages of history no more readily than it would other people. Adams did not believe that all people are born equal, or that social equality could ever be attained; if anything, as Tocqueville later argued and as history corroborated, freedom enhances the unequal distribution of property. Adams did believe that all people are born with equal *rights,* but that was a different matter and what he as a revolutionary took from Locke's creed.

He furthermore did not believe, as did Jefferson, in an ideology of individual liberation from all forms of exterior constraint or control (at least not until humankind had mastered a sense of interior integrity obviating its need for such constraint or control). Adams did not believe in slavery, or in states' rights to decide upon whether or not to permit slavery; unlike Washington, Jefferson, and Madison, he owned no slaves. And, curiously for one who in his day was considered conservative but today would be viewed as liberal, he believed that responsible government could not be divorced from the dynamics of society or the marketplace; government is an inherently collective enterprise whose goals must transcend the ambitions and ethos of mere individualism. Whereas for Jefferson the promise of American life was a birthright of personal fulfillment unimpeded by government, for Adams it was a legacy of public commitment made possible by government.

Given these differences, one could see that Jefferson and Adams had opposing views on what America should be, on the American vision. They were, indeed, the two poles of the American Revolution. Of course, Jefferson's views won out. Ellis concludes that "by the early twentieth century, one did not need to be a brilliant logician or profound historian to recognize that Jeffersonian political beliefs had led directly, if inadvertently, to unprecedented levels of social and economic inequality, the enshrinement of private greed as a natural right by the American plutocracy—the so-called captains of industry—and the doctrinaire rejection of government's authority to do anything about it." The appreciation of Adams and of the value of his beliefs had receded into history. He had been left behind by the times. Or, as Ellis conjectures, perhaps he was, in the cyclic, spiraling process of history, ahead of his time:

> Memorials will only be erected to him . . . when the rhetoric of Jeffersonian liberalism ceases to dominate mainstream American culture; when the exaltation of "the people" is replaced by a quasi-sacred devotion to "the public"; when the cult of the liberated individual is superseded by the celebration of self-denial; when national development must vie for seductiveness with conservation; when the deepest sense of personal satisfaction comes not from consumption but production; when the acceptance of national and personal limitations seems less like defeatism than a symptom of

maturity. In this sense, the time of John Adams has passed and not yet come again.

Who knows? perhaps the pendulum of history has already begun to swing back toward Adams. Recent times have witnessed a small Adams revival, starting in the 1950s with the publication of *The Adams Papers* (400,000 items from Adams' letters and diaries). When in 1976 the historian Robert Rutland reviewed the several modern editions of the papers of the Founding Fathers, he found there a fresh scholarly consensus: "Madison was the great intellectual . . . Jefferson the . . . unquenchable idealist, and Franklin the most charming and versatile genius, but Adams is the most captivating founding father on most counts." Within the liberal, republican tradition they commonly shared, Jefferson and Adams played out a youth-authority dynamic with each other no less than the two together represented the spirit of youth revolting against the authority of the old order. They played out this dynamic philosophically and in other ways too; Adams even described the young Jefferson who served with him in the Continental Congress as having been "but a boy to me. . . . I am bold to say I was his preceptor in politicks and taught him everything that has been good and solid in his whole political conduct." But the youth and authority principles are historically reciprocal, and as authority gives rise to youth, so too youth turns to and into authority. Indeed, Adams' day may yet lie ahead.

## The Canvas of History

The idea of freedom as an expression of interior integrity is the only one consistently good for the person and society because, short of that, freedom is neither qualitatively complete nor about psychological wholeness. Two hundred years of American democracy have shown that there is a great difference between the Jeffersonian freedom of the *individual* and a more comprehensive freedom of the *person*. While the former is a purely social condition—the individual is free relative to whatever restrictions society imposes upon him—the freedom of the person is a spiritual condition limited only by the degree of one's interior integrity.

The Jeffersonian idea of freedom is essentially negative, defined by what it is not. It is freedom from encroachments by church or state, freedom for the individual to be left alone to pursue happiness. Indeed, it is essentially the freedom *to be* an individual, a self-contained identity responsible only to itself. But is this really freedom *or* identity, especially when our mass-minded consumer culture is so intent upon creating the exact same individual—the exact same ephemeral self—out of millions of people? Liberal democracy combined with modernity has given rise to a conformist mentality in the guise of freedom, a totalitarianism which is especially dangerous because of its seductive appearance. Tocqueville was right. With all its so-called freedom, America has not been able to generate a society which, through its public discourse and the education of its citizenry, can even recognize much less free itself from the tyrannical addictions that grip it.

Genuine freedom encompasses much more than what Americans mean by democracy. The freedom of the person grounds the freedom of the individual in the dimension of character and ethics. Because it is concerned with the person's integrity—with *what kind of person* he is, with the *richness of values* he expresses in connection to others and to life as a whole—it is not negativistic. It involves not merely a declaration of human rights but, Nikolai Berdyaev tells us, a declaration of the human's obligation or duty to display the strength of his personal character. Rather than reveling in an ephemeral self, it reveals a self of substance and purpose. This kind of freedom is the only possible positive alternative to the negativistic freedom of the individual that now prevails in America. It alone provides a viable response to the addictions to height and innocence and to modernity's mechanized, atomized individual and his cog-in-the-wheel mentality. To quote Thomas Merton, "The person must be rescued from the individual." Democracy needs to evolve to the personalistic level of freedom if it is to resolve the problems it has created at the current individualistic level. Indeed, if Einstein is correct, the problems created at any given level of thinking or being can only be resolved from the vantage point of the next higher level.

The freedom of the person, as both Adams and Jefferson knew, is not something that can be instilled by government institutions and political philosophy. It is an expression of integrity that must exist at the core of government institutions and political philosophy. Without it, democracy can easily be thwarted and lose its meaning. In other words, freedom is something even greater than democracy. Men and women who were inwardly free have lived in all kinds of societies, even tyrannies. Their freedom was not dependent on democracy, yet democracy, in order to promote a society that possesses a deep integrity, *is* dependent on the freedom of the person. The freedom of personhood is a theme of many great novels, such as Arthur Koestler's *Darkness at Noon* and Dostoevsky's *The Brothers Karamazov*, the latter of which very much influenced Berdyaev's seminal work on this subject, *Slavery and Freedom*. The notion of a free people spearheading an empire of liberty acquires a different meaning when thought of in terms of this kind of freedom. I doubt that any reframing of the American vision that does not address this kind of freedom could make a significant contribution toward the advancement of American civilization, given the current problems with which it is beset.

It is, however, in the context of history that the idea of freedom as an expression of interior integrity encounters great difficulties. There is, to begin with, a certain opposition between personal freedom and social, historical processes—the same opposition that, as discussed in an earlier chapter, makes the idea of world harmony or a new world order illusory. Berdyaev sheds light upon this opposition as follows (note that his use here of the term "personality" connotes the fullness of personhood, with its spiritual depth and integrity, rather than the superficial personality of the social persona so worshiped in America's cult of personality):

> Personality is independent of the determination of society, it has its own world, it is an exception, it is unique and unrepeatable. And at the same time personality is social, in it there are traces of the collective unconscious. It is man's way out of isolation. It belongs to history, it realizes itself in society and in history. Personality is communal; it presuppposes communion with others, and community with others. The profound contradiction and difficulty of human life is due to this communality. . . . Man's difficulty is rooted in the fact that there is no correlation and identity between the inward and the outward, no direct and adequate expression of the one in the other. This is indeed the problem of objectivization. When he objectivizes himself in the external man enslaves himself to the world of objects; and at the same time, man cannot but express himself in the external, cannot dispense with his body, cannot but actively enter into society and history.

In other words, man is both spiritual and worldly, and the two dimensions are experienced as opposites. The Christian mystics attempt to resolve this problem—the "problem of objectivization"—with their teaching that one should aim to be in the world but not of it. Similarly, the Buddhists teach that one should be in the world and should even be at one with the world, but should be detached from desire for its objects and pleasures. Adams' way of dealing with this problem was by self-denial, that is, by denying himself satisfactions that would jeopardize his integrity (for example, the satisfaction of being adulated, something from which he himself admitted he suffered).

The opposition between personal freedom and social, historical processes makes the possibility of personal freedom finding a "home" in democracy about as likely as its finding one in any other collective form. Personhood, Berdyaev insists, "transfers the centre of gravity of personality from the value of objective communities—society, nation, state—to the value of [subjective] personality." Although personhood "presupposes a going out from self to another and to others" and "cannot but have some sort of community in view," the moment it becomes collectivized in some rigid form—such as a national program—and sacrifices its unique quality of being a living experience among persons, it turns into an objectivized "thing" and loses its freedom and integrity. It is taken out of the spiritual realm and loses its spirit. This is not to say that large social bodies cannot, hypothetically, become sensitive to the needs of personhood. Merely, those needs cannot be met by a broad-brush approach to reform on the collective level of those bodies, by some sort of "New Deal." They must be met by each person. The only kind of community and democracy that can serve personhood are those which resist the slavery of collectivization and nourish the spiritual and ethical development of the person.

Indeed, practically speaking, how likely is this kind of community and democracy to emerge? If such a vision is not utopian (and it is not, for it does not aim to artificially remove the suffering or disharmony inherent in life), then it certainly seems fantastic and fanciful. Its actualization presupposes exactly the kind of moral courage, integrity, and self-reliance on the part of the person that was championed not only by the Puritans and Adams, but Emerson, Thoreau, and certainly Lincoln. The person must develop his or her own inner voice of conscience in place of external authority. Society must become, as Neumann put it, a "Community of Free Individuals." Here lies the great problem: what America most needs in order to transform its endangered Lockean democracy has thus far been beyond humanity's reach. Jung writes:

> [M]ankind is, in essentials, psychologically still in a state of childhood—a stage that cannot be skipped. The vast majority needs authority, guidance, law. This fact cannot be overlooked. The Pauline overcoming of the law falls only to the man who knows how to put his soul in the place of [socially instilled] conscience. Very few are capable of this ("Many are called, but few are chosen"). And these few tread this path only from inner necessity, not to say suffering, for it is sharp as the edge of a razor.

For this reason, the reconceptualization of the American vision is concerned with a problem of the human condition on the largest scale and in the profoundest sense. It is fair to say that if America were to resolve this it would resolve a central problem of history itself, of why civilizations ultimately disintegrate or collapse. Adams and Jefferson alike were pessimistic about the question of America's longevity. They thought, as was standard for students of history in their day, that the United States would go the way of other nation-states and civilizations. This was the law of history: all nations have a natural, limited lifespan. Much as an individual, they develop their energies and talents in youth, reach their maturity and high point in midlife, then decline into old age, and sooner or later pass away. The reason for this is that they become corrupted by their worldly successes, so that, sapped of their earlier energy and work habits, they descend into depravity. "Former ages have never discovered any remedy against the universal gangrene of avarice," Adams wrote, "and the steady advance of Wealth . . . has overturned every Republic from the beginning of time." Of course, Toynbee and others have shown that it is more complex than this, but the general premise is correct, namely, that adhering to or indulging in past adaptations in the face of new challenges results in disintegration or collapse. The difference between the views of the Founding Fathers and modern historians is only with respect to the nature of the law behind the rise and fall of civilizations. It is correct that civilizations fall when they lose their integrity. Then, as Toynbee illustrated, they disintegrate. But Toynbee also made it clear that a timely creative response can alter the course of history, that there is no fixed law for the decline and demise of civilizations as there is for individuals. As McLuhan later said in regard to this matter, "There is absolutely no inevitability as long as there is a willingness to contemplate what is happening." To state it another way, if freedom speaks to the recognition of necessity, then survival speaks to the necessity of recognition.

But even without a fixed law of termination, the pessimism of Adams and Jefferson is still well-justified. There has yet to be a republic that did not in time lose its integrity, that is, disintegrate. The hope that the United States can survive long enough to permit the development of personalistic freedom and integrity needed to catapult its republic as a whole to this next level of freedom, can only be met with pessimism among those familiar with history. As Jung stated, humanity simply has not yet evolved to that level. And yet, curiously, the necessity to evolve there seems to be the fateful and imminent challenge facing America. One wonders, will the United States become a fossilized dinosaur along with the other extinct nations of the earth, or will necessity, the mother of invention, compel it to adapt and evolve successfully? Given that a number of prominent thinkers have imagined this challenge itself to be the next great "leap in being" that man must take, one wonders whether the forces of history and evolution, in having brought the leading nation of Western civilization and the world to this precipice, have not conspired to somehow merge together the destinies of all three—nation, civilization, and world. It seems as if history's challenge to America to graduate from its childhood is identical to the challenge facing mankind to graduate from *its* childhood; these challenges are, in essence, one and the same. As Edward Edinger remarked, "America is a great experiment in which the ability of the world to survive is foreshadowed. With all the ethnic groups in this nation, and the human conflicts these bring, we are not only a melting pot, but a microcosm of the world. If we fail to 'make it work' here, it does not bode well for the rest of the world, itself so divided."

If it is indeed America's fate or calling to be at the leading edge of humanity in taking this next evolutionary leap of consciousness, then the vision of the Founding Fathers will have presaged it in a way that even they could not have foreseen; their vision would have been prescient in spite of its innocent assumptions. They spoke of a New Order of the Ages—*Novus Ordo Seclorum*—but, as discussed earlier, what they had in mind was a new social order based upon democracy. Their greatest hope was that democracy would spread throughout the world, creating the empire of liberty of which Jefferson spoke. Breaking with the old order of monarchies and oligarchies, humankind would finally on a global scale have representative governments in which men would rule themselves and be free. This was not an idea of a single world government; the greatest expanse that the Founding Fathers hoped America might directly subjugate was the Western hemisphere, and even annexing more than Canada—that is, extending the United States into South America—was in large part only a Hamiltonian fantasy. One could, however, say that this was an idea of "world Americanism," meaning that the *model* of America would become a world phenomenon, with the world looking to America as its authoritative guide and leader.

The innocence of this idea lay in the assumption that its actualization would really introduce a new order of the ages, a condition for mankind that would be a radical break from the past. True, democracy has liberated men in the social, economic, and political spheres—an accomplishment not to be minimized. But as Tocqueville already knew in the mid-nineteenth century, democracy would not significantly change the condition of human consciousness and the inner quality of life; in some key respects it would even lead to their deterioration. The liberties of American life would create new confusions that would tend to make men less free rather than more. As Erik Erikson reflected in the mid-twentieth century, "The American feels so rich in his opportunities for free expression that he often no longer knows what it is he is free from. Neither does he know where he is not free."

Another innocent notion is that a radical break from the past in international affairs would result from the new world order or global Americanism created by democracy. In fact, as former Secretary of State James Baker said, this new world order is already evolving and can be observed in the rapidly increasing democratization of the world. But relations between the nations of the world are not all that different than they were a hundred years ago. Nations are as nationalistic and conflict-oriented as they ever were, if not more so. McLuhan observed that nationalism, being a heightened awareness of separate tribal identities and geographical boundaries, is a pre-twentieth-century level of consciousness that has not yet caught up to the contemporary consciousness of the global village. But it thrives, and in fact, with the fall of the British and Soviet empires, has even increased: in 2001 there were 188 nation-states in the world in contrast to 72 in 1946. This proliferation of nations and nationalism naturally generates wars. As C. Wright Mills wrote only a decade after the end of the Second World War, "All over the world, the warlord is returning. All over the world, reality is defined in his terms." The Marxist influence on his views may have led him to misconstrue the reasons for this, but he accurately identified the trend. Indeed, the number of wars being waged at any given time has greatly escalated. There were 64 armed conflicts in the first half of the twentieth century compared to over 100 in just its last decade (though needless to say, the mortality due to war in the first half of the century far surpassed that of the second half). Terrorism has also dramatically increased.

The democratization of the world promoted by the United States and accelerated by the collapse of the Soviet Union has thus far done little to assuage the trend of nationalism. By allowing ethnic groups formerly without their own states the option of self-determination, the spread of democracy has even made the impulse toward nationalism more realizable. Balkanization has increased too as independence movements have divided nations into small, quarrelsome, ineffectual states. As the Israeli leader Shimon Peres remarked, the current trend of the world is toward global cooperation in economic affairs and nationalism in political affairs; we may therefore need two solutions—two models—to deal with the relations between nations. In short, humanity is still operating according to its childhood model of international relations, and the democratization of the world, though still in progress, has had little positive effect upon this.

A New Order of the Ages as envisioned by the Founding Fathers has thus largely come about, and what has not yet come about can be anticipated based upon what has. The New Order of the Ages is not so new after all. But what the historian Thomas Kuhn revealed about the process of scientific innovation may be said about other areas of innovation too: it is common that a new model or paradigm that explains something heretofore unknown is, at first, but a "promise of success." Visionary though it may be, it is almost always incomplete and rudimentary at first, a preliminary glimpse of what could be. A new paradigm isn't born as a *fait accompli.* It needs to be tested over time, and as this is done, its details are fleshed out and the paradigm is more fully articulated. As anomalies emerge, the paradigm must be adjusted in order to continue to be explanatory. Some established beliefs are discarded, some new ones adopted. If the anomalies are profound enough to begin limiting the paradigm's effectiveness, the search to resolve them may lead to the birth of another new paradigm. That such a process might need to occur with the American vision was not altogether beyond the imagination of the Founding Fathers. Jefferson called for periodic revolutions, and Adams, in contemplating the spiraling nature of history, speculated that America might only be a single turn in the age-old, recurring pattern of rise and fall that moves the human condition ahead a few notches with each cycle. Indeed, perhaps the American vision would not even be actualized by the United States, but by some descendent or beneficiary further down the road of history.

Certainly, if the inner, core meaning of the American vision—the only dimension of meaning that has yet to be realized and that would have any real significance in today's world—points to a revolution in consciousness such as described above, then we are speaking about a very dramatic leap in the human condition. A revolution in which the freedom and integrity of the person would become the ruling principles of society would be a new order of the ages resembling only one other such new order in recorded history. That one was not just a major event in the world of public affairs, that is, in the polis or society, but in the scheme of human evolution. Voegelin, one among numerous historians and philosophers writing about this development, refers to it as the *periagoge,* a Platonic term which means "conversion" or "turning around." It represented a radical shift in the consciousness of man, a reorientation of how man experienced himself in relation to the universe. Although it primarily involved a redefinition of the nature of religious experience, it was inherently also a redefinition of the nature of human freedom, thus lending weight to Hegel's famous observation that "The history of the world is none other than the progress of the consciousness of freedom." It occurred in the context of religious experience because this was (and one may argue, continues to be) the stage upon which the search for freedom takes place in its most profound sense.

The *periagoge* was, indeed, a religious conversion. For millennia man had believed in the divine as cosmic forces "out there"—animal-gods, planets, or nature (the sun, moon, earth, wind, ocean, etc.). With this dramatic change in consciousness, man now believed in the divine as Something transcendent or beyond the worldly, no longer just "out there" and certainly not out there in limited, fixed forms, but also "in there," within the psyche or soul. In fact, the psyche itself had been discovered; man's soul, formerly a rather compact structure, was now differentiated or opened up, so that it became a new center through which the divine could be experienced. This was one of the most momentous events in the history of consciousness. Man in his relationship to the divine had gone "out there" to the cosmic forces of the physical universe and now had turned around and descended into the transcendent depths of his soul, where he discovered in a most liberating way that *he* was the primary agent of the divine. Voegelin writes the following about this event:

> The discovery of the truth that is apt to challenge the truth of the cosmological empires is itself a historical event of major dimensions. It is a process which occupies about five centuries in the history of mankind, that is, roughly the period from 800 to 300 B.C.; it occurs simultaneously in the various civilizations but without apparent mutual influences. In China it is the age of Confucius and Lao-tse as well as of the other philosophical schools; in India, the age of the *Upanishads* and the Buddha; in Persia, of Zoroastrianism; in Israel, of the Prophets; in Hellas, of the philosophers and of tragedy. . . . [It is] the one great epoch that is relevant for all mankind, as distinguished from the epoch of Christ which supposedly is relevant for Christians only.

The discovery of divinity's ultimate transcendence and of the psyche as the instrument for experiencing this transcendence had not only profound spiritual and psychological implications, but social ones too. The measure of what was important in and for society became no longer man nor the divine in its old, cosmological sense, but man as representative of divine truth. Man and society became the vehicle for the divine, a connection that came to be symbolized in the idea of "the city," be it the city of God, the heavenly city on earth, the city on a hill. The historical expressions of this idea were, of course, Jerusalem, Athens, and Rome. This idea resurfaced in the American vision: America was to become the new heavenly city on earth. One can even argue that the American vision is a re-visioning of this same aspect of the original *periagoge*. Indeed, the American vision offers its own distinct rendition of the idea of the heavenly city. As the psychologist Marvin Spiegelman has pointed out, the extroversion of the American psyche predisposes it to seek "God among us" rather than "God within us" (as is the orientation, for example, in India). Thus, what stands out in the American vision is its ultimate goal of the spiritual brotherhood of man.

This brings us back to our original premise: the re-visioning of the American vision implies a return to and yet a new understanding of that goal. The spiritual brotherhood of man can only happen if enough persons are related to each other with inner freedom and integrity to make a widespread, social difference. If the *periagoge* marked the transition from outerdirected to inner-directed religious experience, then the American vision marks the hypothetical transition of the latter from being a privilege for the few to a priority for the many. Providence here might genuinely avail itself to many because it is, as theologians agree, a phenomenon most inclined to become evident in the personal realm; it is through their personal freedom and integrity that many might now indeed discover the mysterious will and workings of God. And what could more manifest the will and workings of God in the world than the spiritual brotherhood of man? Understood in this way, the American vision of the brotherhood of man, if ever realized, would be as great a transformation of consciousness as the *periagoge*. It would genuinely introduce a New Order of the Ages, but not the kind that is limited to or dependent upon a social or collectivistic world order; this new order, although certainly expressing itself socially, would be what Voegelin would describe as a new order of being.

Such a transformation of consciousness has been, in one aspect or another, a subject of interest for a number of thinkers, among them Toynbee, Jung, Neumann, Karl Jaspers, Lewis Mumford, Teilhard de Chardin, F.S.C. Northrop, Berdyaev, McLuhan, Julian Huxley, Pitirim Sorokin, and Sarvepalli Radhakrishnan. Some of these thinkers even see this transformation as a natural and teleological development driven by the principles of evolution; to them it only makes sense that man should evolve into a more ethically differentiated and conscious creature. However, even if such a transformation is bound to occur, it would in all probability be too far off on the event-horizon of history to speak about in any but the vaguest terms. But, in the final analysis, it is not necessary to speak about it at all. The crucial ingredient of this transformation, whether it occurs tomorrow or a thousand years from now, is each person's ethical and conscious self-examination. If each person attends to this, the rest should take care of it-self. Even social movements or organized collective efforts in which people join together to improve society would have a different impact because they would be undergirded by personal introspection. About this, there is nothing vague. It is, after all, a basic premise of democracy as well. Jefferson and Adams knew well that an enlightened citizenry depends upon the ongoing ethical and conscious self-examination of its individual members.

## Conclusion

In 1998, Pizza Hut filed a lawsuit in federal court against Papa John's in what was to become a protracted and heated series of conflicts between the two chains. Pizza Hut charged Papa John's with unfair competition and deceptive advertising, in particular, a television commercial in which Papa John's boasted that it had better pizza and used better ingredients than Pizza Hut. The commercial featured one of the founders of Pizza Hut touting his new role as a Papa John's franchisee and explaining that he liked Papa John's pizza so much that he had decided to come over and join Papa John's. Shortly after, Pizza Hut retaliated with its own commercials attacking Papa John's, and the latter filed a countersuit.

What is interesting about this episode—and it is just one illustration of American business in action—is the intensity of emotion that fueled it and the spiritual principles that were enlisted to give it an aura of importance. In television interviews, the CEOs of both corporations made it very clear what the legal case was about. It was not just about pizza. Nor was it just about money and profits. It was about *truth*. Asked what this truth was, both CEOs said it was about *better* pizza. This was not a game the two companies were playing, the CEO of Papa John's passionately argued. It was *war*. Indeed, listening to them one would think that they were two generals defending the very existence of their nations. Moreover, one could hear in the tremor of their voices a visionary zeal, as if they were not only Founding Fathers protecting their child-visions but prophets with a message of profound inner truth and significance.

This episode shows on the one hand how far America has digressed from its vision and on the other, paradoxically, that it can never digress very far at all. Such an episode would not likely occur in a nation like Belgium, for example, where there is no deeply ingrained, national messianic vision. Such visionary zeal would appear absolutely ridiculous and out of place there, not only because it is attached to pizza and profits, but because there is simply no psychological and cultural context for it. In America, people know about visionary ambition; it is ingrained in the American psyche. The American vision is part and parcel of the American character and collective unconscious. And even if the vision has become diffused in the American culture so that people no longer recognize it, it surfaces wherever ambitions can merge together and one ambition can become the cloak for another. That is why this episode illustrates on the one hand how far America has digressed from its original vision, and yet on the other, how it can never digress very far at all.

The diffusion of the American vision—be it through the cults of novelty, freedom, happiness, or prosperity—is a problem because people end up living their lives with a loss of vision of what is important and what they should *really* be fighting for. They lose sight of what it is that they should be making "better," and their efforts at improvement are directed towards things that no matter how much improved, still leave their souls hungry. In its essence, the American vision is not so different from the ancient and classical visions it draws its inspiration from, and when presented in its true form, it can be very clear and honest about what is important and what should be made better. Listen to these words by Lyndon Johnson as he outlined his vision of the Great Society:

> The Great Society is a place where every child can find knowledge to enrich his mind and to enlarge his talent. It is a place where leisure is a welcome chance to build and reflect, not a feared cause of boredom and restlessness. It is a place where the city of man serves not only the needs of the body and the demands of commerce but the desire for beauty and the hunger for community. . . . It is a place where men are more concerned with the quality of their goals than the quantity of their goods, where the demands of morality, and the needs of the spirit, can be realized in the life of the nation.

Johnson's vision was derailed, among other things, by the race riots of the 1960s and the debilitating effects of the Vietnam War, but he had the right idea. It was based, like the vision of the Founding Fathers, on the great society or the noble city that the Athenians and Romans built at the height of their civilizations. But unfortunately, a look backwards was all that this idea could amount to; it was and is still not substantially rooted in contemporary American society. The American vision remains just that: a *vision*.

Johnson's words today sound like ancient echoes in the deserted streets of a city that the American has yet to inhabit.

We are now beginning what is already being hailed as the second American century. Such centuries are only fleeting moments in the infinite expanse of time, but for a nation, they are important. We need to decide: how do we want to be remembered in the historic journey that, if Toynbee and others are correct, will advance humanity to a more evolved level of consciousness? We need to decide: will we protect and deepen our democracy in order to help us—and perhaps the world—arrive at that level of consciousness, or will we continue to let it be eaten away from the inside by the many things that threaten it? Indeed, it is our duty to respond to this challenge creatively. At present, it is not clear whether we will wake up and seize this challenge as best we can, or remain unconscious. Our fate sleeps as we do, and at least for now, waits.

# ★ Notes ★

Page vi, George Washington, letter to London Carter, October 27, 1777, in *Writings of George Washington from the Original Manuscript Sources 1745–1799*, edited by John C. Fitzpatrick, U.S. Government Printing Office, Washington, DC, 1933, Vol. 9, pp. 453–454.

Page vi, St. John of the Cross, *The Ascent of Mount Carmel*, translated and edited by E. Allison Peers, Image Books, Garden City, NY, 1958, Book I, Chapter 13, verse 11.

## Introduction

Page xi, Heraclitus, "On the Universe." The often-cited aphorism, *Ethos anthropoi daimon*, has been interpreted in a variety of ways; "Character is fate" is one of the more common and succinct. For other variations plus commentary, see W. H. S. Jones' translation of "On the Universe" in *Hippocrates*, Heinemann, London, 1923–31, Vol. 4, p. 507; John Mansley Robinson, *An Introduction to Early Greek Philosophy: The Chief Fragments and Ancient Testimony with Connecting Commentary*, Houghton Mifflin, Boston, 1968, p. 102; and James Hillman, *The Soul's Code: In Search of Character and Calling*, Random House, New York, 1996, pp. 256–57.

Page xi, Jacques Barzun, cited in Michael Kammen, *People of Paradox: An Inquiry Concerning the Origins of American Civilization*, Alfred A. Knopf, New York, 1972, p. xi.

Page xii, C. G. Jung, "The Complications of American Psychology" (1930), in *Civilization in Transition*, Vol. 10 of *The Collected Works of C. G. Jung*, translated by R. F. C. Hull, Bollingen Series XX, Princeton University Press, 1964, 1970, 1978, p. 514.

Page xv, Arnold Toynbee: see *A Study of History*, revised and abridged edition by Arnold Toynbee and Jane Caplan, Portland House, New York, 1972, 1988, p. 72.

# Part I: America's Heroic Ideal

Page 1, Ernest Becker, *The Denial of Death,* The Free Press, Macmillan, New York, 1973, pp. 4–5.

Page 1, Ernst Barlach, *Der Tote Tag: Drama in Funf Akten,* Cassirer, Berlin, 1912; cited in Erich Neumann, *The Origins and History of Consciousness,* with a foreword by C. G. Jung, translated by R. F. C. Hull, Bollingen Series XLII, Princeton University Press, 1954, 1970, 1973, p. 174.

Page 2, Daniel P. Moynihan, "ABC World News Tonight," December 4, 1988.

Pages 2–3, C. G. Jung, "The Complications of American Psychology," in *Civilization in Transition,* pp. 512–13.

Pages 3–4, Alfred Adler, *Social Interest: A Challenge to Mankind,* Faber and Faber, London, 1938, p. 48.

Pages 5–6, Sean Penn, "The Charlie Rose Show," KCET TV, Los Angeles, January 18, 2001.

Page 6, the books by Bennett and Wattenberg: William Bennett, *Book of Virtues,* Simon and Schuster, New York, 1993, and Ben J. Wattenberg, *Values Matter Most,* Free Press, New York, 1995.

Page 6, high school survey: the annual "Who's Who Among American High School Students Survey," 1996.

Page 7, Bob Dylan, "Love Minus Zero/No Limit," on *Bringing It All Back Home,* Warner Bros., 1965; also cited in Bob Dylan, *Lyrics, 1962–1985,* a Borzoi Book, Alfred A. Knopf, New York, 1973, 1985, 1994, p. 167.

## *Chapter 1  Two Souls Within the Human Breast*

Page 9, Thomas Jefferson, letter to John Adams, June 27, 1813, in *The Writings of Thomas Jefferson,* edited by Albert Ellery Bergh, Thomas Jefferson Memorial Association of the United States, Washington, DC, 1907, Vol. XIII, pp. 279, 280.

Page 9, Johann Wolfgang von Goethe, *Faust,* Part I (1808), translated with an Introduction and Notes by Peter Salm, Bantam, New York, 1962, 1985, p. 69, line 1112. The two souls Faust is talking about in this line refer to what is described in Chapter 10 as the soul and the spirit, and as a pair are different from, though related to, what I am describing here as the spirits of youth and authority.

Page 10, C. G. Jung, see "The Psychology of the Child Archetype" (1940, 1951), in *The Archetypes and the Collective Unconscious,* Vol. 9, Part I of *The Collected Works of C. G. Jung,* translated by R. F. C. Hull, Bollingen Series XX, Princeton University Press, 1959, 1969, 1977.

Page 11, James Hillman, "Senex and Puer," in James Hillman, ed., *Puer Papers,* Spring Publications, Dallas, Texas, 1979, 1991.

Page 12, Arthur Webster, personal communication, 1974, 1998.

Page 13, Eric Voegelin: see "The Beginning and the Beyond: A Meditation on Truth," in *What is History? and Other Late Unpublished Writings,* Vol. 28 of *The Collected Works of Eric Voegelin,* Louisiana State University Press, Baton Rouge, London, pp. 178, 184.

Page 13, on the connections between Babylonia and ancient Israel: see Samuel Noah Kramer, *The Sumerians: Their History, Culture, and Character,* University of Chicago Press, Chicago, London, 1963, pp. 292–296.

Page 14, David Hume, *An Inquiry Concerning Human Understanding, With a Supplement, An Abstract of A Treatise of Human Nature* (1758), edited with an Introduction by Charles W. Hendel, Liberal Arts Press, New York, 1955, 1957, pp. 92–93.

Page 14, examples of mythological images of the union of youth and authority, or *puer* and *senex:* James Hillman, "Senex and Puer," *Puer Papers,* p. 31.

Page 15, Erik H. Erikson, *Childhood and Society,* second edition, W. W. Norton, New York, 1950, 1963, pp. 285–287.

Page 15, Michael Kammen, *People of Paradox: An Inquiry Concerning the Origins of American Civilization,* Alfred A. Knopf, New York, 1972.

Pages 15–17, Arthur M. Schlesinger, Jr., *The Cycles of American History,* Houghton Mifflin, Boston, 1986.

Page 16, John Adams: see Joseph J. Ellis, *The Passionate Sage: The Character and Legacy of John Adams,* W. W. Norton, New York, 1993, pp. 235–236.

Page 18, C. G. Jung, "The Psychology of the Child Archetype," in *The Archetypes and the Collective Unconscious,* p. 161.

Page 19, Daniel J. Boorstin, *The Lost World of Thomas Jefferson,* University of Chicago Press, Chicago, 1948, 1993, p. 3. Jung also, incidentally, wrote about the underlying barbarism or brutality of the American psyche; see "America Facing Its Most Tragic Moment," in *C. G. Jung Speaking: Interviews and Encounters,* edited by William McGuire and R. F. C. Hull, Picador/Pan Books, London, 1980.

Page 20, Geoffrey Gorer, *The American People: A Study in National Character,* W. W. Norton, New York, 1948, pp. 28–29; 32, 33.

Page 21, James Hillman, "Senex and Puer," *Puer Papers,* pp. 30–38.

Pages 22–23, on the decline of Rome: see Max I. Dimont, *Jews, God and History,* Signet, 1962, p. 149 ff.

Page 23, Arnold Toynbee, *A Study of History,* revised and abridged edition by Arnold Toynbee and Jane Caplan, Portland House, New York, 1972, 1988, pp. 267–268.

Page 23, C. G. Jung, *Mysterium Coniunctionis: An Inquiry into the Separation and Synthesis of Psychic Opposites in Alchemy* (1955–56), Vol. 14 of *The Collected Works of C. G. Jung,* translated by R. F. C. Hull, Bollingen Series XX, Princeton University Press, 1963, 1970, p. 358.

Page 25, on the Civil War: Howard Zinn, *A People's History of the United States*, HarperCollins, New York, 1980, 1990, p. 232.

Page 25, Abraham Lincoln, response in August 1862 to Horace Greeley's editorial in the New York *Tribune* demanding emancipation; cited in Howard Zinn, Ibid., p. 186.

Page 26, Garrett Hardin, "The Tragedy of the Commons," in *Science*, Vol. 162, Cambridge, Massachussetts, 1968. See also his *Exploring New Ethics for Survival*, Viking Press, New York, 1972.

Page 26, on democracy and tolerance: see Allan Bloom, *The Closing of the American Mind*, Simon and Schuster, New York, 1987, 1988, pp. 28–29. See also John Locke, *An Essay Concerning Human Understanding*, Book IV, Chapter III, section 18.

## *Chapter 2  The Revolutionary*

Page 29, Joseph Addison, *Cato: A tragedy, as it is acted at the Theatre-Royal in Drury Lane*, J. Tonson, London, 1713.

Page 29, Bob Dylan, in *Biograph*, CBS Inc., 1985, p. 31.

Page 30, on the traditional sense of heroism: for an interesting discussion on its differences from the modern sense, see John Ralston Saul, *Voltaire's Bastards: The Dictatorship of Reason in the West*, Vintage Books, Random House, New York, 1992, 1993, pp. 318–357.

Page 30, Herman D. Hover, *Fourteen Presidents Before Washington: The American History You Never Learned in School*, Dodd, Mead & Co., New York, 1985, p. 21.

Page 30, Max Weber, *On Charisma and Institution Building: Selected Papers*, edited and with an Introduction by S. N. Eisenstadt, University of Chicago Press, Chicago, London, 1968, p. 48.

Page 31 Robert Grudin, *The Grace of Great Things*, Ticknor and Fields, New York, 1990, pp. 73–74. It is to be noted that the connection of integrity, or *integritas*, with wholeness begins with St. Thomas Aquinas. See Umberto Eco, *The Aesthetics of Thomas Aquinas*, translated by Hugh Bredin, Harvard University Press, Cambridge, Massachussetts, 1988, pp. 98–102.

Page 31, John Beebe, "Integrity in the Analytic Relationship," a workshop in the Analyst Training Program of the C. G. Jung Institute of Los Angeles, January 28, 1996. Beebe's most illuminating *Integrity in Depth* (Texas A&M University Press, College Station, Texas, 1992) examines the history and psychology of the idea of integrity, and also includes a discussion of Grudin and Thomas Aquinas.

Page 31, Jefferson on slavery: see Joseph J. Ellis, *American Sphinx: The Character of Thomas Jefferson*, Alfred A. Knopf, New York, 1997, pp. 86–88.

Page 31, George Washington, cited in Richard Brookhiser, "A Man on Horseback," in *The Atlantic Monthly*, Vol. 277, No. 1, January 1996, Boston, p. 64.

Page 33, Richard Hofstadter, *The American Political Tradition and the Men Who Made It*, Random House, New York, 1989, pp. 13–15. Originally published by Alfred A. Knopf, New York, 1948, 1973.

Page 34, John Adams, letter to Thomas Jefferson, February 2, 1816; cited in Daniel Boorstin, *The Lost World of Thomas Jefferson*, p. 202.

Page 34, John Cotton, cited in Reinhold Niebuhr, *The Irony of American History*, Charles Scribner's Sons, New York, 1962, pp. 22–23.

Page 34, Horace White, cited in Richard Hofstadter, *American Political Tradition*, p. 5.

Page 34, James Madison, *Federalist Papers*, number 51.

Page 35, Paine and Adams on legislative government: cited in Howard Zinn, *A People's History*, p. 70; see also Richard Hofstadter, *American Political Tradition*, pp. 13, 11.

Page 36, *Seneca's Morals*, translated into English by Roger L'Estrange, 1682.

Pages 36–37, Thomas Jefferson, "Syllabus of an Estimate of the Merit of the Doctrines of Jesus, Compared With Those of Others," in *The Complete Jefferson*, assembled and arranged by Saul K. Padover, Duell, Sloan, & Pearce, New York, 1943, p. 948.

Page 37, Jefferson's version of the gospel of Jesus: "The Life and Morals of Jesus of Nazareth," in *The Writings of Thomas Jefferson*, Vol. XX, edited by Albert Ellery Bergh, Thomas Jefferson Memorial Association, Washington, DC, 1907.

Page 37, John Adams, diary entry of August 14, 1796; cited in Daniel Boorstin, *The Lost World of Thomas Jefferson*, p. 156.

Page 37, Max Weber, *The Protestant Ethic and the Spirit of Capitalism*, Charles Scribner's Sons, New York, 1958, pp. 52, 53.

Page 37, D. H. Lawrence, *Studies in Classic American Literature*, Viking Press, New York, 1961.

Page 37, Benjamin Franklin, "The Art of Virtue," in *The Autobiography of Benjamin Franklin*, Houghton Mifflin, Boston, 1973.

Page 38, Christopher Lasch, *The Culture of Narcissism: American Life in an Age of Diminishing Expectations*, Warner Books, New York, 1979, pp. 110–111 (includes citation and discussion on Franklin's "art of virtue").

## Chapter 3 The Frontiersman

Page 39, J. Frank Dobie, cited in *A Treasury of American Folklore*, edited by B. A. Botkin, foreword by Carl Sandburg, American Legacy Press, New York, 1944, p. 1.

Pages 39–40, Davy Crockett, from *Davy Crockett's Almanac, of Wild Sports in the West, Life in the Backwoods, & Sketches of Texas*, Vol. I, No. 3, Nashville, Tennessee, 1837, p. 40. Published by the heirs of Col. Crockett. Reprinted in *A Treasury of American Folklore*, pp. 27–28.

Page 40, B. A. Botkin, Ibid., pp. 2–3.

Page 41, Thomas Jefferson, cited in Mark Gerzon, *A Choice of Heroes*, Houghton Mifflin, Boston, 1982, p. 19.

Page 41, Joseph J. Ellis, *American Sphinx: The Character of Thomas Jefferson*, p. 212.

Page 42, Daniel Boorstin, *The Lost World*, pp. 225, 241. On Jefferson's views on happiness in general, see pp. 53, 226.

Pages 42–43, Richard Slotkin, *The Fatal Environment: The Myth of the Frontier in the Age of Industrialization, 1800–1890*, Atheneum, New York, 1985, pp. 72–73.

Page 44, Walter Noble Burns, *The Saga of Billy the Kid*, 1925, p. 145; cited in B. A. Botkin, *A Treasury*, p. 70.

Page 45, Botkin's typology: B. A. Botkin, Ibid., p. 2.

Page 45, Oscar Wilde, letter of April 19, 1882 to Norman Forbes-Robertson, written from St. Joseph, Missouri on the occasion of Jesse James' death; in *The Letters of Oscar Wilde*, edited by Rupert Hart-Davis, Harcourt, Brace & World, New York, 1962, p. 113.

Pages 46–48, C. G. Jung, "Mind and Earth" (1931), in *Civilization in Transition*, pp. 45–49; and "The Complications of American Psychology," *Civilization*, pp. 513–514.

Pages 46–48, Robert M. Pirsig, *Lila: An Inquiry into Morals*, Bantam Books, New York, 1991.

Page 48, George P. Murdock, "The Common Denominator of Cultures" (1945), in *Culture and Society*, Pittsburgh University Press, Pittsburgh, 1965.

## *Chapter 4  Contemporary Heroic Idealism*

Page 50, W. B. Yeats, "The Second Coming," in *The Collected Poems of W. B. Yeats*, Macmillan, New York, 1956, p. 184; originally published in 1921.

Page 51, Henry Kissinger, in an interview by Oriana Fallaci; cited in James Oliver Robertson, *American Myth, American Reality*, Farrar, Straus and Giroux, New York, 1980, 1992, p. 6.

Page 51, Thayer Greene, "America's Loss of Innocence: Bicentennial Reflections," in *Psychological Perspectives*, Vol. 7, No. 2, Los Angeles, Fall 1976, p. 147.

Pages 52–53, Jeff Greenfield, "I'm Just That Simple," in *Time*, June 10, 1996, p. 56.

Page 54, on the 1999–2000 NFL season: see Mark Starr and Alison Samuels, "A Season of Shame," in *Newsweek*, May 29, 2000, pp. 56–60.

Page 54, citation of priest in incident of Massachusetts father: *Newsweek*, December 25, 2000/January 1, 2001, p. 100.

Page 54, interview with Celtic player: "ABC World News Tonight," October 13, 1998.

Page 56, Bill Bradley, cited in Ruth Shalit, "Air Bradley," in *The New Republic*, December 8, 1997, p. 22.

Page 56, Andrew Samuels, "Can the Post-Jungians Survive?," in *Psychological Perspectives*, Issue 31, Los Angeles, Spring–Summer 1995, p. 57.

Pages 56–57, Garry Wills, cited in *Life*, collector's edition: "Celebrating Our Heroes," 1997, Time, Inc., "Hall of Heroes," p. 31.

Page 57, Edward Edinger, in "An American Jungian: Edward F. Edinger in Conversation with Lawrence Jaffe," Part 2: "The Psyche in Culture," produced and directed by Dianne D. Cordic. This is a videotaped interview that is available from the C. G. Jung Bookstore and Max & Lore Zeller Library of the C. G. Jung Institute of Los Angeles.

Page 57, Lance Morrow, "Kennedy Going on Nixon," in *Time*, May 18, 1987, p. 90.

Page 58, Daniel Jonah Goldhagen, *Hitler's Willing Executioners: Ordinary Germans and the Holocaust*, Alfred A. Knopf, New York, 1996.

Page 60, Robin W. Winks, "Traitors of Their Class," in *The New York Yimes Book Review*, April 16, 1989, p. 1.

Page 61, Vincent Bugliosi, *Outrage: The Five Reasons Why O. J. Simpson Got Away With Murder*, W. W. Norton, New York, 1996.

## Part II: The High Life

Page 65, John Adams, letter to Benjamin Rush, April 12, 1807.

Page 65, James Hillman, "Peaks and Vales: The Soul/Spirit Distinction as Basis for the Differences between Psychotherapy and Spiritual Discipline," in James Hillman, ed., *Puer Papers*, p. 57.

Page 67, Michael Kammen, *Mystic Chords of Memory: The Transformation of Tradition in American Culture*, Alfred A. Knopf, New York, 1991, p. 308.

Page 68, Erik Erikson, *Childhood*, pp. 102–106.

Page 68, John Kennedy, cited in *Life*, "Celebrating our Heroes," Time, Inc., 1997, p. 43.

Page 69, Benjamin C. Bradlee, *Conversations with Kennedy*, W. W. Norton, New York, 1975, p. 10.

### *Chapter 5 The Commercialism of America's Heroic Ideal*

Page 71, Calvin Coolidge, from a speech in 1920; cited in *Newsweek*, December 20, 1999, p. 59. Coolidge's comment, a truism of contemporary times, brings to mind Lewis H. Lapham's observation that "The complex mechanisms of the modern world depend as certainly on the faith in money as the structures of the medieval world depended on the faith in God" (cited in *Harpers Magazine*, New York, April 1996, p. 9).

Page 71, Bob Dylan, cited in Christian Williams, *Bob Dylan: In His Own Words*, Omnibus Press, Book Sales, London, New York, 1993, p. 110.

Page 72, "In democracies nothing is greater. . . .": Alexis de Tocqueville, *Democracy in America*, Vol. II, translated by Frances Bowen, Introduction by Alan Ryan, Everyman's Library, Alfred A. Knopf, New York, 1945, 1972, 1994, pp. 155–156.

Pages 72, "When, on the contrary. . . .": Alexis de Tocqueville, Ibid., pp. 129, 130.

Page 72, Murray B. Levin, *Political Hysteria in America: The Democratic Capacity for Repression*, Basic Books, New York, 1971, p. 233.

Page 73, "The same equality that allows. . . .": Alexis de Tocqueville, *Democracy*, pp. 138–139. The last sentence of this passage is taken from the more modern translation by George Lawrence, edited by J. P. Mayer, Anchor Books, Garden City, NY, 1969, p. 538.

Pages 73–74, "In America. . . .": Alexis de Tocqueville, translation by Frances Bowen, *Democracy*, p. 136.

Page 74, William H. Kennedy, "The American Unconscious," Centerpoint Foundation, St. Louis, Missouri, 1974, pp. 32–33.

Page 75, "a philosophy and a mode of thought. . . .": Daniel Boorstin, *The Lost World of Thomas Jefferson*, p. 241.

Page 75, "by refusing to declare. . . .": Daniel Boorstin, Ibid., pp. 202–203.

Page 76, Thomas Jefferson, cited in Paul Tough, "Does America Still Work?," *Harper's Magazine*, New York, May 1996, p. 35.

Page 77, Fritz Redl, "Adolescents—Just How Do They React?," in *Adolescence: Psychosocial Perspectives*, edited by Gerald Caplan and Serge Lebovici, Basic Books, New York, 1969, p. 90.

Page 77, statistic on the prosperity of American households: cited in Jeffrey R. Gates, "Capitalism and Human Dignity: The Ownership Imperative," in *America*, Vol. 175, No. 11, October 19, 1996, pp. 16–19. Gates' figures are taken from the Federal Reserve and the Internal Revenue Service.

Page 78, *The I Ching or Book of Changes*, the Richard Wilhelm translation rendered into English by Cary F. Baynes, Foreword by C. G. Jung, Bollingen Series XIX, Princeton University Press, 1950, 1967, 1977, p. 232. An interesting discussion of the fantasy of unlimited possibilities is also presented from a Western point of view by the French sociologist Émile Durkheim in his *Suicide: A Study in Sociology*, translated by John A. Spaulding and George Simpson, edited with an introduction by George Simpson, Free Press, Macmillan, New York, 1951, 1966, 1967, pp. 246 ff.

Page 79, on America as the world's leading arms broker: see James Burnett, "U.S. Weapons Buyers," in *George*, October 1999, pp. 70–72.

Page 79, John Ralston Saul, *Voltaire's Bastards: The Dictatorship of Reason in the West,* Vintage Books, Random House, New York, 1992, 1993, p. 153.

Page 80, statistics on military portion of the federal budget: *Historical Statistics of the United States, Colonial Times to 1970,* Part 2, U.S. Bureau of Census, Washington, DC, 1975, p. 1116; *Statistical Abstract of the United States,* U.S. Department of Commerce, Economics and Statistics Administration, Bureau of the Census, Washington, DC, 1998, p. 358.

Page 80, on the recklessness of the latter part of the Gilded Age: see H. W. Brands, *The Reckless Decade: America in the 1890s,* St. Martin's Press, New York, 1995.

Pages 80–81, statistics on income during the Roaring Twenties and unemployment during the Depression: Howard Zinn, *A People's History of the United States,* pp. 373–74, 393; Merle Curti, *The Growth of American Thought,* Harper and Row, New York, 1943; George Thomas Kurian, *Datapedia of the United States, 1790–2000: America Year by Year,* Bernan Press, Lanham, Maryland, 1994, p. 90; www.westegg.com/inflation.

Page 81, on the economic trends of the 1970s: see Jay Shartsis, "It Was the Worst of Times," in *Financial Post,* Toronto, Canada, October 12, 1999, pp. D1, D4; reprinted from *Barron's.*

Page 82, statistic on credit card debt: "ABC World News Tonight," March 25, 1997.

Page 82, statistic on federal debt: "Debt: Federal Government," in *Statistical Abstract of the United States,* U.S. Department of Commerce, Economics and Statistics Administration, Bureau of the Census, Washington, DC, 1998.

Page 82, statistic on corporate debt: John Ralston Saul, *Voltaire's Bastards,* p. 377.

Page 82, on the change in the model of the economy in the 1990s: see Robert J. Samuelson, "'Judgment Calls': The Dirty Secret About Today's Economy," in *Newsweek,* May 1, 2000, p. 78.

Page 83, Mario Cuomo, *More than Words: The Speeches of Mario Cuomo,* St. Martin's Press, New York, 1993, pp. 79–80.

Pages 83–84, John Ralston Saul, *Voltaire's Bastards,* p. 371. It is to be noted that much of Saul's research was undertaken in the late 1980s and his book was first published in 1992. This was a difficult period economically and, of course, the model of the "new economy" with its stock market boom had not yet begun to take effect. Saul was operating under the assumption that the great growth period of the world economy had reached its peak and was "a short-lived anomaly" (p. 371). I have omitted his reference to this because clearly his conclusion was premature. The global economy's most recent growth spurt coincidentally began just after the publication of Saul's book. Nevertheless, his basic argument in the passage cited here— that the developing world's rate of population growth leads to impoverishment, that even in the West production needs can't help but eventually reach a saturation point, and that our expectons of constant rapid growth with huge profits will undermine us—is still relevant.

Page 84, C. G. Jung, "Americans Must Say 'No'," in *C. G. Jung Speaking: Interviews and Encounters,* edited by William McGuire and R. F. C. Hull, Picador/Pan Books, London, 1980, p. 63.

Pages 84–85, on the cost of investigations by independent counsels: taken from "ABC World News Tonight," March 31, 1997. This report was in turn based on the General Accounting Office's *Financial Audit of the Independent Counsel Expenditures for the Six Months Ended September 30, 1996.* Figures on the investigation of Henry Cisneros taken from Gloria Borger, "Adults and Adultery," in *U.S. News & World Report,* September 7, 1998, p. 33.

Page 85, statistics on food consumption and waste: taken from "ABC World News Tonight," July 1, 1997.

Pages 85, figure on carbon emission levels: *Time,* October 13, 1997, p. 36.

Page 86, C. G. Jung, letter dated March 9, 1959, in *C.G. Jung Letters,* Vol. 2: 1951–1961, selected and edited by Gerhard Adler in collaboration with Aniela Jaffé, translation from the German by R. F. C. Hull, Bollingen Series XCV: 2, Princeton University Press, 1953, 1975, p. 492.

## Chapter 6  Heroic Mania

Page 87, Roland Barthes, *Mythologies,* selected and translated by Annette Lavers, Paladin, Granada Publishing, Great Britain, 1957, 1972, 1973, p. 71.

Page 87, Bob Dylan, "Dark Eyes," on *Empire Burlesque,* Special Rider Music, 1985; also cited in Bob Dylan, *Lyrics, 1962–1985,* p. 500.

Pages 88–89, Marshall McLuhan, *Understanding Media: The Extensions of Man,* Mc-Graw-Hill, New York, 1964; see also, with Quentin Fiore, *War and Peace in the Global Village,* Bantam Books, New York, 1968.

Pages 89–90, Alexis de Tocqueville, *Democracy,* pp. 98–99.

Page 90, Thomas Hobbes, *The Leviathan, or The Matter, Form, and Power of a Commmonwealth, Ecclesiastical and Civil,* Everyman's Library, J. M. Dent, London, E.P. Dutton, New York; first published in London in 1651.

Page 90, Ferdinand Toennies, *Community & Society [Gemeinschaft und Gesellschaft],* Transaction Books, New Brunswick, NJ, 1988; originally published in the United States by Michigan State University Press, East Lansing, Michigan, 1957.

Pages 90–91, Alexis de Tocqueville, *Democracy,* pp. 136–137.

Page 91, statistics on anxiety disorders: taken from Mary Ellen Lerner, "Facing Your Fear," in *USA Weekend, The Arizona Republic,* September 29–October 1, 2000, p. 8; based on findings of the National Institute of Mental Health. The study by the World Health Organization is also cited by Mary Ellen Lerner.

Page 91, on the existential dimension of anxiety: in addition to Søren Kierkegaard's classics, *Fear and Trembling* (1843), *The Concept of Dread* (1844), and *The Sickness Unto Death* (1849), see Rollo May, *The Meaning of Anxiety,* W. W. Norton, New York, 1950,

1977, and Ernest Becker, *The Denial of Death.* Reading these with an awareness of the modern cult of motion and speed as a backdrop, one can easily see how this cult races headlong toward an escape from existential anxiety that only sublimates, masks, and postpones recognition of it.

Page 92, Alvin Toffler, *Future Shock,* Random House, New York, 1970.

Pages 93–94, Nancy Gibbs and Michael Duffy, "Election '96," in *Time,* Canadian issue, November 4, 1996, p. 24.

Page 94, William Safire, "The Charlie Rose Show," KCET TV, Los Angeles, September 19, 1995.

Page 95, John Ralston Saul, *Voltaire's Bastards,* p. 369. Saul cites Laura Parker in *International Herald Tribune,* Business Section, 1, February 2, 1989, Washington Post Service.

Page 97, material on Yucca Mountain: taken from "Life & Times," KCET TV, Los Angeles, September 16, 1997.

Page 98, Arthur M. Schlesinger, Jr., *The Disuniting of America,* W. W. Norton, New York, 1991, 1992, pp. 45–46.

Pages 98–88, C. G. Jung, *Memories, Dreams, Reflections,* recorded and edited by Aniela Jaffé, translated by Richard and Clara Winston, Vintage Books, Random House, New York, 1965, p. 277.

## Chapter 7 The Imitation of Heroism

Page 100, C. Wright Mills, *The Power Elite,* Oxford University Press, New York, 1956, p. 71. Compare this to an advertisement for Cleveland Amory and Earl Blackwell's *Celebrity Register* (1959), in which celebrities are described as "the 'names' who, once made by news, now make news by themselves"; cited in Daniel J. Boorstin, *The Image or What Happened to the American Dream,* Atheneum, New York, 1962, p. 61, description of *Celebrity Register* on p. 273. Boorstin's book remains an outstanding study on celebrity in particular and the culture of images in general in spite of the fact that it was written four decades ago.

Pages 101–102, on the historical antecedents of modern celebrity in the royal courts of Europe: see John Ralston Saul, *Voltaire's Bastards,* pp. 499–505.

Pages 102–103, financial figures on paparazzi photographs: taken from "Turning Point," ABC, March 27, 1997 and "NBC Nightly News," September 1, 1997.

Pages 103–104, *InStyle Magazine,* October 1997, p. 62.

Page 104, the account of James Doohan: taken from "Trekkies," TMC (The Movie Channel), August 31, 2000.

Pages 104–105, Marshall McLuhan, *Understanding Media: The Extensions of Man,* pp. 287, 261.

Pages 105–106, Neal Gabler, "The Celebriticians," in *George,* December/January 2000, pp. 110, 111.

## Chapter 8  Heroic Tunnel Vision

Page 107, Nikolai Berdyaev, *Slavery and Freedom,* translated from the Russian by R. M. French, Charles Scribner's Sons, New York, 1944, p. 92.

Page 108, Alexis de Tocqueville, *Democracy,* pp. 134–135.

Page 110, C. G. Jung, *Mysterium Coniunctionis: An Inquiry into the Separation and Synthesis of Psychic Opposites in Alchemy* (1955–56), Vol. 14 of *The Collected Works of C.G. Jung,* p. 370.

Page 111, Abraham's encounter with God: Genesis 18: 25, King James Version.

Pages 111–12, Erich Fromm, *Psychoanalysis and Religion,* Bantam Books, New York, 1950, 1972, pp. 49–50.

Pages 112–13, on the Book of Job and God's dark side: see Chapter 10 in Jack Miles' Pulitzer Prize-winning *God: A Biography,* Alfred A. Knopf, New York, 1995, and C. G. Jung's provocative *Answer to Job* (1952), in *Psychology and Religion: West and East,* Vol. 11 of *The Collected Works of C. G. Jung,* translated by R. F. C. Hull, Bollingen Series XX, Princeton University Press, 1958, 1969, 1973. The latter essay is also available as a separate volume published by Princeton University Press, Bollingen Paperback Editions, 1973.

Page 113, Stephan A. Hoeller, "Jung, Gnosis and the American Psyche," a public lecture delivered at the C. G. Jung Institute of Los Angeles, November 5, 1993.

Page 113, financial figure on self-improvement industry: based on research by Marketdata Enterprises; cited in Daniel McGinn, "Self Help U.S.A.," in *Newsweek,* January 10, 2000, p. 43.

Page 113, quotation from self-help book editor: Barbara Quick, "Tales From the Self-Help Mill," in *Newsweek,* August 31, 1992, p. 14.

Page 114, Jean Piaget, "The Mental Development of the Child," in *Six Psychological Studies,* Vintage Books, Random House, New York, 1968, p. 64.

Page 115, Alphonse D'Amato, *Power, Pasta and Politics: The World According to Alphonse D'Amato,* Hyperion, New York, 1995.

Page 115, John Adams: see Joseph J. Ellis, *The Passionate Sage: The Character and Legacy of John Adams,* W. W. Norton, New York, 1993, pp. 123, 202.

Page 116, Paul Tillich, *Faith and Doubt,* George Washington University, Washington, D.C., 1962.

Page 116, St. Paul, Hebrews 11:1, King James Version.

Page 116, Eric Voegelin, *The New Science of Politics,* University of Chicago Press, Chicago, London, 1952, 1987, p. 122.

Page 117, on St. Thomas Aquinas: see Thomas Merton, *The Ascent to Truth,* Harcourt Brace Jovanovich, New York, 1951, 1979, pp. 323–325. Aquinas' work is the *Summa Theologica.*

Page 117, Jacob Heilbrunn, "A Sideshow in America's Culture Wars," in *The Los Angeles Times*, Section M, July 20, 1997, p. 1.

Page 117, quotations from William Jennings Bryan: cited, respectively, in Jacob Heilbrun, Ibid., p. 6 and Richard Hofstadter, *The American Political Tradition and the Men Who Made It*, p. 263. On the subject of anti-intellectualism in America, see also Richard Hofstadter, *Anti-Intellectualism in American Life*, Alfred A. Knopf, New York, 1963, 1966, 1974.

Pages 117–18, on opposition to teaching the theory of evolution by school boards in the South: see Peter Keating, "God and Man in Oz," in *George*, October 2000, p. 82 ff; "Darwin in Kansas," in *America*, September 18, 1999, p. 3; and Michael Shermer, "75 Years and Still No Peace," in *The Humanist*, September 2000, p. 3.

Page 118, statistics on mainstream and evangelical Protestants: taken from Harold Myerson, "Try the 60s. Try the 80s," in *LA Weekly*, August 23–August 29, 1996, p. 22; based on Thomas B. Edsall, in *The Washington Post*.

Page 120, Alexis de Tocqueville, *Democracy in America*, p. 143.

## *Chapter 9 The Escape from Heroism*

Page 122, Nikolai Berdyaev, *Slavery and Freedom*, p. 59.

Pages 122–123, on peak experience: see Abraham Maslow, *Religion, Values, and Peak Experiences*, Ohio State University Press, 1961, *Toward a Psychology of Being*, D. Van Nostrand, New York, 1968, and *The Farther Reaches of Human Nature*, Viking Press, New York, 1971.

Page 123, David Cole Gordon, *Self-Love*, Penguin Books, Baltimore, 1968, 1972, pp. 48–49.

Page 125, Meister Eckhart: see *Meister Eckhart: A Modern Translation*, by Raymond B. Blakney, Harper and Row, New York, 1941, pp. 82–91 and footnote 1, pp. 315–316.

Page 125, Marshall McLuhan, in George Sanderson and Frank Macdonald, *Marshall McLuhan: The Man and His Message*, Fulcrum, Golden, Colorado, 1989, p. 139.

Page 126, Bill Clinton: press conference, Mexico, May 6, 1997.

Page 126, Department of Health and Human Services survey: reported on "CBS Evening News," September 8, 1997.

Page 126, other government survey: reported on "CBS Evening News," October 7, 1996.

Page 126, Fyodor Dostoevsky, *The Gambler*, University of Chicago Press, Chicago, 1972. Also interesting is the depiction of Dostoevsky's compulsion in Anna Dostoevsky, *Dostoevsky Portrayed by His Wife*, translated and edited by S. S. Koteliansky, Dutton, New York, 1926.

Page 126, *Newsweek*, May 8, 1989.

Page 127, statistics on gambling in casinos: "ABC World News Tonight," March 5, 1996.

Page 128, Malcolm X, *The Autobiography of Malcolm X*, with the assistance of Alex Haley, Ballantine Books, New York, 1965, 1973.

Pages 128–29, *Benet's Reader's Encyclopedia*, fourth edition, edited by Bruce Murphy, HarperCollins, New York, 1948, 1996, p. 85.

Page 131, U.S. government statistic on heroin addiction: cited in "ABC World News Tonight," March 26, 1997.

Pages 131–32, George F. Will, in *Newsweek*, May 8, 1989.

## Chapter 10  The Metaphor of Depth

Page 133, James Hillman, *The Soul's Code: In Search of Character and Calling*, pp. 48, 53.

Page 133, Patsy Jefferson (Martha Jefferson Randolph), cited in "Thomas Jefferson," a documentary by Ken Burns, PBS, on KCET Television, Los Angeles, February, 1997. On the passing of Jefferson's wife, see also Joseph J. Ellis, *American Sphinx: The Character of Thomas Jefferson*, Alfred A. Knopf, New York, 1997, pp. 66–67.

Page 134, Thomas Jefferson, "Head-and-Heart Dialogue," letter to Maria Cosway, October 26, 1786, in *The Complete Jefferson*, pp. 823–831.

Page 135, Thomas Jefferson, Ibid., pp. 827–828.

Page 135, on the metaphors of height and depth: for an interesting comparative treatment, see James Hillman, "Peaks and Vales: The Soul/Spirit Distinction as the Basis for the Differences between Psychotherapy and Spiritual Discipline," in James Hillman, ed., *Puer Papers*, pp. 54–74.

Page 136, Blaise Pascal, *Pensées*, Vol. 13 in *Oeuvres de Blaise Pascal*, edited by Leon Brunschvicg, Librairie Hachette, Paris, 1904, IV, 277, p. 201. English translation in *The Concise Oxford Dictionary of Quotations*, Oxford University Press, New York, 1981, p. 181.

Page 136, Ralph Waldo Emerson, cited in *Life*, "Celebrating our Heroes," Time, Inc., 1997, p. 6.

Page 137, James Hillman, *Re-Visioning Psychology*, Harper and Row, New York, 1975, 1977, p. 159. Hillman cites Plato, *The Republic*, 621a, and *Timaeus*, 47e–48e; Francis M. Cornford, *Plato's Cosmology*, Routledge, London, 1966, p. 164; and Paul Friedlander, *Plato*, Vol. 3, translated by H. Myerhoff, Princeton University Press, Bollingen Series, p. 382.

Page 139, Allan Bloom: see *The Closing of the American Mind*.

Page 140, George Santayana, *Life of Reason*, Scribner's, New York, 1905.

Pages 141–42, Bob Dylan, "Ballad in Plain D," on *Another Side of Bob Dylan*, Warner Bros., 1964; also cited in Bob Dylan, *Lyrics, 1962–1985*, p. 143.

Page 142, Henry David Thoreau, *Walden* (1854), Barnes & Noble, New York, 1993, pp. 76, 80.

# Part III: The Underside of Innocence

Page 143, Genesis 3: 22–24, Revised Standard Version.

Page 143, James Hillman, "Abandoning the Child," in *Loose Ends: Primary Papers in Archetypal Psychology*, Spring Publications, Zurich, 1975. This quotation does not appear in this publication, but is on the audiotape of Hillman's lecture with the same title, Spring Audio, Inc., 1992.

Page 143, Allan Bloom, *The Closing of the American Mind*, p. 75.

Page 144, Bertrand Russell, *An Inquiry into Meaning and Truth*, Penguin Books, Baltimore, 1965, p. 13.

Page 145, the Talmud and God's banishment of man from the garden of Eden: see the first tractate of the Talmud, the *Tractate of Baruchas*, for the treatment of Genesis.

Page 146, the Talmud and God's foreknowledge of the future: see *The Living Talmud: The Wisdom of the Fathers and Its Classical Commentaries*, selected and translated with an essay by Judah Goldin, New American Library, New York, 1957, pp. 141–142.

Page 146, Paul, 1 Corinthians 15:45.

Page 146, on the idea of the *tzaddik*: see Charles Poncé, *Kabbalah*, Straight Arrow Books, San Francisco, 1973, pp. 86–87, and Martin Buber, *Tales of the Hasidim: The Early Masters* (1947), and *Tales of the Hasidim: The Later Masters* (1948), Schocken Books, New York.

Pages 146–47, R. W. B. Lewis, *The American Adam: Innocence, Tragedy, and Tradition in the Nineteenth Century*, University of Chicago Press, Chicago, 1955, pp. 5, 102–105, 120–126, 147–152, and 197–198.

Page 147, Ralph Waldo Emerson, *Journals*.

Page 147, Guilford Dudley III, "America: Its Wars and Mythologies," in *Psychological Perspectives*, Issue 26, Los Angeles, 1992, p. 97 ff. Dudley's treatment of American innocence and the American character in general is excellent.

Page 147, Henry James, *Christianity: The Logic of Creation*, 1857.

## Chapter 11 The Historical Roots of American Innocence

Pages 150–51, on the significance of the pyramid: Richard S. Patterson and Richardson Dougall, *The Eagle and the Shield: A History of the Great Seal of the United States*, Office of the Historian, Bureau of Public Affairs, Department of State, Washington, DC, 1976, p. 85.

Page 152, on ancient Israel's system of government and the belief by some scholars that it influenced the Founding Fathers: taken from Max I. Dimont, *Jews, God and History*, Signet Books, New York, 1962, pp. 47–48.

Page 152, on the historical influences on Jefferson: see Joseph J. Ellis, *American Sphinx: The Character of Thomas Jefferson*, Alfred A. Knopf, New York, 1997, pp. 31–32, 57–59, 115.

Page 152, Thomas Jefferson, in *The Writings of Thomas Jefferson*, Vol. II, edited by Albert Ellery Bergh, Thomas Jefferson Memorial Association, Washington, DC, 1907, p. 249.

Page 153, Daniel Boorstin, *The Lost World of Thomas Jefferson*, p. 238.

Page 153, on the eye of God: quotation from Zechariah 4:10 taken from Revised Standard Version. See also Proverbs 15:3, Ezekial 7:8–9, and Revelation 5:6. Reference to Horus taken from R. T. Rundle Clark, *Myth and Symbol in Ancient Egypt*, Grove Press, New York, 1960, p. 221. For commentaries on the larger psychological implications of this symbol, see Edward F. Edinger, *Ego and Archetype*, Penguin Books, Baltimore, Maryland, 1972, 1973, 1974, pp. 282–285; Edward F. Edinger, *The Creation of Consciousness: Jung's Myth for Modern Man*, Inner City Books, Toronto, 1984, pp. 42–52; and George R. Elder/The Archive for Research in Archetypal Symbolism, *An Encyclopedia of Archetypal Symbolism: The Body*, Vol. 2, pp. 133–137.

Page 154, on the conservatism of the Founding Fathers: see Daniel Boorstin, *The Genius of American Politics*, University of Chicago Press, Chicago, 1953.

Page 154, on the pyramid as unfinished: Richard S. Patterson and Richardson Dougall, *The Eagle and The Shield*, pp. 78, 92.

Page 154, Edward Johnson, *Wonder Working Providence of Zion's Saviour*, 1650.

Page 154, Thomas Paine, *Common Sense*, 1776.

Pages 154–55, Department of State publication on the history of the seal: Richard S. Patterson and Richardson Dougall, *The Eagle and the Shield*, pp. 84–85.

Page 155, Thomas Jefferson, "Notes on Virginia," in *The Writings of Thomas Jefferson*, edited by Albert Ellery Berg, Vol. II, Thomas Jefferson Memorial Association, Washington, DC, 1907, p. 207.

Page 155, Reinhold Niebuhr, *The Irony of American History*, Charles Scribner's Sons, New York, 1962, p. 26.

Page 156, Nikolai Berdyaev, *Slavery and Freedom*, pp. 88, 89.

Page 156, Rollo May, *Power and Innocence: A Search for the Sources of Violence*, Norton, New York, 1972, p. 51.

Page 157, Benjamin Franklin, *The Autobiography of Benjamin Franklin*, Houghton Mifflin, Boston, 1973, p. 108.

Page 157, on the use of the ideas of Providence and Manifest Destiny in the Mexican War: see Howard Zinn, *A People's History of the United States*, pp. 149 (citation of

John O'Sullivan) and 152–153 (citations of the *New York Journal of Commerce* and Senator H. V. Johnson).

Page 157, Bob Dylan, "With God on Our Side," on *The Times They Are A-Changin'*, Warner Bros., 1963; lyrics also presented in Bob Dylan, *Lyrics, 1962–1985*, p. 93.

Page 157, James Hillman, *The Soul's Code: In Search of Character and Calling*, p. 216.

Pages 157–58, Nikolai Berdyaev, *Slavery and Freedom*, pp. 88–89.

Page 158, on St. Augustine's view of Providence: see Gerhart Niemeyer, "Are There 'Intelligible Parts' of History?," in *The Philosophy of Order: Essays on History, Consciousness and Politics*, edited by Peter J. Opitz and Gregor Sebba, Klett-Cotta, Stuttgart, Germany, 1981, pp. 309–311.

Page 158, W. H. Vanstone, *The Risk of Love*, Oxford University Press, 1978, pp. 6, 92; also cited in Gerhart Niemeyer, "Intelligible Parts," p. 311.

Page 159, John Locke, *The First Treatise of Government*, sections 39, 56, 63, 86, 88, 89; *The Second Treatise of Government*, sections 4, 6, 25, 135, 136 (footnote reference to Richard Hooker's *Ecclesiastical Polity*).

Page 159, Thomas Paine, "Rights of Man, Part II," in *The Writings of Thomas Paine*, edited by Philip S. Foner, Vol. 2, New York, 1945, p. 408 ff.

Page 160, citation from earlier draft of Declaration of Independence: see Julian P. Boyd, *The Declaration of Independence: The Evolution of the Text*, Princeton, 1945, p. 19.

Pages 160–61, Daniel Boorstin, *The Lost World of Thomas Jefferson*, p. 130.

Page 161, on the Greek origins of the idea of natural rights: see Leo Strauss, *Natural Right and History*, University of Chicago Press, Chicago, 1953, 1959. In particular, see Chapter III, "The Origin of the Idea of Natural Right."

Pages 161–62, Joseph J. Ellis, *American Sphinx: The Character of Thomas Jefferson*, p. 59.

Page 162, Immanuel Kant, cited in Jaroslav Pelikan, *The Christian Tradition: A History of the Development of Doctrine*, Vol. V, University of Chicago Press, Chicago, 1971, 1989, p. 125.

Page 162, C. Wright Mills, cited in Todd Gitlin, "Critic and Crusader: The Exemplary Passions of C. Wright Mills," in *Los Angeles Times Book Review*, Sunday, May 28, 2000, p. 3.

Page 163, C. G. Jung, *Civilization in Transition*, Vol. 10 of *The Collected Works of C.G. Jung*. See particularly the essays in Part III.

Page 163, John Ralston Saul, *Voltaire's Bastards*, p. 18.

Page 164, Andrew Burstein, in "Thomas Jefferson," a documentary by Ken Burns.

Page 164, on Jefferson's naturalistic view of society: see Daniel Boorstin, *The Lost World of Thomas Jefferson*, p. 166.

Page 165, Daniel Boorstin, Ibid., pp. 196, 197.

Page 165, John Locke, cited in Leo Strauss, *Natural Right and History*, University of Chicago Press, Chicago, 1953, 1959, p. 202.

Page 165, Joseph J. Ellis, in "Thomas Jefferson," a documentary by Ken Burns.

## Chapter 12  Jefferson's Bastards

Page 166, Henry James, *Christianity: The Logic of Creation*, D. Appleton and Co., New York, 1857.

Page 166, Thomas H. Huxley, *American Addresses*, D. Appleton and Co., New York, 1877, p. 125 ff.

Pages 167–68, Eric Voegelin: see *Order and History*, Vol. 1, *Israel and Revelation*, Louisana State University Press, 1956, p. 429.

Page 168, on the Hebrew origins of the idea of progress: see Thomas Cahill, *The Gifts of the Jews*, Doubleday, New York, 1998.

Page 168, D. H. Lawrence, *Studies in Classic American Literature*, Penguin Books, London, New York, 1923, 1951, 1961, pp. 60, 58.

Page 169, Jefferson on the second American Revolution: letter to Joseph Priestley, March 21, 1801.

Page 170, on Kennedy's New Frontier and his call for a new generation of leadership: so central was the theme of novelty to his platform that he used the word "new" in his Democratic Convention acceptance speech 27 times; see Peter Keating, "Kennedy Led Us to the New Frontier," in *George*, August 2000, pp. 49–57.

Page 171, Herman Melville, cited in Joseph L. Henderson, "American Characteristics of Classical American Literature," in *Shadow and Self*, Chiron Publications, Wilmette, Illinois, 1990, p. 214.

Page 174, John Locke, *Second Treatise of Government*; cited in Leo Strauss, *Natural Right and History*, University of Chicago Press, Chicago, 1953, 1959, pp. 226, 241.

Pages 174–75, Leo Strauss, Ibid., pp. 248, 249, 251.

Pages 175–76, Murray B. Levin, *Political Hysteria in America: The Democratic Capacity for Repression*, Basic Books, New York, 1971, p. 244. (I have taken the liberty of correcting two minor grammatical or typographical errors in Levin's passage.)

Page 176, Alexis de Tocqueville on public opinion: *Democracy in America*, pp. 10 ff., 257–263.

Page 176, John Kenneth Galbraith, cited in *The Washington Post*, Book World, Vol. XXV, No. 35, Sunday, August 27, 1995, p. 10; based on Studs Terkel, *Coming of Age: The Story of Our Century By Those Who've Lived It*, New Press, 1995.

Page 176, Louis Hartz, *The Liberal Tradition in America*, Harcourt Brace, New York, 1956, p. 9.

Page 177, Leo Strauss, *Natural Right and History*, p. 61.

Page 178, Harold Rothwax: see *Guilty: The Collapse of Criminal Justice*, Random House, New York, 1996.

Page 178, John Locke: see *An Essay Concerning Human Understanding*, Book IV, Chapter III, section 18.

Page 179, on corporate abuses in the category of business practices: see John Ralston Saul, *Voltaire's Bastards*, Chapters 16 and 17.

Page 179, Denis Diderot, *Encyclopedie*, Vol. 2, "Morality of Richness."

Pages 179–80, Michael Sandel, *Democracy's Discontent: America in Search of a Public Philosophy*, Harvard University Press, Cambridge, Massachusetts, 1996, 1998. George Will gives an excellent summary of this book in his review, "The Politics of Soulcraft," in *Newsweek*, May 13, 1996, p. 82.

Page 180, P. J. O'Rourke, *Parliament of Whores*, Vintage Books, Random House, New York, 1991, 1992, p. 84.

Page 180, Baron de La Brède et de Montesquieu: see Lettre LXXXIX in *Lettres Persanes* (1721), Folio, Paris, 1981, p. 215.

Page 180, François Voltaire: see "Poem on the Disaster of Lisbon."

Page 180, Jefferson on happiness: see Daniel Boorstin, *The Lost World of Thomas Jefferson*, pp. 53, 226.

Pages 180–81, Clay Jenkinson, in "Thomas Jefferson," a documentary by Ken Burns.

Page 181, Thomas Jefferson, cited in "Thomas Jefferson," Ibid.

Page 182, Philip Slater, *The Pursuit of Loneliness*, Beacon, Boston, 1970, 1976, 1990.

Page 182, Alexis de Tocqueville, *Democracy in America*, p. 136.

Page 183, 1996 government survey: cited in "CBS Evening News," September 26, 1996.

Page 183, Bob Dylan, in Mikal Gilmore, "Bob Dylan at Fifty," *Rolling Stone*, May 30, 1991, p. 60.

Page 183, Thomas Merton, *Seeds of Contemplation*, New Directions Books, New York, 1961.

Page 183, Alexis de Tocqueville, *Democracy in America*, p. 136.

Pages 184–85, Arnold Toynbee, *A Study of History*, revised and abridged edition by Arnold Toynbee and Jane Caplan, Portland House, New York, 1972, 1988, pp. 171, 174, 176, 179. "The ineffably sublime works" is a quotation from Goethe, *Faust*, line 249, and "abomination of desolation" is from Mark 13:14.

Page 186, Jerry Seinfeld, cited in Tim Appelo, "10 Reasons We Already Miss Seinfeld," in *TV Guide*, January 17–23, 1998, p. 37.

## Chapter 13 The Land of the Overrated Child

Page 187, Ovid, *Metamorphoses*, IV, 18–20, Vol. I, translation by Frank Justus Miller, third edition, Harvard University Press, Cambridge, Massachussetts, 1916, 1984, p. 181.

Page 187, Richard Stengel, "Carried Away with Kids," in *Time*, September 9, 1996, p. 34.

Page 187, Neil Postman, *The Disappearance of Childhood*, Random House, New York, 1982, 1994, p. 98.

Page 188, Ralph Waldo Emerson, "Old Age."

Pages 188–89, George Boas, *The Cult of Childhood*, Spring Publications, Dallas, Texas, 1966, 1990, pp. 15, 71, 21, 88 (and note in Appendix, 114), 101, 48, 8–9.

Page 189, Friedrich Nietzsche, *Thus Spoke Zarathustra*, translated by R. J. Hollingdale, Penguin Books, New York, 1961, 1969, p. 55.

Page 189, on the reality of childhood in history: see Ivan Illich, *Deschooling Society*, Harper and Row, New York, 1970, p. 38 ff.

Page 190, on the symbolic nature of the child archetype: see C. G. Jung, "The Psychology of the Child Archetype," in *The Archetypes and the Collective Unconscious*, p. 161, footnote 21, and James Hillman, "Abandoning the Child," in *Loose Ends: Primary Papers in Archetypal Psychology*, Spring Publications, Zurich, 1975, pp. 8–12.

Page 190, George Boas, *The Cult*, p. 9.

Page 190, statistics on child labor in 1880 and at the beginning of the twentieth century: taken from Howard Zinn, *A People's History of the United States*, pp. 261, 338.

Page 191, Hermann Keyserling, *America Set Free*, Harper, New York and London, 1929, p. 267.

Pages 191–92, statistics on children: taken from Cornell West, "The Charlie Rose Show," KCET TV, Los Angeles, June 8, 1998; Mike Males, *The Scapegoat Generation*, Common Courage, 1996; Camille Sweeney, "Portrait of the American Child," in *The New York Times Magazine*, October 8, 1995, pp. 52–53 (cited in James Hillman, *The Soul's Code*, p. 84); Marian Wright Edelman, President, Children's Defense Fund, "The Charlie Rose Show," KCET TV, Los Angeles, 1998; CDC study reported on CNN, August 13, 1998; "ABC World News Tonight," April 4, 1997; "Nightline," ABC, September 9, 1994; the U.S. Advisory Board on Child Abuse and Neglect, study reported on "ABC World News Tonight," April 26, 1995.

Page 192, Michel Foucault, *Madness and Civilization: A History of Insanity in the Age of Reason*, Pantheon Books, Random House, New York, 1961, 1965, p. 252.

Pages 193–94, "Milestones," in *Time*, March 3, 1997.

Page 194, studies of pedophiles: see A. Bentovim, *Trauma Organised Systems: Sexual and Physical Abuse Within Families*, Karnac, London, 1992, and G. G. Abel, J. V. Becker, M. Mittelman, J. Cunningham-Rathier, J. Rouleau, and W. Murphy, "Self-reported

Sex Crimes in Non-incarcerated Paraphilias," in *Journal of Interpersonal Violence,* 1987, Vol. 2, pp. 3–35.

Pages 194–95, Richard Corliss, "Who's Bad?," *Time,* September 6, 1993, p. 56.

Page 195, material on ritual abuse: cited in Leon Jaroff, "Lies of the Mind," *Time,* November 29, 1993, p. 59.

Pages 196–97, C. G. Jung, *Memories, Dreams, Reflections,* Vintage Books, Random House, New York, 1961, 1965, pp. 233–234.

Page 197, on the history of love and marriage in traditional cultures: see Denis de Rougemont, *Love in the Western World,* Princeton Publishing, Oak Bluffs, Massachussetts, 1983.

Page 197, Rollo May, *Love and Will,* Doubleday, New York, 1969, 1989.

Page 197, M. Scott Peck, *The Road Less Traveled: A New Psychology of Love, Traditional Values and Spiritual Growth,* Simon and Schuster, New York, 1978: see Section II, "Love."

Page 199, James Hillman, "Abandoning the Child," in *Loose Ends: Primary Papers in Archetypal Psychology,* p. 15.

Page 199, Meredith B. Mitchell: see *Hero or Victim?,* published by Meredith B. Mitchell, Sherman Oaks, California, 1993.

Page 199, statistics on marriage and divorce rates: U.S. Census Bureau, June 1985 report, and "ABC World News Tonight," June 2, 1997.

Page 200, material on adult children of divorce: study cited in "ABC World News Tonight," June 2, 1997.

Page 200, statistics on abortion clinic incidents: "ABC World News Tonight," January 20, 1995.

Page 202, Karl Menninger, *Man Against Himself,* Harcourt, Brace and World, New York, 1938, 1966, p. 227.

Pages 203–4, initiation of female gang members: see Christian E. Molidor, "Female Gang Members: A Profile of Aggression and Victimization," in *Social Work: Journal of the National Association of Social Workers,* Vol. 41, No. 3, May 1996, pp. 253–254.

Page 204, 1995 study on gangs: conducted by the University of Southern California and reported on MacNeil/Lehrer, August 31, 1995.

Page 204, Robert Bly, *The Sibling Society,* Addison-Wesley, New York, 1996, pp. 6, 46–47, 126–127, 128.

Page 205, Paul Taylor, *The Washington Post,* Sunday, August 27, 1995.

Pages 205–6, Michael E. Kinsley, *Big Babies,* William Morrow, New York, 1995.

Page 206, Sigmund Freud, *New Introductory Lectures on Psycho-Analysis* (1932), translated by W. J. H. Sprott, in *Great Books of the Western World,* Vol. 54 (*The Major Works of Sigmund Freud*), edited by Mortimer J. Adler, Clifton Fadiman, and Philip W. Goetz, *Encyclopaedia Brittanica,* Chicago, 1952, 1994, p. 837.

Page 206, Robert Hughes, *Culture of Complaint: The Fraying of America,* Oxford University Press, New York, Oxford, 1993, p. 8.

Page 207, Al Gore, *Earth in the Balance: Ecology and the Human Spirit,* Houghton Mifflin, Boston, New York, 1992, pp. 226–232.

Page 207, Lawrence Kohlberg and Carol Gilligan, "The Adolescent as Philosopher: The Discovery of the Self in a Postconventional World," in *Twelve to Sixteen: Early Adolescence,* edited by Jerome Kagan and Robert Coles, W. W. Norton, New York, p. 157.

Page 207, Robert S. McNamara, with Brian VanDeMark, *In Retrospect: The Tragedy and Lessons of Vietnam,* Times Books, New York, 1995.

Page 208, C. G. Jung, "The Psychology of the Child Archetype," in *The Archetypes and the Collective Unconscious,* p. 179.

## *Chapter 14 The Metaphor of the Eternally Young Hero*

Page 209, Robert A. Nisbet, *Social Change and History: Aspects of the Western Theory of Development,* Oxford University Press, London, 1969, p. 4.

Page 209, Mick Jagger and Keith Richards, "Sympathy for the Devil," on *Beggars Banquet,* ABKCO Music, 1968; also cited in *The Rolling Stones, Singles Collection: The London Years,* published by ABKCO Music, 1989, p. 64.

Pages 209–10, James George Frazer, *The Golden Bough: A Study in Magic and Religion,* abridged edition (one volume), Macmillan, New York, 1922, 1951, p. 309.

Page 211, Richard Lacayo, "Smashing Camelot," *Time,* November 17, 1997, pp. 44–45.

Page 211, Mircea Eliade, *The Myth of the Eternal Return or, Cosmos and History,* translated by Willard R. Trask, Princeton University Press, Bollingen Series XLVI, Princeton, New Jersey, 1949, 1954, 1965, 1971, pp. 39, 42.

Page 211, Elizabeth Gleick, "So Happy Together?," *Time,* August 19, 1996, p. 48.

Page 212, Michael Burlingame, *The Inner World of Abraham Lincoln,* University of Illinois Press, Urbana, Chicago, 1994, pp. 73, 323.

Page 213, Lyndon Johnson, in Michael R. Beschloss, *Taking Charge: The Johnson White House Tapes, 1963–1964,* Simon and Schuster, New York, 1997.

Page 213, Gerald Posner, *Case Closed: Lee Harvey Oswald and the Assassination of JFK,* Random House, New York, 1993.

Page 213, Giambattista Vico, in *The New Science of Giambattista Vico,* translated by T. G. Bergin and M. H. Fisch, Cornell University Press, Ithaca, New York, 1968, p. 129.

Page 213, Hans Vaihinger, *The Philosophy of 'As If,'* translated by C. K. Ogden, second edition, Routledge, London, 1935, p. 12.

Page 214, James Hillman, *Re-Visioning Psychology,* p. 18.

Page 214, Seymour Hersh, *The Dark Side of Camelot*, Little, Brown, Boston, 1997.

Page 214, on the Kennedy administration's conspiratorial efforts against Cuba and in Vietnam: see Howard Zinn, *A People's History of the United States*, pp. 432, 463–465.

Page 214, Guilford Dudley III, "America: Its Wars and Mythologies," in *Psychological Perspectives*. Issues 26, Los Angeles, 1992.

Page 215, "The X-Files," Fox, November 16, 1997.

Page 216, statistics on Elvis Presley fan clubs and public tours of Graceland, and material on marketed vials of sweat: *Time*, August 4, 1997, pp. 63, 65, 66.

Page 216, David Halberstam, cited in "Elvis + Marilyn: 2 × Immortal," in *American Way*, American Airlines Magazine Publications, Dallas, Texas, August 15, 1995, p. 74; based on the book accompanying the 1995 art exhibit with the same title.

Page 216, on the Dionysian cult: see Walter Otto, *Dionysus: Myth and Cult*, Indiana University Press, 1965, or Spring Publications, Dallas, Texas, 1981; and W. F. Jackson Knight, *Elysion: Ancient Greek and Roman Beliefs Concerning a Life After Death*, Rider, London, 1970, pp. 76–79.

Page 217, C. G. Jung, "Flying Saucers: A Modern Myth," in *Civilization in Transition*, p. 314.

Page 219, "Saturday Night Live," CBS, December 13, 1986.

Page 220, James Hillman, *Puer Papers*.

## Chapter 15  The Explosion of Innocence

Page 221, James Grotstein, "Forgery of the Soul," in *Evil, Self and Culture*, edited by C. Nelson and M. Eigen, Human Sciences Press, New York, 1984, p. 211.

Pages 221–22, James Thomson, Jr., in "The American Experience: LBJ," PBS, September 4, 1994.

Page 222, H. Norman Schwarzkopf, cited in *Newsweek*, September 28, 1992, p. 61; based on *It Doesn't Take a Hero*, with Peter Petre, Linda Grey/Bantam Books, New York, 1992.

Page 222, C. G. Jung, *Mysterium Coniunctionis: An Inquiry into the Separation and Synthesis of Psychic Opposites in Alchemy* (1955–56), Vol. 14 of *The Collected Works*, p. 546.

Pages 223–24, William Appleman Williams, *Empire as a Way of Life: An Essay on the Causes and Character of America's Present Predicament Along with a Few Thoughts About an Alternative*, Oxford University Press, New York, 1980, 1982, pp. 68–69, 73–76, 102–110, 136–142, 165–167, 129. See also his *The Roots of the Modern American Empire*, Random House, New York, 1969, and *The Tragedy of American Diplomacy*, Dell, New York, 1972.

Page 224, on Herbert Hoover: see William Appleman Williams, *Empire as a Way of Life*, pp. 153–154.

Page 224, Philip Foner, *The Spanish-Cuban-American War and the Birth of American Imperialism*, Vols. I and II, Monthly Review Press, New York, 1972.

Page 225, Howard Zinn, *A People's History of the United States*, pp. 307–308. Chapter 12 of this book, "The Empire and the People," provides a brief but excellent treatment of the subject of American imperialism. The citations from the Philadelphia *Ledger*, William James, and Mark Twain as well as some of the other material on Cuba and the Philippines are taken from here.

Page 226, Thayer Greene, "America's Loss of Innocence: Bicentennial Reflections," in *Psychological Perspectives*, Vol. 7, No. 2, Los Angeles, Fall 1976, p. 147.

Pages 226–27, on the messianic idea in Judaism: see Joseph Klausner, *The Messianic Idea in Israel from its Beginning to the Completion of the Mishnah*, translated by W. F. Stinespring, Macmillan, New York, 1955; Sigmund Mowinckel, *He That Cometh: The Messianic Concept in the Old Testament and Later Judaism*, translated by G. W. Anderson, Basil Blackwell, Oxford, England, 1956; Gershom Scholem, *The Messianic Idea in Judaism and Other Essays on Jewish Spirituality*, Schocken, New York, 1971; and Max I. Dimont, *Jews, God and History*, Signet, New American Library, New York, 1962, pp. 48, 271–278.

Pages 227–28, on the messianism of different nations: see Reinhold Niebuhr, *The Irony of American History*, pp. 72, 68–69; Emanuel Geibel, in "Deutschlands Beruf," a famous poem in the nineteenth century; Nikolai Berdyaev, *The Russian Idea*, Lindisfarne Press, Hudson, New York, 1992 (originally published in 1947).

Page 228, George Washington, First Inaugural Address.

Page 228, Thomas Jefferson, letter to James Madison, April 27, 1809.

Page 228, James Madison, letter to Thomas Jefferson, 1787.

Page 228, James Monroe, special message to Congress, May 4, 1822.

Page 228, John Quincy Adams, cited in William Appleman Williams, *Empire as a Way of Life*, p. 61.

Page 228, James K. Polk, cited in William Appleman Williams, *Empire as a Way of Life*, p. 89.

Page 228, Abraham Lincoln, Second Annual Message to Congress, December 1, 1862.

Page 229, William McKinley, based on an account of what he told a group of ministers who visited the White House; taken from Howard Zinn, *A People's History of the United States*, pp. 305–306.

Page 229, Theodore Roosevelt, 1904; cited in William Appleman Williams, *Empire as a Way of Life*, p. 111.

Page 229, William Howard Taft, 1912; cited in William Appleman Williams, *Empire as a Way of Life*, p. 111.

Page 229, Woodrow Wilson, submission of the World War I peace treaty to the Senate; this quotation is also inscribed on Wilson's tombstone in Washington National Cathedral in Washington, DC.

Page 229, Franklin Delano Roosevelt, 1933; cited in William Appleman Williams, *Empire as a Way of Life*, p. 143.

Page 229, Harry Truman, cabinet meeting, September 1945; cited in William Appleman Williams, *Empire as a Way of Life*, p. 182.

Page 229, John F. Kennedy, cited in William Appleman Williams, *Empire as a Way of Life*, p. 199.

Page 229, Ronald Reagan, in *The Wit and Wisdom of the Great Communicator*, edited by Frederick J. Ryan, Jr., Collins, San Francisco, 1995.

Page 230, Jean Piaget, "The Mental Development of the Child," in *Six Psychological Studies*, Random House, New York, 1968, pp. 66, 77.

Page 230, John Locke, 1691; cited in William Appleman Williams, *Empire as a Way of Life*, p. 15.

Page 231, Reinhold Niebuhr and Alan Heimert, *A Nation So Conceived: Reflections on the History of America from Its Early Visions to Its Present Power*, Charles Scribner's Sons, New York, 1963, pp. 126–127, 145.

Page 231, Herman Melville, *White Jacket*, New American Library, New York, 1988.

Page 231, Rollo May, *The Cry for Myth*, W. W. Norton, New York, 1991, p. 92.

Page 231, Adolf Guggenbühl-Craig, "America's Political Fantasies," in *Spring 52: A Journal of Archetype and Culture*, Spring Publications, Dallas, Texas, 1992, p. 62.

Page 232, on the complex of Nazi Germany: see Michael Gellert, "The Eruption of the Shadow in Nazi Germany," in *Psychological Perspectives*, Issue 37, Los Angeles, Summer 1998, pp. 72–89.

Page 232, Rollo May, *Power and Innocence: A Search for the Sources of Violence*, W. W. Norton, New York, 1972.

Pages 233–34, statistics on violence: based on www.fbi.gov; *Statistical Abstract of the United States*, U.S. Department of Commerce, Economics and Statistics Administration, Bureau of the Census, Washington, DC, 1997; p. 94; *Crime State Rankings*, edited by Kathleen O'Leary Morgan, Scott Morgan and Mark Uhlig, Morgan Quitno Press, Lawrence, Kansas, 1998, p. 326; George A. Gellert, *Confronting Violence: Answers to Questions About the Epidemic Destroying America's Homes and Communities*, Westview Press, HarperCollins, Boulder, Colorado 1997, pp. 1, 4, 91; "NBC Nightly News," October 12, 1998; "Telling Stories: How Television Skews Our View of Society, and Ourselves," an interview with George Gerbner by Derrick Jensen, in *The Sun*, August 1998, pp. 13, 16.

Page 234, Rollo May, *Power and Innocence: A Search for the Sources of Violence*, pp. 166–167.

Page 234, Thomas Jefferson, letter to Edward Rutledge, July 18, 1788, in *The Life and Selected Writings of Thomas Jefferson*, Modern Library, New York, 1944, p. 448.

Page 235, Marshall McLuhan, in George Sanderson and Frank Macdonald, *Marshall McLuhan: The Man and His Message*, Fulcrum, Golden, Colorado, 1989, pp. 198, 3.

Page 235, Franz Alexander and William Healy, *Roots of Crime: Psychoanalytic Studies*, Knopf, New York, 1935, p. 283.

Page 236, on the use of fairy and folk tales as an aid in child development: see Bruno Bettelheim, *The Uses of Enchantment: The Meaning and Importance of Fairy Tales*, Random House, New York, 1989.

Page 237, George Gerbner, in "Telling Stories: How Television Skews Our View of Society, and Ourselves," an interview by Derrick Jensen, in *The Sun*, August 1998, pp. 16, 17.

## Chapter 16  The Metaphor of America's Darkness

Page 238, Richard Wright, *White Man, Listen!*, Anchor Books, Doubleday, New York, 1957, 1964, pp. 71–72.

Page 238, Aeschylus, *Agamemnon*, lines 179–183 in most translations. I have not been able to find the translation Kennedy used, but it is not inconceivable that, as a renowned lover of the Greek classics, he paraphrased these lines in his own words, which ring true to most translations. Kennedy's speech: Indianapolis, Indiana, April 4, 1968; cited in "Robert F. Kennedy: A Memoir," Discovery Channel. The same lines appear in an almost identical form at the memorial at Kennedy's gravesite at Arlington National Cemetery.

Page 240, data on Native Americans: taken from William Denevan, *Native Population of the Americas in 1492*, University of Wisconsin Press, 1992; Jeffrey S. Dosik, "The First Americans: Indian Groups," from Peopling of America Exhibit, Ellis Island Immigration Museum, 1995; *Handbook of American Indians*, 1906.

Page 242, Marshall McLuhan, in *Playboy*, New York, March 1969, Vol. 16, No. 3, pp. 66, 68.

Page 243, C. G. Jung, "The Psychology of the Child Archetype," in *The Archetypes and the Collective Unconscious*

Page 243, Robert Bosnak, in "Image, Active Imagination, and the Imaginal Level: A *Quadrant* Interview with Robert Bosnak," *Quadrant: The Journal of Contemporary Jungian Thought*, XXV:2, 1992, p. 24.

Page 245, historical study on slavery: Robert Fogel and Stanley Engerman, *Time on the Cross: The Economics of American Negro Slavery*, Little and Brown, Boston, 1974.

Page 245, Andrew Hacker, *Two Nations*, Ballantine, New York, 1992, p. 48.

Page 245, Gunnar Myrdal, *An American Dilemma: The Negro Problem and Modern Democracy*, Harper and Bros., New York, 1944.

Page 246, statistics on neighborhoods: taken from Andrew Hacker, *Two Nations*, p. 36.

Page 246, statistics on white and African-American levels of unemployment: *The Washington Post*, December 9, 2000, p. E1.

Page 246, statistics on white and African-American levels of poverty: *Statistical Abstract of the United States 2001*, U.S. Department of Commerce, Bureau of the Census, Washington, D.C.

Pages 247–48, William H. Grier and Price M. Cobbs, *Black Rage*, Basic Books, New York, 1968, pp. 171, 61–62, 73–74, 52–54.

Page 250, Frantz Fanon, *The Wretched of the Earth*, Penguin Books, Baltimore, 1973, p. 40.

Page 250, James Baldwin, "Stranger in the Village" (1953), in *The Oxford Book of Essays*, edited by John Gross, Oxford University Press, New York, 1991.

Page 251, statistics on crime: Marc Mauer of the Sentencing Project ("ABC World News Tonight," October 4, 1995); Andrew Hacker, *Two Nations*, p. 182.

Page 251, Christopher Lasch, *The Culture of Narcissism*, Warner Books, New York, 1979, p. 128.

Page 252, statistic on the Cryps and the Bloods: taken from William Shawcross, "The Cryps and the Bloods," *The Spectator*, May 28, 1988, p. 10.

Page 252, Marshall McLuhan, *Understanding Media: The Extensions of Man*, p. 74.

Page 252, study on student violence: cited in George A. Gellert, *Confronting Violence: Answers to Questions About the Epidemic Destroying America's Homes and Communities*, p. 93.

Page 253, rap singer: KRS-One, "Tomorrow's New York," *The New York Times*, September 9, 1989.

Pages 255–56, Michael Ortiz Hill, "Dreaming in Black and White," in *The Los Angeles Times Magazine*, December 11, 1994, p. 27.

Page 256, C. G. Jung, in "Mind and Earth" and "The Complications of American Psychology," in *Civilization in Transition*, and *C. G. Jung Speaking: Interviews and Encounters*, edited by William McGuire and R. F. C. Hull, Picador/Pan Books, London, 1980.

Page 257, Michael Ortiz Hill, "The Boundaries of Our Dreams: Cultural Diversity, Deep Ecology and the Edge of the Psyche," a public lecture delivered at the C. G. Jung Institute of Los Angeles, June 30, 1995.

Page 258, Erik H. Erikson, *Childhood and Society*, p. 327.

Page 259, Wynton Marsalis, in "Jazz," a documentary by Ken Burns, PBS, on KCET TV, Los Angeles, January 8, 2001. I have taken the liberty of making Marsalis' passage, originally given in context of an oral interview, more easily readible in text form, but its essential meaning is unchanged.

Page 259, C. G. Jung, "The Complications of American Psychology," in *Civilization in Transition*, p. 508.

Page 261, C. G. Jung, "After the Catastrophe," in *Civilization in Transition*, p. 197.

Page 261, Elie Wiesel, "The Charlie Rose Show," KCET TV, Los Angeles, December 22, 1999.

Page 261, Marshall McLuhan, in George Sanderson and Frank Macdonald, *Marshall McLuhan: The Man and His Message*, p. 90.

Page 262, on practices of the U.S. Department of Agriculture: see *Jet*, September 15, 1997, Vol. 92, No. 17, p. 16; *Wall Street Journal*, May 1, 1998, p. A1; admission on "ABC World News Tonight," report in late November 1998.

## Chapter 17 The Implosion of Innocence

Page 264, W. B. Yeats, "The Second Coming," in *The Collected Poems of W. B. Yeats*, Macmillan, New York, 1956, p. 184; originally published in 1921.

Pages 265–66, Alan M. Dershowitz, *Sexual McCarthyism: Clinton, Starr and the Emerging Constitutional Crisis*, HarperCollins, New York, 1998.

Page 266, Perry Miller, *The Life of the Mind in America: From the Revolution to the Civil War*, Harcourt, Brace and World, New York, 1965; see "Book Two: The Legal Mentality."

Page 266, William H. Kennedy, "The American Unconscious," Centerpoint Foundation, Nashua, New Hampshire, 1974, p. 72.

Page 266, Thomas Jefferson, letter to John Colvin, September 20, 1810, in *The Writings of Thomas Jefferson*, edited by Paul Leicester Ford, Vol. X, New York, 1892–99, p. 146. Jefferson's comment brings to mind Aristotle's observation on the need to keep a flexible attitude toward the law: "Even when laws have been written down, they ought not always to remain unaltered" (*Politics*, Book II, Chapter 8).

Pages 266–67, the Johnathan Prevette incident: "A Kiss Isn't Just a Kiss," *Time*, October 7, 1996, p. 64.

Page 267, John Ralston Saul, *Voltaire's Bastards: The Dictatorship of Reason in the West*, pp. 322–323.

Page 267, statistic on lawyers: *Statistical Abstract of the United States, 1999*, U.S. Department of Commerce, Bureau of the Census, Washington, DC, 1999, p. 424; see chart entitled "Employed Civilians by Occupation, Sex, Race and Hispanic Origin: 1983 and 1998, U.S. Bureau of Labor Statistics. It is to be noted that a significantly smaller figure, 681,000 lawyers, is given in the *Occupational Outlook Handbook: 2000–01 Edition*, U.S. Department of Labor, Bureau of Labor Statistics, Washington, DC, 2000.

Page 267, Learned Hand, *The Spirit of Liberty: Papers and Addresses of Learned Hand*, Alfred A. Knopf, New York, 1952, p. 189; cited John Ralston Saul, *Voltaire's Bastards*, p. 324.

Page 268, George Harrison, "Sue Me, Sue You Blues," on *Living in the Material World*, Harrisongs Music, 1973.

Page 268, Vincent Bugliosi, *Outrage: The Five Reasons Why O. J. Simpson Got Away With Murder*, W. W. Norton, New York, 1996.

Page 268, Thomas Jefferson: see the opening quotation of Chapter One.

Page 269, on the Clinton administration's health care reform program: see Scott C. Ratzan, "Reform Undone by a Failure to Communicate," in *American Medical News*, November 7, 1994, Vol. 37, No. 41, p. 42; and Franklin Foer, "After Meritocracy," in *The New Republic*, February 5, 2001, p. 21.

Page 270, C. G. Jung, *Memories, Dreams, Reflections*, p. 154.

Page 270, T. T. Paterson, *Management Theory*, Business Publications, London, 1966.

Page 271, polls illustrating American cynicism: cited in CNN news report, October 2, 1996; Jean Bethke Elshtain, "Authority Figures," in *The New Republic*, December 22, 1997, p. 11; *U.S. News and World Report*, October 9, 1995, p. 47.

Pages 271–72, Jean Bethke Elshtain, *The New Republic*.

Page 272, Bill Clinton, press announcement, December 19, 1998.

Page 272, Jonathan Lear, "Freudian Slip," in *The New Republic*, September 28, 1998, p. 29.

Page 272, Marie-Louise von Franz, *Puer Aeternus: A Psychological Study of the Adult Struggle with the Paradise of Childhood*, Sigo Press, 1970, 1981, p. 33.

Page 273, DNA corroboration of Jefferson's relationship with Sally Hemings: Eugene A. Foster, M. A. Jobling, P. G. Taylor, P. Donnelly, P. de Knijff, Rene Mieremet, T. Zerjal, and C. Tyler-Smith, "Jefferson Fathered Slave's Last Child," in *Nature*, Vol. 396, November 5, 1998, pp. 27–28. See also Eric S. Lander and Joseph J. Ellis, "Founding Father," in *Nature*, Vol. 396, November 5, 1998, pp. 13–14.

Page 273, Thomas Jefferson, letter to M. Pictet, February 5, 1803, in *The Writings of Thomas Jefferson*, edited by Albert Ellery Bergh, Vol. X, pp. 356–357.

Page 273, James Fallows, *Breaking the News: How the Media Undermine American Democracy*, Pantheon Books, Random House, New York, 1996.

Page 273, Edwin Diamond and Robert A. Silverman, *White House to Your House: Media and Politics in Virtual America*, MIT Press, Cambridge, Massachussetts, 1995.

Page 274, John Ralston Saul, *Voltaire's Bastards*, pp. 496–497.

Pages 274–75, on the state of world affairs during the Lewinsky episode: see "As the World Churns" editorial in *The New Republic*, October 5, 1998, pp. 9–10; "Antarctic Ozone Hole Reaches Record Size," in *Science News*, October 17, 1998.

## *Chapter 18  The Sacrifice of Innocence*

Page 276, Bob Dylan, "Where Are You Tonight? (Journey Through Dark Heat)," on *Street Legal*, Special Rider Music, 1978; also cited in Bob Dylan, *Lyrics, 1962–1985*, p. 413.

Page 276, Thomas Jefferson, citation inscribed in the Thomas Jefferson Memorial, Washington, DC.

Pages 276–77, James Hillman, *Loose Ends: Primary Papers in Archetypal Psychology*, pp. 40–42; the references to Plato, Paul, and Augustine (*Enarrationes in Psalmos*, XLVI, 2) are taken from here.

Page 276, Jefferson on Plato: see Daniel Boorstin, *The Lost World of Thomas Jefferson*, pp. 161–62.

Page 277, Hannah Arendt, *The Origins of Totalitarianism*, Harcourt Brace Jovanovich, New York, 1951, 1973, p. 474.

Page 278, Marshall McLuhan, in George Sanderson and Frank Macdonald, *Marshall McLuhan: The Man and His Message*, p. 32.

Page 278, James Hillman, *The Soul's Code: In Search of Character and Calling*, p. 247.

Page 279, Martin E. Seligman, "Why Is There So Much Depression Today?," a report given to the American Psychological Association, 1988. The investigations upon which this report are based were supported in part by NIMH grant 19604, NIMH grant 40142, NIA grant AG05590, and a grant to Seligman from from the MacArthur Foundation Research Network on Determinants and Consequences of Health-Promoting and Health-Damaging Behavior. Rollo May provides an interesting treatment of this research in "The Age of Melancholy," in *The Cry for Myth*, pp. 120–123.

Page 280, M. Esther Harding, *Psychic Energy: Its Source and Its Transformation*, Foreword by C. G. Jung, Princeton University Press, Bollingen Series X, Princeton, New Jersey, 1947, 1963, 1973, p. 250.

Page 280, Marie-Louise von Franz, *Puer Aerternus*, pp. 68–69.

Page 280, James Hillman, *Puer Papers*, p. 108.

Page 280, Robert A. Johnson with Jerry M. Ruhl, *Balancing Heaven and Earth: A Memoir*, HarperCollins Publishers, New York, 1998, pp. 280–281.

Page 281, Robertson Davies, *Fifth Business*, Viking Press, New York, 1970.

Page 281, Allan B. Chinen, *Beyond the Hero: Classic Stories of Men in Search of Soul*, Jeremy P. Tarcher/G.P. Putnam's Sons, New York, 1993.

Page 281, C. G. Jung, *Memories, Dreams, Reflections*, pp. 180–181.

# Part IV: The Fate of America

Page 283, John Adams, letter to James Warren, April 22, 1776; cited in *Papers of John Adams*, edited by Robert J. Taylor, Cambridge, 1977.

Page 283, Abraham Lincoln, Second Annual Message to Congress, December 1, 1862, in *Complete Works of Abraham Lincoln*, edited by John G. Nicolay and John Hay, Francis D. Tandy Co., New York, 1905, Vol VIII, p. 131.

Page 283, anonymous quote: compare to the apocryphal Gospel of Thomas, verse 70: "If you bring forth what is within you, it will save you. If you do not bring forth what is within you, it will destroy you."

Page 284, Arthur M. Schlesinger, Jr., *The Cycles of American History*, Houghton Mifflin, Boston, 1986.

## Chapter 19  America in the Third Millennium

Page 287, Deuteronomy 4:7–9, King James Version.

Page 289, Federico Fellini, acceptance speech for Lifetime Achievement Award, Academy Awards, Los Angeles, March 29, 1993.

Page 289, Leo Strauss, *The City and Man*, Rand McNally, Chicago, 1964, p. 3.

Page 291, Benjamin Rush, letter to John Adams, February, 1812.

Page 292, Joseph J. Ellis, *The Passionate Sage: The Character and Legacy of John Adams*, W. W. Norton, New York, 1993, pp. 47, 53, 174–175.

Page 293, James Hillman, *The Soul's Code: In Search of Character and Calling*, 1996.

Page 293, John Beebe, "Integrity in the Analytic Relationship," a workshop in the Analyst Training Program of the C. G. Jung Institute of Los Angeles, January 28, 1996. See also Beebe's *Integrity in Depth*, Texas A&M University Press, College Station, Texas, 1992.

Page 293, Erich Neumann, *Depth Psychology and a New Ethic*, foreword by C.G. Jung, Shambhala, 1969, 1990, pp. 26, 94, 93.

Pages 294–95, on John Adams' beliefs: see Joseph J. Ellis, *The Passionate Sage: The Character and Legacy of John Adams*, pp. 106–107, 132, 133–134, 156–157, 135, 140–141, 165, 223.

Page 295, "by the early twentieth century. . . .": Joseph J. Ellis, Ibid., pp. 220–221.

Pages 295–96, "Memorials will only be erected. . . .": Joseph J. Ellis, Ibid., p. 232.

Page 296, Robert Rutland, "Recycling Early National History Through the Papers of the Founding Fathers," in *American Quarterly*, XXVIII, 1976, pp. 250–262; also cited in Joseph J. Ellis, Ibid., p. 230.

Page 296, John Adams, letter to Benjamin Rush, 1809; cited in *The Complete Jefferson*, assembled and arranged by Saul K. Padover, Duell, Sloan, & Pearce, New York, 1943, p. 890, footnote 3.

Page 296, on the Jeffersonian freedom of the individual: one is reminded of Walt Whitman's words, "Underneath all, individuals,/ I swear nothing is good to me now that ignores individuals,/ The American compact is altogether with individuals,/ The only government is that which makes minute of individuals . . . ." ("By Blue Ontario's Shore," in *Leaves of Grass, Comprising All the Poems Written by Walt Whitman Following the Arrangement of the Edition of 1891–2*, Book 23, Stanza 15, Modern Library, New York, 1963, pp. 278–279). The individualism that was extolled as a virtue in the days of Jefferson and Whitman must be seen against the backdrop of its absence in predemocratic, monarchistic times, just as the virtue of personhood today must be seen against the backdrop of the individualism of the last two hundred years.

Page 298, Nikolai Berdyaev, *Slavery and Freedom,* translated from the Russian by R. M. French, Charles Scribner's Sons, New York, 1944, p. 48.

Page 297, Thomas Merton, *New Seeds of Contemplation,* New Directions, New York, 1961, 1962, 1972, p. 38.

Page 298, "Personality is independent. . . .": Nikolai Berdyaev, *Slavery and Freedom,* pp. 46–47.

Page 299, "transfers the centre of gravity. . . .": Nikolai Berdyaev, Ibid., p. 42.

Page 299, Erich Neumann, *Depth Psychology,* p. 19.

Page 299, C. G. Jung, "The Relations Between the Ego and the Unconscious" (1916, 1935), in *Two Essays on Analytical Psychology,* Vol. 7 of *The Collected Works of C. G. Jung,* translated by R. F. C. Hull, Bollingen Series XX, Princeton University Press, Princeton, New Jersey, 1953, 1966, 1972, p. 239.

Page 300, John Adams, letter to Benjamin Rush, June 20, 1818; cited in Joseph J. Ellis, *The Passionate Sage: The Character and Legacy of John Adams,* p. 238.

Page 300, Marshall McLuhan, in George Sanderson and Frank Macdonald, *Marshall McLuhan: The Man and His Message,* p. 219.

Page 301, Edward Edinger, personal communication, in "Symbols of Transformation," a course in the Analyst Training Program of the C. G. Jung Institute of Los Angeles, 1992.

Page 302, Erik H. Erikson, *Childhood and Society,* second edition, W. W. Norton, New York, 1950, 1963, p. 321.

Page 302, James Baker, "The Charlie Rose Show," KCET TV, Los Angeles, 1998.

Pages 302, Marshall McLuhan: see Marshall McLuhan and Quentin Fiore, *War and Peace in the Global Village,* Bantam Books, New York, 1968.

Page 302, statistics on nation-states in the world: *The World Almanac,* World Almanac Books, Mahwah, New Jersey, 2000.

Page 302, C. Wright Mills, *The Power Elite,* Oxford University Press, New York, 1956, p. 171.

Page 302, statistics on wars: see Melvin Small and J. David Singer, *Resort to Arms: International and Civil Wars, 1816–1980,* Sage Publications, Beverly Hills, California, 1982, pp. 87–92, 226–229; Peter Wallensteen and Margareta Sollenberg, "Armed Conflict, 1989–1998, *Journal of Peace Research,* September 1999.

Page 302, on the increase in terrorism: see "The Rise of World Terrorism," *U.S. News & World Report,* July 8, 1985.

Page 302, Shimon Peres, press conference, National Press Club, Washington, DC, February 16, 1993.

Page 303, Thomas S. Kuhn, *The Structure of Scientific Revolutions,* International Encyclopedia of Unified Science, Volume II, Number 2, University of Chicago Press, Chicago, 1962, 1970, pp. 23–24, 52–53, 66, 68–69.

Page 303, John Adams: see Joseph J. Ellis, *The Passionate Sage: The Character and Legacy of John Adams,* p. 239.

Page 304, Georg Wilhelm Friedrich Hegel, *The Philosophy of History* (1857), translated by J. Sibree, in *Great Books of the Western World,* Vol. 43 *(Hegel, Kierkegaard, Nietzsche),* edited by Mortimer J. Adler, Clifton Fadiman, and Philip W. Goetz, *Encyclopaedia Britannica,* Chicago, 1952, 1994, p. 168.

Page 304, Eric Voegelin, *The New Science of Politics: An Introduction,* University of Chicago Press, Chicago, London, 1952, 1987, p. 60. See also Section 6 of Chapter II, pp. 66–70.

Page 305, J. Marvin Spiegelman, personal communication, in "The Psychology of Transference," a course in the Analyst Training Program of the C. G. Jung Institute of Los Angeles, 1994.

Page 306, material on legal case involving Pizza Hut and Papa John's: Louise Kramer, "Pizza Hut Hauls Rival to Court over Ads," in *Advertising Age,* August 17, 1998, Vol. 69, No. 33, p. 4 and Louise Kramer, "Papa John's Blasts Rival Pizza Hut's Ad Imagery: Commericial Uses Footage from Smaller Chain's Spot," in *Advertising Age,* January 25, 1999, p. 4; interviews with the respective CEOs of Pizza Hut and Papa John's aired on "Fortune," CNN, March 10, 1999.

Page 307, Lyndon Johnson, cited in Henry Louis Gates, Jr., "A Pretty Good Society," in *Time,* November 16, 1992, p. 84, and "The American Experience: LBJ," PBS, September 4, 1994. It is to be noted that Johnson's speech mixes up the language of St. Augustine. What Johnson is actually talking about is the "City of God." The "city of man," according to Augustine, is the typical city of the world, modeled upon Babylon—godless, sinful, and "in a chronic condition of civil war." (Augustine, *The City of God,* Book XVIII, Chapter 2, abridged version from the translation by Gerald G. Walsh, S. J., Demetrius B. Zema, S. J., Grace Monahan, O.S.U., and Daniel J. Honan, with a condensation of the original Foreward by Etienne Gilson, edited, with an Introduction, by Vernon J. Bourke, Image Books, Doubleday, New York, 1958, p. 392.).

# ★ Acknowledgments ★

A number of people have shared in the long process that gave birth to this book, and I am deeply grateful for their kindness and contributions. Naturally, it goes without saying that the views expressed in the book are solely my responsibility and not necessarily ones with which they agree.

My good friend Gary Granger was involved from the outset, patiently listening to my thoughts, meticulously reading successive drafts, and generously making himself available with his erudition. In general, the world needs more selfless people of his kind. My brother George Gellert carefully read the manuscript, too, and made invaluable observations and suggestions. He was also very supportive with his love and good will. My loving wife, Ann Walker, was not only a good listener and a shrewd reader, but a partner whom I could always count on for a rich dialogue and for her gifted insight. She also graciously put up with the inconveniences of being with someone whose thoughts were often preoccupied.

I am especially indebted to the Ann and Erlo van Waveren Foundation for its generous research grant; such assistance always helps a writer in matters of morale and not just financially. Kimberley Cameron of the Reece Halsey North Literary Agency has been everything one can hope for in an agent—committed, diligent, and wise. Her faith in this book made a huge difference. My publisher, Don McKeon, moved the book along in a smooth and timely fashion, and gave it his full attention and enthusiasm. My editor, Don Jacobs, did a fine job polishing the manuscript and getting it into its final form. Jeanne Hickman, Kristen Gustafson, Jane Graf, Allyson Bolin, and the other staff at Brassey's were also very helpful.

The late Marie-Louise von Franz, whose *Puer Aeternus* is the foundation for practically all studies on the psychology of eternal youth, generously responded to my research queries. The late Edward Edinger significantly contributed to my process of inquiry by imparting one of his favorite methods of analyzing the collective unconscious. James Hillman's landmark essay, "Puer and Senex" (in his *Puer Papers*), explains basic principles at work in the polarity that is in part the subject of this book. Selwyn Mills and the late Max Weisser, though not having written about this particular polarity, influenced my thoughts about it with their pithy and humorous book, *The Odd Couple Syndrome.*

Brahm Canzer, another good friend, was of invaluable assistance on my chapter on economic trends, helping me to make sense of them in a historical and psychological context. Donald Benson similarly was an indispensable resource for this chapter, availing me of his keen understanding in matters of the American economy. Paul Babarik, always a wellspring of learnedness in social psychology, sifted through the manuscript and provided the benefit of his reactions. Connie Zweig has my gratitude for many helpful suggestions. Marvin Spiegelman, Sheldon Freedman, John Dobbs, Joe McNair, Donald Sloggy, Mel Gottlieb, and Jeffrey Dosik of the Ellis Island Immigration Museum helped with material on a wide range of topics. Aryeh Maidenbaum, David Deneau, and Charles Goodman, read an early draft of some chapters and made valuable comments. The chapter on race relations was delivered as a lecture at the 1998 California Spring Conference of Jungian Analysts and to the Los Angeles Chapter of the Employee Assistance Professionals Association; the comments I received from both were also helpful.

Bradley TePaske and Lore Zeller graciously helped with proofreading. I am indebted to Paul Kugler, Martha Kaplan, Agi Orsi, Daniel Ostroff, and Etan Lorant for their assistance, too. The librarians at the Santa Monica Public Library came to know me both in person and by my voice on the telephone, and were remarkably helpful in locating information and resources. The librarians at the Los Angeles Public Library were a great asset, too, particularly in finding obscure documents. Steven Blaize, Patricio Libenson, Ziliang Tan, and Ken Ho excellently serviced my computer needs.

Gilda Frantz, a wise old soul with a big heart, was a steady source of encouragement and a friend through thick and thin. Warner Carr, Eliane George, Jerry Barclay, Martha Assima, Charles Zeltzer, Arlene TePaske

Landau, Melissa Miller, René Engel, Rose-Emily Rothenberg, Paula Smith-Marder, and Sheila Zarrow were also consistent in their support and warm enthusiasm. Michael Dafter and Peter Dafter have my love for their good cheer and more. Dianne Cordic and Lior Warner gave generously of their deep insights. Friends at the C. G. Jung Institute of Los Angeles, too many to mention by name, contributed through a sharing of ideas and their collegial support. Going back some years to my student days, I remain indebted to three professors—Arthur Webster, the late Denis Diniacopoulos, and the late Marshall McLuhan—for their lasting influence. And last but very far from least, I am grateful to Dr. Neil Martin of the University of California at Los Angeles for his special assistance.

# ★ Index ★

# ★ About the Author ★

Michael Gellert is Director of Training at the C. G. Jung Institute of Los Angeles, and a Jungian analyst in private practice in Santa Monica, California. He was formerly a humanities professor at Vanier College, Montreal, and taught religious studies at Hunter College of the City University of New York. He has also been a mental health consultant to the University of Southern California and *Time,* and managed an employee assistance program for District Council 37, the labor union for employees of the City of New York. His previous book is *Modern Mysticism: Jung, Zen and the Still Good Hand of God.* He lives in Santa Monica, California.